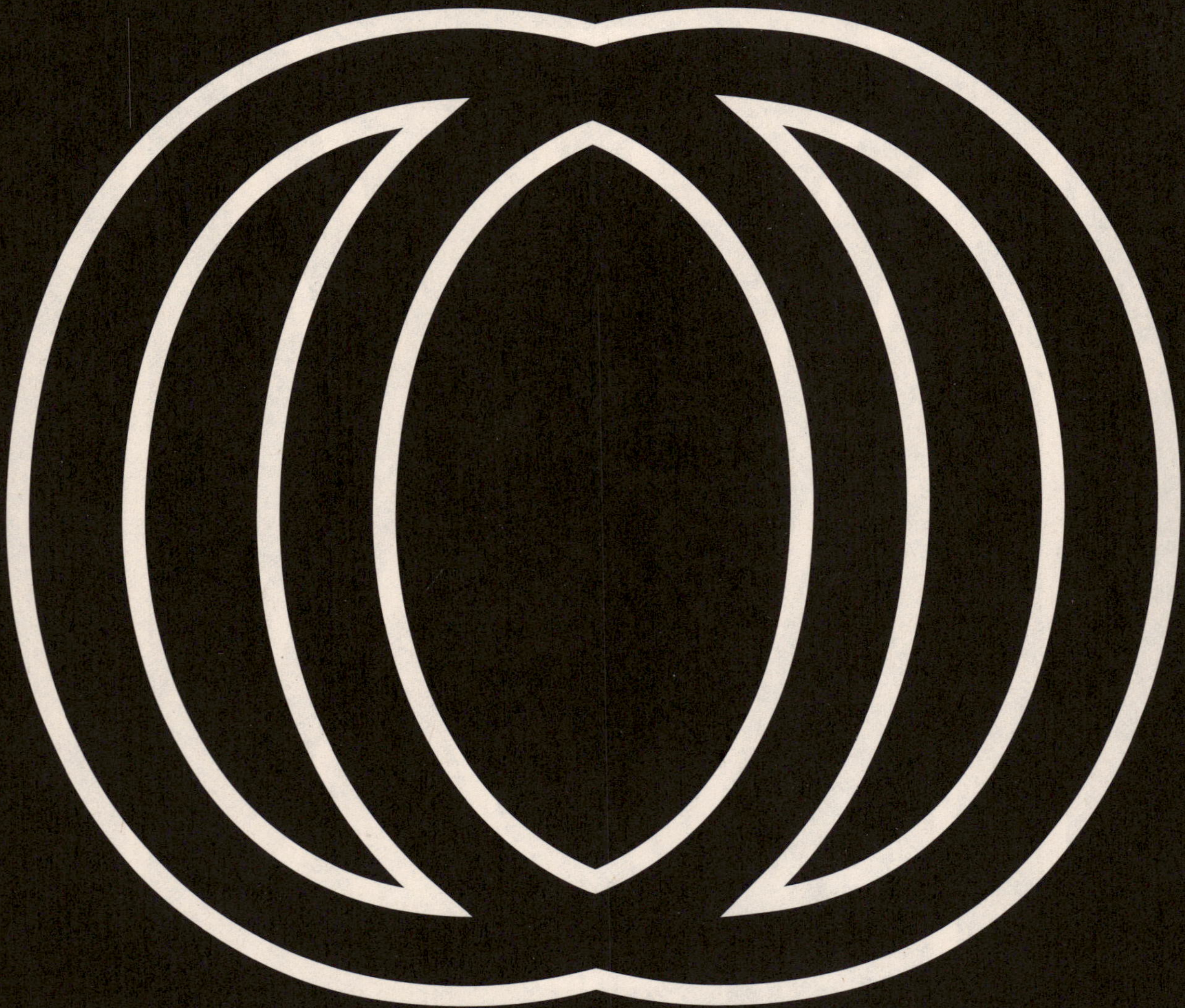

R

DEATH AND LIFE OF FICTION
MODERN MONSTERS
Taipei Biennial 2012 Journal

Taipei Fine Arts Museum
Spector Books

THE MUSEUM OF THE MONSTER THAT IS HISTORY

THE MUSEUM OF ANTE-MEMORIALS

THE MUSEUM OF THE INFRASTRUCTURAL UNCONSCIOUS

THE MUSEUM OF GOURD

THE MUSEUM OF CROSSINGS

THE MUSEUM OF RHYTHM

FOREWORD

Hai-Ming Huang

Since the Taipei Biennial 2012 came to a close, the world has been visited with unprecedented changes and natural disasters that defy easy understanding: Global warming has led to extreme climatic events and the rapid melting of polar ice. The swift expansion of capitalism has caused a global economic crisis and a widening gap between rich and poor. Beset by strange and unpredictable changes, extreme weather conditions, earthquakes and tsunamis, typhoons and floods, the earth has become a planet in deep distress. In such circumstances, what is the function of art? And what can an art biennial accomplish?

Many cognoscenti in the global art community have predicted the decline of the biennial, yet it lives on, like a cat with nine lives. An increasing number of second-tier cities have leapt on the bandwagon with fervor. The biennial continues to serve as an important vehicle for representing cities in the realm of the arts, and raising their profiles. The many people who take part in biennials harbor a variety of expectations and imagine a wide range of possibilities for what these events can be. In recent years, "biennial research" has become a prominent field of academic study. The global phenomenon of the biennial and the culture it has engendered are proving enormously influential in the development of contemporary art round the world. Ultimately, what is it that a biennial can give us? The series of Taipei Biennials we have presented in recent years has attempted to respond to these crucial questions.

Curated by Anselm Franke of Berlin, the Taipei Biennial 2012 featured forty-five artists and art groups. Additionally, it hosted six "mini-museums" at which individual curators or curatorial teams gathered artists of their own choosing. Altogether, around seventy artists participated, and approximately one-third of the works were conceived and created specifically for the event, making this the largest Taipei Biennial yet. The exhibition covered floors one to three of Taipei Fine Arts Museum, with an auxiliary exhibition space at the Paper Mill in the Shilin district. The exhibition as a whole attempted to reflect the many problems and processes of modern history through an Asian perspective and to explore the global, even the universal, historical experience with the unfettered attitude of contemporary art.

Every exhibition has a beginning and an end. After an exhibition has closed, it leaves behind an archive of documentation, and it is extended in the form of publications. This journal, published two years after the 2012 Taipei Biennial, allows it to live on in another form. The product of long hours of organization and communication between the curator and editors, this journal is both substantive and enlightening. Its publishing involved a multitude of details and could only be realized through the long efforts of many talented people. I offer my true gratitude not only for the generous contributions of the authors of each text, but also to the curator, the editor-in-chief, and all the personnel involved. By keeping their eyes on the horizon and their noses to the grindstone, they have made the Taipei Biennial Journal a publication of meaning and merit.

Hai-Ming Huang, Director, Taipei Fine Arts Museum

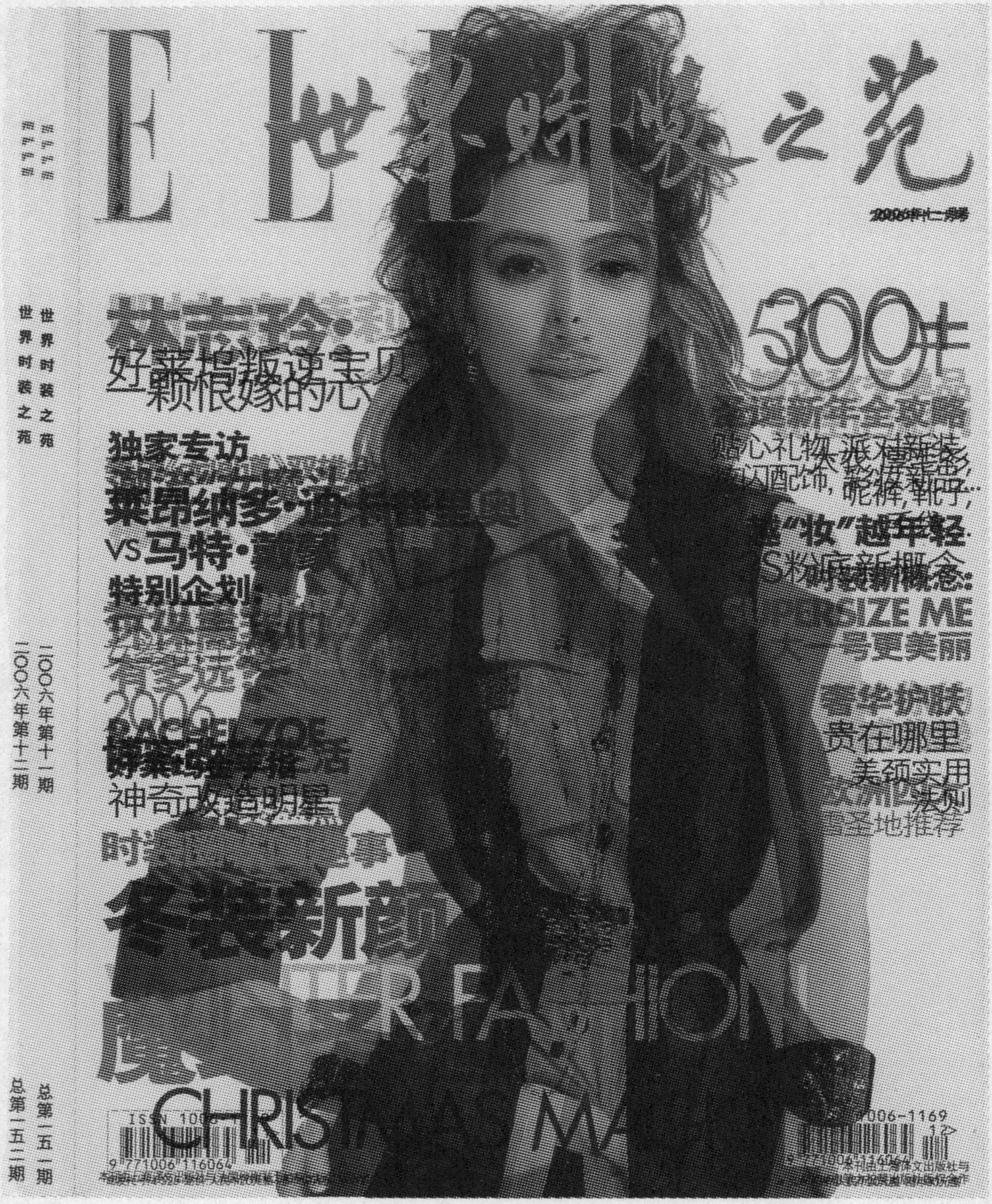

Willem Oorebeek, *More ELLE*, 2012, lithography on paper, mounted on dibond, 115 × 92 cm.

MONSTER AS GEOMAGNETISM

Brian Kuan Wood

Shortly after the most optimistic months of the 2011 Egyptian revolution, I asked the artist Maha Maamoun how things were looking in Cairo. I will never forget her response: Well, we were so, so happy when things broke open and all this darkness and disease, corruption and sewage started coming out for the first time. It was a kind of exorcism. But then, it never stopped! It just kept spewing out. And now we are drowning in this sewage.

So much for clarification. So much for revolutionary, emancipatory rupture. This is rupture as leak—as oil spill, as Fukushima and Chernobyl. You thought the monster was some dictator, but actually it isn't even human—it is a system, a structure, a substance, a chemical, an ideology, an economy, a process, a fear, a ghost, a language, a border, an event, a story, a history. And it has infected all of us. It goes by many names, and it shows its face most clearly when the prospect of emancipation presents itself, even if just for a moment, before being dragged back into the ocean of history. You thought making a rupture, a massive incision, a strike at the structural and ideological heart of the system would shake loose its injustices so that they might be held up against a metric of judgment. You thought you would be liberated, but in fact something much worse was set free.

Revolutions are almost always followed by a difficult period where a new social idea is forced to confront the immense power of the status quo, of tradition as such, of accepted norms, and ultimately of history itself as the diabolical mask of entrenched habits. History shows its face as a potent medium of justification that refreshes and reboots its precedents and antecedents. It is the substratum of ethical consciousness and it does not go down without a fight. It swiftly morphs, adjusting the bounds of identity to accommodate new information. And when hard-pressed, it will overwhelm with more violence and more sewage any attempt to compromise it. And in most cases it will do so until the only remaining solution is to just seal the leak. Go back to the way things were. The problem isn't the sewage but the leak itself. All these kids causing trouble. Let's keep everything tied up and as it was. Get ready for a globally deterritorialized geomagnetic regime that constantly adjusts and reconstitutes itself through a peace and pacification that is an essentially conservative restoration of tradition, virally producing new taboos, new methods of sealing, of hiding, of avoiding, of enthusiastic amnesia, of weird plastic fundamentalisms, of phantasmagorical forgetting and distraction.

But even this won't work. It is here that the face of the monster offers some relief, because the monster lives precisely at the point of an impasse. It settles in and goes to work at the very spot where it is simultaneously impossible to move forward or go backward—impossible to expel a structural violence built into history, but also impossible to withdraw into the safety of a tradition that has already been evacuated. The sheer violence and the absolutely unsustainable, lethal force of the old regime has already been revealed. Once leaked, it cannot be put back, tied up, neutralized, or undone. The monster appears when you are utterly paralyzed, overwhelmed on the one side by the scale of atrocities, and on the other by the impossibility of a certain romantic idea of revolution that thinks it is actually possible to come out the other side winning.

We are now inside of this realization, and we look to the monster as an enlightened barbarian par excellence. It presents a terrifying new project with regard to the handling of history, to the prospect of confronting its horrors, of accounting for its losses. We return again to an insistence upon clarification, to staring horror in the face, to deriving some perverse pleasure from swimming in its sewage, from jumping into its darkness, from facing and being consumed by the force of its evil—knowing that this is the actual material through which any real emancipation would need to be forged. This becomes further complicated when methods of clarification appear as the most violent—and yet we know that the regime has already entered our bodies, that we have already been made too violent even for ourselves. And it is here that David Der-Wei Wang has located the form of the monster in literature, in its use of subjectivity and voice, in subjective accounts that thematize and impress trauma as expression.

The essays gathered in this volume should be read as a close parallel and interpellation of the curatorial concept put forward by Anselm Franke for the Taipei Biennial 2012. Franke's sly redirection of the force of darkness against taboo, against closure, is almost necrological. It is a clumsy rush into the cemetery. It is a call to greet care and solemnity by opening all graves. Let us mock processes of sober clarification and accounting with destruction. Let us discover new synthetic pleasures in the impossibility of any absolute horizon for total reconciliation. Let's dance with ethical catharsis, with smashing pipes, and go for a swim in the sewage. Beyond the perversity of loving truth or death for its own sake, let's look for the thrill of standing with Chelsea, Assange, Snowden, Poitras, Greenwald, and forcing the spill.

We are curious. Let's see what leaks. If madness marks a limit point where the liquidation of meaning becomes total, the dissolution of any boundary between subjective expression and objective clarification becomes the beginning of a new form of life. Let us protect against yet another restoration by countering its pull into oblivion, precisely by giving madness its due form. Why not insist almost stupidly upon yet another round of clarification, this time to clarify madness as such—and as us. Rather than safety or freedom, let us clearly demand a new ethical madness.

This collection of writing around the works and themes of the Biennial is brought together in an attempt to identify what such a demand might constitute. And it attempts to embrace a further complication that appears when memorializing mechanisms are transposed onto a present time where the politics of spectacle and visibility already demonstrate a very particular latent claim to heal existential and historical wounds. It is how progressive democracies redeploy information-based economies to create symbolic registration mechanisms that function to absorb the pain and guilt of historical losses. This is a symbolic regime that identified an interchangeability between linguistic or semiotic devices, a spotlight or a category filter, and the erasure of people and places. It converts history from a sequence of events into a mnemonic device with an infinite capacity for sympathy by way of spectatorship and distribution as registration. It is a far more confusing quagmire than the map-territory relations we know from the internet. Because it reformulates the position of the dead in relation to the living by mobilizing the medium of memory as the connective tissue that holds them together. It pacifies the anger and regret, the sense of lack, by offering formats of expression, turning a framed photo of a loved one on the mantle into a sixteen-channel immersive art installation documenting exhaustive autobiographical research into one's own ancestors at various municipal archives. And these formats of expression are most destabilizing when they appear to, and often do, supersede functions of accounting and justice traditionally performed by larger officiating bodies such as states. This is a privatization of mechanisms of justice that function at the precise point where justice itself can only rely on symbolic and semantic relations to heal wounds that are in essence relational.

We are only now beginning to see how this enormous investment in symbolic modes of registering losses and cataloging injustices has another effect, namely, the unfurling of a Ponzi scheme that modernity has been running the whole time. Because modernity always had to bury what could not connect. To stay alive, it had to run a campaign of using anything—from the nation-state to food packaging—to absorb the rootedness of identity into modular abstraction schemes to market rationality, even to itself.

Some like to call this capitalism, but now it appears that when we talk about markets and libidinal forces, we are no longer talking about capitalism at all but about something else that it has given way to or unleashed from inside itself. And this something else seems to take the form of a feedback loop. Deleuze, after the liberatory demands of 1968, wrote about desire as a recursive machine, but we are now inside a planetary internet that has already captured and deployed a certain kind of liberty of economic expansion, which has hit its terrestrial limit. And now that it is on the prowl for another terrain of capture, it begins to take hold of time. But not time in the abstract, and not labor time or leisure time or production time, but another time that is stickier and longer—time as a means of accumulating historical identity. It is a feedback loop of identification that does not latch onto desires as such—for goods, commodities, lifestyles, or images—but rather onto one's very soul. It seizes one's identity and mobilizes its meaning effects by feeding it back onto itself to produce amplified, accelerated, attenuated iterations of one's own basic composition and historical makeup. It is a mistake to look to financial speculation as the folding and deployment of that time, when it is in fact biography. The monster feeds on biography. It draws its maps by forming connections across distances, and the legibility and availability of these connections must feed upon characteristics that cannot be altered in order to stabilize a network that can only be relational insofar as the nodes are not. Just watch as the sect becomes a new nation. As the people around you dress and behave more and more like you than you thought you did. As you start to constantly run into people from your past. As your history starts to haunt you more than you ever thought possible.

The interesting thing is that this functions at the level of an identity that is not chosen, but rather historically received. It is not the cultural identity that we choose, or even buy on the market in fashion or in fantasy, but actually the one we are born with and can never change. The one thing you can only be and always will be will be the thing you will fall into. In cultural studies, most thinking on identitarian issues takes for granted a subject that is to some extent free to negotiate identity as something that can slip and shift around in a kind of soapy postmodern bathwater, but this thing is truly coming from another place. Maybe its ancestor was called fascism, but that was a political ideology, and this thing does not come from people. It comes from something else. It comes from deep inside the liberal project loaded into economy and spun into a planetary internet.

It is your history, your search history and your birth history and the movements of your family and the language they supposedly speak. This is cultural production as historical retrograde construction, autonomous only from people and individual subjects because it comes down from the top and rushes into the present from a time you thought had passed. And you are not in control of it any more than you are in control of where you were born and to what parents and in what country. No wonder China expects 5 percent of its GDP to come from cultural industries in the coming decades. They know this is the heartbeat of a phase of exchange and consolidation that we can no longer call capitalism and that we don't have a new name for, however monstrous it is. You can dress in drag all you want but we all know that whatever this is will never allow you to be anything but that kid from the village, so you better face up to it.

Or not. Another response is to spin off its surface. If you can twist your body at just the right moment when it tries to subsume you, you just might slide across its skin and get a feel of its face. Commit that shape to memory and reproduce it in as many ways as you can until you recognize it as the face of the beast. Feed it back its own tail and don't fall into the loop when you plug that thing into its own mouth. Tell the folks back at the village to go eat it or dress them all in drag. Paint it wrong. Make it not what it is. Don't be what it wants you to only be. Think about George Psalmanazar. Take that money from the free zone, accept it, get some security for yourself, but always, always shove that tail right back into the dragon's mouth because if you don't, you'll be a tasty dinner. Welcome to the diabolical cultural production of the twenty-first century that is nothing but the monster of history.

MODERN MONSTERS

David Der-Wei Wang

In ancient China, there was said to be a monster called *Taowu*, a creature that looked like a tiger but had "a human's face, a tiger's feet, a pig's teeth, and a tail as long as eighteen feet." Aside from its vicious nature, *Taowu* was known for its power to see the past and the future, so as to make the best of its own life. From such origins, *Taowu* went through various incarnations over the centuries, to the point where it became identifiable with humans of evil inclination and, more intriguingly, with history itself. Since the seventeenth century, the meaning of *Taowu* has taken on yet another dimension: as a fictional account of history.

The metamorphosis of *Taowu* from monster to historical *and* fictional account, while indicative of the amorphous power of the Chinese imaginary, points to *one* way in which history came to take its form. In view of the incessant outbursts of violence and brutality from one generation to another, one has to ponder: Could history be regarded as both an embodiment and an indictment of monstrosity? If so, to what extent has the contemplation of history entailed insight as well as indifference? This paradox becomes all the more poignant in modern times, when monstrosity has assumed an unprecedented multitude of forms. Particularly in view of the massive scale of violence and pain that Taiwan and the rest of the world have undergone over the past few centuries, one senses that the line between understanding and complicity has never been so difficult to discern.

The mutual implication of history and artistic representation, to be sure, has always motivated human creativity. But never have we seen such a moment as we have in modern times, when official history has been so dictated by the ideological and institutional machines as to verge on make-believe, and representational art so arrested by a desire to reflect the past and future as to appropriate the functions of traditional history with respect to facts.

The monster *Taowu* is invoked because it is a mythopoetic figure deeply ingrained in the Chinese imaginary. The monster is known for its ferocious nature, multiple incarnations, and divinatory power. In classics such as the *Shenyi jing* (The Classic of the Fantastic and the Strange), *Taowu* is described as a creature which "looks like a tiger, with hair two feet long." *Taowu*, however, became identified with human evils as evinced by accounts in the *Zuozhuan*, *Shangshu*, and *Shiji*. It is said that Prince Zhuanxu's son, Guen, was of such wayward nature that he earned himself the monstrous name of *Taowu*. Together with three other evils of the time, this human *Taowu* was tamed and exiled to the frontiers, where it would scare away ghostly mountain spirits of the *Chimei*—only evils being able to withstand other evils.

Even more pertinent to our concern is the fact that *Taowu* was known for its power to see the past and the future, so as to make the best of its own life. As scholars have noted, in the Xia, Shang, and particularly Chu mythological traditions, *Taowu* appears to have been a creature with divinatory power, and it was therefore worshiped as a tribal totem. Because of its ferocious nature and mysterious visionary ability, *Taowu* was made one of the guardian creatures of the imperial tombs in the Chu region. Most significantly, somewhere along the way *Taowu* acquired cognitive identity with history itself. One finds in Mencius the following statement:

> The Sheng of the Chin [Jin], the T'ao U [*Taowu*] of Ch'u [Chu], and the *Spring and Autumn Annals* of Lu are the same kind of work ... and the style is that of official historian.

As the *Zuozhuan* indicates, thanks to its fiendish nature *Taowu* compels the ancients to "remember and recount [their] wickedness so as to take precaution." In other words, the monster was invoked as an "objective correlative," so to speak, to the human account of bygone experience, registering that which is immemorial and yet unforgettable in Chinese collective memory, and cautioning against any similar mishaps in the future.

My genealogical foray into the ancestry of *Taowu* culminates in a modern Taiwan connection. In Taiwan in the fall of 1957, the émigré mainland Chinese writer Jiang Gui (1908–1980) published a novel titled *Jin taowu zhuan* (A Tale of Modern Monsters). This novel chronicles Communist activities in a small town in Shandong Province from the twenties through the forties, and it culminates in a macabre riot costing hundreds of lives. For Jiang Gui, the function of *Taowu*, or history, is to "record evil so as to admonish." He sees in the image of *Taowu* a liminal zone where the inhuman and the human mingle, a region that is politically and morally anomalous. Jiang Gui is not the first writer to equate fiction with *Taowu*; he derived the idea from a late Ming novel, *Taowu xianping* (An Idle Commentary on Monsters, 1629) by Li Qing (1602–1683). Moreover, an early Republican writer, Qian Xibao, incorporated the term into the title of his novel *Taowu cuibian* (A Compendium of Monsters, 1916). Still, as Jiang Gui would have it, at a time when history is dominated by ideological camps, it is fiction, not history, that serves the function of recording evil so as to admonish.

Jiang Gui's fictional invocation of *Taowu*, though based on his diasporic experience in Taiwan, can be brought to bear on far more complex experiences and representations that the world has undergone. Two hundred miles southeast of mainland China and sparsely populated before the sixteenth century, Taiwan had traditionally been regarded as on the margins of the margins of Chinese politics and culture. It would nevertheless serve as an unlikely pathway through which China entered a succession of global modernities. Between the sixteenth and the late nineteenth century, when China was undergoing a final dynastic cycle and settling into an increasingly confused stagnation, the island had already diverged onto a fateful path of its own. It was alternately inhabited or dominated by ruthless pirates, scheming exiles, venturesome settlers, Ming loyalists followed by Qing pacifiers, to say nothing of Dutch and Spanish colonizers. In 1895, Taiwan was ceded to Japan, as a result of a Chinese defeat in the First Sino-Japanese War. Over the next five decades, Taiwan became Japan's most treasured colony and a testing ground for Japanese cultural and political assimilation. In 1945, at the end of the Second Sino-Japanese War, Taiwan was returned to China; but then, reverting to its traditional role, Taiwan became the refuge of the Nationalist government after the Chinese Communists took over the mainland in 1949.

Thanks to these experiences, Taiwan constitutes a contact zone where conflicting legacies, impulses, and ideological forces are brought into play. Taiwan was first forced into its "modern" existence at the turn of the twentieth century, when Japan initiated its colonial regime. The next five decades were to see, in both cultural and political spheres, strenuous conflict and compromise between colonial discourse and indigenous consciousness; between modern viewpoints achieved via Japanese mediation and revolutionary thoughts brought back from China; between fascination with the novelty of a colonizer's culture and loyalty to Chinese tradition. Taiwan was both the "Island of Beauty," or *Formosa* as early foreign explorers saw it, and the "Orphan of Asia," as viewed by Wu Zhuoliu (1900–1976), the pioneer of post-1945 Taiwanese literature. So Taiwan came to illuminate an entire array of modern issues, ranging from postcolonial critique to oppositional cultural politics, from hybrid modernity to the circulation of cross-cultural capital—issues that concern us even today.

Through the prism of Taiwan, we come to appreciate the anomalous and polymorphous nature of *Taowu* anew. We recognize that though the professed goal of history lies in leading virtue to the exclusion of evil, the act of historical writing is made possible ironically by the continued accumulation—inclusion—of that which is immoral and therefore excludable. This historical vision generates its own antithesis: insofar as its moral *telos* holds true and valid in the long run, history, as a narrated account of bygone events, performs its function negatively, as an agency revealing vice, waste, and anomaly.

Taowu has been associated with monsters, outlaws, the historical account of evil, and the fictional representation of that historical account; it now takes on the form of various artistic projects. Through the multitude of representations of the monster, we find ourselves imagining past inhumanity in the hope of a future in which such inhumanity can scarcely be imagined. And yet at any fold in time we may come to realize that without the imagination of past violence, we are unprepared to recognize it in its future incarnations, and for this reason all modernities bear the imprint of primitive savagery. Walter Benjamin's statement resounds: "There is no documentation of civilization which is not at the same time a document of barbarism."

A monster haunts the human struggle for self-betterment. How to come to terms with this monstrosity by way of teasing out its hidden divinatory force remains a task as urgent in our millennium as it was in ancient times.

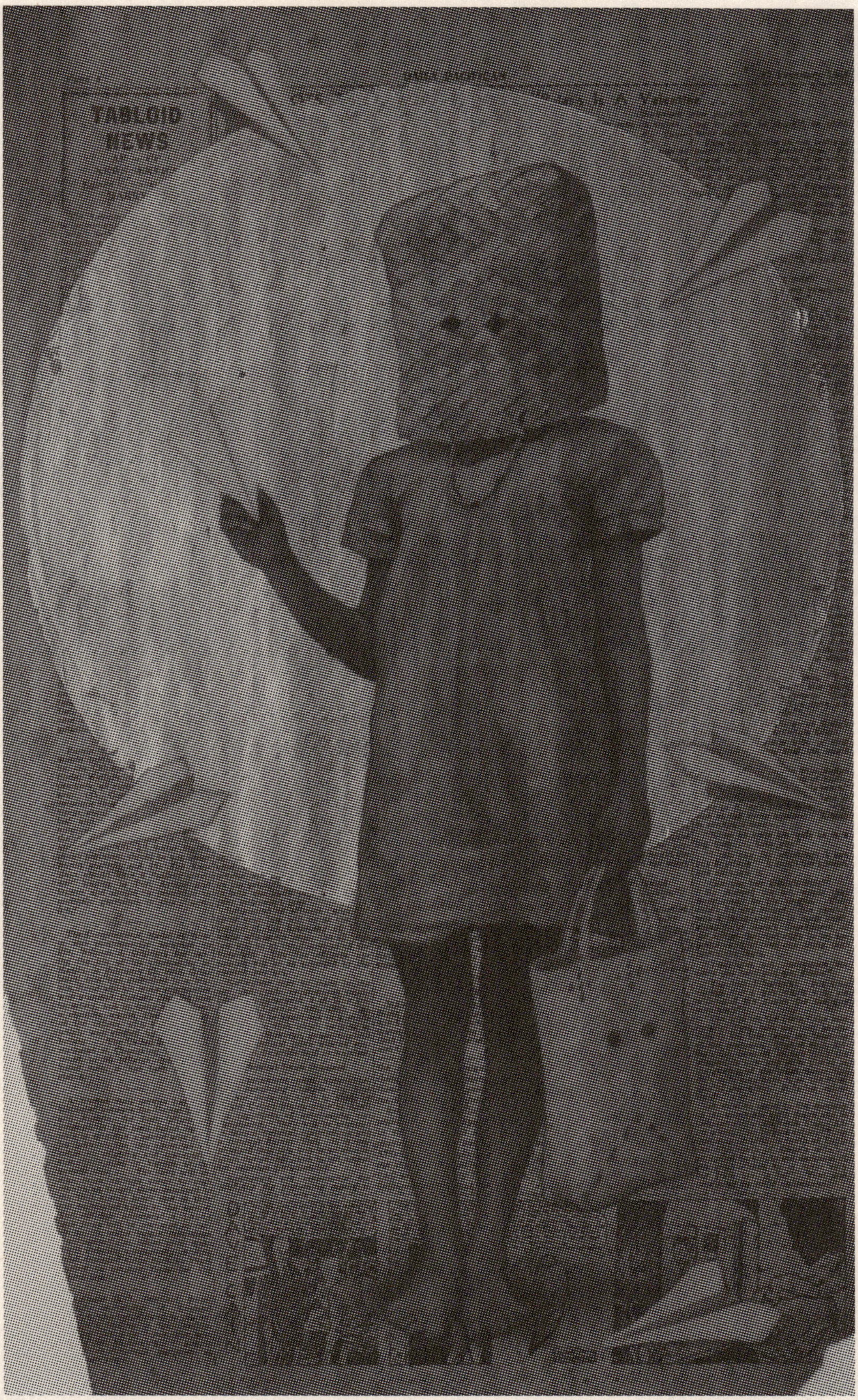

Joven Mansit, *Tabloid News*, 2012, oil on 1940s newspaper, 47.5 × 29.5 cm. Courtesy of Joel Ruiz Butuyan Collection. The Makapili was a militant group formed in the Philippines during World War II to give military aid to imperial Japan. The Makapili are best remembered for aiding the Japanese by pointing out insurgents while covering their heads with a *bayong* in order to conceal their identity.

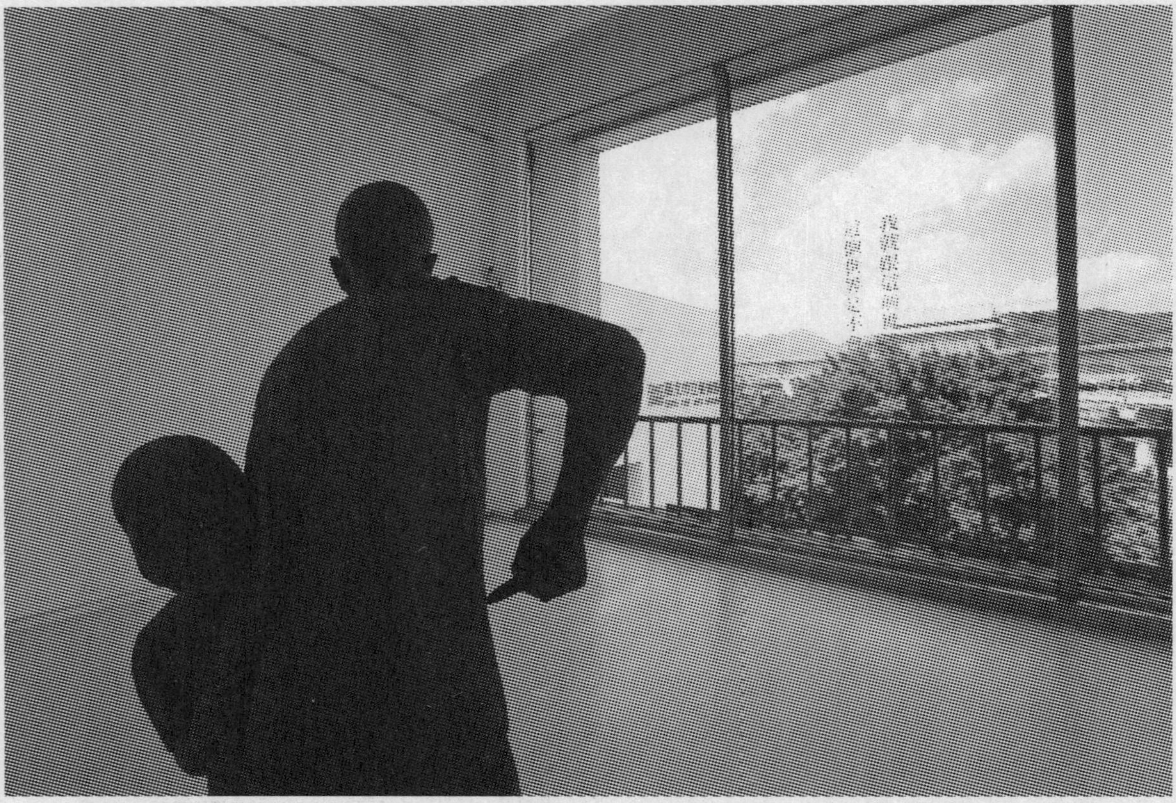

Teng Chao-Ming, *A Monument for The (Im)possibility of Figuring It Out*, 2012, fiberglass casting sculpture, digital archival print documents, newspaper clippings. The film *A Brighter Summer Day* (1991), by seminal Taiwanese director Edward Yang, is one of the main cinematic representations of Taiwan's White Terror period (1949–1987). Set in Taipei in the years 1959 to 1961, the film is based on a real-life story: the murder of a schoolgirl by her boyfriend — both fifteen years old — which was considered the first juvenile murder case after 1949. With this film, Yang attempts to create a representation of a period in Taiwan's history that is deliberately ignored and forgotten. He also considers the actual murder to be an inevitable result of the societal structure and political environment, and he uses the incident as a narrative tool to describe the logic of Taiwanese society in that period.

PREFACE TO *WHIRLWIND* (ORIGINALLY TITLED *A TALE OF MODERN MONSTERS*)

Jiang Gui

Over the past thirty years, I have written five novels. I wrote the first when I was twenty. That was a twisted romantic tragedy. At the time, Hong Xuefan was running a publishing house on Sima Road in Shanghai. I submitted it to him, and he printed it for me. The work was really childish, and afterward I often felt embarrassed about it. After the first printing of two thousand copies sold out, I was hoping to revise it for a second run, but just at this time Hong Xuefan passed away. Modern Publishing House closed its doors and stopped printing. The second book I wrote was also a love story. Mr. Wang Tongzhao took it and printed it in *Qingdao News*. The Nanjing Book Company was looking into buying the publishing rights, but price negotiations failed, and it was cancelled. That book was called *White Coffin*.

In 1926 I witnessed firsthand the behavior of the Communist Party in Hankou, and after I returned to Nanjing the next year, that memory remained fresh in my mind for many years. Two decades later I wrote my third novel, *Black Face*. I considered the Communist Party to be the "opposite face of light," something that inevitably had no future to speak of. But in terms of technique, I was not very satisfied with this work. After a certain amount of time, I consigned it to the flames.

In the spring of 1937, when I was in Xuzhou, I wrote my fourth novel, *Breaking the Siege*. It described a group of minor civil servants fleeing from Nanjing to Luoyang during the February 28 Incident. My motive was to champion resistance to the Japanese. After I finished the manuscript, I sent it to a literati friend of mine living in Shanghai. (This person is already a ministerial-level official in the Red Regime, and I am unwilling to mention his name.) When full-scale war broke out after the Marco Polo Bridge Incident, I went to serve in battle. Eventually, I ended up behind the lines, and had no means to affect the book's fate.

In the summer of 1941, I saw this book in the shop window of World Books on Wuku Street in Chongqing, and discovered that it had already been published by World Publishing Company. I immediately purchased twenty copies to give away to friends and relatives. I personally liked this novel quite a lot, but for many years I haven't had a copy in my possession.

In the winter of 1948, I moved to Taiwan to escape the Red Army. I could find no gainful employment, and my wife was invalided with illness. My life had sunk to its most senseless state since the day I was born. When I looked back at all that had transpired, it felt like a dream. And the greatest wound of all was that many other people had also tasted the "death of a nation." Because of the numerous things I had personally seen and heard over the previous thirty years, I thought I ought to know what the Communist Party was. I recorded a whole series of recollections, trimming them down and adding subplots, until I had composed a complete story. Every day I would arise at four in the morning and write for three hours. Working without a day of interruption for four months, I completed my fifth novel in a flash at the age of forty-one.

Publishing industry statistics reveal that New Literature novels still do not achieve sales comparable to traditional Chinese episodic novels. According to my own analysis, the reasons are twofold: (1) Traditional episodic novels employ purely Chinese syntax and chapter structures, and can be appreciated by both the elite and ordinary people. Thus, they have found acceptance among the vast majority of readers. (2) The stories are completely engrossing in their plot development, and truly achieve the goal of entertainment. Indeed, the old term for the novel was *xianshu* ("leisure book").

I think that if we disconnect literature from the purpose of propaganda and consider publishing as fundamentally a form of business, the problem of sales is something the writer cannot ignore. We must use the goal of entertainment to achieve the goal of propaganda. Particularly today, in the modern age of fierce struggle between freedom and enslavement, the writer guided by political objectives can no longer ignore general readers. You have to give them the things they need to read, those salacious, dark, tainted colorations, in order to create an opening, and achieve the maximum advantage.

That is why I adopted the strong form of the episodic novel, and in the end added battle scenes, in the hope of conforming to the interests of most readers. Even though what I wrote wasn't a purely traditional episodic novel, I deliberately moved in that direction. How effective this will be, I do not know.

This book describes the diseased state of previous years through the decline and fall of a prominent family. And this state of disease is the breeding ground of the Communist Party. It has wormed its way in through this crack. In this way, you can always imagine what role is played here: warlord, bureaucrat, local tyrant, venal gentry, prostitute, bandit, decadent literati,

Japanese soldier, vagabond, and many other minor characters playing petty roles. Their entanglements with the Communists, direct or indirect, their cooperation, intentional or unintentional, their incursions, tangible or intangible—this is what has jeopardized the Republic of China. Naturally, in its current form the Communist Party has a multitude of faces. And the little corner that I depicted is a mere gathering of brigands. But with a single spot one glimpses the whole leopard. I think this will suffice.

Here, there is nearly no upright individual. With an effort, I inserted the die-hard loyalist (KMT member) Fang Bagu to represent the decency of our people, to leave the reader a thread of hope. Sadly, she wages her battle in isolation. Her powers are too weak, and she is swallowed by the undertow. But in the current state of affairs, this view is quite accurate. Right now, to talk about resisting the Communists, one must concede the leadership of the KMT. This is a real problem, not a theoretical one. And in Old Auntie Ximen and Old Man Cao of Wu Village, the pen of the author inadvertently discovered two truly benevolent souls. But the reader will be able to comprehend on his own that they are even more isolated than Fang Bagu, even weaker. Because the Old Auntie has her own bodhisattva, a final strand of rope on which to rely, and gains release in the end. What the end of Old Man Cao is, it's really unnecessary to retell.

When I finished writing this book, I thought that as in times past I could immediately find a place that would publish it. I searched for a while but began to understand that such was not the case at all. In this place, most works of literature are paid for by the authors themselves, and I happened to be without the means for this. Consequently, I placed my book on the shelf for several years. Now, world opposition to Communism is more progressive than a few years ago, and Free China is already on the eve of its counteroffensive. The unveiling of this book to the world can no longer be delayed. Thanks to the assistance of a good friend, I have first printed five hundred copies to give away to various parties as a commemorative edition. I leave it in paper form, awaiting formal publication at some later date.

The book was originally titled *Whirlwind*, but as I learned that another book had already been so named, I adopted its current title. According to legend, the emperor Zhuanxu had a wayward son named Taowu. The word "*Taowu*" can also mean "broken wood." In my judgment, this is largely the same as the "Useless Tree" of Zhuangzi. Both were originally meant to be metaphorical. By association, *Taowu* is also thought of as a monster. The history of the ancient Kingdom of Chu is also called *Taowu*, meaning to “recount evils so as to admonish.” In popular fiction, there is a work entitled *Taowu Saga*, which tells of the evil deeds of Wei Zhongxian and Madame Ke, with the goal of moral improvement. As I approach fifty, the year when one realizes one’s fate, I look back on half a life of impecunity, but have no time for regret. While I stand in awe of virtuous behavior, I have no intention of glorifying any virtue of my own. The purpose of this work is also to “recount evils so as to admonish.”

HEADLESS LANDSCAPES

Jow-Jiun Gong

1989: Flourishing, but Still …

Early on in *The Man from Island West* (1989), Ah-Ming, naked and standing upside down, shares the screen with a seated Ah-Chiang. The obscure wanderer Ah-Ming (upside down) and the indigenous youth Ah-Chiang (seated) carry on a conversation, out of focus. As he is framed in the film, the protagonist Ah-Ming is inverted with his back to the camera, and his head is cut off from view. He says: "Countless things drive me crazy." Ah-Chiang responds: "What are you talking about?" From his upside-down position, Ah-Ming tumbles over onto a round rock on the beach. "I want to rush straight ahead and embrace all sorts of things, but nobody will accept it." When he finishes saying this, he runs, naked, into the ocean waves. Not long after, he suddenly jumps up in the water and shouts this incomplete sentence: "Flourishing, but still …"

This shout, or one might call it a scream, breaks out from the crashing waves. Comparably, Hou Hsiao-hsien's *A City of Sadness*, also released in 1989, engages in a survivors' narrative and violent criticism of a violent period of history, through the off-key slur of the deaf Lin Wen-Ching, and through cinematography. Both films stammer inarticulately, possessing a remarkable correspondence of theme, despite their different modes of execution. What is dissimilar in *The Man from Island West*, however, is that when facing the vast, enshrouding violence of modern society and modern history, it adopts a narrative tense closer to the historical present, from the angle of a "survivor," establishing a fragmented, incomplete aesthetic narrative of desolation. And parallel to this aesthetic narrative of desolation, *The Man from Island West* overlays numerous shots of the sea coast of eastern Taiwan, as well as a level of allegorical voice-over narration throughout the whole film. As this essay will highlight, these voice-overs seem to be neither the portrayal of a specific incident as myth, nor the construction of an origin myth, so much as they are a special form of allegory meant to intimate to the audience a variety of possible "explanations."

As the philosopher Walter Benjamin said of the writer Franz Kafka, while he was neither a prophet nor the founder of a religion, he was nonetheless the creator of allegories. He combined supreme mystery with great succinctness.[1] For Kafka, reality and the modern world were a "swamp world," in which people were shackled by intangible powers and a web of laws. An extreme degree of alienation existed between people and the outside world, and between one person and other people. The village in which Kafka lived was just such an alienated world. "Modern man lives in his own body," and yet "the body slips away from him, is hostile toward him." Indeed, a man may wake up and find himself transformed into vermin. Nevertheless, in many of his writings Kafka led the reader on a return to the ancient prehistoric world, a place full of clarity and purity, where fairy tales and folk songs, children, animals, and fairies lived together harmoniously and joyously in the wild, underground and in holes beneath the earth.[2]

The Man from Island West, the first film Huang released after returning from ten years of life abroad, is filled with animalistic vision, as can be seen from a consideration of the film's protagonist Ah-Ming. When Ah-Ming returns to his hometown, arrangements are made for him to live in a chicken coop. In addition, the film is full of chickens, ducks, dogs, snakes, sheep, bats, and fables featuring pigs and frogs. It is rife with the tracks of animals. Ah-Ming first appears from a cave. He scrambles, crawls, and climbs up cliff faces, mountain slopes, the ocean, streams, and unpeopled country lanes. Twice he submerges his whole body in a mountain stream. Then he returns to his cave, passing a night of typhoon gales there, and encounters his father's apparition. Finally, when crawling face-down in a messy pile of grass, he finds his father's abandoned grave. These images make us feel something akin to "losing our heads," because Ah-Ming represents the eyes of those who have returned home after being "decapitated" by modern civilization. When he says, "Countless things drive me crazy," it is as if his skull has melted and become one with the scenery, lending the role of main character to the voiceless, faceless "scenic shots" that occasionally appear. Yet this main character only possesses an enormous mass and body, but no head.

Headless Landscapes and the Discovery of Emptiness

In contrast to the air of collective tragedy in *A City of Sadness*, expressed as landscape shots of eagles circling in the distance around the mountains and vales of Jiufen, how should we view these "scenic shots" in *The Man from Island West* that resemble either photographic panoramas or landscape paintings? How do we understand their distinctively melancholic ambiance in the film, and their "anti-panorama," "anti-landscape" frames of reference? Did Ming-Chuan Huang, or perhaps Ah-Ming, "discover" the long-neglected scenery of Taiwan's east coast? As Karatani Kojin observes in *Origins of Modern Japanese Literature*, the "discovery of scenery" in modern Japanese literature was in fact an epistemological inversion. If not for the construction of an "interior landscape" through the use of narrative and the framing of a certain private, specific experience, the "discovery of landscape" would have been impossible.[3] Yet in the eyes of Ah-Ming, the fractured mindset reflected in his outburst "Flourishing, but still ..." demonstrates, as Benjamin commented in *Der Erzähler (The Storyteller)*, that modern humanity has no "experiences" to speak of, but merely the corporeal expression of "shock." He only has a body, but no head. After he returns home, he only has the silence and emptiness of his decapitated state. This is quite unlike ancient times when those who had gone traveling and returned home or hometown figures knowledgeable in local lore naturally became storytellers because of the fullness of their experiences, sharing their knowledge with their neighbors.[4] This "headless landscape"—the mountains, ocean, rivers, seaside caves, and wilds of Aohua on Taiwan's eastern coast where Ah-Ming roamed—form a matching, mirror image with the headless state of his own interior landscape. If the many long-distance outdoor scenes in *A City of Sadness* may be described as "empty landscape shots," the outdoor scenes in *The Man from Island West* constantly illuminate the fragmented phrase "Flourishing, but still ..." breaking like waves, constituting coordinate points linking it with the physical landscape, and not merely "empty landscapes."

The rediscovery of "empty landscapes" substantively involves the issue of the critique of violence. *Bodo* (1993) and *Flat Tyre* (1998) may be generally understood to engage in quite direct criticism of the "mythical violence" of the modern military authoritarian system, of the mythical idols of fascism, and of the two states of "law-making" and "law-preserving" violence. As Walter Benjamin asserted in the conclusion of his essay *Critique of Violence*: "Once again all the eternal forms are open to pure divine violence, which myth bastardized with law. It may manifest itself in a true war exactly as in the divine judgment of the multitude on a criminal."[5] Consequently, I am of the view that Huang's three films *The Man from Island West*, *Bodo,* and *Flat Tyre* might most accurately be described not as a "myth trilogy," but a "critique of mythical violence." This is because the narratives of landscape paintings, travel, ethnic groups, war, and fascism all have their own ongoing mechanisms of mythical violence. "But all mythical, lawmaking violence, which we may call executive, is pernicious. Pernicious, too, is the law-preserving, administrative violence that serves it."[6] Thus, in *Bodo* we encounter a penetrating treatment of military mythical lawmaking, and in *Flat Tyre* a trenchant critique of fascist mythical law-preserving violence.

The remaining question is, what is "divine violence?" Benjamin remarks: "Divine violence, which is the sign and seal but never the means of sacred dispatch, may be called 'sovereign' violence." I feel that *The Man from Island West* possesses a theological dimension, demanding further consideration from the perspective of divine violence. "Mythical violence in its archetypal form is a mere manifestation of the gods. Not a means to their ends, scarcely a manifestation of their will, but first of all a manifestation of their existence."[7] Thus, Ming-Chuan Huang's critique of violence, and his criticism of fascist figures and idols in *Bodo* and *Flat Tyre*, are criticisms of "mythical violence in its archetypal form." But can we say that *The Man from Island West* builds a certain variety of archetypal myth? Amid the fragments of crumbling mountains and the sea, how is it possible to construct a myth of modern society? In this regard, what indeed is the dividing line between "mythical violence" and "divine violence?"

Divine Violence:
The Phantom Off-Screen Narrative

Unlike *Bai Gong Tu (All Kinds of Workers)*, the documentary series on ordinary laborers he was also filming at the time, which aimed at absolute realism, *The Man from Island West*—Ming-Chuan Huang's first feature film after returning home from abroad—had its main character Ah-Ming returning from his own Ulysses-like odyssey, evincing a certain flavor of self-projection. Moreover, the long allegory told by the unshakable, spectral off-screen voice hovering around Ah-Ming's existence could be described—along with the cross-examination in a church that took place between the film's twenty-forth and twenty-sixth minutes—as one of two theological themes running through *The Man from Island West*. The church interview begins when Ah-Ming sees the numbers "1965" carved into the side of a table, and mumbles to himself: "1965, 1965, when I was ten years old." This reveals the implicit autobiographical nature of the film, as Huang was born in 1955. Afterwards, the pastor says: “Sir, you seem to really need a Bible. The Savior rescues all who believe in Him.” Ah-Ming asks why everyone who goes to church is old, and this clergyman, who solves all the problems in the village, answers: “This is the grace that God bestowed upon them. When they were young, God had not called them yet. It wasn’t until they were in middle age, about twenty five years ago, that God’s grace descended on this place.” Then Ah-Ming asks: “The ancestors of the Atayal didn’t have a God—can they be saved?” The pastor replies: “God is the way, the truth, and life. God is the beginning and the end. Jehovah created a new heaven and a new earth for us, and all the things of the past will not be remembered. All sins will no longer be punished. God’s elect are all humanity, civilized or savage. All people should come to Jerusalem to rejoice, because there, there is no sound of weeping or lamenting.”

Firstly, we should note the implicit autobiographical nature of this passage. Not only is it expressed in the common age of Ah-Ming and Ming-Chuan Huang, but also the voice of the preacher, which is none other than the voice of Huang himself. (Of course, according to the director’s explanation, this is purely a coincidence caused by work environment and method.) Yet this episode seems to comprise a dialogue in which Huang both asks himself questions and answers himself. Furthermore, after the minister is finished speaking, Ah-Ming utters a skeptical, even atheistic, response, full of doubt as to the possibility that the messiah can save: “Is that so?” Secondly, the pastor’s speech paraphrases Isaiah 65:17, a prophecy of the world to come that during the New Testament era was echoed in the visions of John: “And I saw a new heaven and a new earth: for the first heaven and the first earth were passed away; and there was no more sea. And I saw the holy city, new Jerusalem, coming down from God out of heaven …” (Revelation 21:1, 2) These prophecies and visions at most only point out the current state of headlessness and ruin. The sign and seal and aftermath of divine violence cannot portend that now is the time of the Messiah’s salvation. Moreover, the pastor’s words burst with violent irony regarding the history of the Atayal: “The things of the past will not be remembered. All sins will no longer be punished.” This is tantamount to saying their historical consciousness has been wiped out, causing them to fall into a state of collective amnesia, and leading to the day when justice is not miscarried—that is to say, divine violence is no longer manifest, and justice will only be manifest in a new heaven and earth different from the current situation. Finally, the saying “God’s elect are all humanity, civilized or savage” implicitly embraces the narrative or hierarchical divisions found in the "progress" of Western anthropology and Darwinism, embraces the myth of Western modern enlightenment, embraces the "mythical violence" that Walter Benjamin urgently sought to criticize.

In any case, in *The Man from Island West* the historical narrative of the Christian religion and the voice of messianic prophecy seem solely confined within the church. As for whether Huang intends to criticize the apocalyptic, messianic narratives of Christian thought, the answer seems abundantly clear. Beyond the church walls lie scenes of dilapidated villages and ruins, such as burnt, abandoned, and occasionally graffitied cars or overturned motorcycles on the beach, the legend of a ghost in a cave, river valleys, chicken coops, and inarticulate mountainsides. Among the fragments of these shattered scenes there constantly wafts an eerie voice as if from a fable, contrasting with the intermittent presentation of plot amidst the fragmentary scenery of the film. This gives the entire movie a torpor, narrative looseness, temporal superfluity, spatial emptiness, and odd drifting quality typical of Gilles Deleuze's "time-image."[8] Comparatively, this eerie voice from the allegorical narration highlighting the sign, seal, and aftermath of divine violence is simpler and more substantive than Christian prophecy. It does not particularly reference an as-yet unmanifested, transcendent, idealized future, but preserves and explains a variety of possibilities, referring to the past and at times seeming to strongly imply a projection of the present, even not infrequently intimating the direction in which fate may move in the future. Nevertheless, this allegorical voice echoes the fragmented landscape, revealing fractured clues to a Ulyssean homecoming, inducing the minute details of plot from the narrative and the present tense to converge, and thus producing a peculiar effect of resonance between the narrative and the present moment.

The Resonance of Allegory: Problematized Historical Narrative

This is redolent of Benjamin's emphasis on the mode of allegorical expression, which lies not only in its literary meaning but also in the theological meaning it encompasses. In allegorical expression, language is fragmented and discontinuous, symbols are disconnected from their original meanings and significations, the chain of mutual reference between subject and object is broken, language systems collapse and fragment; however, reintegration in the manner of a montage pieces these disintegrated linguistic symbols together again like a constellation, reinitiating linguistic meaning, enabling the transformation of the historical narrative into an act of problematization that cannot be easily converted into fixed collective memory or villainous official history. This kind of historical narrative is frequently a prelude to the violence of bureaucratic administration, legal verdict, and nationalistic warfare. The fragmented language and scenery of allegory manifests the scenes of fragmented ruination from the mundane world. Although it conveys a strong spirit of pure reality, it is also full of melancholy. Here, melancholy constitutes a recurrent motive force of the spirit, through the phenomenon of the mnemonic manifestation of individual moments. By redeeming the past, it forms a constellation of personal memories replacing the holy aura of transcendence of previous times. This is different from Christian messianism; it is the eschatology of Benjamin within a fractured landscape. It does not transcend the fragmentation of the mundane world, yet its voice and stance are sufficient to produce a breach of unfamiliarity and distance. Amidst the tempest of progress, it attempts, like Paul Klee's angel, to transform the fragments of history into a visible constellation.[9]

In my opinion, the precondition for the allegorical mode of expression that Benjamin emphasized is to concede the existence of violence, one that possesses a law-making effect, that is to say, a "divine violence" which is the source of the legitimization of proletarian revolution or general labor strike through the use of violence: in order to create a new heaven and a new earth, in order to establish a new law of justice, it is necessary to engage in total revolution. However, "divine violence" is only manifested in sign and seal and aftermath. If people establish a myth in this way, be it a myth of nationhood, leadership, heroism, war, or law, the violence of this myth will ultimately result in "divine violence," fragmenting it, shattering it, and renewing it. Therefore, the ultimate source of a critique of violence is in fact a "divine violence" that few can anticipate, control, or presume to explain. Benjamin conceded this violence and sought by all possible means to address the historical aftermath of divine violence. If we adopt this perspective in viewing the tale of Maona's exile and homecoming, perhaps we can gain an understanding different from the commonplace cultural or anthropological interpretation, and view it as a cautionary allegory of continuous minutiae and present-tense resonance, instead of a distant myth of ethnic origin.

In the fable of the young man Maona, the sign, seal, and aftermath of "divine violence" involve several specific themes: hunting and violence, the mutual evolution of humans and animals, ghost hauntings, unfamiliar languages, the inability to speak or communicate, the sale of ancestral

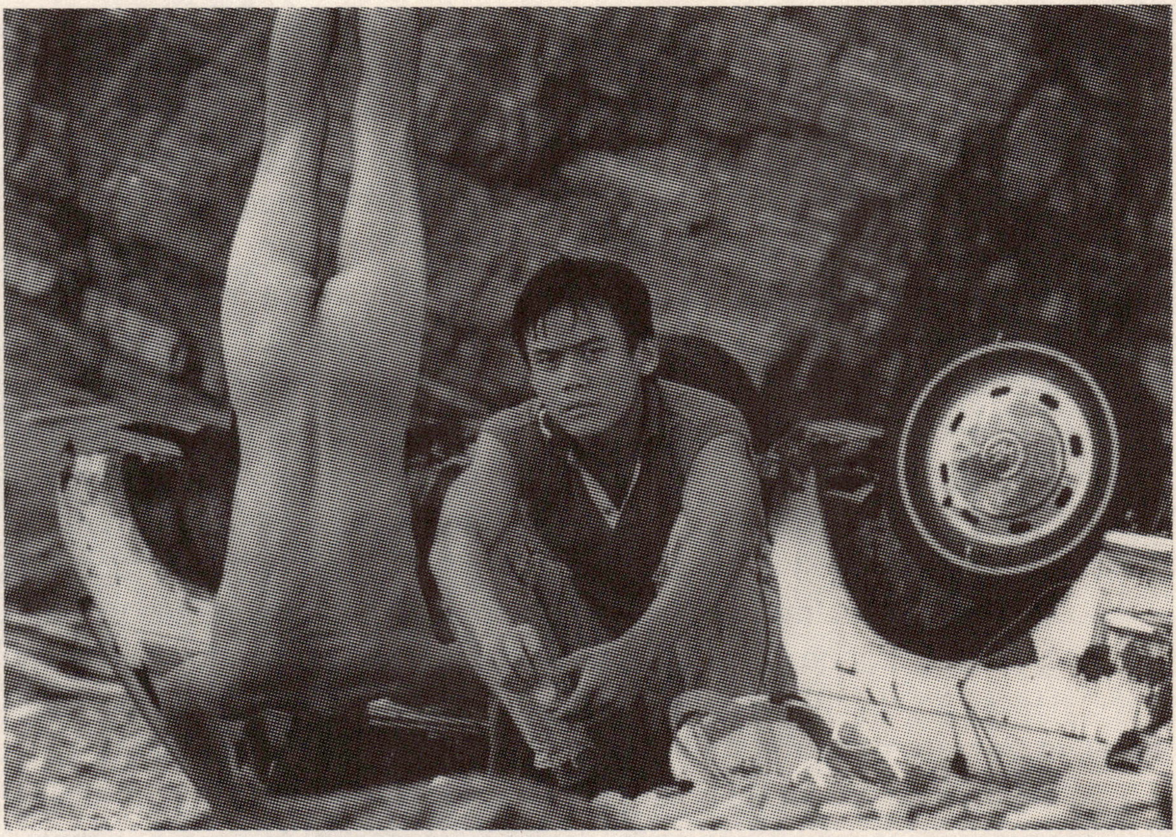

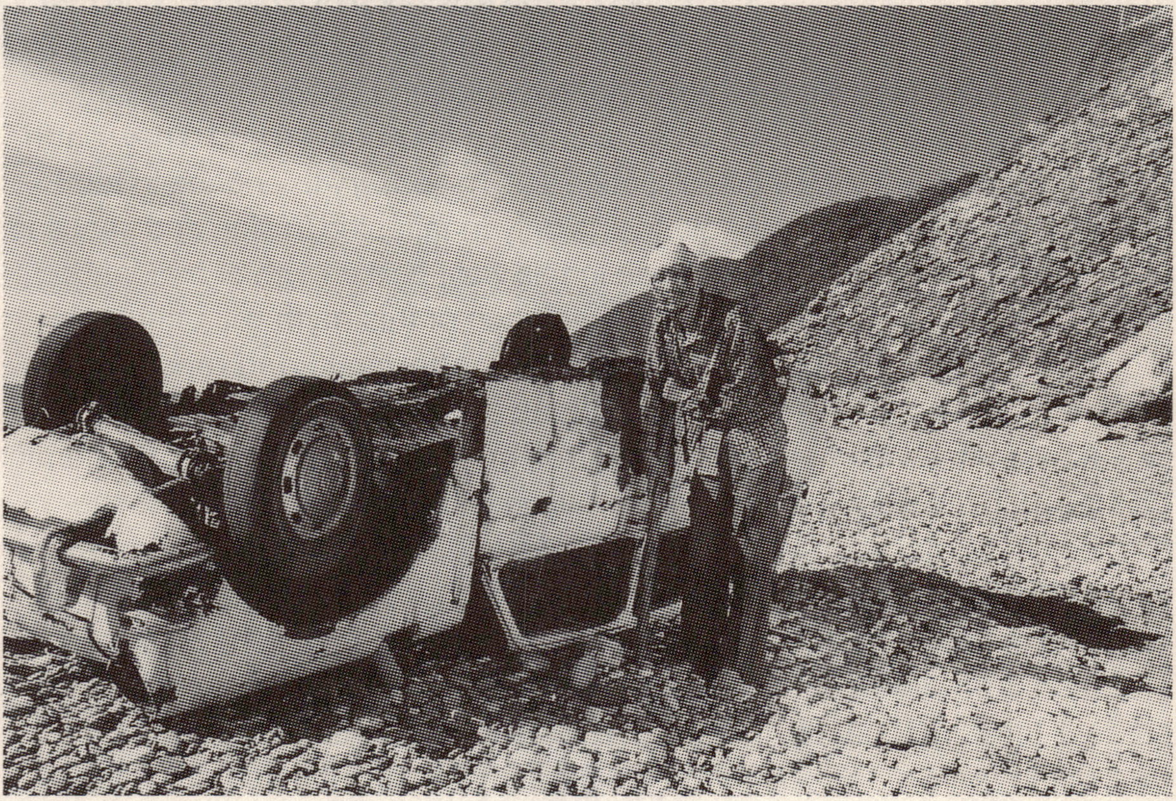

Fig. 1 Ming-Chuan Huang, *The Man from Island West,* 1989, film still, "Ah-Chiang's goal went the opposite direction of Ah-Ming's." © Formosa Filmedia Co.

Fig. 2 Ming-Chuan Huang, *The Man from Island West*, 1989, film still, "A failure suicide paved the way for Ah-Ming's new life." © Formosa Filmedia Co.

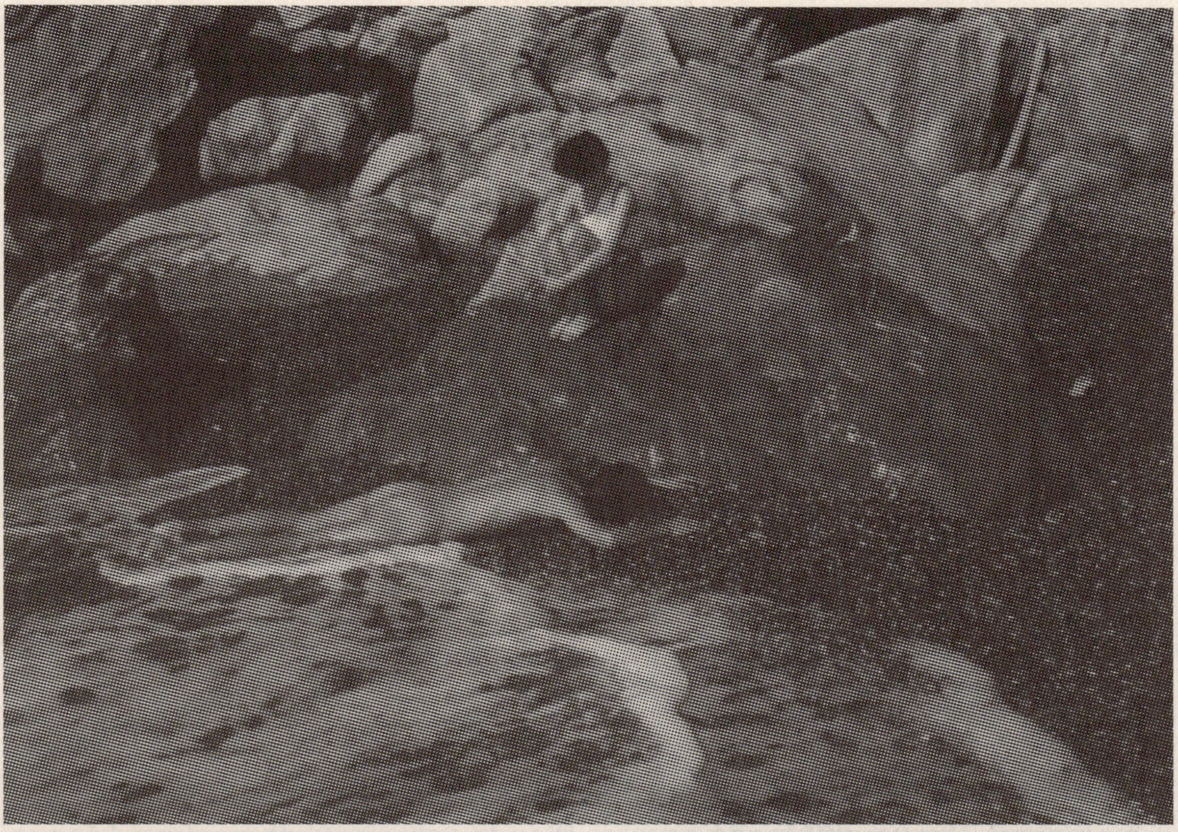

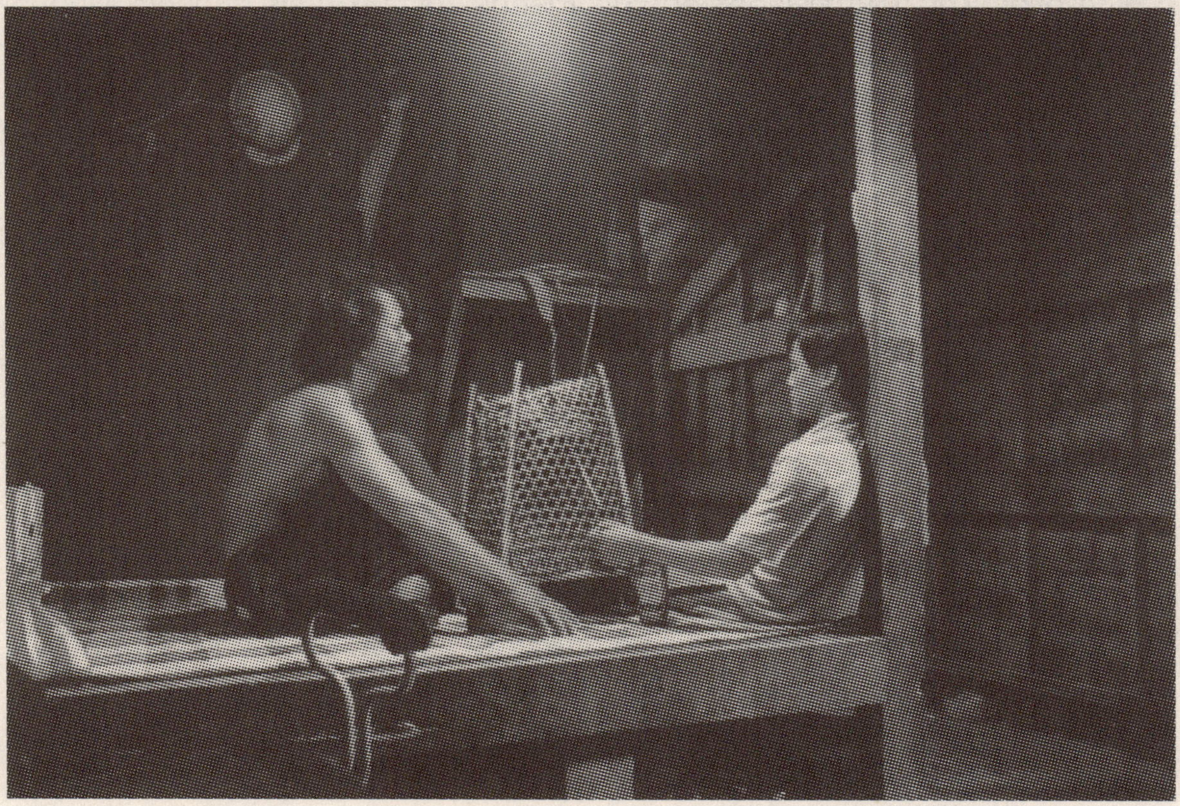

Fig. 3 Ming-Chuan Huang, *The Man from Island West*, 1989, film still, “Reasons of homecoming for Hsiu-Mei and Ah-Ming differed.” © Formosa Filmedia Co.

Fig. 4 Ming-Chuan Huang, *The Man from Island West*, 1989, film still, “Conflicts constantly appealed between the father and son.” © Formosa Filmedia Co.

property, natural disasters, migration, the establishment of a new heaven and earth, self-exile, homecoming, and mutual recognition. At the same time, the narrative voice is that of the ancient Atayal language of the village of Smangus, and the linguistic admixture of Atayal, Japanese, Mandarin, and Taiwanese throughout the film form a special off-screen linguistic orientation. This allegorical ghost story structure and its critique of violence receive far greater weight than the narrative structure of Christian prophecy and messianism in the film. Clearly, the director places the story of Maona, and the voice telling this story, at the core of the film's narrative, just as the images of Ah-Ming's exile and homecoming in a landscape of decapitation form another narrative core. We may view this dual narrative core structure as Ming-Chuan Huang's double-stranded semaphore of allegorical expression.

Double-Stranded Allegorical Narrative Structure

Let us compare these two parallel core narrative strands. (1) Dark tunnel: (Voice-over) The youth Maona and his friends split up while hunting. Maona takes a longer path, and in a trance he comes upon a faraway village. (Image) Ah-Ming, hobbling on a stick, exits the darkness of a high-mountain tunnel and walks into eastern Taiwan, as if entering an alien world. A vertical camera angle of the mountain slope, slowly descending, makes it look like a close-up of a face. Ah-Chiang's father lets Ah-Ming live in his chicken coop and look after the fields.

(2) On the chicken coop bed: (Voice-over) The villagers invite Maona to take part in a hunt for a mountain boar, but when everyone gathers together, they discover he has killed a hunting dog instead. Maona feels ashamed, but is forgiven. (Image) By the wreckage of a fallen car, Ah-Ming lingers all alone. Hsiu-Mei angrily asks why he has trespassed into her swimming area. (Voice-over) On the second day of the hunt, when chasing a big frog, he is unable to subdue it properly, and the frog inflicts Maona's companion with a grievous wound, like a bite from a boar. Everyone is greatly enraged, and they drive him into the big river. (Image) Ah-Ming appears at the side of a river, and is invited to go into the mountains to quarry stones. (Voice-over) Several months later, Maona is rescued by the people of his original village. When they ask him what happened, they discover that he can no longer speak. (Image) The underage prostitute Hsiu-Mei returns home searching for love, but in vain.

(3) Foreign tongues and haunting: (Voice-over) The witch doctor comes to treat Maona, and cuts his tongue with a saber. Not long after, Maona gradually starts to speak, but he talks to himself in a strange language from an outside land. The witch doctor diagnoses him as being haunted by a ghost. (Image) Ah-Chiang complains that the work Hsiu-Mei did in Taipei was unclean.

(4) The lazy boy who sells his ancestral property: (Voice-over) When the boy is direly ill, the witch doctor comes to treat him. (Image) Ah-Ming submerges himself in a stream to cleanse his body. (Voice-over) After consulting the spirits he discovers the boy has sold the ritual vessels of his ancestors, and this has angered them. (Image) Ah-Ming rushes into the ocean, leaping and screaming, "Flourishing, but still ..." Then, a drunken Ah-Chiang argues with his father, declaring his desire to seek a career in Taipei.

(5) God's elect and offending the ancestral spirits: (Image) The pastor and Ah-Ming discuss eschatological redemption. (Voice-over) The witch doctor recognizes that Maona has angered the spirits, bringing on calamity and extending that calamity to his whole people. Maona asks his clansmen to give him local wine, so he might return to health, but his clansmen cannot understand the language he speaks, believing that the ghost has seized him again. Finally, the witch doctor asks the clan to burn him to death. (Image) Ah-Ming, on the beach, digs madly at the sand with his hands. The relationship among Hsiu-Mei, Ah-Chiang, Ah-Ming, and the men from Taipei reaches a climax, and finally Ah-Ming enters a dark tunnel, recalls going mad in a cave when he was young, and calls both the city dwellers and the Atayal men "pigs."

(6) Being burnt to death and flooding: (Voice-over) Maona is surrounded by flames, but before he dies, he suddenly remembers his own tribe's language, and shouts out to his people: "After I die the flood waters will flood the village, the livestock, and the fowl. Nothing with blood and breath will escape. If the prophecy comes to pass, I am innocent." Then, indeed, after Maona dies, a great flood inundates the land for months. The village is completely destroyed. (Image) Ah-Chiang steals Hsiu-Mei's scooter, continues to drink in excess, and dreams of fleeing to Taipei.

(7) Survival and the self-exile of Maona's son: (Voice-over) The surviving villagers do not know what their fate will be, but recalling the prophecy of Maona, they take in his son Yawei Maona and raise him. After he grows up, they ask him to lead the rebuilding of the home the floods have destroyed. Yawei leads some warriors to build a boat, but before departing he tells the people: "You killed my father, and from this day forth, I no longer acknowledge

this people. But to repay your kindness, I will surely lead everyone back home." After forty days and nights, they return to their native island. Then he leaves, never to return. (Image) An interlude of scenery, and Ah-Ming recalling a conversation with his father—his father wanted him to have no fear of snakes and told him not to flee. Then, Ah-Ming and Ah-Chiang confront each other in a tunnel. Images of Ah-Ming's memories constantly surface. His father's breathing reverberates. Finally, amidst flying bats, the spirit of Ah-Ming's father appears in the tunnel. Ah-Ming finally confronts his father, and afterwards he abandons all written words.

(8) Homecoming and silence: (Voice-over) Twenty-five years later, Yawei Manao returns with a head of white hair to his homeland in the east. Though its appearance has changed enormously, the villagers have not forgotten their joy after living through the flood. Every year they hold a rite at the seaside. But the self-exiled Yawei does not dare to mention his brave exploits of the past, when he led the people on their return voyage. He always jokingly calls himself an "outsider," until he dies of old age. (Image) Ah-Chiang gives up hope and sees no way out of his troubles. When he and Ah-Ming speak by the side of the cave, Ah-Ming brings up the question of his own ancestry. Helped by Ah-Chiang's father, he learns that his own father waited forlornly for him to return but finally lost his mind in the cave. Finally, Ah-Ming finds his father's abandoned grave in the woods. Crying bitterly, he acknowledges his homeland. At this time, Ah-Chiang turns hostile toward his father, dragging a traditional woven basket behind a scooter in a state of high dudgeon. When he encounters Hsiu-Mei on a bridge, Hsiu-Mei says: "I'm no longer one of these people here." The screen jumps to the scooter falling down into a steep valley.

(9) Legend and allegory: (Voice-over) A dialogue between what sounds like Hsiu-Mei's voice and that of the narrator of the ancient legend, whom she calls "Papa." The narrator urges insistently that the legend cannot be altered. Here, the narration, and the whole movie, comes to an end.

Headless Landscape and Its Genealogy

The tale of Maona differs from the film's biblically inspired eschatological and messianic narrative in that while Maona issues a prophecy, it constitutes his final words, uttered when he remembers his mother tongue on the brink of death, as he faces being burned alive—it is a prophecy at the simultaneous occurrence of the violence of natural law and the violence of the divine.

Consequently, throughout the entire allegorical tale, not a single transcendent deity or prophet appears. On the contrary, it is the violence exhibited in the wild hunt, the mutual interplay of man and beast, beast and beast, adoption and exile, nurture and punishment, native and alien, language and ghost, forming a set of boundless antinomies. Maona and his son Yawei seem determined to become outsiders, employing a foreign tongue or remaining silent in regard to history. Ah-Ming and his father seem determined to bring into the cave the madness engendered by outside elements, speaking a language that the people of Aohua Village do not comprehend. Ah-Chiang's father, meanwhile, represents the gradual loss of complete narrative ability, becoming embroiled in conflict with the younger generation in a conundrum between tradition and contemporaneity. Finally, it seems that only the entire allegorical narrative voice possesses a certain degree of transcendent status; nevertheless, this voice ultimately does not dare to claim the authority to represent a transcendent god. It merely tells an ancient tale; it is merely a fable. All complicated explanations and meanings await explication from the listener. The entire metaphor reveals a mysterious, minimal "divine violence"; there is no mythical hero able to represent the final law.

Following the release of the movie *Seediq Bale* (2011), the actor and director Leon Dai posted an opinion piece on the internet titled "What Are We Filming?" It offered a comparison between *Seediq Bale* and *Apocalypto* (2007). He felt that the cruel hunting behavior in the indigenous culture of the Mayans signified the value that "for the sake of love, one must suffer to preserve life," and that this value was commonplace in Hollywood film narratives. However, the headhunting (known as *chucao*) that took place in *Seediq Bale* exhibited "excess." "When one head gets chopped off, the audience perhaps is frightened, but can understand. By the time the tenth or eleventh head is chopped off, I think the audience is no longer able to simply understand the cumulative effects of repeated slaughter that might seem reasonable at first. That is to say, through multiple, repeated, detailed display, the director pushes the audience from a perspective cherishing the 'preservation of life' toward the concept of 'life serving beliefs.'"[10]

Dai opines that the value of "life serving beliefs" is not compatible with the mainstream values of either Hollywood or most viewers, and additionally, the film includes many unexplained, slow-paced scenes that have the purpose of debating or contemplating values, and so the headhunting plot creates a chasm separating it from the viewpoints of most viewers, engendering horror and alienation. However, Dai encourages viewers to ruminate on the sense of discomfort in such a viewing experience: Is it because the film returns to a narrative logic and subject entirely alien from modern society that the plot elements of headhunting and "determination to kill" have such a frightening effect? For Dai, this is the major accomplishment of *Seediq Bale* that sets it apart from Hollywood. We should take this opportunity to affirm the existence of a different form of life and a different set of values: "Life must serve beliefs."

Nevertheless, looking at the Wushe Incident from Ming-Chuan Huang's *The Man from Island West*, from Wu He's novel *Remains of Life*,[11] or from the standpoint of the survivors, it is worth deliberating over whether the implications of the term "incident" strictly signify the value of "life serving beliefs." In a critique of violence as original "divine violence," the question of whether the decapitative violence of headhunting represents ultimate justice becomes more complicated with the interjection of the violence of Japanese colonial imperialism. My view is that if we consider the issue from the perspective of the survivor, informed by a differentiation between "divine violence" and "mythical violence," our main focus of concern will be the survivors—the phantom or the lone soul entangled with the phantoms of history—not the will of the hero.

In the history of Taiwanese contemporary art, Ming-Chuan Huang's 1989 narrative of headless landscapes and ghostly allegories was a response to a genealogy that preceded it. The visual narrative of photographer Chang Chao-Tang often placed headless subjects in settings with quite existential auras of absurdity or ruin. Between 1962 and 1964, Chang released *Wuchihshan, Sinchu*, an image of a body with the head hidden from view in a natural landscape; *Panchiao*, a headless shadow against a wall; *Chiangzitrei, Panchiao*, two hands squeezing a head; and *Fujhou, Panchiao*, showing the back of a headless human body against a wall amidst ruins. In his 1970 video self-portrait *Momentary Face*, he constantly shook his head. His *Fangliao, Pingdong* (1973–1985) featured headless frogmen, and from 1986 to 2005 he unveiled such images as *Beitou,* with its upside-down bathers, and *Wufeng, Sinchu,* with its headless livestock. The leftist painter Wu Yao-Chung's self-portrait *Long Night* (1962) depicts the artist clutching his head in a state of melancholia, and in *Mountain Road* (1984), a revolutionary lifts his head and marches forward amid a scene of valor. Hou Tsung-Hui's *Long Fa Tang II* (1983) features the print of a moldy negative of the back of an insane asylum inmate. Hou Chun-Ming's *Hall of Giants* (1990) presents the image of the headless god Xing Tian; and an upside-down Xing Tian, body morphed and doing battle, appears in his *In Search of the Supernatural* (1993). Chen Chieh-Jen's series *Revolt in the Soul and Body* may possess the most vivid historical consciousness regarding historical violence, the narrative of historical events, and the role of the artist's own self-reflection in this process, as well as the most incisive presentation of the state of the survivor. *In Self-Destruction* (1996), Chen placed himself in the scene of a beheading during government suppression of riots in modern China. In *Rule of Law* (1997), he presented himself playing four different roles in the Wushe Incident: a Japanese officer, an indigenous bystander, an indigenous man being tortured, and a head being lopped off. In *Image of an Absent Mind* (1998), two blind believers with amputated legs lift a headless deity as they walk through a wasteland of corpses. In the animated film *Ah-Q* (2002), Kao Chung-Li depicted the ridiculous burden of the Manchurian queue that Chinese men bore in modern history as a reference to the existence of anonymous people in the Third World; headlessness and metal balls taking the place of heads became major images in the film. By 2011, when Wei Te-Sheng portrayed the Wushe Incident in a nearly realistic style in *Seediq Bale*, this genealogy had been extended without interruption, much like the genealogy of modern Chinese fiction documented in David De-Wei Wang's book *The Monster That Is History: History, Violence, and Fictional Writing in Twentieth-Century China*.[12] The vantage point of the survivor and the anonymous individual explored by Ming-Chuan Huang in 1989 and Chen Chieh-Jen in the mid-1990s, and limned by Wu He in *Remains of Life* in 1999, form an undeniable nexus that reverberates down this entire lineage.

1 Walter Benjamin, *Selected Writings of Walter Benjamin* [Chinese language], eds. Chen Yongguo and Ma Hailiang (Beijing: China Social Sciences Press, 1999), 245, 247.

2 Ibid., 246.

3 Karatani Kojin, *Origins of Modern Japanese Literature*, trans. Brett de Bary (Durham, North Carolina: Duke University Press, 1998), Chapter 1, "The Discovery of Landscape," Chapter 2, "The Discovery of Interiority."

4 Walter Benjamin, *Selected Writings*, 292.

5 Walter Benjamin, *Reflections: Essays, Aphorisms, Autobiographical Writings*, trans. Edmund Jephcott (New York: Schocken Books, 1978), 300. "Divine violence" may be interpreted as either "the violence of a deity" or as "holy violence"; because God held no prominent position within Benjamin's understanding of mythology, "holy violence" more properly underscores this aspect of his impersonalized understanding of the divine.

6 Ibid.

7 Ibid., 294.

8 Gilles Deleuze, *Cinéma II: L'image-temps* (1983), Chapter 1.

9 Walter Benjamin, *Selected Writings*, 408, Chapter 9.

10 Leon Dai, "What Are We Filming?", http://litera.ccu.edu.tw/playwriting/?p=105, viewed 09/24/2012.

11 Wu He, *Remains of Life* [Chinese Language] (Taipei: Rye Field Publishing Co., 1999).

12 David De-Wei Wang, *The Monster That Is History: History, Violence, and Fictional Writing in Twentieth-Century China* [Chinese language] (Taipei: Rye Field Publishing Co., 2011).

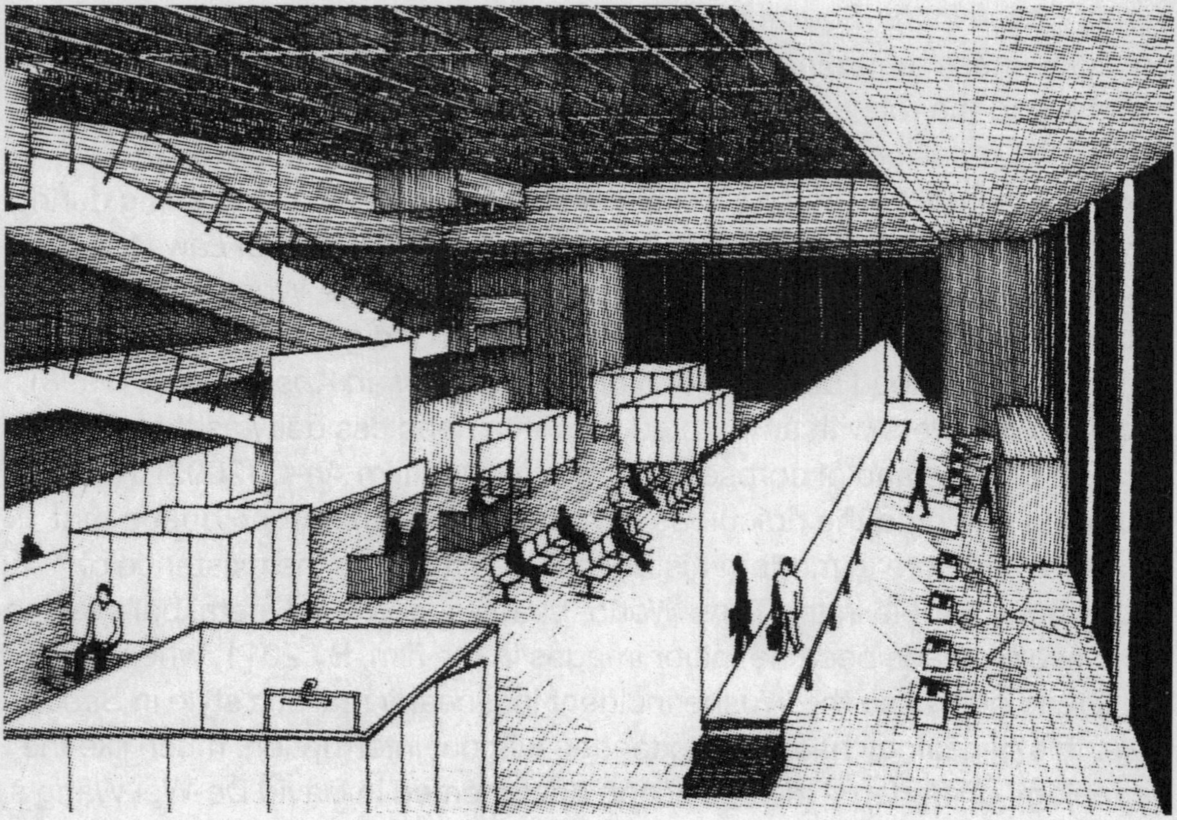

Hannah Hurtzig, *The Waiting Hall. Scenes of Modernity*, 2012, installation and performance. Sketch: Florian Stirnemann; courtesy of Hannah Hurtzig / Mobile Academy Berlin. Entrance into a modern underworld: upon entering the Taipei Fine Arts Museum, visitors walk down a long catwalk and pass by a large screen. Spectators become shadows, projected onto this screen as silhouettes, visible in reverse, from the inside.

INTRODUCTION: DEATH AND LIFE OF FICTION

Anselm Franke

The point of departure for the Taipei Biennial 2012 was the assumption that the monstrosity of modernity could be repurposed to release the political imaginary from its current ideological deadlock. To "talk" to these monsters, to bring them back into animate, dialogic, cultural-political articulation, necessitates that one pass through a realm of order that is on the side of disorder, the "negative" of order, its constitutive fundament, the leftovers of its concrete negations. It means developing a sense that this destruction, this ontological negation, is not something that disappears or is otherwise left behind in the course of linear history, but is something that is actual, that lives on in the present, not merely as a ghost or a specter, but in a concrete way that shapes thinking and structures feeling, that determines the forms available for articulation. It means engaging in a reading of these forms as symptoms of a buried relational past.

In this attempt to speak of, and to, the monstrosity of modernity, the Taipei Biennial turned to a particular monster from ancient Chinese mythology. This monster notoriously shifted its shape within the parameters of the amorphous ancient Chinese imaginary. It was the renowned Taiwanese literary scholar David Der-Wei Wang who, in a recent book called *The Monster That is History*, traced these mutations, following the trail of the monster through Chinese history and into modernity. The Monster That is History: this is not a monster that exhausts itself in a picture. It has no definite graphic image, no specific iconographic tradition. Some representations exist of this fictional creature, but they are sparse and inessential, because this shape-shifting monster is significant not as an image but as a figure of thought and an analytical device.

In his book, David Der-Wei Wang traces the breathtaking journey that the *Taowu* has made through the Chinese cultural imaginary over thousands of years. Like every monster, the *Taowu* is a hybrid: "In classics such as the *Shenyi jing* (The Classic of the Fantastic and the Strange), the *Taowu* is described as a creature that 'looks like a tiger, with hair two feet long. It has a human face, a tiger's feet, a pig's teeth, and a tail as long as eighteen feet.'"[1] Later in the course of its many incarnations, the *Taowu*

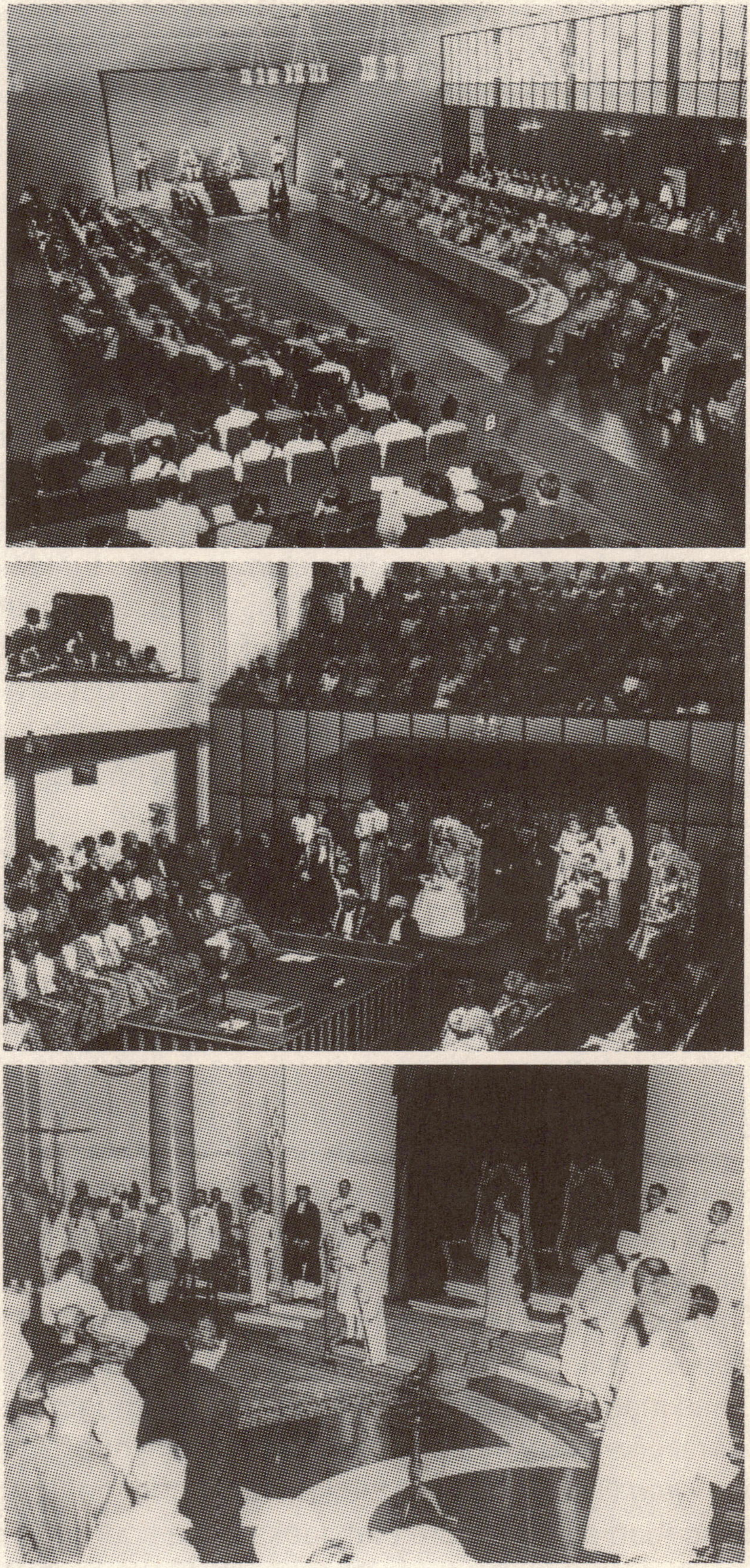

Maryam Jafri, *Malaysia-Ghana-India 1947–1957*. From the photo installation "Independence Day 1936–1967" (2009–present). A series of photographs taken on the first Independence Day of a number of nations in Africa and Asia by artist Maryam Jafri. Jafri emphasizes the identical formal staging of these events, and suggests that the images of them are emblematic of the way the Western model of the nation-state has been desired by and exported to ex-colonies.

was identified with humans of evil inclination, and was "tamed and exiled to the frontiers, since only evil can withstand other evils."

The *Taowu* is a "symbolic exchange," a typical border-equation, an anthropological universal. The *Taowu* became known as a monster that could foresee the future: "As scholars have noted, in the Xia, Shang, and particularly Chu mythological traditions, the *Taowu* is a creature with divinatory powers." The *Taowu* cannot be hunted: it always escapes, it uses its divinatory powers to "make the best of its own life." "Because of its ferocious nature and mysterious visionary ability, the *Taowu* was made a guardian of the imperial tombs in the Chu region. Most significantly, somewhere along the way, the *Taowu* acquired cognitive identity with history itself." Thus, the *Taowu* is an animal that can foresee the future, so it can always run away before the hunters arrive. "Since history reveals both past and future, it is referred to as '*Taowu*.'"

From a monster of evil inclination dwelling in the mountains, guarding the frontiers of empire and later the imperial tombs, the *Taowu* has become identified by Chinese historians and writers with history itself—modern Chinese history in particular, in which one cannot fail to notice a "seemingly endless brutality totted up in dishearteningly large figures," according to David Der-Wei Wang, a modernity that began and continues in crisis.[2] In its different manifestations, this kind of "history" has a common narrative structure: breaking the chains of bondage (imperial, colonial, feudal, or otherwise), this history is about the conquest of history through rational agency itself. It is a fight against monsters. And like all modern histories, it is about the enthronement of human agency against these monsters. And like all these histories of enthronement, this history is haunted, if not overwhelmed, by the vulnerabilities and paradoxes of such agency—which always takes place within a complex nexus of active and passive—and by the instability of its categories.

The Biennial sought an aesthetics of monstrosity that corresponded to the paradoxes of modern agency, and to the structural, abstract, systemic conditioning of modernity. Such an aesthetics folds symptomatic fictions—the common aesthetics of monstrosity as liminal border-figures—into the silent core of normativity and everyday rationality. The "monster" is then not the a-normal, exceptional figuration of a potentially overwhelming force, a threat from the "outside" of social normativity. Rather, in the structural determination of the everyday, the monster is figured as apparatus, as institution, as a-subjective process; the monster is the calculus that binds order to disorder, control to chaos.

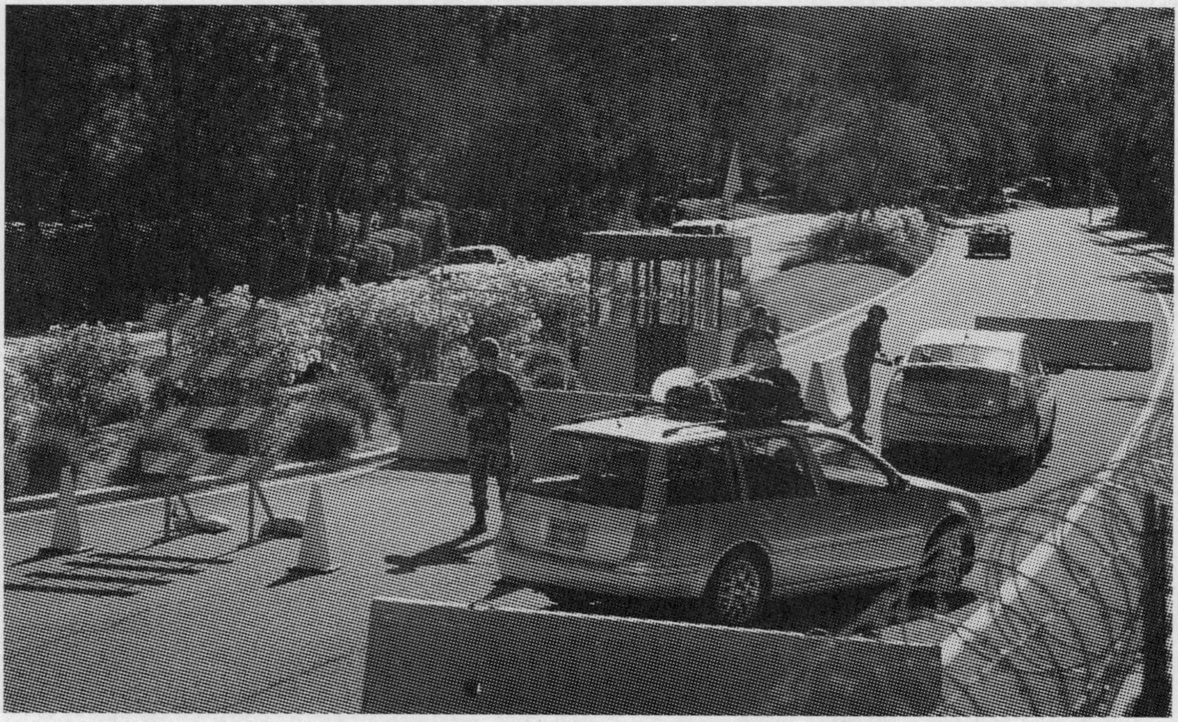

Omer Fast, *5000 Feet is the Best*, 2011, HD video, color, sound, 30 min. Courtesy of gb agency, Paris; Arratia Beer, Berlin. A juxtaposition of footage from two interviews. One is an interview Omer Fast conducted at the end of 2010 with an American ex-drone pilot who talks about the work he did for five years that left him with post-traumatic stress disorder (PTSD). The other is an interview that is staged and portrays a fictional situation in which an interviewer talks to an ex-drone pilot in a hotel room in Las Vegas.

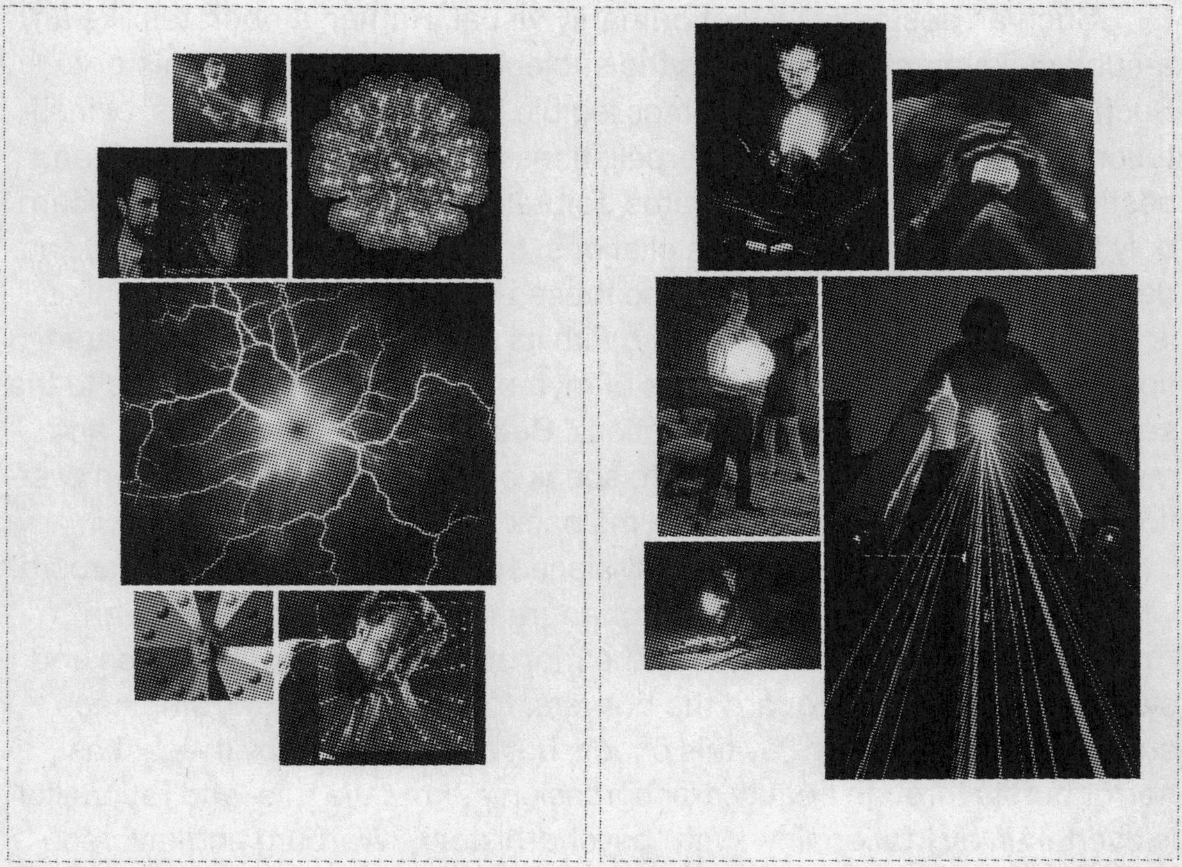

Luis Jacob, *Album II* (panels # 51, 52), 2003–2004, image montage in plastic laminate, 80 panels, each 45.7×30.5 cm. There always remains an incommensurable rest, a gap, a possible locus of resistance: Jacob's *Albums* open up an image-space of iconographic and semantic shifts kept in gestural movement, through which we can experience form not as something stable, but rather as a dialogic event in which subjectivity is formed.

Such an aesthetics is not primarily visual. Rather, it operates like an a-subjective mirror which maps the subject onto the surface of history. Such a-subjective history becomes legible as a system of borders, of institutions and designations, of interpellations and rationalizations. Such an aesthetics seeks to open the gates, to break through borders, which can only be done in dialectical constellations, through foldings, inversions, and deconstructive equations, because these borders are ontological. This is what the narratives of mythology, with its canon of monsters, have traditionally done. Today, the monsters of mythology have been relegated to the secure and fenced off island of "fiction." But "fiction" can be mirrored and mapped onto itself, until it begins to speak of the fence as such. It then overflows the fence, dissolves, and claims back a lost sovereignty.

Just such an aesthetics was envisioned by the art historian Aby Warburg, who saw himself as a "psycho-historian" reading in all cultural facts an "uncanny duality," a "dialectics of the monster": the social structures and symbolizations built to guard the borders, to separate order from chaos, are not merely "haunted" by this chaos, but overwhelmed by it—just as horror bursts through beauty, transgression affirms the rule, and rationality is overtaken by irrationality. With "psycho-history," Warburg endeavored to read history as an imprint at the dialectical tipping points of inversion, contradiction, and collapse. Yet these tipping points were like gates through which he entered a different region, one situated below the scission that runs through opposites, their common "ground" where "history" itself is turned into a psychic tableau, into a diagram of dynamic forces that exhibit themselves as ex-stasis. To de-monster the monstrosity of history in the current moment means to denaturalize this realm of primary relationality—the realm of the unconscious, of emotions, affects, social mimesis, rhythm, and industrialized subjectivations. It means to reinscribe this region of ecstatic history back into the realm of politics.

In ecstatic history, the subject is annulled and negated, rendered transparent, turned into a fleeting effect. It is such anti-subjectivism that is capable of facing "modern monstrosity" in its abstract, machinic form, or as one could say, as that which is already there, structurally given, before an "I" or a "we" occupies its prescribed place and a "self" assumes its form and claims agency—only such anti-subjectivism allows us to see the subject as mediated and historical through and through. What emerges from such a perspective is a view of history that is universalist without leveling particularities—its universalism is "negative" insofar as it maps the discontinuous forces and effects of official historiographies. It is also

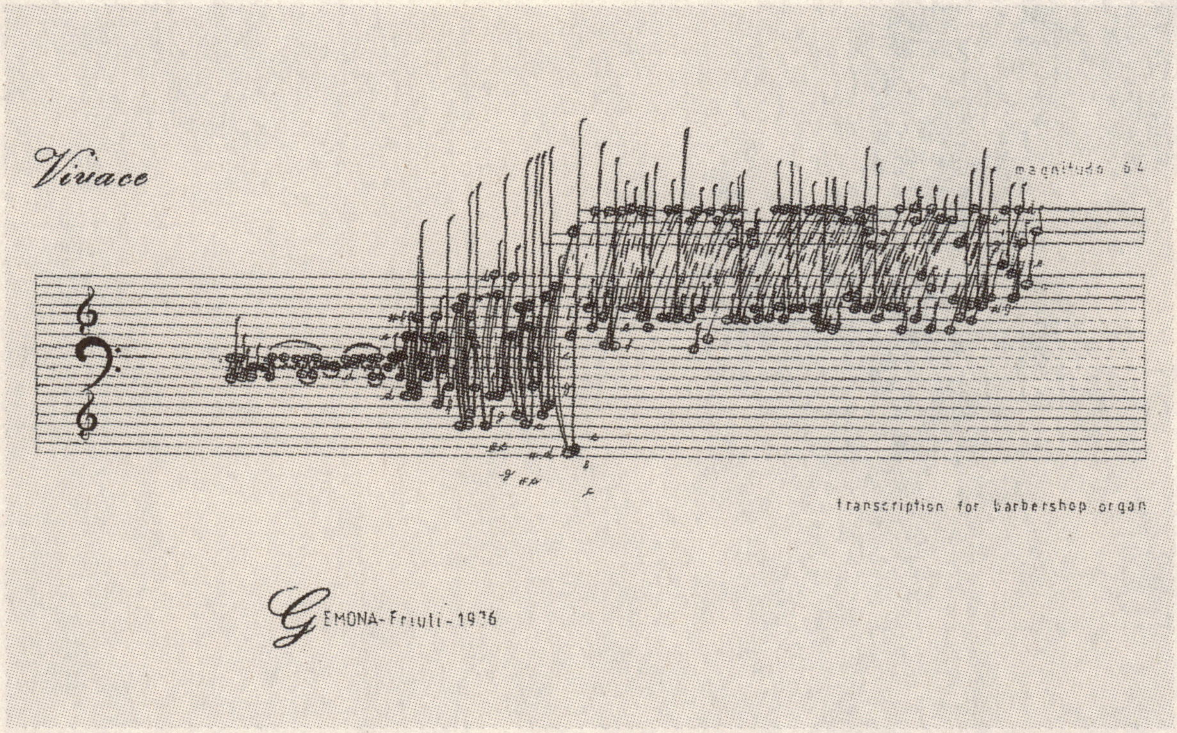

Elisa Strinna, *Seismic Symphonies*, 2008/2012, sound installation, wood, plastic, iron, paper, 210 × 60 × 70 cm, 5 min. *Seismic Symphony — Taiwan* translates earthquake seismograms into a symphony played on a wooden organ. The seismic shock of the 1999 Taiwan earthquake becomes the score.

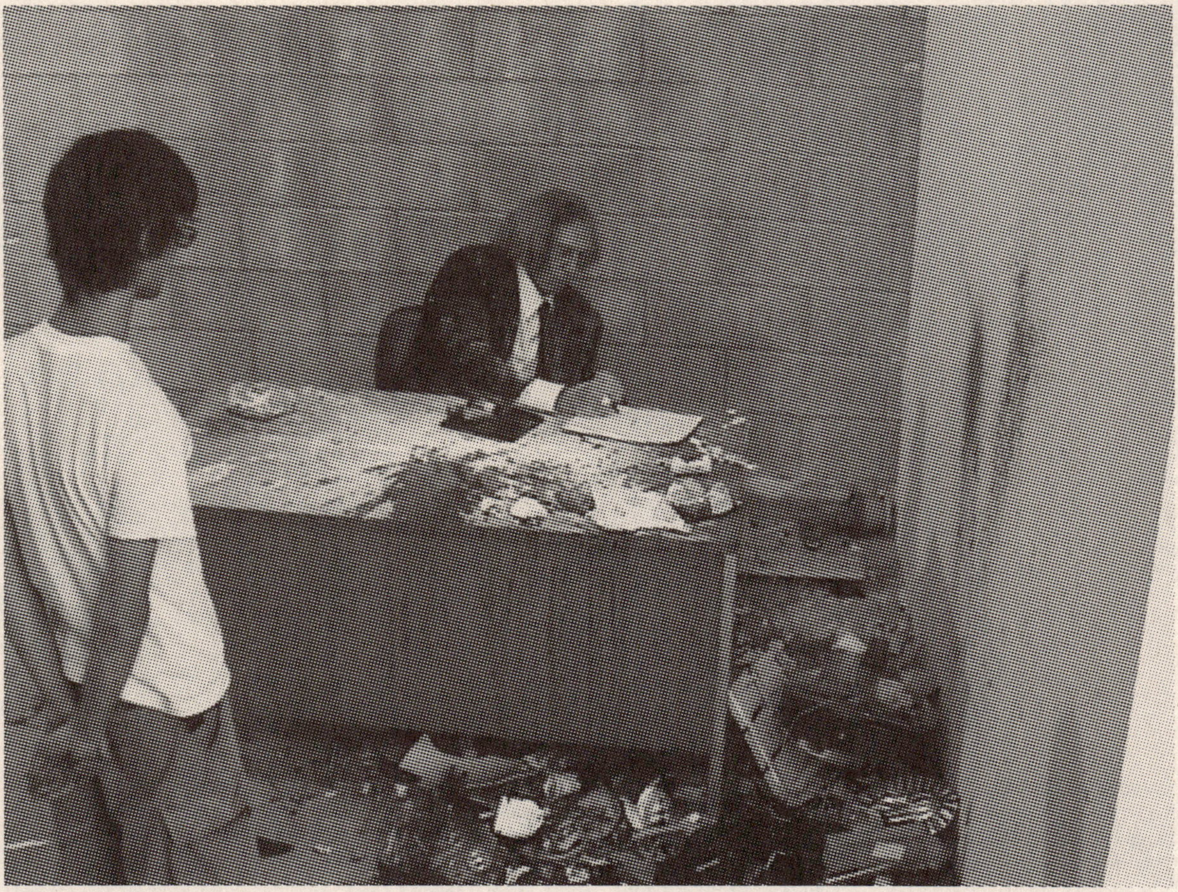

Jimmie Durham, *Smashing*, 2004, video color, sound, 92 min. Like a bureaucrat, Jimmie Durham sits behind his desk and smashes objects given to him, an act certified with an official stamp. Decomposition, destruction, trash: it is through the "objects" that have fallen outside the "order of things" that Durham's work tells us what this order doesn't know about itself.

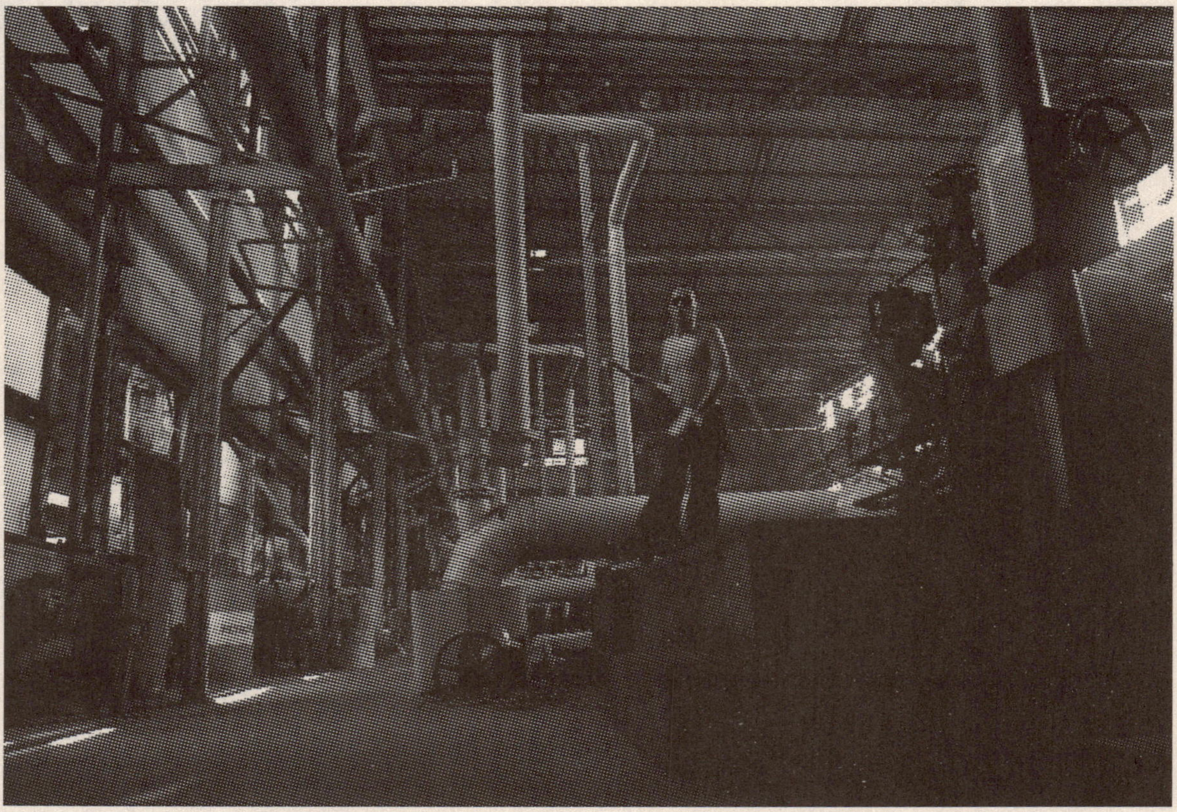

Jompet Kuswidananto, *War of Java. Do You Remember? #2*, 2008, video, black and white, sound, 7 min. The War of Java was fought between 1825 and 1830, sparked by the rebellion of Prince Diponegoro in response to the plans of Dutch colonizers to build a road across land where his parents' tomb was located. In the middle of the nineteenth century, when the Dutch began to build sugar factories in the north coastal region of Java, a particular practice emerged among the plantation workers and sugar farmers. A ritual called "*cembengan*" was created, which accompanied the initial processing of the sugar cane into sugar. This ritual was conducted amidst the large machines that ground the sugar cane. Workers performed a dance that invoked the spirits of their ancestors. In the context of the colonial factory, the ritual addressed the experience of colonialism and factory work as a new cosmological bond, expressed as a bodily-mimetic relation between humans and machines.

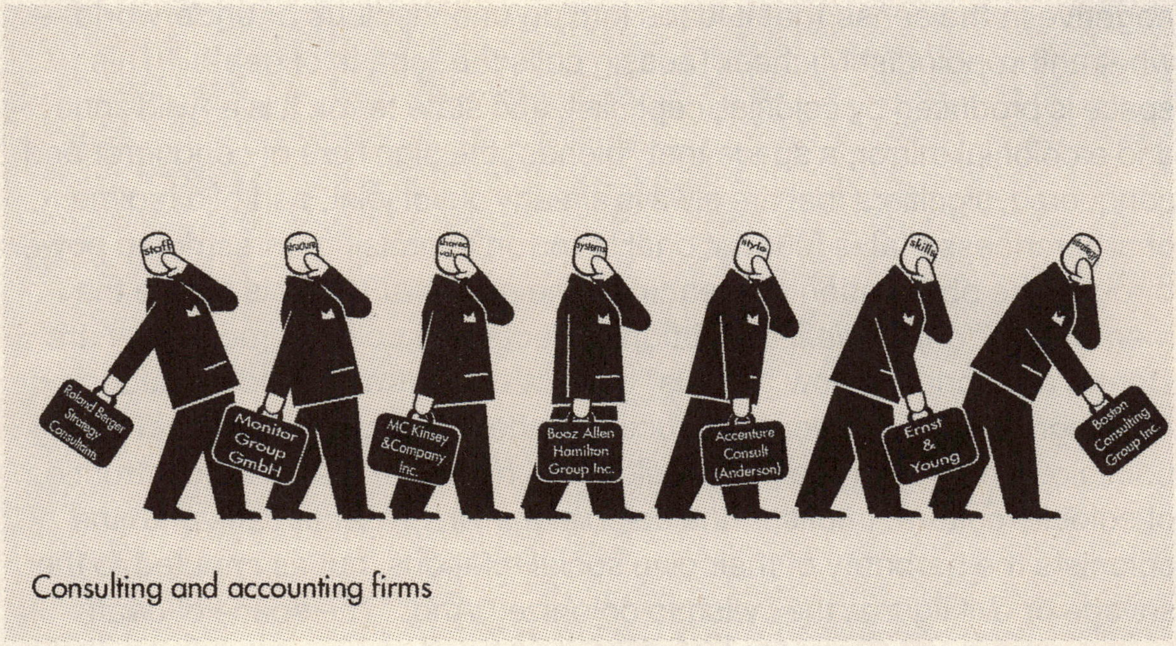

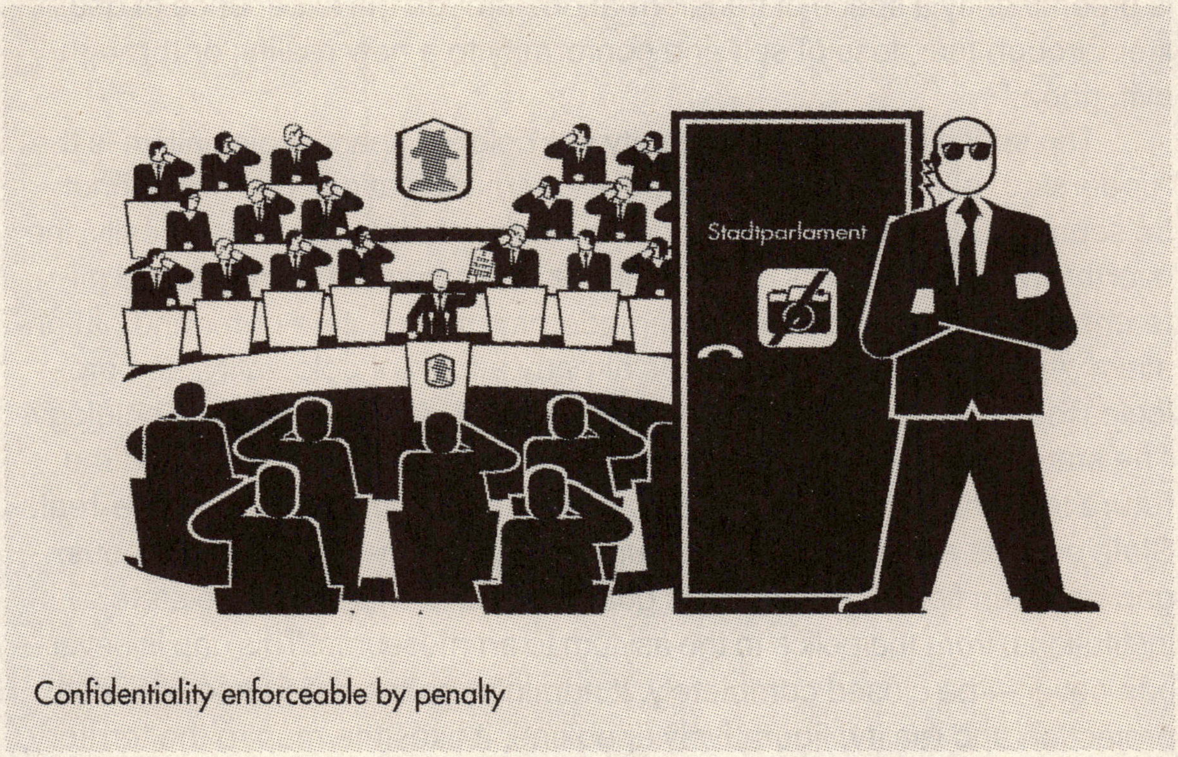

Andreas Siekmann, *Trickle down—Public Space in the Era of Its Privatization*, 2012/2007, digital prints, 460 × 980 cm. Courtesy of Gallery Barbara Weiss, Berlin. Siekmann's work focuses on the restructuring of labor conditions under so-called globalization and the systematic erosion of social structures. He interrogates the present conditions of capitalist exploitation, neoliberal propaganda, and the forms of political camouflage they yield today. This investigation focuses on the close relationship between artistic work, "creativity" as a marketing slogan, urban image-campaigns, and so-called regeneration policies. The backdrop of this work is the increasingly global methods used by the financial industry to make city governments dependent as debtors, thereby systematically undermining politics and public control.

negative in the sense that it leads into an unconscious or underworld—what anthropologist Michael Taussig calls the "space of death." This space is produced by colonial, capitalist, and state terror. It is a "wild zone" and a colonial mirror, a space that "blends" the signifiers of conqueror and conquered, signifiers that are always already out of joint, part of a regime of arbitrariness that is foundational to terror, exercising unrestricted power through the obliteration of meaning. The space of death is where the memories of *ontological* revolutions effected by colonial modernity are stored, memories of how "worlds" have been destroyed and shrouded. An integral part of this very destruction is the destruction of *sense*. Taussig points out the "reciprocating yet distorted mimesis" that the "construction of colonial culture" implies: "*the colonial mirror*…reflects back onto the colonists the barbarity of their own social relations, but as imputed to the savage or evil figures they wish to colonize." And: "The space of death is preeminently a space of transformation: through the experience of death, life; through fear, loss of self and conformity to a new reality; or through evil, good."[3]

The space of death in modernity is a colonial space: colonialism is the "underside" of modernity-as-narrative-of-emancipation. The two cannot be separated, and everything hinges on their entanglement. Historically, the overthrow of direct forms of colonial rule has marked the entry into a different frame of the social order of modernity, that of state order and nationalism. And this form of the state is already a form of coloniality, an ontological homogenization, a map made corporeal, a map turned into ontology. The state colonizes the ways in which the past is remembered and the future imagined. The state is realized as an operative fiction-made-real. State order is established and "naturalized" when the (always precarious) gap between fiction and reality is guarded and managed by the state's institutions, from the police to the asylum to art museums. This gap is never—can never—be closed completely. It administers the difference between projection and reality; figuratively speaking, it fixes the map to the territory, signs to things, names to bodies. The institutions of modern states secure this fixing through various degrees of symbolic and actual violence. They guard and manage the limits of the state's ontology around an empty center of normativity. In the case of totalitarian governments or military dictatorships, the violence is all-pervasive: the state fights its specters by realizing itself as a monstrosity, as an embodiment of the principle of negation. But liberal democratic nation-states are likewise haunted by the primary violence on which they have been (and continue to be) erected,

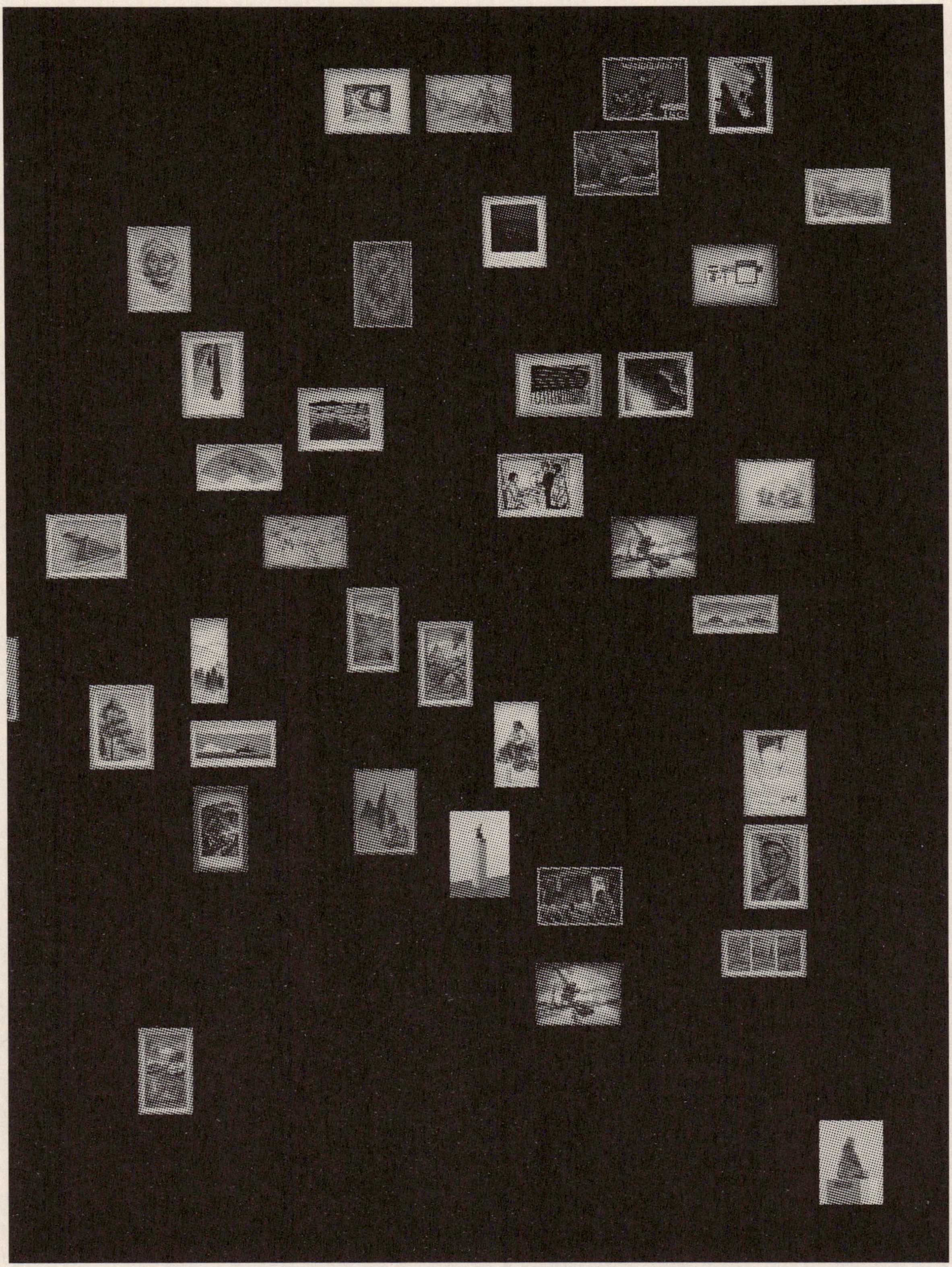

Liu Ding, *The Un-erasable*, 2012, performance, mixed media installation. Courtesy of Galerie Urs Meile, Beijing-Lucerne. Since 2009, Liu Ding has collected "everyday" artworks from online auctions, flea markets, and friends. These include paper-cuts, embroidery, sketches, watercolor paintings, oil paintings, woodcuts, and sculptures, most of whose motifs, styles, and genres are familiar and common. Yet these artworks hold no "special" status, significance, or value. Typically they are gifts or souvenirs, or they decorate homes or hotel lobbies, or they are made as part of an artist's training or by an amateur. They are part of history and our experience of art and aesthetics, but without having a distinct place in art history. And yet they express and reflect the sensibilities, desires, and states of consciousness of their makers just as much as the social context in which they exist.

Jason Dodge, *Anyone*, 2010, ten sheets exchanged by a linen service weekly. *Anyone* consists of a pile of bedsheets from a hotel in Taipei which have been slept on numerous times. This loss of personal information grows as the sheets are washed and replaced on a regular basis during the duration of the exhibition.

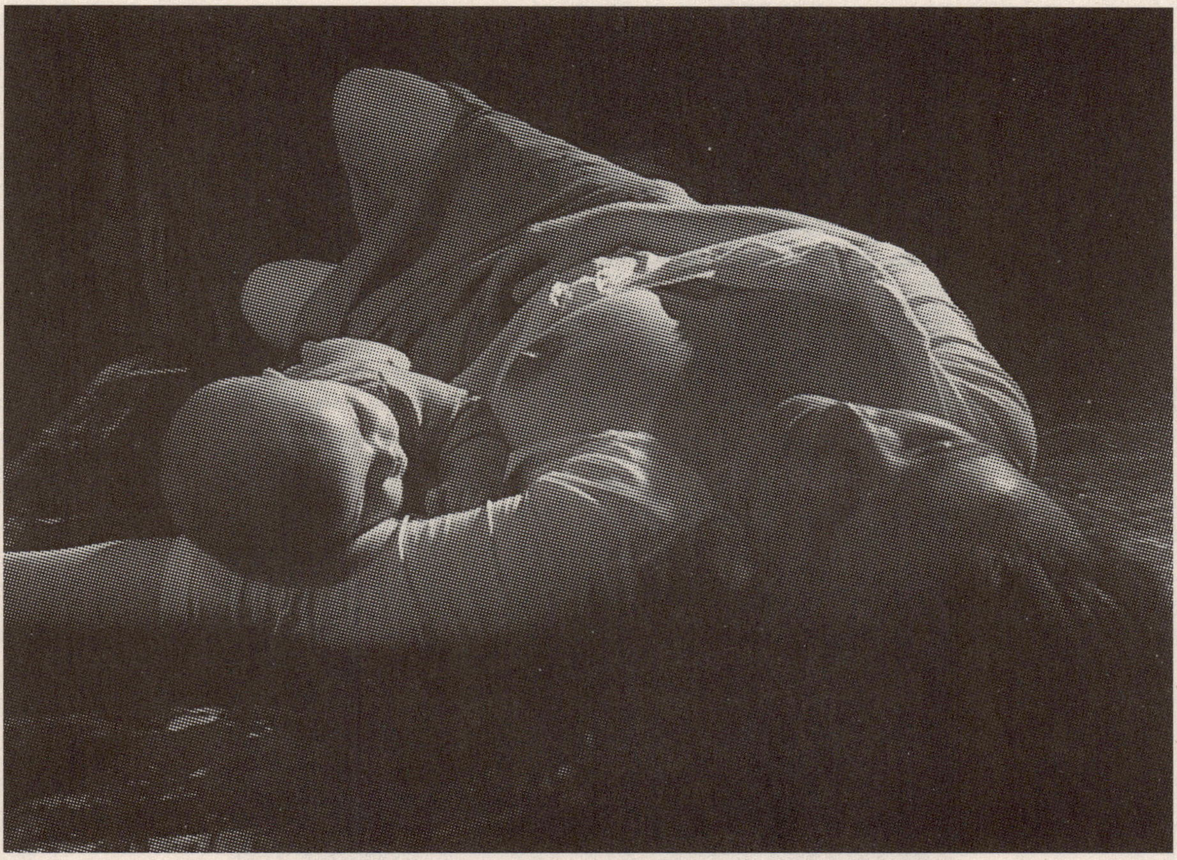

Peter Friedl, *Bilbao Song*, 2010, HD video, color, sound, 5 min 53 sec. Courtesy of Meyer Kainer Gallery, Vienna. *Bilbao Song* shows different historical paintings from various epochs as tableaux vivants. What they have in common is that they are all related to the Basque Country, a part of Spain marked by its struggle for independence, and whose complex history encompasses the internal colonization of Europe, the so-called "minority-question," as well as the world's first aerial bombing of civilians, famously depicted by Picasso in his painting *Guernica*—an iconic picture of both modern atrocity and modernist art.

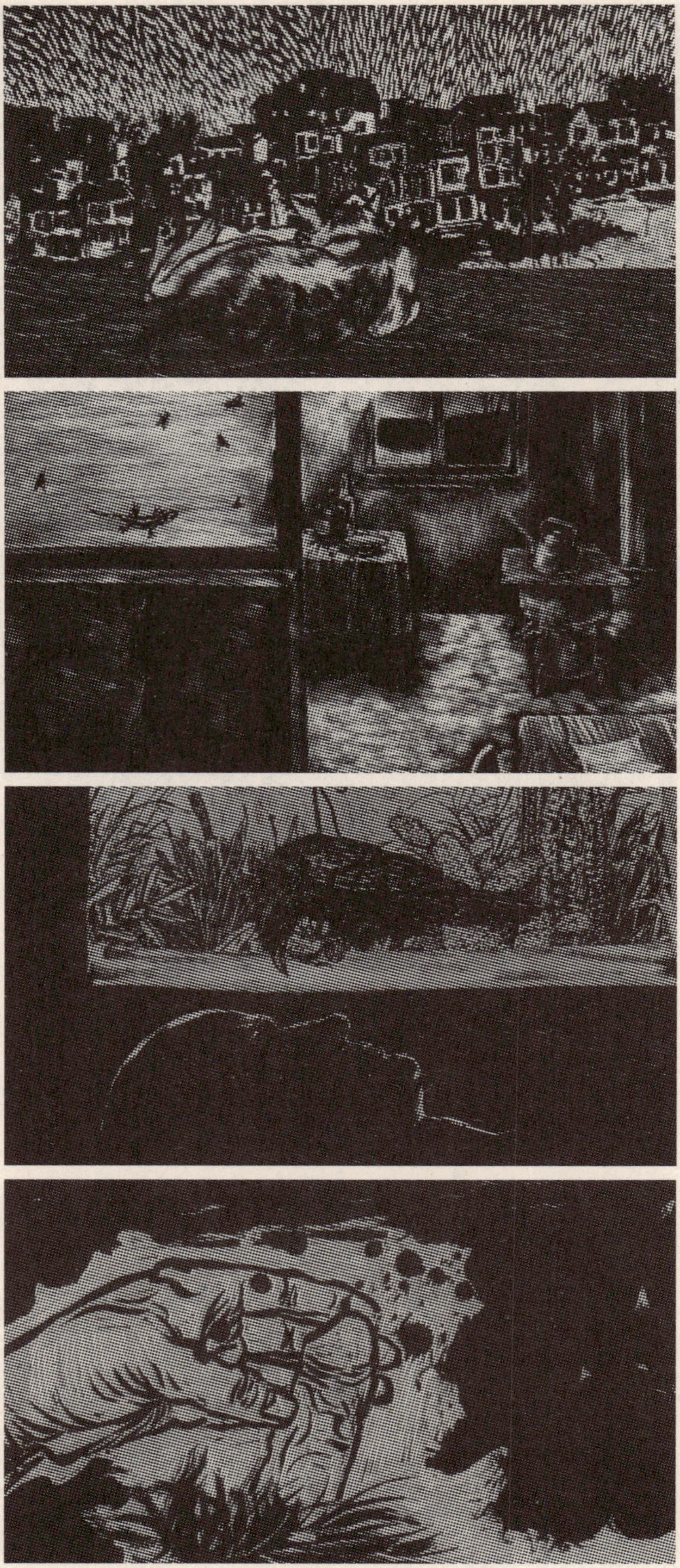

Sun Xun, *Some actions which haven't been defined yet in the revolution*, 2011, animation, 12 min 22 sec. The woodcut is a traditional Chinese technique which is more than two thousand years old and which experienced a revival during the Cultural Revolution in the 1960s and 1970s. The scenes in this animation evoke the metaphor of "cannibalism" as an attitude and mental condition, used by the influential author Lu Xun to describe the decay of Chinese consciousness. Lu Xun wrote *The True Story of Ah Q* in the first half of the twentieth century and was, not coincidentally, also an eminent scholar of Chinese woodcuts.

and also by, on the one hand, modern capitalist dialectics of identitarian division, and on the other, transgressive hybridization. Multiculturalist pluralism has fought against the identitarian in order to reconcile modern state order with hybridity, but while it successfully broke some monocultural monopolies, it also extended identitarian principles and inscriptions into ever new terrains. The "space of death" of modern statehood harbors the memory of the "blind spot" of modern sovereignty: the zone where power is above the law and absolute, and thus, theoretically and in practice, a zone of terror that is experienced as plain war by those outside of its identitarian and symbolic order. Paradoxically, it is also the zone where power testifies to its nonidentity with the people.

Today, modernization is almost universally equated with economic and technological development, while political modernization has become deeply suspect. The belief in a rational conquest of the future has been irretrievably undermined by the catastrophic record that modern schemes for planning, liberation, and rationalization left in their wake. Among these schemes, the monstrosities of the socialist states stand out in historical consciousness. But socialism was followed closely by the fate of former colonies, by the debris of modernization schemes in the third world. The message: there is no longer liberation, there is only techno-capitalist development. The only horizon left is integration into its global infrastructure. It is as if history has conveyed a unambiguous message: dreams of emancipation, a rational society, and collective progress are doomed and will inevitably turn into totalitarian nightmares—as if they were against nature, which will inevitably take its revenge. The declared enemy of the new global alliance has been named "ideology," "state planning," and any politics that represents the dispossessed. Power directed against power, as if enhanced by a principle of negation, appears to turn into more vicious forms of power. The negative evidence left behind by schemes for social and political modernity is the resource on which neoliberalism continues its triumphal conquest. Throughout this conquest, "politics" and democratic planning have not ceased to surrender to economic calculus. Where modern rationality has failed to inject life into its drawing-board utopias, and has instead turned them into life-negating tyrannies, capital now rushes to fill the void, like blood flowing through the veins of the social body of modernity. The narrative-imaginary vacuum of the present bears witness to this shift. We can read the symptomatic imprint of it in social and aesthetic genres, in the flows of desire, in the formatting of emotions and affects. Capital has filled a void in which the oppositions

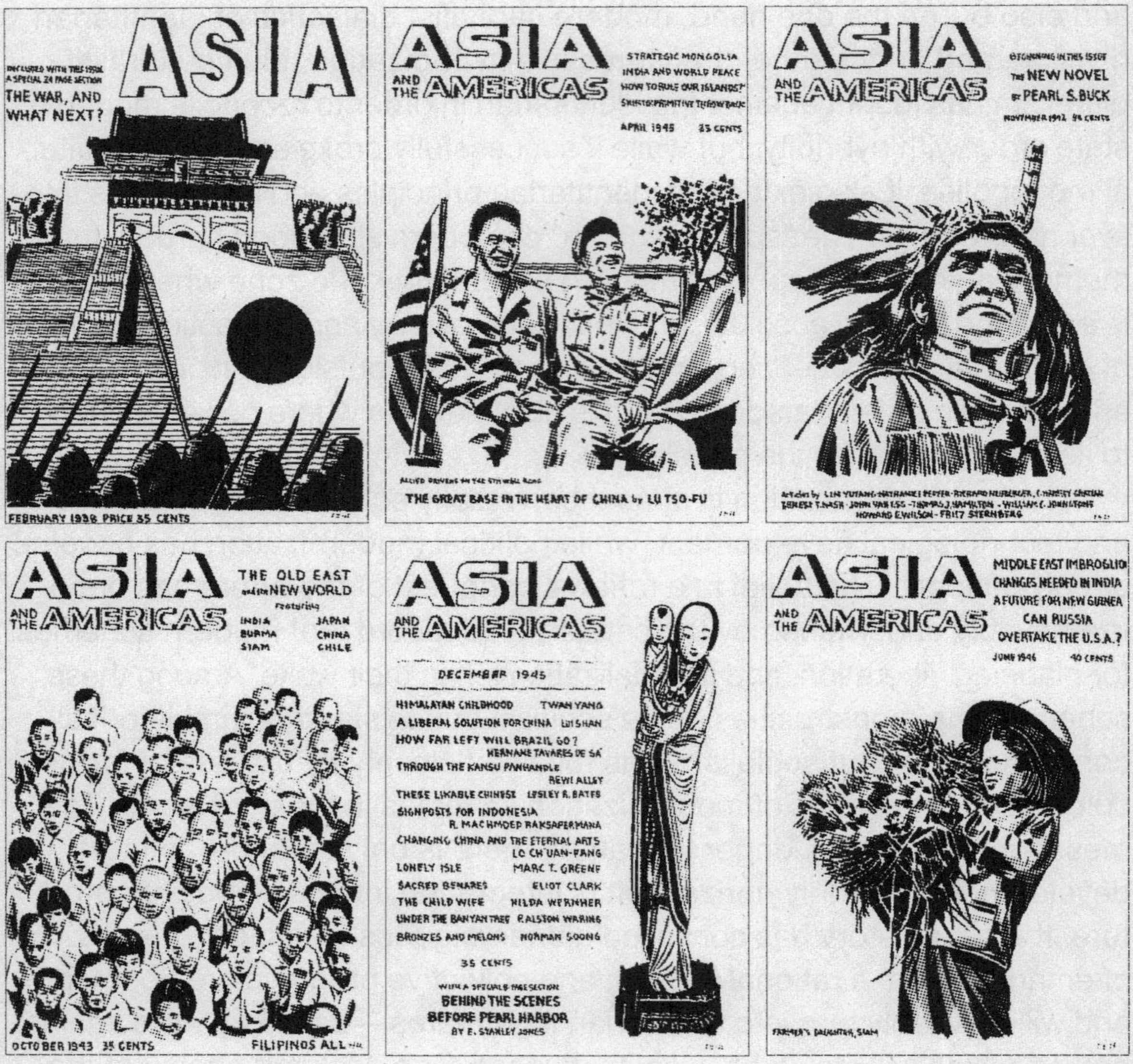

Fernando Bryce, *ASIA* (detail), 2006, ink on paper, a series of fifty drawings, each, 30 × 21 cm or 42 × 30 cm. Collection of Diana and Moisés Berezdivin. Fernando Bryce uses a technique he calls "mimetic analysis." He copies the existing text and image in his own aesthetic style, which is characterized by simple drawings that resemble mid-twentieth century cartoons, and he replaces the texts with handwritten commentaries that have calligraphic traits. This series depicts the American magazine *Asia*, which was later renamed *Asia and the Americas*.

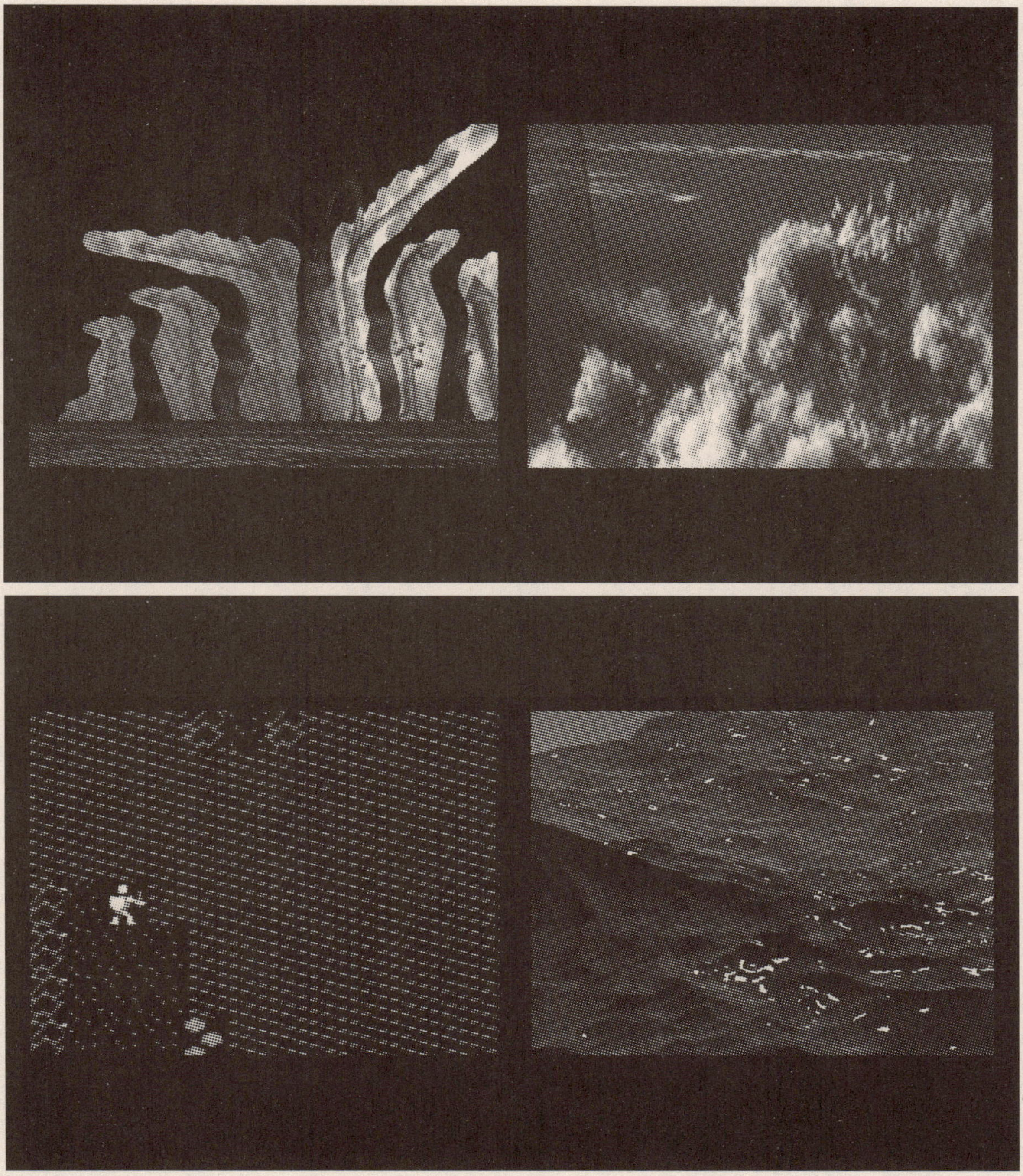

Harun Farocki, *Parallel*, 2012, two-channel HD video installation, color, sound, 17 min. Today, mimesis is increasingly a matter of generative algorithms, and the resulting technologies are increasingly capable of calculating, predicting, and controlling complex processes — from manufacturing, to war, to emotional experiences in the animated worlds of mass entertainment. Underlying Farocki's investigation into the frontiers of innovation in current image-technologies is the assumption that increasingly, we live in technologically produced image-worlds in which images have become what he calls "ideal-typical." In the new mimetic paradigm of digital hyperrealism, reality is no longer the measure of the always imperfect image; instead, the image increasingly becomes the measure of an always-imperfect reality.

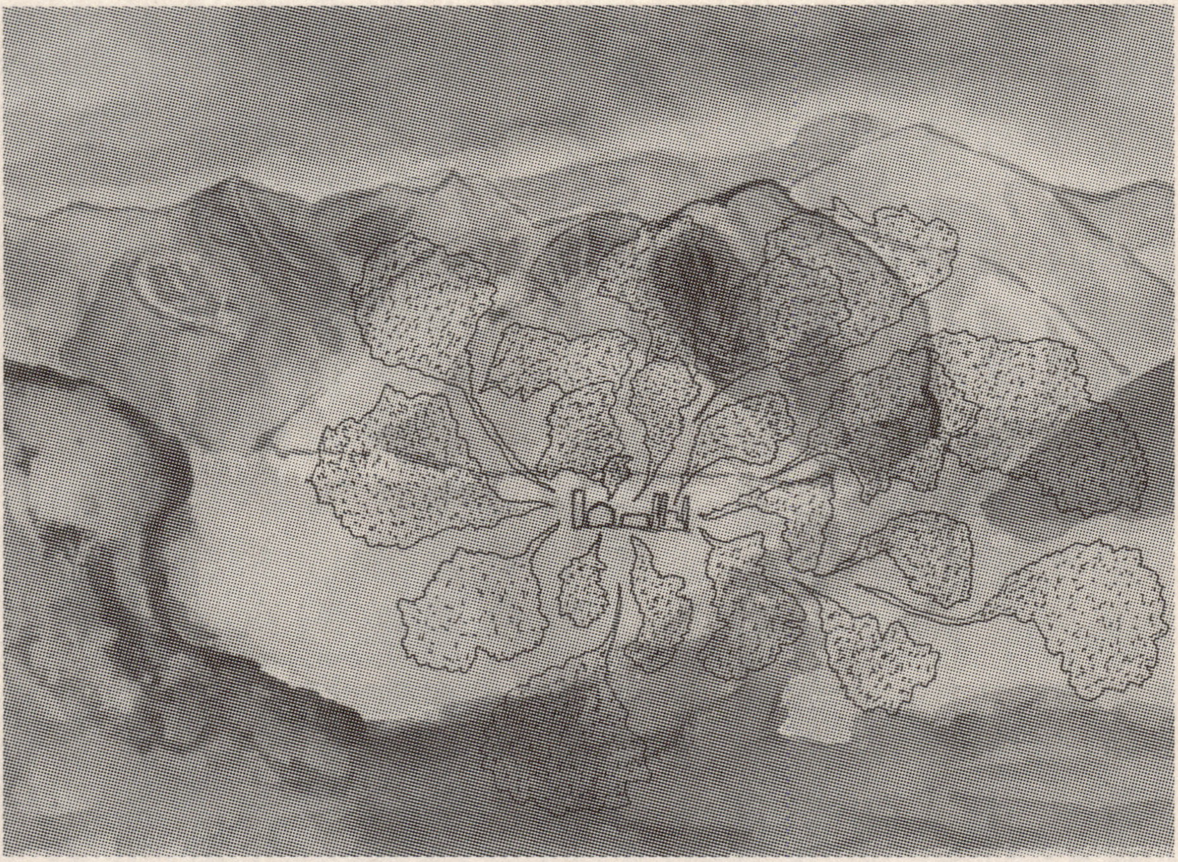

Maria Thereza Alves, Sketch for an unrealized work on the Taroko people's struggle against the Asia Cement Corporation, Hualien, Taiwan, 2012.

and trenches of long sequences of historical struggles progressively collapse. Today, neoliberal hypermodernity is synonymous with countless restorations and revisions which seek to appease the "unnatural monsters" of modernity, outliving the oppositional logic on which they were based. After such appeasement, what kind of modernity are we left with?

To answer this question, artists today are increasingly obliged to become quasi-historians. In the case of the authors and practitioners gathered in the Taipei Biennial 2012, this is not out of an identitarian concern with authenticity, origins, or ancestry, nor out of any safe romantic yearning for a lost golden age. On the contrary: it is because the quest for modernity-as-emancipation is leading a spectral life underneath the surface of the present. The artists in the Taipei Biennial 2012 do not seek to cut all ties with the past, as high modernism called for many times. Instead, they seek to de-naturalize the present and regain alternative choices beyond the existing double binds, to defend difference and certain oppositions against their conflation and collapse into the void. What is this difference that only a recourse to history can uphold? It is the difference that allows us to resist the naturalization of nationalism, to resist our own inscription into the mytho-propagandistic imaginaries of state rationales. It is the difference that allows us to refuse subjectivation by an identitarian order based on divisions into phantasmagoric insides and outsides, and that allows us to question the implicit premises and assumptions on which such orders are based. It is the difference that makes it possible to characterize what "modernity" has become as a present condition, a haunted condition, an increasingly all-encompassing technological inscription, a technoscientific conquest of "nature" that yields monstrous effects in the service of capital.

Taiwan is a country where no layer of colonial or nationalist capture has gone uncontested or been univocally naturalized, from the early days of European colonialism to Chinese migration, Japanese occupation, US hegemony, and the threat of a takeover by the People's Republic of China. Even on the level of sovereignty, Taiwan—the Republic of China—is a head without a body, a non-recognized phantom that has lost its body, the "mainland." Taiwan, in its position in both the world and in modernity, represents paradigmatic "unstable grounds." The Biennial sought to turn this instability from a deficit into a advantage, to question and articulate a common denominator of modernity, a possible ground for a non-identitarian collectivity, the *experience* of modernity as recounted in the space of death.

The space of death as a negative mirror, as a desubjectfying mirror: this concept is reminiscent of the first hall in the mythology of hell in the Daoist tradition. There, the dead encounter the "mirror of evil" or the "mirror of retribution," which takes measure of their deeds and consequently defines their future karma and their punishments in the ten halls of hell. The halls of hell can be imagined as desubjectifying purifiers that transform the soul into a state that enables it to continue its karmic travel. The Daoist underworld, like the thousands of Daoist temples in Taiwan, is meticulously organized into a proto-bureaucratic monstrosity, at times reminiscent of a Kafkaesque corporation or state. Could this relation between, on the one hand, an orderly economy of mimesis, law, inscription, registration, and calculation, and on the other, a profound ontological uncertainty, become a fictionalized account of the paradoxes of modernity and of the ontologically uncertain "state" that is Taiwan? If so, where would fiction end and realism begin? Could the two—the organization of the spiritual underworld and the "inevitable" order of modernity—become a dramaturgical *Kippfigur*, with one turning into an aspect of the other, tied to each other as twin inventions, just as "tradition and modernity" have always been, yet remaining distinct, even incommensurable—not "out there" in the object of study, where they clearly coexist and reciprocate each other just like the duck and the rabbit or the human profile and the vase, but in "subjective experience," that is, in what we take from "history" and bring to bear on the present?

The insecure, "non-naturalized" status of Taiwan means that one does not need to dig deep to reach below the nation as the "skin stretched over the bones of the state"[4] to reach the strata of unpacified, "colonial" memories, the sacrificial logic of ontological violence. After all, the gates between the dead and the living are loosely guarded. Contrary to the rich resources of mythology in Daoism—which has images and narratives to adapt to such encounters—what crosses from underneath here falls into an imaginary-narrative vacuum. There are no, or few, forms available to engage with state order and its paradoxes, forms that could communicate with these aporias and with the symbolic economy of order from its outsides—the very imaginability of an outside or of otherness that enables what we have called the "sense of alternative" on which historical consciousness and the ability to step outside the circle, or to inhabit the void, is built.

David Der-Wei Wang speaks of a "primal scene" of Chinese literary modernity, a scene of decapitation. Here, the numbing of the senses calls

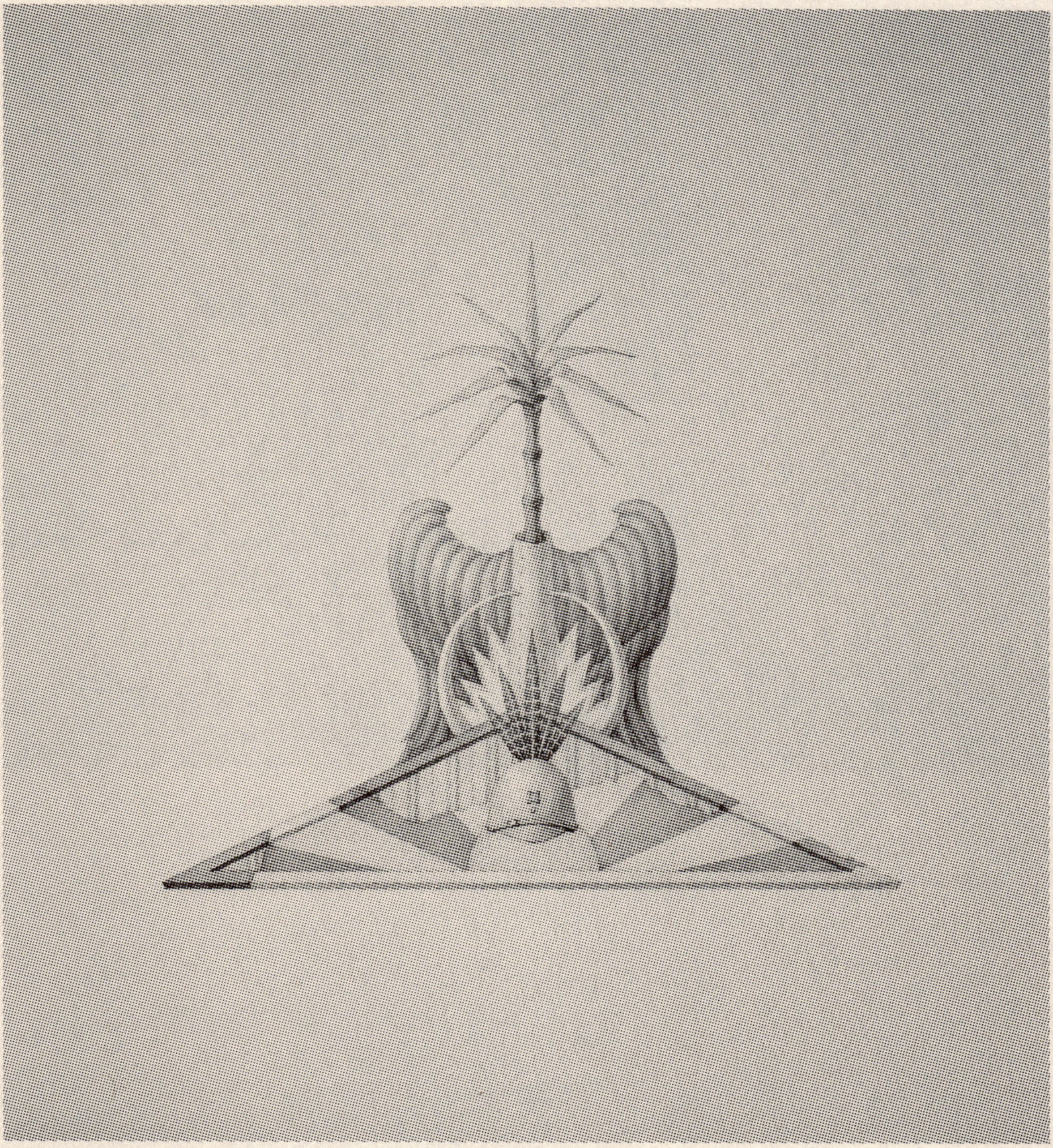

Chia-En Jao, *ARMS*, 2012, pencil on paper, series of thirty drawings, each 40 × 40 cm. The word "symbol" has its roots in the Greek *symbolon*, which originally meant "to throw, or bind, something together." Chia-En Jao's thirty designs of a fictional coat of arms use this symbolic convention as a means to bind together various conflicting elements of Taiwanese history. The coat of arms represented here depicts the rising sun, representing the imperial Japanese dream of "uniting" Asia. Japan took possession of Taiwan in the late nineteenth century from the defeated Qing Dynasty, which had ruled the island since the seventeenth century. This sun rises above the South Pacific Islands, and the (broken) shape of Taiwan's Yushan mountain is visible. The filled-in portions of the triangle are galvanized steel plates, which are commonly used in the construction of factories in Taiwan. Above the red sun is an American helmet, representing US hegemony in Taiwan under the KMT, after Japan's defeat. On top of the helmet are feathers from a Taiwanese Mikado, while in the background is an inferno and black eagle's wings, the imperial symbol par excellence. In the center of the image is an upright cannon, out of which a sugar cane grows—the very first commodity cultivated in Taiwan. Sugar cane piqued imperial interest in Taiwan and triggered the waves of colonization that have defined Taiwanese history up to the present day.

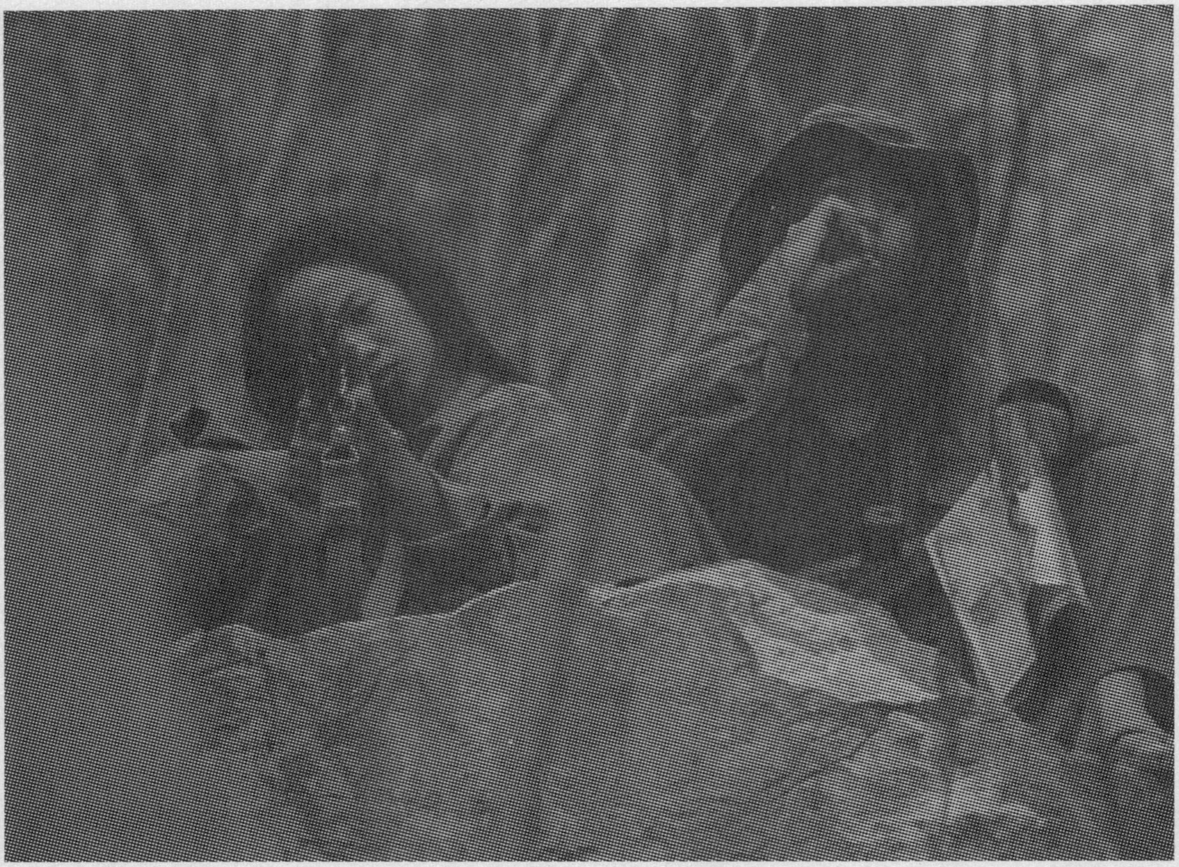

Jakrawal Nilthamrong, *Zero Gravity*, 2012, HD video, color, sound, 28 min. *Zero Gravity* by Jakrawal Nilthamrong is a film about the borderland between Thailand and Burma. It is also about the borderland between fiction and truth, and past and present. In 2000, Ratchaburi Hospital was occupied and the staff was taken hostage by armed Karen guerrillas under the command of "God's Army" from neighboring Burma, the leadership of which was attributed to two twelve-year-old twins. The ten occupying guerrillas were eventually killed by Thai forces, some apparently executed on the spot after their surrender. This incident raised awareness of the political situation in Burma and the war fought by the Karen people in southern Burma, and was credited with sparking today's insurgency in southern Thailand.

forth its cure. A particular "death" gives birth to a form of "fiction": looking at a decapitation, the then student of medicine, Lu Xun, claimed that he decided to became a writer in order to promote a "new culture." It is the passivity of his own people, their voyeurism and complicity, that strikes Lu Xun as he looks at a photograph from the Russo-Japanese war in which a Chinese collaborator is executed. He later describes a spectacle like this in his novella *The True Story of Ah Q*. It is the apathetic gaze of the onlookers from his own "weak and backward" country, the symptomatic subjectivity, which, in "Diary of a Madman," China's first "modern" story, Lu Xun would come to characterize as "cannibalistic"—a consuming subjectivity that must be cured. The cure, for Lu Xun, was the writing of fiction, a kind of fiction that was able to hold up a transformative mirror to society, producing an inversion of commonsensical rationality and inaugurating a new sensibility. But Lu Xun's writing itself inhabits an important ambiguity between horror and spectacle, self-defense and voyeurism, enjoyment and pain, violence and its reinscription. This ambiguity testifies to the role of violence, at the limit of its representation, in the creation and figuration of the body politic. It testifies not only to the savagery that lurks underneath civilization, but also to the savagery enacted in the name of civility itself.

The key image of the Taipei Biennial 2012 could be Francisco Goya's famous etching *The Dream of Reason Produces Monsters*. "El sueño de la razón produce monstruos" is usually translated as "The sleep of reason produces monsters." This etching is part of Goya's infamous satirical series of etchings, *Los Caprichos*. It can be understood as an enlightened allegory of enlightenment and the nightmares of tyranny enlightened people had to face in the world. The monsters appearing to the sleeping artist symbolize irrational superstitions and dream images, since they are animals of the night: owls, cats, and bats. But the text can be translated in two ways: either as "the sleep of reason" or as "the dream of reason." And the animals can also be symbols for wisdom, not merely for nightly deliriums. In this interpretation, it is enlightened rationality itself that produces monstrous knowledge. Today, we hold a similar view of the propagandistic images of progress and hope that defined twentieth-century modernities: they no longer speak of the promise they once held, but rather of the terror they sanctioned.

The task for constructing a narrative-conceptual matrix for the Biennial was to oppose both the identitarian logic of division (inherent in, but not limited to, the modern nation-state and its fictions), and the pressure to mediate this logic within the hypervisibility of the global as part of the circulation of capitalized signs, in which the format of a biennial necessarily partakes. *Modern Monsters / Death and Life of Fiction* was conceived in this vein: as a mirror space, a space of inversions and transgressions, a historiographic device, like a stereoscope through which the double binds of history could become legible. Exhibitions call into question the constitution of reality as a common reality, as a historically conditioned experience, insofar as they are semantic playing fields and testing grounds for the construction of subjectivities, objects, and social imaginaries. The semantic playing field of the exhibition is situated in this nexus between the making and the relation between people and images or things. In art, this nexus takes multiple turns: between artist and material, material and reality, viewer and work. It disrupts and experiments freely, and it can suggest all kinds of mediated relations and shifts between active and passive roles, as long as it is designated as "art" and hence fundamentally tied to the "expression of a subject." The medium itself gives a space to the dialectics between a-subjective processes and subjective agency. An exhibition can be conceived as an exemplary, model-like spatialization of borderlines—conceptual, political, and even ontological—and can transform such lines of division into image-spaces in which the choice they impose is suspended, made explicit, historicized, and "de-monstrated." This means abandoning formalist art histories and the subjectivity of artists as the primary discourses of legitimization, in favor of an analytical approach to historical conditions of appearance, a Bakhtinian aesthetic dialogism which reveals reified, sedimented, or implicated forms as interpellations. In such "dialectical laboratories," the visitor is recruited as the "meridian" at the tipping point of reciprocities and inversions, situated within a *Kippfigur* at the hinge between figures and grounds.

This was what remained of the figure *Taowu* in the exhibition: a mere principle of "de-monstration," which is best described in terms of the motif of the *multistable figure*. It is an art-historical motif that opens onto the realm of mediation and figuration, of *pathos* and *poiesis* and their inversions, of the active and the passive. Monsters are multistable figures in this sense, and modernity, too, is a multistable image. It creates and includes its "other" in its system of oppositions, while it enacts a logic of division and enforced choice at the very same time, compelling us to take sides: either on the side of modernity and hence following its rationale, or on the side of its others and opponents, who are defined and framed by it. This is why it is so difficult to step outside the modern imaginary and its spell: it produces its own opposites and locks them up.

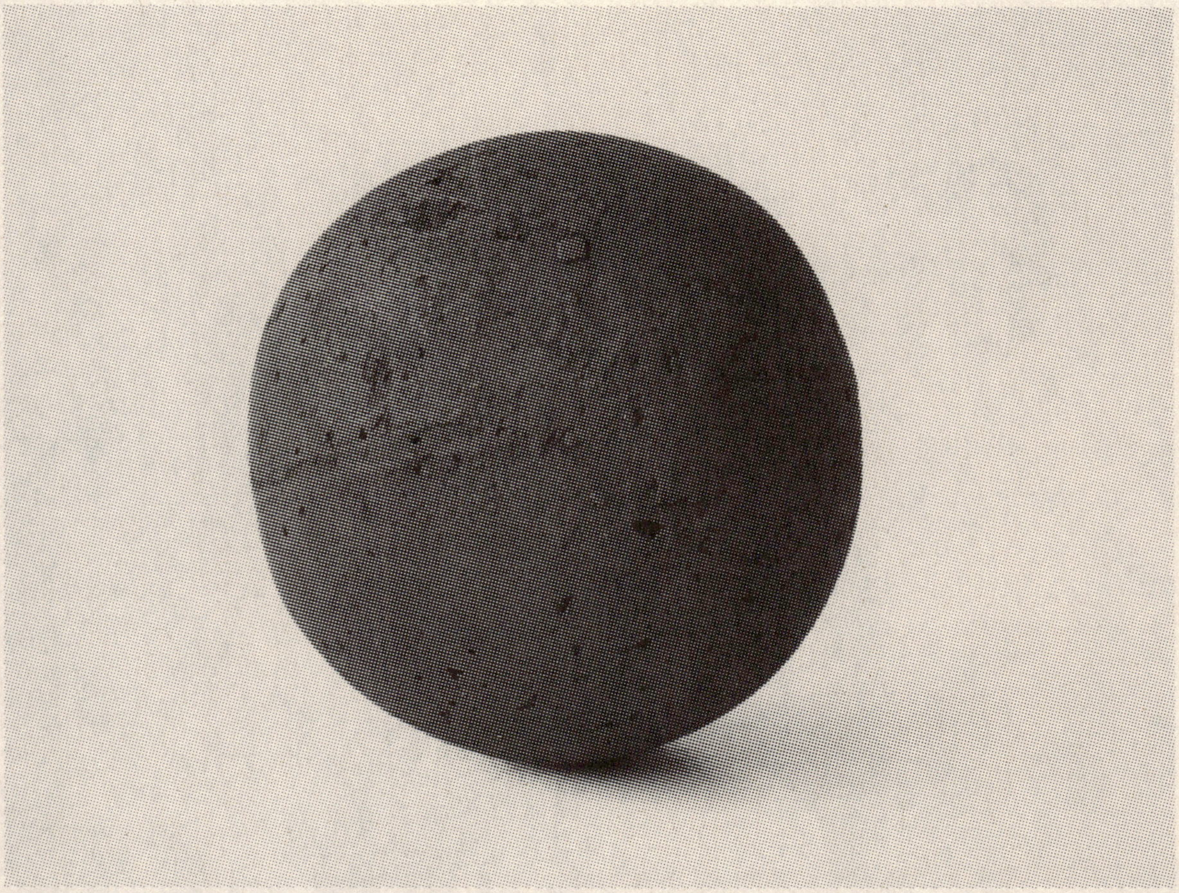

Pratchaya Phinthong, *One of Them (01)*, 2012, installation, a ball made of a rare earth element (ytterbium metal), 10 cm diameter, color print on paper, 42 × 29.7 cm. Courtesy of gb agency, Paris. This image shows one of eight balls produced from rare earth minerals in China by Pratchaya Phinthong. In ancient China, the scientist Zhang Heng was said to have invented a seismograph that worked with extreme precision to detect the occurrence of earthquakes as well as the direction of their source. The seismograph consisted of eight dragons attached to the outside of a closed vessel. Each dragon faced a principle direction of the compass and carried a ball in its mouth. When the ground moved, the ball in the mouth of the dragon facing the direction of the source of the earthquake would move and fall into the mouth of a toad that was seated under the dragon. The mechanism of the seismograph was never unveiled and remained a mystery for the many scientists who produced replicas that never attained the same accuracy. Pratchaya Phinthong links this object to a current economic reality. In mines throughout the globe, seventeen rare earth elements (REEs) necessary for hi-tech gadgets such as flat-screen TVs, smartphones, and hybrid cars are excavated. With the closing of the last US element mine in 2002, the People's Republic of China controls 97 percent of the global trade in these minerals. Recently, China announced that it would be cutting these exports by 70 percent.

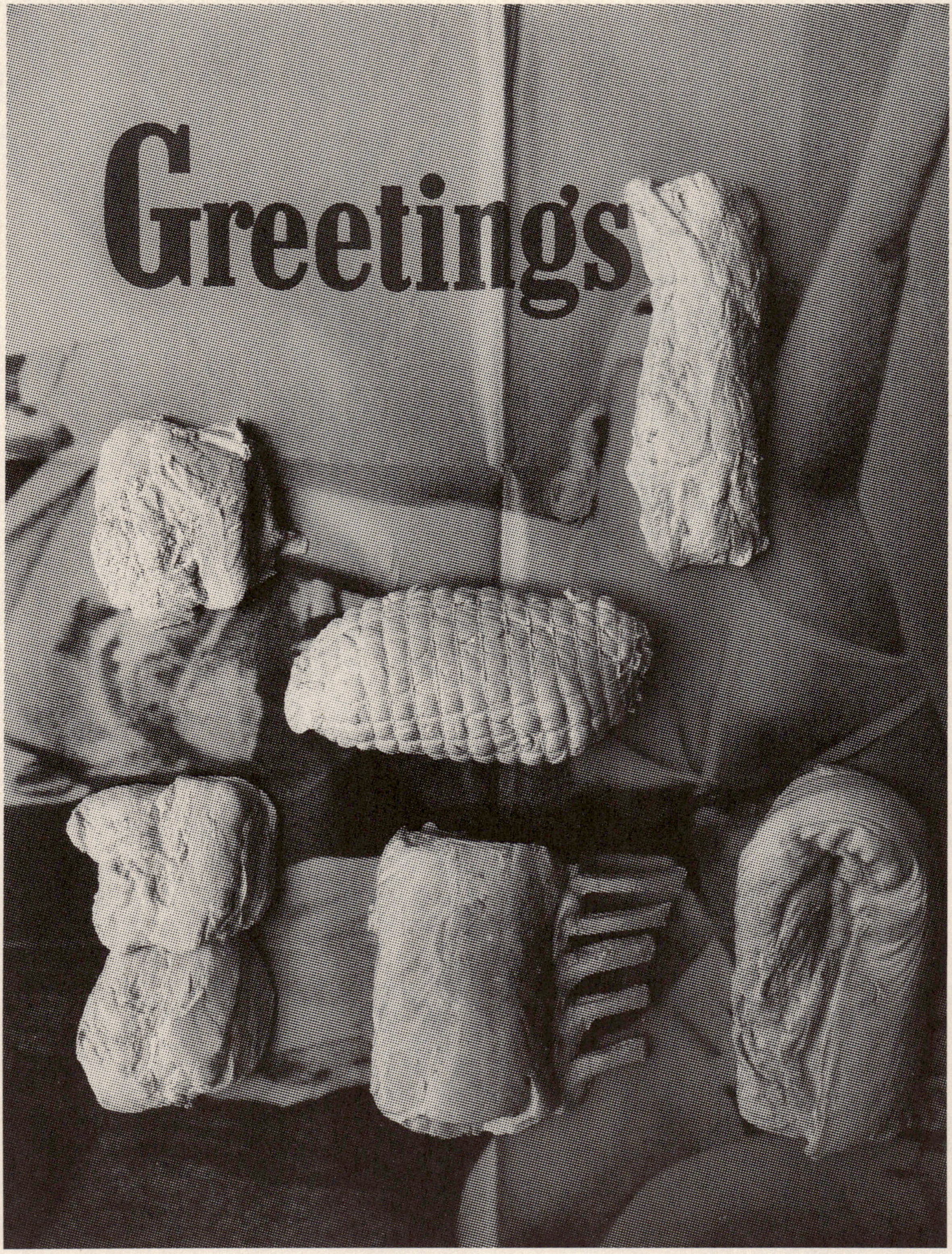

Rosemarie Trockel, *Language Change*, 2012, digital print, 90 × 70 cm.

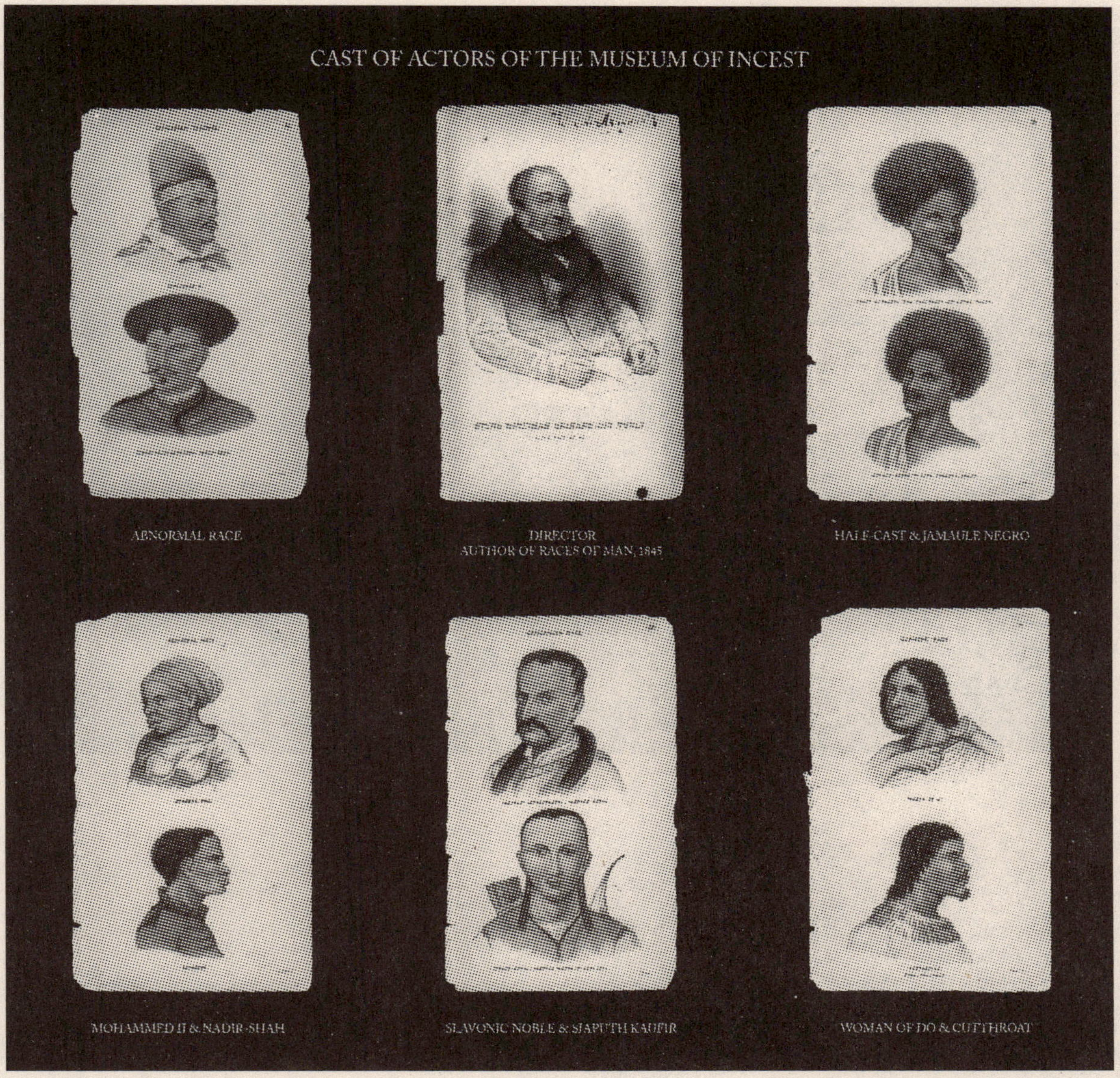

Simon Fujiwara, *The Museum of Incest,* 2009, mixed-media installation, performance, and guidebook, detail. Courtesy of Private Collection Kortrijk, Belgium. Simon Fujiwara's fictional *The Museum of Incest,* is situated in the Olduvai Gorge in Tanzania, the place where Science has located the so-called Cradle of Civilization. Just as the development of humankind is based on a collection of historical remains, in this work the history and development of incest are pieced together based on objects from an imagined time when incest was prevalent or unavoidable. Though incest tends to be left out of most museums, here the artist approaches incest as a natural phenomenon in the development of mankind. The installation consists of two vitrines containing objects, a large mural, a video in which the artist introduces the museum, and a printed museum guide. Simon Fujiwara plays the role of the designer of the museum.

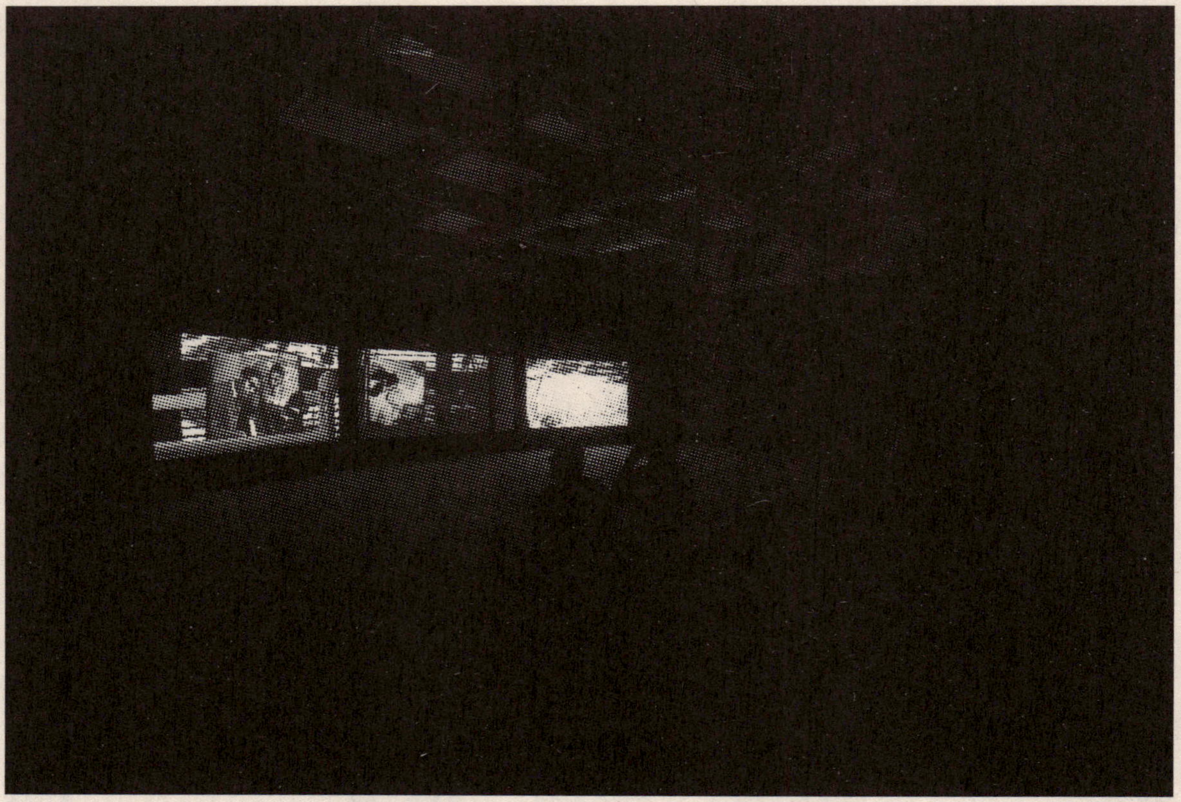

John Akomfrah, *The Unfinished Conversation*, 2012, three-channel HD video installation, color, sound, 46 min. *The Unfinished Conversation* by John Akomfrah is a cinematic installation devoted to Stuart Hall, a theorist of cultural identity and difference who exerted great influence on Akomfrah and the movement in which he participated. Hall arrived in the UK from Jamaica (then still a British colony) in the 1950s. He graduated from Oxford and became a decisive voice on the New Left, along with intellectuals such as E. P. Thompson and Raymond Williams. *The Unfinished Conversation* focuses on Hall's "formative years" in the 1950s and '60s. It explores, for instance, the crucial role of the Soviet invasion of Hungary in 1956, which caused a Europe-wide exodus from Communist parties; and the Suez Crisis, when Britain, France, and Israel invaded Egypt the year after Egyptian president Nasser recognized the People's Republic of China and nationalized the Suez Canal, one of the world's economic arteries. For Hall, identity is never a finished product or a given reality. Rather, it is an ever-changing relation that emerges in-between subjects and history—as an "unfinished conversation."

The exhibition featured double-sided images inviting a permanent shift between what counts in a specific context as "figure" and "ground." It suggested a similar changing of perspectives in relation to "fiction" and "reality"—fiction read not merely as unreal or make-believe, but as a form of registering what is otherwise inexpressible and memorable. In turn, we must learn to understand the "really-real" of modernity as a powerful fiction: the idea, for instance, of "nature" as a realm opposed to "culture," or the "really-real" of the modern state and disciplinary bureaucracy, or the phantasmagoric objects of consumerism.

"Culture," the imaginary, the symbolic order—today they are trapped within a spectral globalism and an anachronistic nationalist deadlock. Language, imagery, narratives, the entire vocabulary of practice and thus the very infrastructure of consciousness is confined to conditions that, in the face of technological realities, do not pay tribute to, and are far from politically mastering, the collective body that is today given in technology. This disconnect between "culture" and "systemic conditions" underlines the fact that the question of modernity today is not primarily a "cultural" question—and according to the old argument against the false consciousness and "interiority" of bourgeois culture, it of course never was. Modernity is a certain logic of scission, a matrix, a particular relation between construction and destruction, between map and territory. It is primarily systemic, machinic, and abstract, a question of the enrollment and addressability of subjects and things in its maps. The anonymous power of modernity overrides experience, values, morals, culture, and subjectivities. It is technological, but understood in a wider sense: it embraces the kinds of fixations, inscriptions, calculations, and automatizations that stabilize and make events predictable—only in order to create a greater potential for other entities to be displaced, mobilized, and to circulate.

What is left is modernity in the form of maps: the kind of maps that do not represent a reality that is external to them, but that inscribe and transform that reality. The maps of modernity are based on reductions, standardizations, and homogenizations, on a particular dialectics between fixity and mobilization. They used to be made according to essentialist classifications, reductions, and objectivist identification. Today, they have become algorithmically enhanced data-maps, and they expand into the complex matter of life. In his work *Parallel*, artist and filmmaker Harun Farocki traces iconographic aspects of the rapid rise of digital technologies as they evolve into a global surveillance system that rather literally seeks to out-mimic a complex and always imperfect reality. No longer is reality the measure of the map. Instead, the map increasingly becomes the measure of reality, now designed to control flows and movements, and to register *deviation*. Increasingly, irregular movements are monitored as potential threats. Appeasing the monster of the great transformation, of the communist mastery over history, capitalist modernity puts reality under clinical quarantine. The technoscientific maps of this modernity are means of political control, to be sure, but they are also a sort of immune system, the armament of a system in a state of permanent war.

1 Unless otherwise indicated, all quotes about the *Taowu* come from David Der-Wei Wang's book *The Monster That is History: History, Violence, and Fictional Writing in Twentieth-Century China* (Berkeley: University of California Press, 2004).

2 David Der-Wei Wang, *The Monster That Is History.*

3 Michael Taussig, "Culture of Terror—Space of Death: Roger Casement's Putumayo Report and the Explanation of Torture," *Comparative Studies in Society and History*, vol. 26, no. 3 (July 1984): 467–497.

4 "Nation is a skin stretched over the bones of the state": An Interview with Hamid Parsani, by Jon Soske, May 2013, http://internalfrontiers.wordpress.com/2013/05/14/nation-is-a-skin-stretched-over-the-bones-o

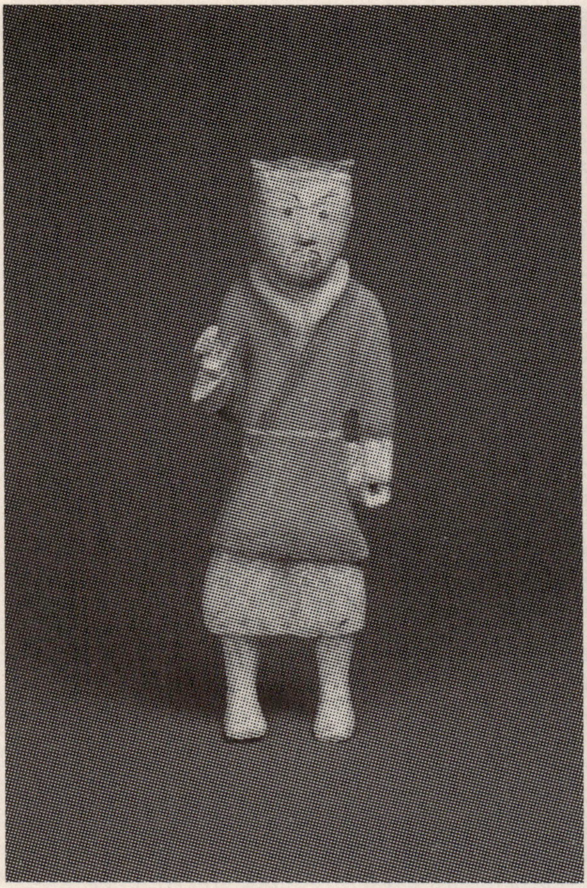

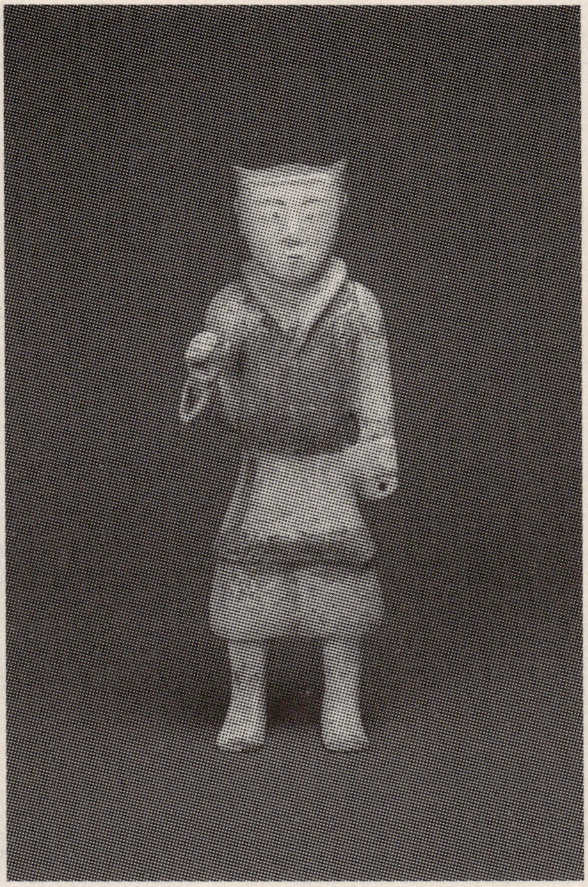

Yu-Cheng Chou, *AURORA*, 206 BC–220 AD/2012, pottery figurine. Courtesy of The AURORA Art Museum. *AURORA* is a cooperation between the artist and a company based in Taiwan that holds a world-renowned collection of Chinese antiques. A group of objects from this collection is shown, but they are displayed very differently from the way "antiques" are usually presented. Rather than underscoring the status of the antiques as "treasures from the past," Chou's display renders them "spectacularized," placed in a postmodern-style vitrine under moving lights. How is value produced through context and aura, and what does the evaluation—and de-valuation—of the past mean in the present? These questions are further enhanced by the content of the vitrine: figurines of servants meant to function as grave goods, or helpers for the dead in the afterlife.

IN DEFENSE OF THE TERROR: AN INTOLERABLE REVOLUTION

Sophie Wahnich

> I want never to forget how I was forced to become—for how long?—a monster of justice and intolerance, a narrow-minded simplifier, an arctic character uninterested in anyone who was not in league with him to kill the dogs of hell.
> —René Char[1]

In Éric Rohmer's film *The Lady and the Duke* (2001), the French Revolution is seen through the eyes of Grace Elliott. This friend and former lover of the duc d'Orléans, before being imprisoned herself during the Terror, was confronted with two of those events that have given the Revolution its savage reputation: the massacres of September 1792 and the death of the king. During these massacres, Grace Elliott crossed Paris in a carriage. After having managed not to faint at the sight of the duchesse de Lamballe's head—whose well-known face was paraded in front of Elliott's carriage atop a pike—she cried in delayed shock when she reached her home and explained what she had seen. Faced with the impending death of the king, she hoped right until January 21, 1793 that the revolutionaries would not dare to kill him, and interpreted the cries of the people that she heard from her residence in Meudon as a demonstration to prevent his execution. After his death she went into mourning, and would not get over her anger at the duc d'Orléans, who had not only done nothing to oppose the king's death, but had actually voted for it. Revolutionary violence was imprinted on human bodies, whether in the institutional no man's land of the September massacres or in the context of the inventive institution of the king's trial. Grace Elliott's reactions were both sensitive and moral: fear, anger, and sadness are the expression of an emotional and normative judgment. We can well imagine that she found these two events "insufferable."

Elliott's point of view, which was also that of Edmund Burke and Hippolyte Taine, was expressed in the memoirs she later wrote and that were eventually published in 1859. But today, through the effect of this historical film, it has also become a contemporary point of view on the French Revolution.

If we cannot maintain that this vision of the Revolution is completely dominant today—since it is certainly not detested by all its heirs—we have to admit that the film's reception, both before and after its release in September 2001, was highly positive, not just on account of its aesthetic innovations but also for its ideological standpoint. Marc Fumaroli, in an article for *Cahiers du Cinéma* in July 2001, saw it as a key film on "the bloodiest and most controversial days in our history,"[2] and constructed a parallel between the prisons of the Terror and the Nazi-era extermination camps:

> When she meets up in prison with duchesses, countesses, laundrywomen and actresses, all condemned to the scaffold for the mere fact of their birth or their allegiance, she is almost happy to share their fate, just as a "goy" *résistante* would have been in the Drancy transit camp in 1942–43.[3]

We see here the conscious construction of a new reception of the French Revolution which, out of disgust at the political crimes of the twentieth century, imposes an equal disgust towards the revolutionary event. The French Revolution is unspeakable because it constituted "the matrix of totalitarianism" and invented its rhetoric.[4]

The social and ideological cleavages that form the fabric of the revolutionary event have constantly plagued its representations. There have always been counterrevolutionaries—and they were perceived as such. Today,

THE MUSEUM OF THE MONSTER THAT IS HISTORY

however, what is more surprising is that these counterrevolutionary representations can pass as majoritarian, commonplace, and—like Eric Rohmer's film—be considered both by critics and the public as historically correct. We are no longer in an age in which different standpoints argue over an event that resists interpretation, but rather one of unquestioned detestation of the event. Since the French Revolution includes what the British call the "Reign of Terror," and the French simply "the Terror," not only can it no longer be seen as a historical movement which is redeemable en bloc, but it can in fact be rejected en bloc. The French Revolution is a figure of what is politically intolerable today, as it had already become in 1795.

But is this disgust and rejection based on any reflective and critical stance? One small anecdote makes it possible to doubt this. At the Sorbonne, allegedly the stronghold of Jacobin historians, Michel Vovelle replaced Albert Soboul in 1985. The following year he offered to organize a "calf's head dinner" for postgraduates on January 21. This is a traditional republican ritual in which the calf's head represents the head of the king: the people, gathered at a banquet, replay the king's death in carnival mode. Vovelle's proposal met with an icy reception. For the majority of students, even those enrolled in the Sorbonne's course on the history of the Revolution, it seemed indecent. The merry chuckling of Michel Vovelle was met by an embarrassed and incredulous silence. The calf's head ritual had become non-contemporary, without time being taken to assess it properly. It was impossible now to "replay" the severed head—that kind of thing was shocking, or troubling at the least. To my mind, this collective banquet belongs to the "obligatory expression of sentiments,"[5] i.e., to "a broad category of oral expressions of sentiments and emotions with a collective character":

> This in no way damages the intensity of these sentiments, quite the contrary … but all these collective expressions, which have at the same time a moral value and an obligatory force for the individual and the group, are more than simple manifestations … If they have to be told, it is because the whole group understands them. More than simply an expression of one's own sentiments, these are expressed to others, since they have to be expressed in this way. They are expressed to oneself by expressing them to others and for their benefit. This is essentially a matter of symbolism.[6]

This republican symbolism, however, came undone in the 1980s and 1990s. When the bicentennial celebration came round, the question of revolutionary violence returned to disturb some of the certainties that had newly imposed themselves since the Liberation. Until this time, the French had no need to be ashamed of the revolutionary event; they even had to be proud of it—proud of the French republican invention, a counter-model to the Vichy regime, and proud above all of the Declaration of the Rights of Man and of the Citizen, which served as a reference point for the rebirth of international law and the famous Universal Declaration of Human Rights. At the time of the bicentenary of the French Revolution, however, 1789 and 1793 were disassociated, the challenge to the Ancien Régime was separated from the invention of the Republic—and in short, the wheat had been sorted from the chaff. 1789 was celebrated; but 1792, the fall of the monarchy and the invention of the Republic, remained in the shadow of Valmy. As for 1793, the preference was to merge its "fine anticipations" with those of 1789. The abolition of slavery and the rights to education and public assistance were removed from their context without any investigation of how these irrefutable values were bound up with the Terror. Democracy in France today does not seem to sit well with its foundation. "At a time when democracy has become the sole perspective of contemporary societies, it is essential for attention to focus on its inaugural moment, 1789, and not on the dark days of 1793," proclaimed Patrice Gueniffey,[7] one of the main current detractors of the Revolution, before going on to ask:

> Who would dare today to celebrate the Terror with the frankness of Albert Mathiez,

THE MUSEUM OF THE MONSTER THAT IS HISTORY

James T. Hong and Anselm Franke

Monstrosity in modern times surely comes in plentiful forms, but its most poignant face is not modern fiction, but actual violence enacted in the name of rationality. *The Museum of the Monster That Is History* is devoted to the violence on which modern states and social orders are based. It looks at the violence that foregoes any "modern" organization of society (which never disappears at its margins within and without) and in those institutions that guard them. It highlights the monstrosities exerted in the name of reason and order, or in the name of a lesser evil to serve a greater perceived good. State-sanctioned forms of terror are monstrous not merely because of the scale of destruction afforded by modern technologies, but more so because of their "normality." While perhaps considered unfortunate, state terror is still accepted as necessary and legitimate at a given moment within a particular regime, or in the name of a universalist science. And indeed while modern history is characterized by radical ruptures and permanent transformations, it is in the insistent irrationality of officially sanctioned, systemic terror, as experienced in colonial subjugation, genocide, imperial wars, cultural destruction, and disciplinary measures, that we must locate its actual and strikingly consistent continuity. Turning towards this continuity in modern history reveals that there is a particular systemic economy of terror necessitated by the rule of "modern reason" itself, and hence official terror is not an exception, but rather modernity's history-making rule. This side of modern rationality presents us with a symptom running counter to the promise of progress: modernity as the permanent invention of a barbarity that hides behind the mask of civilization, order, and rationality.

The Museum of the Monster That Is History comprises various contributions. *Taiwan WMD* identifies weapons of mass destruction as its monstrous historical subject. The international community has taken steps to ban or at least control the spread of WMDs (weapons of mass destruction), but Taiwan is not officially a part of this international community. And since Taiwan (ROC) was born as a state of emergency in a state of exception, WMDs are especially well-suited for just such states and just such who writes in 1922 that it was "the red crucible in which the future democracy was elaborated on the accumulated ruins of everything associated with the old order"?[8]

In this vision, subsequent to the bicentenary but in the same spirit, democracy could no longer have anything to do with this "red crucible." The possibilities of appropriating the event today are encumbered by a sensitivity to bloodshed, to political death meted out and decided: responsibly assumed.

By this evocation of blood, doubt is introduced as to the value of the revolutionary event. We have seen on magazine covers, and in productions for a wide audience, questions that might formerly have been thought peculiar to inveterate monarchists. "Was it necessary to kill the king?," asks *Le Nouvel Observateur* in January 1993. "Would you French television viewers of today have decided to kill the queen?," asks Robert Hossein at the end of his show about Marie-Antoinette. These questions have the value of interesting symptoms.

By applying the Kantian categorical imperative to judge past events, two hundred years after the facts, these questions involve people today in the historical situation of 1793. They have to put themselves in the place of the Convention members who actually had to judge this question, in the place of contemporaries of the event who had to discuss it and decide their political position. This amounts to inventing a mode of historicity that could be called the concatenation of presents, or of situations. Readers are no longer mere inheritors of an event in which they were not protagonists. If they do indeed want to be its heirs, then they are led to play a part in it. In other words, every heir of the republican foundation could be morally included in the category of regicides, or in what the Thermidorians called "men of blood." Who today, even among republicans, would assume such a designation? Kant's

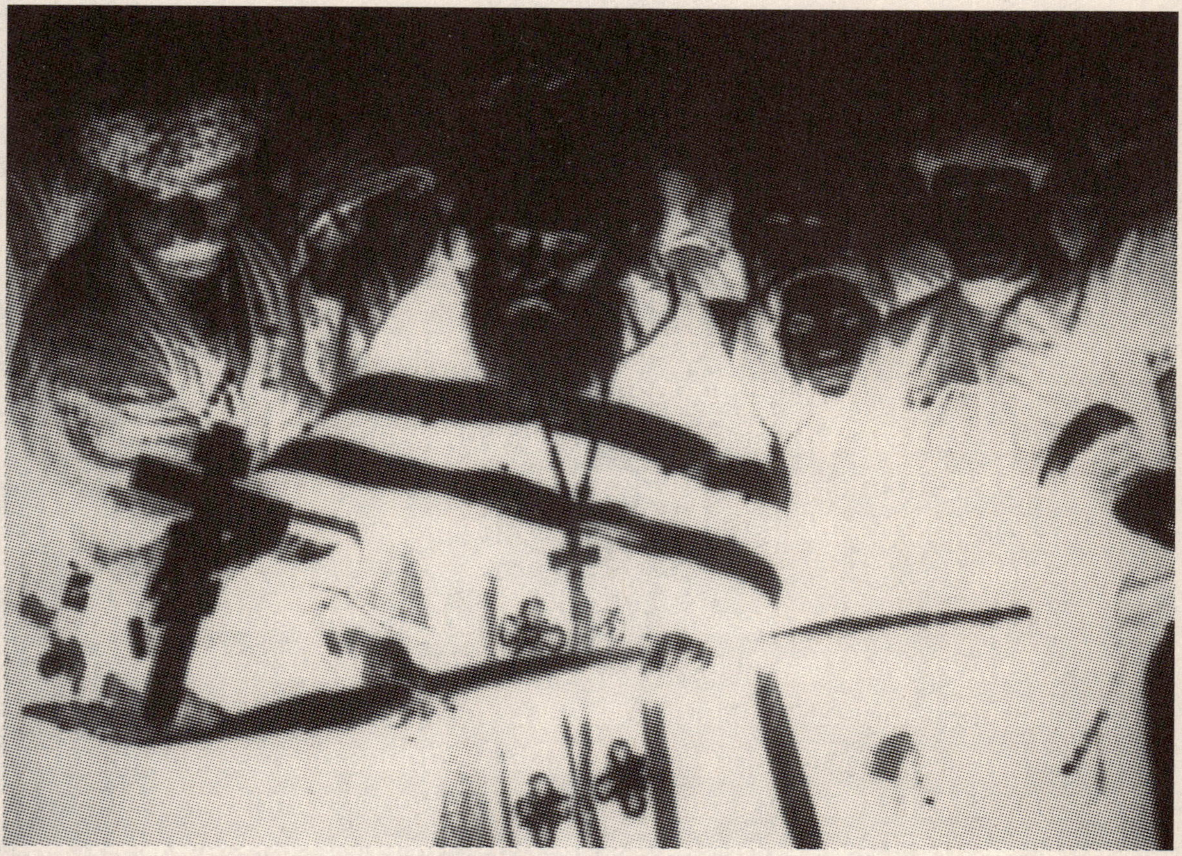

Yervant Gianikian and Angela Ricci Lucchi, *Triptych of the 20th Century*, 2002–2008, video, five-screen installation in loop, 4 min 50 sec.

emergencies. Compiled by James T. Hong, with contributions by Tony Wu and Kelvin Park, this exhibit presents the rarely documented and much-contested history of these types of weapons within and around Taiwan.

The end of World War II signaled both the creation of modern Asian states and the inauguration of their state-supported WMD programs, which were kick-started by Japanese WWII research units, such as Unit 731 in China and Unit 31 in Taiwan, and by preparations for the coming Cold War. One such example is *The Report of G.*, which outlines WWII Japanese experiments with the glanders bacterium, a weaponized horse disease, on primarily Chinese prisoners. Prepared by Japanese biological warfare scientists for the US government in 1949, this report impeccably represents the utilization of medicine, science, and rationality for the efficient production of terror.

Supplementing these exhibits, *The Museum of the Monster That Is History* dedicates a series of vitrine displays to particular historical aspects of "the rationality of terror": one is dedicated to the Great Famine in China, conceived by scholar Jie Li; another to decapitation as an iconographic and political motif which persists both in Chinese history and in modernity at large; and another to the Irishman Roger Casement, who served the British government and authored two famous "reports" on systematic colonial terror in the Congo and the Amazon around the turn of the twentieth century. During WWI the British would execute Casement as a traitor.

Cultural theorist and artist Bavand Behpoor, together with graphic designer Reza Abedini, contribute an installation on the "martyrs museum," a form of museum found worldwide which palpably exemplifies the fundaments of modern states in martyrdom, as the sacrifice of individuals and their bodies. The museum that they restage in parts, however, is the rather particular Shiraz Martyrs Museum in Iran, which addresses itself to foreigners but is hardly visited by them, and relies in several respects on a *metaphysics of absence*—in opposition to Western concepts of the museum. Their "translated" martyrs museum hosts a variety of "typical" objects and accompanying martyr narratives that in themselves *exhibit* the gap between the systemic rationale and individual history.

Another section of the museum is devoted to the role of traitors: those who betray the norms of their respective countries or communities and "cross" enemy lines. In the popular imagination, they are either embodiments of evil or larger-than-life personalities. The traitor here is literally looked upon as a "figure," represented by an idiosyncratic selection of known and unknown figurines in the accessible size of twelve inches. This size seems commentary on the French Revolution is familiar enough:

> The revolution of a gifted people which we have seen unfolding in our day may succeed or miscarry; it may be filled with misery and atrocities to the point that a sensible man, were he boldly to hope to execute it successfully the second time, would never resolve to attempt the experiment at such cost—this revolution, I say, nonetheless finds in the hearts of all spectators (who are not engaged in this game themselves) a wishful participation that borders closely on enthusiasm, the very expression of which is fraught with danger; this sympathy, therefore, can have no other cause than a moral predisposition of the human race.[9]

Moral reverse projection onto the French Revolution, however, ends up making the position of a nonparticipating spectator impossible. Yet it is the "play" of the actor—in both the theatrical and historical sense of the term—that is required in Robert Hossein's production. Here, too, spectators cannot remain spectators; they in fact become actors by voting for or against the death of Marie-Antoinette, and in this way collude in a simulacrum of popular consultation that leads to denying one of the very characteristics of the event, namely its irreversible character.

"To suggest putting Louis XVI on trial is a counterrevolutionary idea," Robespierre declared. "It is making the Revolution itself a subject of litigation."[10] And putting the king's trial on trial certainly means reopening such litigation; it explicitly means using the faculty of judgment rather than of understanding. The moral mechanism here stands in the way of historical curiosity. The object is no longer to understand the meaning of the death meted out to the man whom Saint-Just described as "foreign" to humanity and the community. Nor is it to know what such an event succeeded in establishing, in terms of sovereignty. The question, rather, is settled in advance. What is played out here is the figure of historical evil, of the inability to settle political conflicts peacefully—i.e., without inflicting violence on the body, without putting to death. To be a happy heir to the French Revolution means becoming complicit with a historical crime. The event's character as a political laboratory is thus eroded in favor of a moral question. Scholarly historical debate—in the historicist sense of the term—becomes a forbidden zone. The decontextualizing and naturalizing of the sentiment of "humanity" are made to reign in the eternal present of a moral condemnation.

This replay of the event in the mode of judgment—moral and normative, sensible and emotional, in a context of aestheticization—leads the Revolution to appear insufferable to the very people who, in terms of classic political sociology, are not supposed to be its detractors. From now on the Revolution finds critics not only just on the right of the French political spectrum but also on the left, among the heirs of Jean Jaurès and the Socialist International.

1 René Char, "Recherche de la base et du sommet. Billets à Francis Curel, II" (1943), *Œuvres complètes* (Paris: Gallimard, 1983), 633.

2 Marc Fumaroli, "Terreur et cinéma," *Cahiers du cinéma*, July–August 2001, 42.

3 Ibid., 44.

4 Thus François Furet can write: "Today the Gulag leads us to reflect afresh on the Terror, by virtue of its identical project," and again: "Solzhenitsyn's work … ineluctably locat[es] the issue of the Gulag at the very core of the revolutionary endeavor," *Interpreting the French Revolution* (Cambridge: Cambridge University Press,1978), 12.

5 Marcel Mauss, *Essais de Sociologie* (Paris: Minuit, 1969), 88.

6 Ibid.

7 Patrice Gueniffey, *La politique de la Terreur. Essai sur la violence révolutionnaire* (Paris: Fayard, 2000), 10.

8 Ibid.

9 Immanuel Kant, *The Conflict of the Faculties*, trans. M.J. Gregor (New York: Abaris Books, 1979), 153.

10 Robespierre, *Pour le Bonheur et pour la Liberté, Discours*, eds. Yannick Bosc, Florence Gauthier, and Sophie Wahnich (Paris: Éditions La Fabrique, 2000),194.

to be the most appropriate for contemplating and perhaps appreciating their treasonous accomplishments.

The museum then presents a display contemplating the "economy of death" by looking at the "price tags" and the monetary values of life. Just as a nation's currency is relative to its strength and influence, so too is the value of its citizens. We imagine that all human lives are priceless, but we know that economic reality—represented, for instance, by compensation payments—speaks of another truth.

The passage of time does not heal all wounds, and it cannot settle all accounts or resolve all disputes. So the final two exhibits offer attempts at preparing the ground for reconciliation and opening new chapters in history. As governments change, technologies advance, and the identities of perceived perpetrators adapt, symbolic atonements and scientific research seek to document, to uncover, and to put on record, as a prelude to possible forgiveness. *Apologies*, compiled by James T. Hong, presents the "official apologies" of statesmen and perpetrators from various contexts throughout the twentieth and early twenty-first centuries. The *Mineral Geology of Genocide*, shot by Paulo Tavares, Eyal Weizman, and Steffen Krämer, documents a cutting-edge forensic investigation of mass graves in Guatemala, in an attempt to reconstruct the unwritten, silenced history of state-sanctioned violence.

Curated by James T. Hong and Anselm Franke.
Participating artists: Reza Abedini, Bavand Behpoor, James T. Hong, Jei Li, Kelvin Kyung Kun Park, Eyal Weizman / Paulo Tavares / Steffen Krämer, Tony Chun-Hui Wu, Yao-Chung Wu, and anonymous contributors.

THE BLOODY LATTE: VAMPIRISM AS A MASS MOVEMENT

Ian Svenonius

The penchant for a culture to imbibe drinks and drugs en masse, in a collective ritual-orgy, is a phenomenon transcending mere fashion.

This, *in itself*, is unworthy of remark; the quest for transcendence through intoxication is as old as history itself. The cultural particularity of the proclivity is what is striking: the strange uniformity of every epoch's beverage cult.

Personal taste amounts to little; instead, for each era, there's a distinctive mass hysteria for the imbibing of a particular beverage or substance.

The favored drinks at this juncture in American history are indisputably coffee from Starbucks and the vodka of Absolut. The popularity of these drinks stems from their value as symbolic war booty from recent conquests. A culture's adopted beverage represents the blood of their vanquished foe.

Drink is transubstantiation à la the Catholic cannibalism of Christ's blood and body. The smell of coffee is the odor of the Sandinista hospital maimed by Contra bombs. Ice-cold vodka is the blood of the Russians, raped and murdered by capitalism.

And so it has been throughout history. Each imperial culture imports a liquid memento from its vanquished foe to serve as a totem of its power and glory. Tea, the Englishman's beverage, is falling out of favor as England's neocolonial hold on the subcontinent wavers. For two centuries the English supped on their well-steeped leaves and tasted the sweat of the slaves of the Empire. Now, tea is for old mums, while beer swilling "lads" form the visible majority. The British love their beer; a cold pint brings fond memories of dead Germans, falling out of the sky in The Battle of Britain.

Beer first attained great popularity in America immediately after the First World War, when the US had tipped the scales against the Kaiser in the last days of the conflict. That war had been highly unpopular to a then-isolationist nation, with American involvement cynically contrived by Anglophiles in government. The war transformed the country profoundly, much to the consternation of the activists who opposed it.

The women who had raged for abolition and suffrage now turned their eyes to alcohol, successfully banishing it in 1920. Prohibition, then, was unconsciously a moral crusade against imperialism and the blood sucking and chest beating that followed the Treaty of Versailles. Of course, beer made a comeback, especially after the depression hit and veterans needed to boost self-esteem by slurping the entrails of the wretched Kraut. A cold beer in a bar with one's buddies brought one's thoughts to the bread lines in Berlin, with all their one-legged soldiers.

Beer was big in Germany one thousand years earlier, when King Otto pushed back the Slavic Wend and Magyar interlopers from the East. For the German, it is essentially the blood of the Slav. Its popularity was reinforced when Frederick the Great struck into the breadbasket of Poland, expanding Prussia, a conquest that led to German domination of the continent under Bismarck.

Years later, to invoke the German's bloodlust, an Austrian man named Hitler held meetings in Munich beer halls, and cited the loss of those wheat fields, now occupied by Slavs.

When Hitler rose to power, after the "Beer Hall Putsch," he allied himself with the Italian dictator Mussolini, who dreamed of imperial glory in Africa. The Italian conquest of Ethiopia, the birthplace of coffee, resulted in the espresso craze in Italy. During the Second World War, every Italian soldier carried an espresso maker in his mess kit. The Starbucks aesthetic—

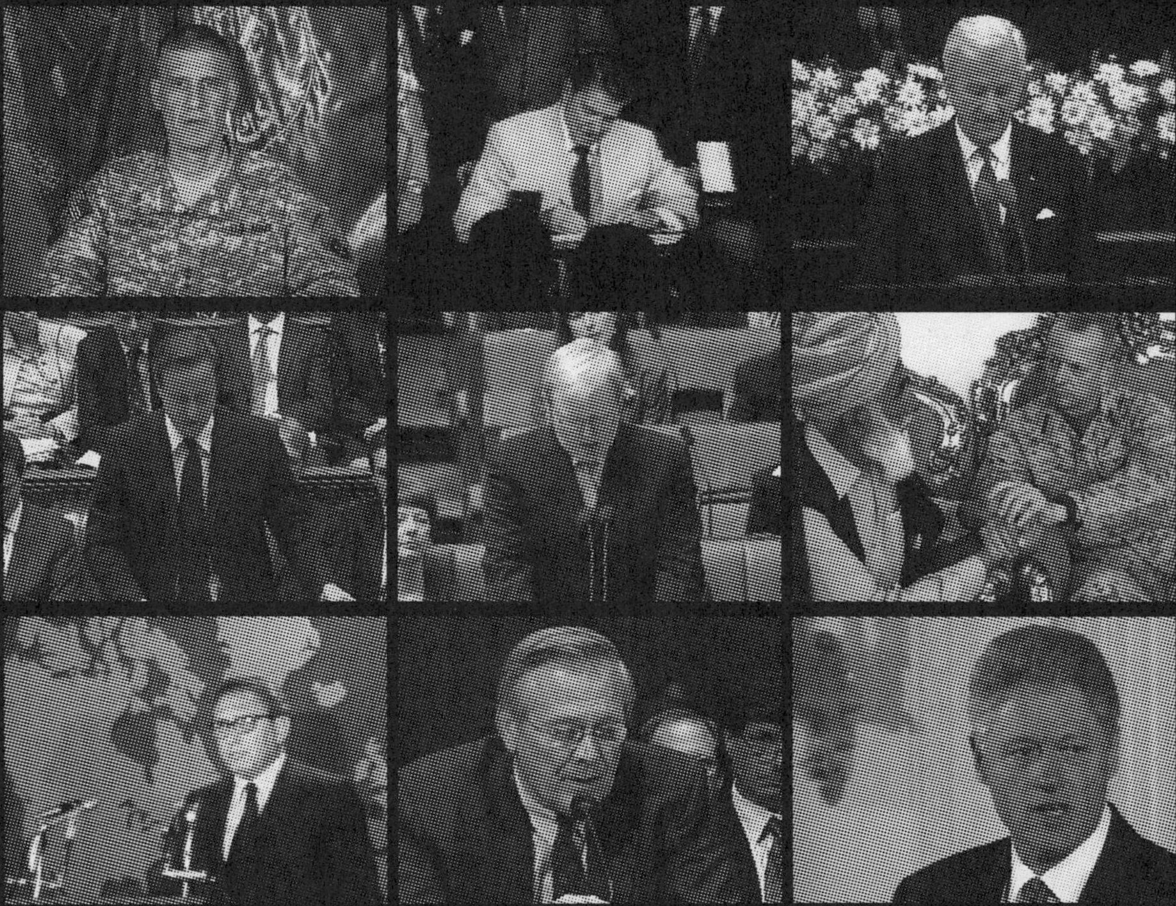

James T. Hong, *Apologies*, 2012, single-channel video.

Apologies by
John Allen, Commander, International Security Assistance Force.
Benigno Aquino III, President of the Philippines.
Willy Brandt, Chancellor of the Federal Republic of Germany.
Gordon Brown, Prime Minister of the United Kingdom.
David Cameron, Prime Minister of the United Kingdom.
Edward I. Cassidy, Cardinal, Commission for Relations with Judaism, Vatican.
Richard A. Clarke, US Counterterrorism Chief.
Bill Clinton, President of the United States.
Recep Tayyip Erdoğan, Prime Minister of Turkey.
Ichiro Fujisaki [藤崎一郎], Japanese Ambassador to the United States.
Robert Gibbs, White House Press Secretary, US.
Stephen Harper, President of Canada.
Viktor Ilyukhin, Commission on Security of Russia.
Carsten Jacobson, Spokesperson, International Security Assistance Force.
Naoto Kan [菅直人], Prime Minister of Japan.
Henry Kissinger, US Secretary of State.
Nada Kolundzija, Member of the Serbian Parliament.
Junichiro Koizumi [小泉純一郎], Prime Minister of Japan.
Peter Lavoy, US Acting Assistant Secretary of Defense for Asia and Pacific Security Affairs.
Ma Ying-Jeou [馬英九], President of the Republic of China.
Louis Michel, Belgian Minister of Foreign Affairs.
Tomiichi Murayama [村山富市], Prime Minister of Japan.
John Nicholson, US Army Commander.
Victoria Nuland, US State Department Spokesperson.
Ronald Reagan, President of the United States.
David Rodriguez, Commander, International Security Assistance Force.
Kevin Rudd, Prime Minister of Australia.
Donald Rumsfeld, US Secretary of Defense.
Boris Tadic, President of Serbia.
Peter Wall, Head of British Army.
Richard von Weizsäcker, President of the Federal Republic of Germany.
Ryuichiro Yamazaki [山崎隆一郎], Japanese Ambassador to the Philippines.
Tjeerd de Zwaan, Dutch Ambassador to Indonesia.

garish, fascistic murals combined with Futurist mechanization of the workforce and absurdist shouting—can be traced to Mussolini.

America's love of coffee has always been tied to its affection for conquest. Coffee fueled the "winning of the West" and the usurpation of the former colonies of Spain at the turn of the century. Guatemala, Salvador, Nicaragua, Colombia, etc., have all been virtual colonies since then, with frequent US-armed interventions to ensure servitude.

These nations constitute the mainstay of our coffee supply, and much blood has been spilled to maintain it. Coffee was the blood of the Indian, and gave one the adrenal rush needed to achieve "manifest destiny." Coffee was "Joe," as in Joe Nobody or John Doe, as the racist dehumanization of the native peoples refuted any necessity for their identification.

This name was changed to "Java" in the '60s, when the US helped install the dictator Suharto in Indonesia, who murdered so many of his subjects at the behest of anxious multinationals. Although this was a proxy war, not directly fought by the US, coffee's taste still reflects the power imparted by the struggle. Its flavor was enriched and it grew in popularity. Whether from india or indonesia, coffee was the blood of the vanquished and it tasted good.

Now, in the global economy, coffee is grown across the entire subjugated Third World. When Starbucks sells a bag of beans, it's always marked with the region from whence it sprang, making the consumer an imperial cannibal connoisseur.

Coca-Cola is another toast of imperial conquest; it initially drew its flavor from the coca plant from Central America, but switched to another regional flavor (tamarind root) when this was outlawed. Coca-Cola's ascendancy coincided with the Spanish-American War and the annexation of Puerto Rico, Cuba, etc. It was often mixed with rum, the sugar-based flavor of those very islands.

Coke was provided to all American soldiers during the Second World War as a way to "blood" the army. Coke plants in Germany changed their trade name to FANTA, so as to deflect charges of corporate two-timing in the war effort. FANTA was orange, a flavor homage to the smashed Republican army in Spain, where the German army first honed its killing skills. When a German drank an orange pop, he was gnawing the jugular of an anarcho-syndicalist in Valencia.

Vodka is the refined fruit of the peasant's potato. Under the Tsars, Russia's border relentlessly expanded, from the Baltic to the Black Sea, and then on to the Pacific. Conquered people, pressed into serfdom, were manifest in the vodka favored by the Russian ruling class, both before the execution of the Tsar and then later with Stalin.

Vodka can actually be made from a variety of grains and fruits, appropriate to the vast and varied lands of Muscovite conquest. For the Russians, this drink, the blood of Swedes, Finns, Lithuanians, Ukrainians, Uzbeks, and Khazars, became suddenly, under the creed of Communist internationalism, the celebration of fratricide. This accounts for the existential mania and depression that famously accompanies modern Russian drunkenness.

With the Cold War concluded, and Russia under the yoke of exploitive capitalism, vodka is more and more beloved by Americans, who gulp it smugly as proof positive of their power to sculpt the earth. Sweden, the traditional nemesis of Tsarist Russia, is the producer par excellence of this trophy drink.

As we can see, the cultural specificity of the blood represented by a drink is contingent on the race or nationality of the person drinking it. So, while a German drinking a beer would be enjoying the life force of the Slav, an American popping a Bud would be eating the guts of that same German man. Similarly, a toast using expatriate brand Bacardi rum is a celebration of the assassination of Che in Bolivia, while a splash of Habana Club, the Cuban national brand, is the bloody froth from the surf at the Bay of Pigs.

And so it goes: tequila's worm is the dead Yankee at the Alamo, as "gusano" or "worm" is the Latin revolutionaries' name for the *Yanqui* imperialist. Even the introduction of Perrier to America coincided with the death of the nationalist de Gaulle and the subsequent

TAIWAN WMD

A recent history of weapons of mass destruction with a focus on Taiwan (The Republic of China)

Compiled by James T. Hong

1945
Chiang Kai-Shek wants to be the second nuclear power.

1949
The Kuomintang (KMT) loses Mainland China, and the Communists found the People's Republic of China (PRC). The KMT and the PRC inherit Japanese WWII chemical and biological weapons facilities. (Unit 31, a subdivision of the notorious Japanese biological warfare outfit Unit 731, was based in Northern Taiwan.) The Japanese also leave behind mustard gas, lewisite, and phosgene. The Soviets test their first nuclear bomb. The PRC loses to the KMT on Kinmen Island.

1950
US President Harry Truman declares Taiwan neutral territory and sends the Seventh Fleet to the Taiwan Strait.

1950–1953
During the Korean War, the US military purportedly uses biological weapons against the Communists. They also prepare for the use of nuclear and tactical nuclear weapons against North Korea and China.

1950s
China and Taiwan's biological weapons (BW) and chemical weapons (CW) programs begin in earnest. Various KMT strategies to invade China fail.

1952
Chiang Kai-Shek pushes for the nuclear bomb.

1954
US and Taiwan sign mutual defense treaty.

1954–1955
US President Eisenhower threatens the PRC with a nuclear attack during the First Taiwan Straits Crisis. The nuclear threat succeeds, and the PRC backs down.

1955–1956
First nuclear program in Taiwan established at National Tsing Hua University (NTHU). Taiwan founds the Atomic Energy Council (AEC) to promote the peaceful use of nuclear energy. Taipower creates the Atomic Power Research Commission. NTHU starts the Graduate Institute of Atomic Science.

1956–1958
Taiwan opens its first nuclear reactor, provided by the United States, at NTHU.

1958
During the Second Taiwan Straits Crisis (or "823 Artillery Bombardment"), the US prepares nuclear weapons for attacking China. China is pushed to pursue its own nuclear program.

1960
US nuclear bombs first deployed at Tainan Air Base, according to the *Bulletin of the Atomic Scientists*.

1964
China's first nuclear test, at Lop Nur, pushes Taiwan to produce its own nuclear weapons. China pledges "no-first-use of nuclear weapons at any time and in any circumstances." It is unclear if this also applies when attacking Taiwan, since China regards it as a renegade province.

1965
The predecessor of the military-run Chungshan Institute of Science and Technology (CSIST) is established. The proposed First Institute would become the Institute for Nuclear Energy Research (INER).

1967
Taiwan launches the $140 million Hsin Chu Program: procuring and operating a heavy-water reactor, a heavy-water

compliance of France with NATO. (The boycott of an intransigent and undefeated foe's imported foodstuffs follows a similar repressed logic, as with Cuban rum or French wine during the Iraq War.) Wine was championed by the Gauls upon the disintegration of its drinkers, the imperial Roman occupiers. The Romans snatched it from their Greek competitor, whose empire they had eclipsed, while the Greek slave states begat their wine from the stamping feet of their war captives, and so on, ad infinitum to the prehistoric dawn of life on the planet.

Food rituals have always been centered on hierarchy and power. The cow is ingested because it is essentially defenseless against us. We assert our primacy over nature by ingesting it in a gory ceremony of flesh chewing. The animals we admire are felines and canines, bears and eagles: predators like us. This is an ancient warrior's ethic, echoed in the American craze for Nazi memorabilia. The milk of the breast is the first liquid imbibed by the newborn child. The baby learns that his mewing automatically summons the mother, whereupon she administers the juice of subjugation from her teat. Therefore the taste of liquid is psychically paralleled with subjugation and enslavement even in the semiconscious baby state.

Once again, while Stoker's *Dracula* ostensibly addresses the genetic concerns of the European upper classes, vampirism—an ancient legend shared by many different cultures—is also a mass movement, enjoyed by every conquering race.

production plant, a reprocessing research lab, and a plutonium separation plant.

1964–1969
Taiwan purchases uranium from South Africa, nuclear plans from Canada, and other nuclear-related information from France and Germany.

1967–1969
Approximately fifty-five nuclear bombs are deployed at Tainan Air Base, according to the *Bulletin of the Atomic Scientists.*

1969
INER purchases a small heavy-water reactor (40 megawatts) from Canada. Dubbed the "Taiwan Research Reactor" (TRR), it becomes operational in 1973 and serves mainly to facilitate the procurement of elements to produce plutonium. Twenty-four people are exposed to a US sarin weapon on Okinawa. US President Nixon ends the US biological weapons program.

Late 1960s
Secret locations in southern Taiwan are used to enrich uranium and plutonium.

1970
South Korea begins its own nuclear program.

1971
Taiwan (ROC) loses its seat to the PRC in the United Nations. Since the United Nations does not recognize Taiwan as a sovereign state, it is not eligible for membership in nonproliferation treaties or export-control regimes that require statehood.

1972
US President Nixon visits China. Taiwan cannot join the Biological and Toxin Weapons Convention (BTWC), the Chemical Weapons Convention (CWC), or the Australia Group, an export-control cooperative.

1974
The last US nuclear bombs in Tainan are moved to the Philippines. India tests its first nuclear device.

1972–1974
The CIA concludes that Taiwan is working toward nuclear weapons capability and will be capable of producing a nuclear weapon within five years.

1975
Chiang Kai-Shek dies. South Korea signs the Nuclear Non-Proliferation Treaty and ends its nuclear program.

1976
The US pressures Taiwan to stop its nuclear program. Premier Chiang Ching-Kuo publicly promises that Taiwan will not acquire its own reprocessing facilities or engage in any activities related to reprocessing. International Atomic Energy Agency (IAEA) officials inspect the activities of the INER. They discover discrepancies: the Canadian-supplied TRR; other suspicious equipment from the US, Germany, and France, including US-supplied heavy water; uranium from South Africa; and technical information from Norway and Israel.

1977
The US pressures Taiwan to dismantle its reprocessing facilities and return US-supplied plutonium.

1978
US President Jimmy Carter normalizes relations with the PRC. Taipower's first nuclear reactor begins producing electricity. The US deploys some 2,400 nuclear bombs in Asia, primarily in Guam, South Korea, Okinawa, the Philippines, and Taiwan. A US nuclear monitoring team detects that Taiwan has a secret uranium enrichment program at CSIST. Chiang Ching-Kuo sends a cable to the US Department of State claiming that Taiwan is not developing nuclear weapons, "in line with their agreement."

1979
The US Congress passes the Taiwan Relations Act and withdraws its military forces from Taiwan. Weaponized anthrax leaks from a military facility in the Soviet Union, killing at least one hundred people. The Soviet Union develops a significant BW program (which Russia probably still maintains today).

1982
The US and China issue a third joint communiqué, in which the US declares that it will limit arms sales to Taiwan.

1983
The Special National Intelligence Estimate reports that Taiwan had "an aggressive, high-priority program to develop both offensive and defensive [CW] capabilities"—but this information is deleted from the declassified version of the estimate.

1987
The INER begins building a multiple-hot-cell nuclear facility, in violation of commitments made in 1976.

1987–1988
Col. Chang Hsien-Yi, Deputy Director of the INER and a CIA spy, defects and reveals Taiwan's plans. The CIA estimates that Taiwan was within one or two years of developing a nuclear bomb. President Chiang Ching-Kuo dies. US government agencies and IAEA inspectors shut down the Taiwan Research Reactor (TRR) and the hot cell. President Lee Teng-Hui promises US President Ronald Reagan that Taiwan will agree to end its nuclear weapons program conclusively and verifiably.

1988
Various intelligence sources suspect a biological weapons leak in northwestern China.

1990
It is reported that a series of accidental explosions at INER in the late '80s released cesium 137, cobalt 60, and plutonium 238 into the Dahan River, a water source for an estimated five million Taiwanese.

1991
Rear Admiral Thomas Brooks identifies Taiwan as a "probable" CW possessor in testimony before the US Congress.

1992
Local Taiwanese media reports that recycled, radioactive building materials were used in the construction of residential buildings in northern Taiwan from 1982–1984. The AEC covered up the issue for at least seven years.

1993
According to a Russian intelligence report, "Taiwan does not have biological weapons … [however], it has shown signs of conducting biological research of an applied military nature." US intelligence still believes that Taiwan maintains a BW program, possibly including anthrax, plague, yellow fever, typhoid, cholera, tuberculosis, typhus, smallpox, and botulinum toxin. The US accuses the PRC of having an offensive BW program.

1995
The US Office of Technology Assessment reports that Taiwan has BW.

1996
US President Clinton deploys two aircraft battle groups to waters off of Taiwan in response to Chinese ballistic missile tests.

1998
According to a US Arms Control and Disarmament Agency report, Taiwan has been upgrading its biotechnology capabilities by purchasing sophisticated biotechnology equipment from the US, Switzerland, and other countries. A Canadian analysis claims that Taiwan has developed thirty-six strains of bacteria and viruses for weaponization. In response, the Taiwan Ministry of National Defense (MND) denies developing BW. Pakistan conducts its first nuclear weapon test.

2000
The US Commerce Department fines Saint-Gobain Performance Plastics, Inc.

THE WAY STATION TRILOGY (1987–2012)

Kao Chung-Li

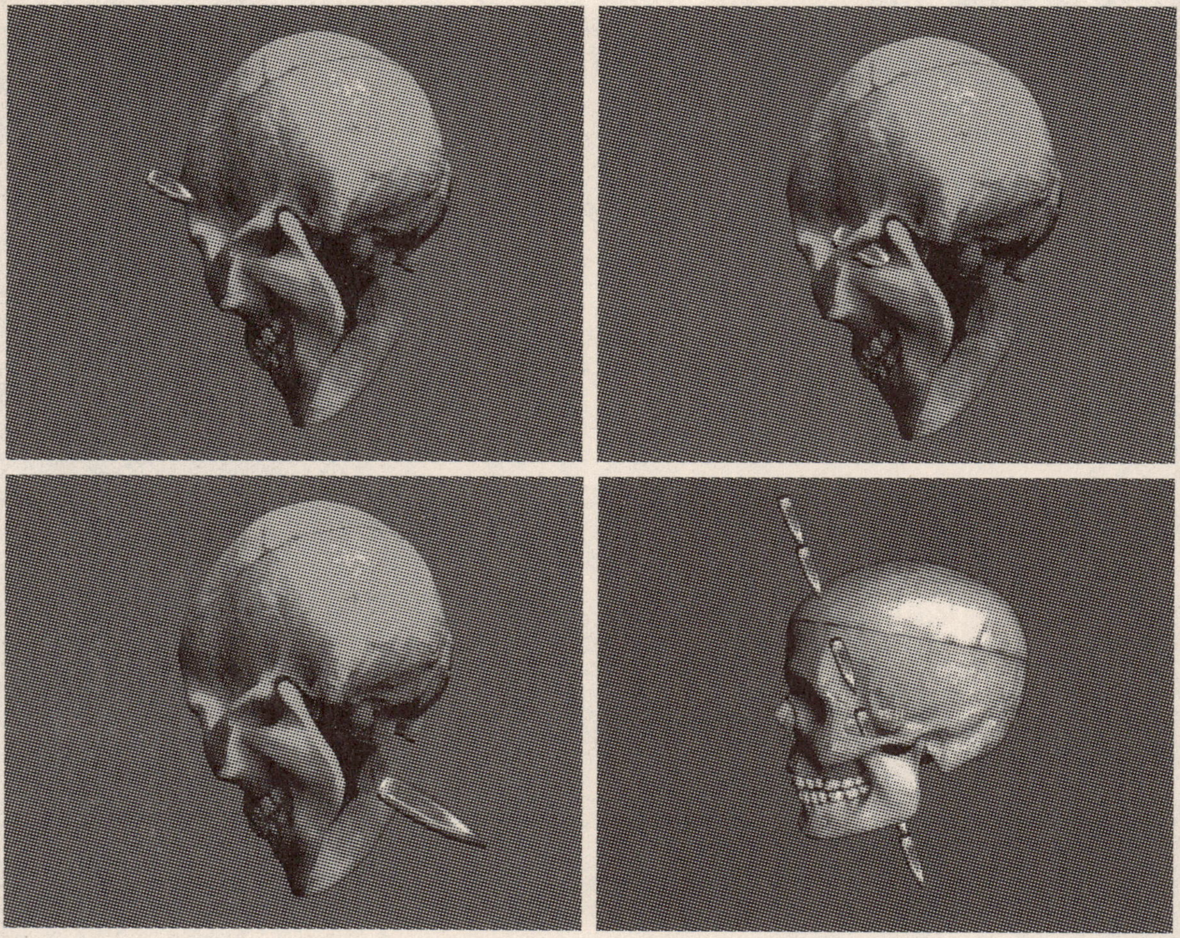

Kao Chung-Li, *The Way Station Trilogy*, 1987–2012, single-frequency projection, 41 min.

In the Xubang Campaign, a pivotal battle in the Chinese Civil War, my father Gao Wenbin was shot in the head. To this day, that 7.7 mm bullet is still buried inside his cranium, clearly visible under X-ray, looking exactly like a miniature ship.

My film *The Way Station Trilogy* comes in three parts. Part One, "Clouds, Moons, and Eight Thousand Miles: A Home Movie," is an 8 mm film completed in 1987. Part Two, "The Taste of Human Flesh," is made from a slideshow and was completed in 2010. Part Three, "Hey, Wake Up, You Little Rascal!," is a pencil animation short completed in 2012. All three parts are based on the experiences of my father. The film begins with his life and recollections, and moves toward my own life and growth mingled with a reflection on his.

My father appears in all three parts, supplying anecdotes through his constantly mumbling recollections, while I try my best to probe the depths of those recollections and arrive at the truth. There are actually two temporalities in this film. One is forward-flowing, from past to present, as witnessed by my father. The other flows

$697,500 for exporting export-controlled, dual-use, Teflon-coated valves and pumps to Israel and Taiwan.

2001 ☢

The BBC reports that the Taiwanese navy has used some sixty thousand depleted uranium (DU) rounds in maneuvers over recent years. The US government maintains that "China is believed to possess an offensive biological warfare capability based on technology developed prior to its accession to the BWC [Biological Warfare Convention]." Weaponized anthrax spores sent through the mail kill five in the US.

2002 ☣

The US Commerce Department fines Sigma-Aldritch $1,760,000 for exporting biological toxins to various countries, including Taiwan.

2003 ☣ ☠

President Chen Shui-Bian reveals the existence of Taiwan's Institute of Preventive Medical Research (IPMR), operating under the auspices of the National Defense Medical Center. The IPMR, located some twelve miles southwest of Taipei, supposedly no longer produces biological weapons of mass destruction and instead researches defenses against biological warfare attacks, which still requires creating weaponized strains. The US fines the Hamilton Sundstrand Corporation $171,500 for selling centrifugal pumps that can be used for producing chemical and biological weapons to China, Taiwan, Israel, and Saudi Arabia. The US and other allied nations invade Iraq in a search of WMD.

2004

Taiwanese President Chen Shui-Bian pledges that Taiwan will never develop weapons of mass destruction and urges China to do the same. The American Institute in Taiwan (AIT) reports on Ching Hwee International Trading Company's export of dual-use tools to North Korea (source: WikiLeaks).

2005 ☣ ☠

The AIT investigates two Taiwanese companies for shipping dual-use machine tools to Syria. The shipping invoices stipulated that the machines were "not to be used for WMD purposes" (source: WikiLeaks). The AIT reports on a new level-4 pathogens ward in Taiwan: "Trudil explained that level-4 pathogens are 'genetically-engineered bugs that can destroy the world,' far more dangerous than anthrax, SARS, or avian influenza. He said Taiwan already had an operational level-4 laboratory, and that he had recently arranged a tour of these facilities for US DOD and CDC personnel in exchange for DOD allowing Taiwan MND and CDC to tour the US level-4 ward located at Fort Detrick, Maryland. (AIT ECON and COMM were unaware of these visits. Reftel's report on the DOD tour noted that the Taiwan facility claims to have a sample of a smallpox strain that produces a 100% fatality rate.) Trudil noted that there is currently only one other level-4 ward in the world, located in Siberia" (source: WikiLeaks). According to official PRC and Taiwan military sources, the Taiwanese military, supported by the Taiwan Army Chemical Corps, CSIST, and the National Defense University, stockpiles chemical weapons and has three thousand chemical weapon combat troops.

2006

North Korea claims to have successfully conducted a nuclear test.

2007 ☣ ☠

The AIT reports that Taiwan has the ability to develop chemical and biological weapons and may be secretly developing biological weapons (source: WikiLeaks). President Ma Ying-Jeou claims that Taiwan will never develop WMD. The AIT reports that China has become Taiwan's sole acknowledged source of Chemical Weapons Convention (CWC)-restricted schedule two (S2) chemical imports (source: WikiLeaks).

2008

South Korea purportedly destroys its own stockpile of 3,126 tons of chemical weapons, mostly nerve agents, in accordance with the CWC.

2006–2009

Various governments and entities ponder ways of integrating Taiwan into international export-control organizations without Chinese interference.

2009

North Korea conducts a second nuclear test.

2010

Taiwan-based Axiomtek Co. Ltd. is fined NTD 600,000 for illegally exporting a controlled Strategic High Tech Commodity to Iran (source: WikiLeaks).

2011 ☢

Taipower admits that nuclear waste leaked on Orchid Island.

backward, to the past. Ultimately, I attempt not to buttress my father's recollections with any prevailing historical perspective, but simply to rewrite history through the life of a ninety-three-year-old man.

As the film draws to an end, I employ the three-in-one image of slave ship, bullet, and ark to cast the Chinese Nationalist-Communist Civil War as the pivotal point that changed the nature of modern warfare, moving it toward the goal of shaping the progress of history. Before the Chinese Civil War, modern warfare was no more than fights between Western powers over spoils—that is, wars between "The Comfy of the Earth." The Chinese Civil War, circa 1948, was the first war that mobilized "The Wretched of the Earth" against the new imperialist surrogate rule by the Comfy.

Actually, all groups—be it societies, old historical groups, or new groups that are still writing their histories—are shaped by telling their stories to themselves or to others. At the present moment, Taiwan is simultaneously new and old. Here in Taiwan, we do not know how to imagine ourselves, even as this imagination will ultimately decide whether Taiwan is to be reunited with the Mainland, secede into independence, or maintain the status quo (one of the several forms of the official stance of "one China, different interpretations"). The way Taiwan ultimately goes, however, will be dictated by a story that both the Taiwanese and others can accept and support. The Taiwanese will have to orient themselves according to that story, so that they can have some kind of stability in the future. An ark that accommodates a common historical identity can only be built upon planks of internationalism and riggings of historical perspective.

Michel Foucault says that reality is political. If so, memories and stories not only open up the prospect of realpolitik, but also turn political reality into a tool for one's own use.

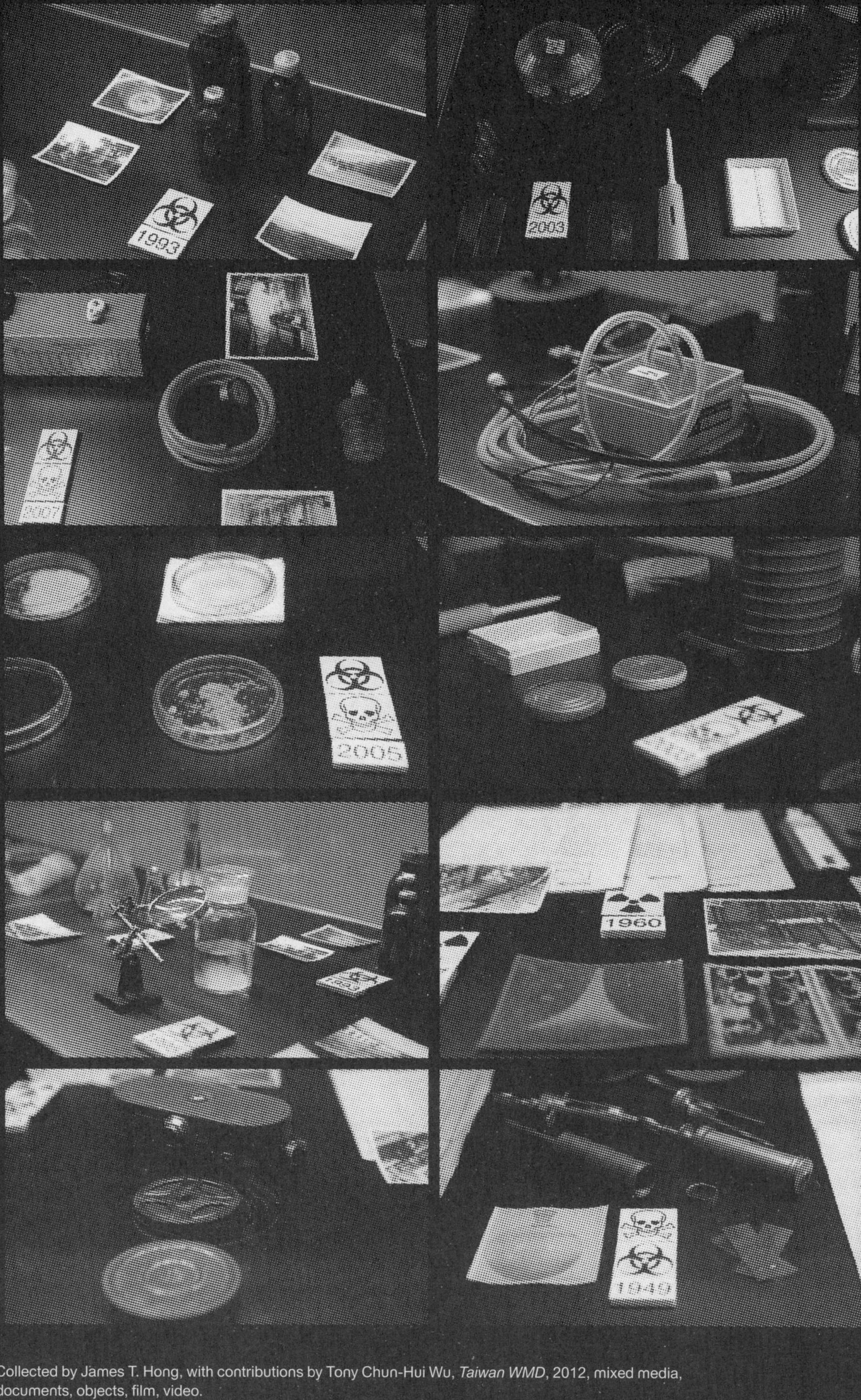

Collected by James T. Hong, with contributions by Tony Chun-Hui Wu, *Taiwan WMD*, 2012, mixed media, documents, objects, film, video.

FUZZ-BOMBED: BEING A SPECTATOR AT THE TAIPEI BIENNIAL

David Barton

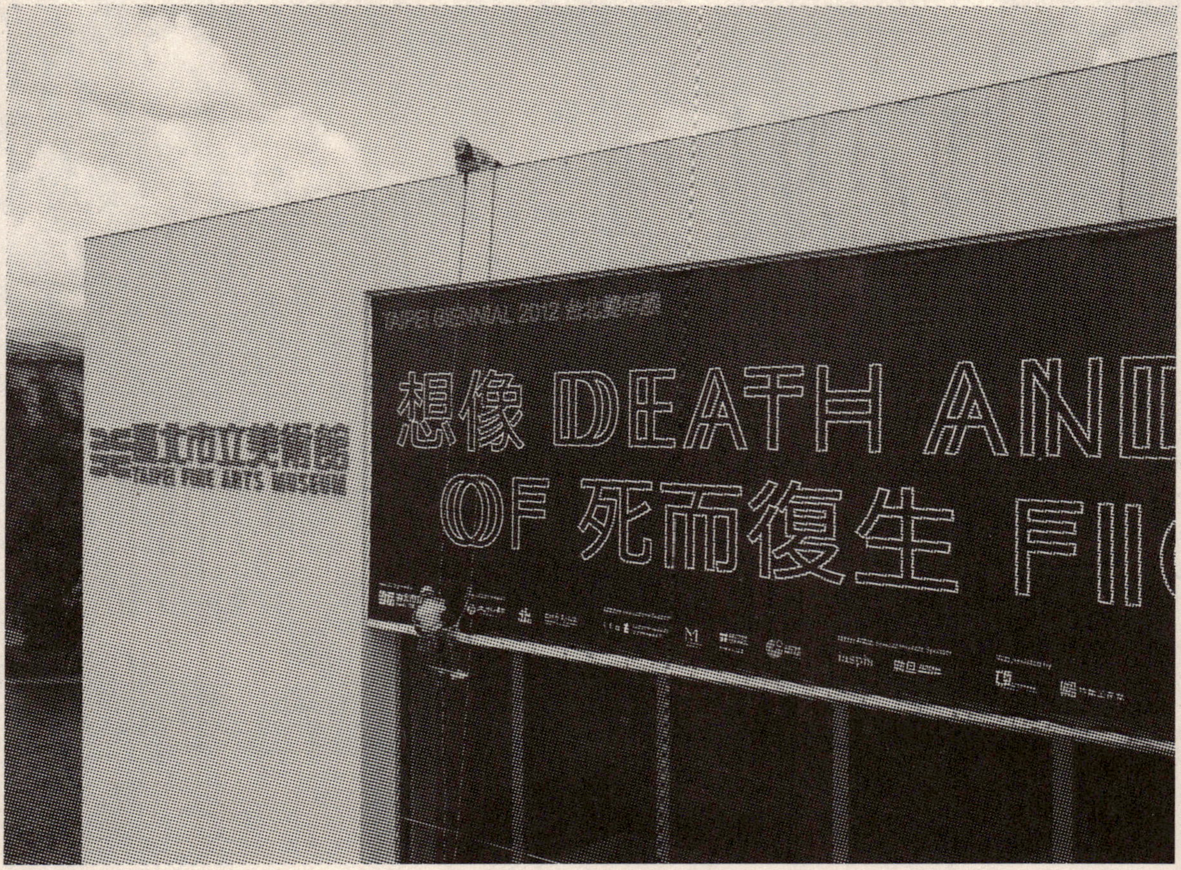

Exile, politics, and cinema combine in a film on a Japanese left-wing Red Army militant and a Japanese filmmaker devoted to the Palestinian cause, both in hiding in Beirut for decades. *The Anabasis of May and Fusako Shigenobu, Masao Adachi, and 27 Years Without Images* combines globalism and landscape filmmaking, or "*fukeiron*," (Tokyo, Beirut, and Palestine). Fusako Shigenobu was the leader of the extremist wing of the Japanese Red Army, a terrorist organization. Her daughter, born in hiding in Lebanon, grew up in a war zone far from Japan. "Through filming landscapes, Masao Adachi sought to reveal the structures of oppression that underpin and perpetuate the political system." Why are these Japanese people in the Middle East? Why have they joined a transpolitical martyrdom? How do they imagine themselves? How do we imagine them? Are they heroes? They are a militant, a child of a militant, and a militant filmmaker. Are they terrorists? Was the child, May, recruited? How does this become cultural fodder for a museum? Is the museum a recruitment center?

According to the Apple online dictionary, the stages of the recruitment process include: job analysis and the development of candidate specifications; the sourcing of candidates through networking, advertising, or other search methods; matching candidates to job

PHOTOGRAPHY OF THE GREAT LEAP FORWARD AND GREAT FAMINE

Jei Li

How might photographs testify to a momentous epoch like the Great Leap Forward and the Great Famine? Perusing Chinese newspapers and magazines from 1958 to 1962, one would be hard-pressed, amidst the abundance of harvest images, to find any hint of the widespread famine. Was this because the totalitarian state's propaganda apparatus monopolized all cameras? Or was it because there was a unique, and naive, photographic culture in Maoist China, which was isolated from the rest of the world? Drawing mainly from photography magazines of the late 1950s and early 1960s, this exhibit shows that journalistic, social, and amateur photography all grew during the Great Leap Forward. Thousands of professional photographers went to the countryside to take pictures of the "laboring people" and to "bear witness" to miracles, while affordable domestic-made cameras became available for the first time.

Yet in this Chinese photography culture, the "Great Leap" did not mean that people could photograph whatever they wanted. At a time when all texts and images were subject to pathological over-reading and were considered expressions of their makers' ideological stance, any image that intimated poverty or hunger would have been labeled counterrevolutionary, a sacrilege against the pursuit of an ideal Communist society. Yet political oppression and terror were not the only explanations for the absence of famine images. Many patriotic photographers sought to create proud and dignified images of China and her people, breaking away from the humiliating, backward, and savage images of the Chinese as seen through the "imperialist" lens. Moreover, utopian visions were not held by Mao Tse-Tung alone, but were also internalized by many of the famine's victims through mass-media propaganda. These victims believed that toil and hardship in the present would lead to an eternal happiness in the future. People used a variety of media to express their utopian dreams—painting, poetry, photography, film, and radio, as well as their laboring bodies in the fields. They sketched out sublime pictures on a "poor and blank" Chinese countryside. Not merely propagandistic "fakery" or "lies," photographs from this period were concrete visualizations of these projected hopes, which were eventually brutally trampled, along with tens of millions of lives.

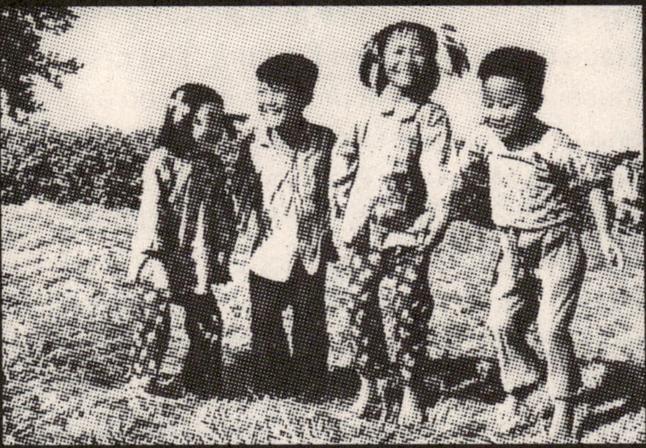

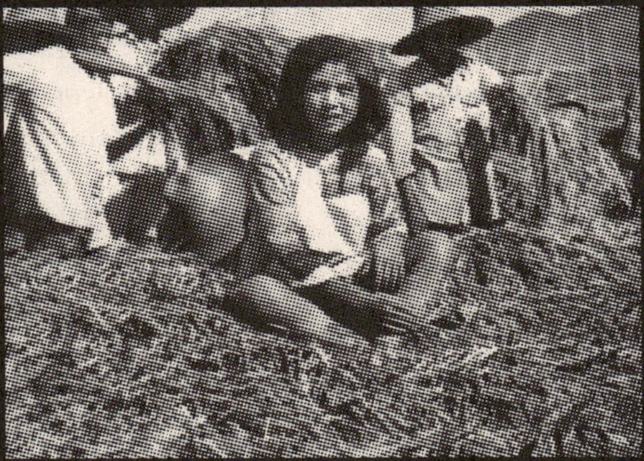

Fig. 1 Yu Dengjian, *Rejoicing on an Early Rice Sputnik*, from *Popular Photography*, September 1958.
Fig. 2 Ge Yongkun, *The Girl on the Rice Paddy*, from *People's Pictorial*, October 1958.

requirements and screening individuals using testing (skills or personality assessment); assessment of candidates' motivations and their fit with organizational requirements through interviewing and other assessment techniques. The recruitment process also includes the making and finalizing of job offers and the induction and onboarding of new employees. At the Taipei Biennial 2012, the spectator becomes a potential recruit—examined, networked, advertised (literally put on screen as he or she enters the museum). For what job? Check your spectatorship at the door and realize that you are a historical artifact of the twenty-first century being processed for your worthiness as a participant in the overarching theme of the Biennial, "The Museum of the Monster That Is History," which is also the name of Station 18[1], and which derives from the title of a book on Chinese history by scholar David Der-Wei Wang, *The Monster That Is History*.

Recruitment is not new to the history of poetry and theater (think Bertolt Brecht). However, it is relatively new to the history of the place of the museum in culture. The new museum recruitment process is based on skills and personality assessment. At the Taipei Fine Arts Museum's Biennial, you are essentially exposed to three forms of Rorschach test: representations of autism, torture (mainly decapitation), and camouflage. These three psychic states could be expressed as flight into mental illness, fight to survive a sure death, and the need to simply hide. The engine of this exposure, the industrial military engine that makes this recruitment necessary, is "Modernity."

If one visualizes this anonymous power of systemic modernity, it is difficult to come up with a better image than the giant mimetic planet in the film *Solaris*, by the great Russian filmmaker Andrei Tarkovsky. This planet traps, abstracts, and deploys the disparate psychic monsters of every space station recruit to which it is exposed. This mimesis is the power of the Biennial: technological, machinic mimesis and its recruitment of the spectator, a systemic "fixing," or an antisystemic "mobilization" of human agency. However, one cannot simply be mimetically fixed or mobilized. First, the spectator has to become de-objectified, dereified, has to become a fluid agency which can then be either fixed or mobilized. One has to be made a fluid transparency, recognizing the self of oneself as an alien, an abstraction, an impostor, a space station recruit.

Modernity and the monster of history (which, according to David Der-Wei Wang, have become a double bind, meaning that modernity has become the monster of history and not the escape from this monster, as promised by the Enlightenment) demand that a double consciousness be installed in the spectator, if said spectator is to become a prospective recruit, fixed or mobilized, pro or con. The Biennial announces as much when the spectator enters the museum and walks down a long catwalk, abstracted, projected onto a large scrim screen. Those within the museum witness this spectator de-objectified, silhouetted, screened for recruitment. So it is confirmed, from Ecclesiastes to Benjamin, that Modernity has heralded one significant technological change: we are no longer dust, we are scrims of film, not shadows in a cave even, we are reproducible silhouettes, transparencies. Whether catapulted light on silver nitrate or digital positrons, Modernity no longer experiences the primitive fear of soul-stealing apparatuses, it lives in them, the second consciousness of modernity relies on their iridescence, the soul made eternally digital, as its only hope of relevance, fixed or mobilized, pro and con simultaneously.

It is an age of aesthetic crisis in which "Damien Hirst and Jeff Koons discuss the future of art," as French author of the disillusioned Enlightenment Michel Houellebecq puts it in his novel *The Map and the Territory*. This could be a banner under which the Taipei Biennial seeds its roots of rebellion. The Taipei Biennial heralds the end of the age of "aesthetic rationalism," as Tim Reiss has it, where beauty is framed as a fetishistic commodity: a diamond-encrusted skull by Damien Hirst, or a mold of Michael Jackson and his chimpanzee Bubbles by Jeff Koons. At the very least, aesthetic rationality, the judgment of the beautiful, is coming under attack. Beauty now stands

On August 15, 1958, *The People's Daily* published on its front page a photograph of four children called *Rejoicing on an Early Rice Sputnik* (Fig. 1). The rice paddy, located in Macheng County in Hubei Province, reputedly produced a record 15,000 kilograms of rice: "So dense are the rice stalks in this high-yield experimental field, children could stand on it like a sofa." Reprinted in *People's Pictorial* and *Popular Photography*, this image soon became a model for other photographers (see Fig. 2), as well as for artists (see Fig. 3), journalists, and poets. Above all, it was a model for the cadres of People's Communes throughout China. To stage such images, communes were required to surrender their subsistence grain to the state as surplus, which directly caused the ensuing famine. Thus, images of abundance not only elided the larger scarcity, but also contributed to an unprecedented catastrophe through their very production.

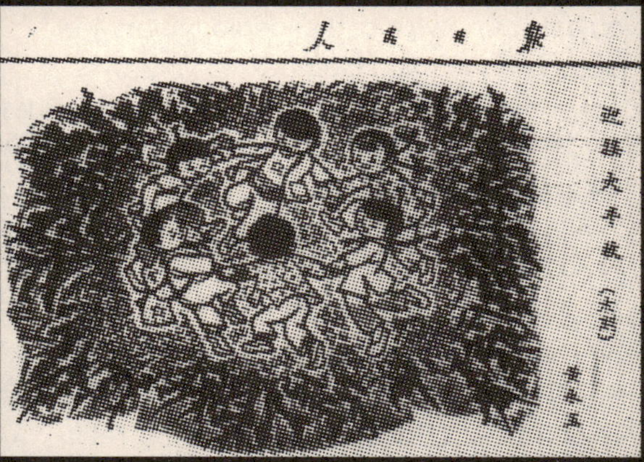

Fig. 3 Huang Yongyu, *Greeting the Great Harvest*, from *People's Daily*, October 4, 1958.

The Bloomsbury edition of Frank Dikötter's 2010 book *Mao's Great Famine* featured on its cover a photograph of a skinny boy in rags with a begging bowl (Fig. 4). This photograph first appeared in a 1946 issue of *Life Magazine* (Fig. 5) and depicted the victim of a famine in Hunan that took place prior to the Communist Revolution. Chosen for the "Family of Man" exhibition at New York's MoMA, this image also travelled to the American pavilion at the Moscow World's Fair of 1959. It was criticized by the Soviet hosts, who demanded its removal. The story of the picture's removal, accompanied by reprints of the image, circulated widely in the American press, alongside speculation about the Chinese famine. In this way, the photograph came to represent the Great Famine outside of China.

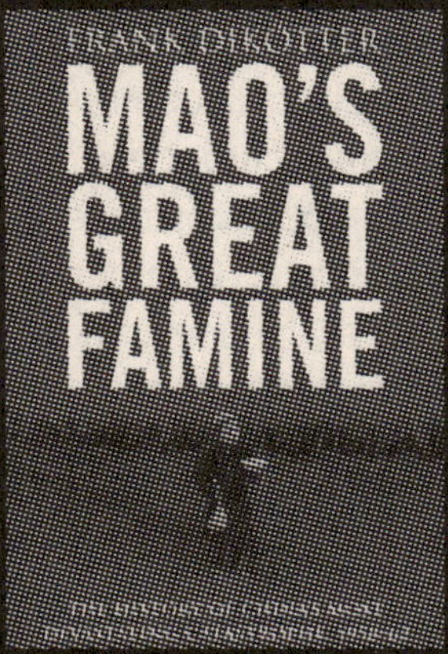

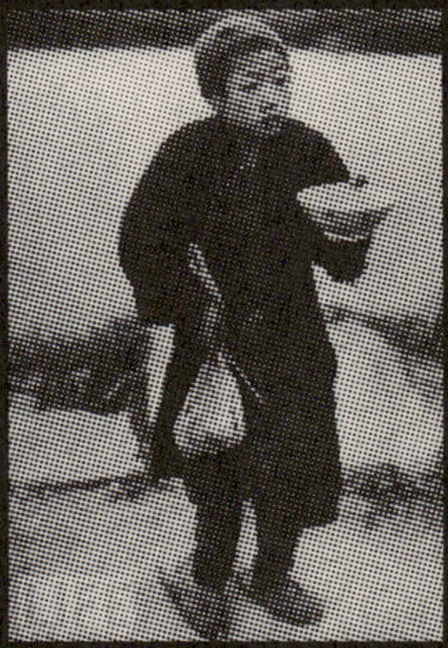

Fig. 4 Cover of the first Bloomsbury edition of Frank Dikötter's book *Mao's Great Famine*, 2010.
Fig. 5 George Silk, *Ragged Child Begging for Food During Famine,* Hunan Province, China, May 1946. © George Silk/Time Life Pictures/Getty Images.

Along with photojournalists, social photographers were also exhorted to abandon their previous "bourgeois" aesthetic standards and go to factories and to the countryside to serve the proletariat. Photographers who had storefronts were expected to transform their display windows, formerly "bedecked with jewels," into bulletin boards to promote socialist building projects.

Chinese factories only began producing domestic cameras, from brands like Shanghai, Great Leap, and Happiness, in 1958. These domestic-made cameras were a fraction of the price of imported cameras. In the inaugural issue of *Popular Photography*, Shi Shaohua proclaimed that photography was no longer "the toy of the elite," but rather "an indispensable part of socialist construction and mass culture." He continued: "In many factories, schools, work units, and even in some rural areas, amateur photography clubs are being established like bamboo shoots after the rain."

Popular Photography held several reader photo competitions. It published work by readers to both encourage amateur photography and critique unwanted tendencies like "naturalism" and "formalism."

as besotted with itself as the drowning Ophelia or the narcissistic hordes of K-pop bands, while biennials do battle—recruit agents to do battle—over the rotting corpse, literally, of the use value of history.

So to be a spectator at the Taipei Biennial is to be one of its characters/victims/witnesses, all triangulated together: headless, in camouflage, a traitor, a collector of transparencies, not the Baudrillard kind, not virtual but subjective transparencies, meaning animistic decentered transparencies, where with the Chinese author Lu Xun you are a decapitation fetishist, an Andy Warhol lover of car crashes, electric chairs, gas chambers, germ warfare, and Dead Leaf butterflies. And you only realize with a shock, the shock of the residual spectator you thought you were supposed to be, that you saw nothing beautiful. That you are simply a witness and an agent, a recruit to Capital confronting itself. Modernity is not beautiful, it's a death drive.

It's all about what you can let go of. The show consistently asks the spectator to let go—of ego, the earth, guilt, innocence, fear, life. Why else would we be in an inner-city Guatemalan cemetery exhuming a mass grave of disappeared, shot-in-the-head, politically active young men and women from the Reagan era of the 1980s? Why, if not to say, "Alas, poor Juan, I knew him well," and to allow that skull held in that researcher's hands to become your own skull. How much can you give up to fight the monster of History that is Modernity? Are you recruited yet?

This seems to be the historical question addressed to the end of the narrative of the ideology of the beautiful. Station 7 (Yervant Gianikian and Angela Ricci Lucchi), open-skull brain surgery on a wounded soldier; Station 10 (Rajkamal Kahlon), anatomical drawings of skulls on official autopsy reports and death certificates from US military bases in Iraq and Afghanistan; Station 18, Guatemala, a gun-shot-shattered skull; Station 13 (Kao Chung-Li), an X-ray of a skull with a bullet lodged in it from the time of the Chinese Civil War; Station 37 (Luis Jacob), X-ray photographs of skulls, fractures, and fireworks. Gun-shot-shattered skulls from around the world, decapitation, and the fireworks in the brain of blunt trauma riddle this show with exactly how much can you give up before the slate is wiped clean and you can be pleasantly imprisoned in the Okinawan sanatorium of autism. Autistic aestheticism seems to be the desired ascetic evolutionary leap from Rational Aestheticism, at least as a stage. This is a Beckettian sublime that one can't help but cheer for. The clutter of history, as the clutter of the three floors of the Biennial invites, actually wills the spectator to an eternal sunshine of the spotless mind.

The monkey eating the germ warfare gruel, Station 18, is you, and you, like Oliver Twist, should be forced to ask for more. You haven't given up enough yet. Not until you have cooked and eaten your own child, as a section of Station 18 devoted to the Great Famine in China in the late 1950s demonstrates. It's like getting fuzz-bombed, first cooking and eating your kid, the art part, then getting made into an exhibit as an enemy of the state that made you eat your own kid, the ideology part, then photographed manacled next to your overcooked kid half in the pot, half out, at your side, as surprised proof that the state cares or better that anyone cares, the end of the art part. The Chinese man, who, like Saturn, has devoured his own child, is already listening to the autistic side, the other side, he appears to have become another Asian Muselmann. This Station relates closely to Station 46 (Sun Xun), "Some Actions Which Haven't Been Defined Yet in the Revolution," in which a series of woodcuts evokes the metaphor of cannibalism as an attitude and mental condition, used by the influential author Lu Xun to describe the decay of Chinese consciousness. The spectator learns that besides being an "eminent scholar of Chinese woodcuts," Lu Xun, again in Station 18, received the historical insight that led to his becoming a writer by watching the decapitation of a traitor and being struck by the passive crowd of Chinese onlookers. The suggestion is the Chinese world was cannibalizing its own subjectivity in the twentieth century. And we should reread Lu Xun.

The alternative to "how much can you give up" as a spectator at the Taipei Biennial is

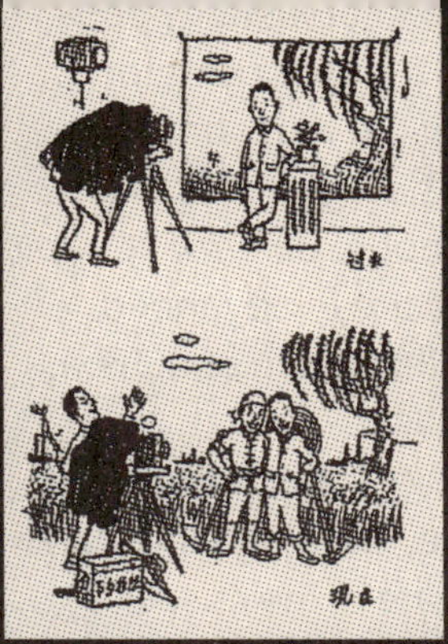

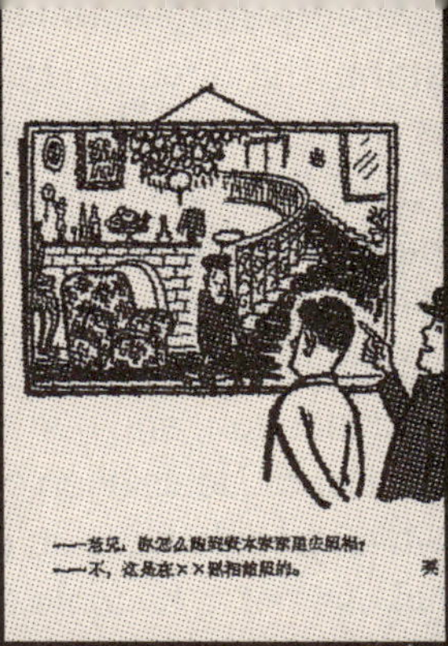

Fig. 6 Ying Tao, *New People, New Phenomena, New Landscapes* (cartoon), from *Popular Photography*, July 1958.
Fig. 7 Ying Tao, *Elder Brother …* (cartoon), from *Popular Photography*, August 1958. The caption reads: "Question: Elder Brother, how come you went to a capitalist's house to have your photo taken? Answer: I didn't. I had it taken at XX photo shop."

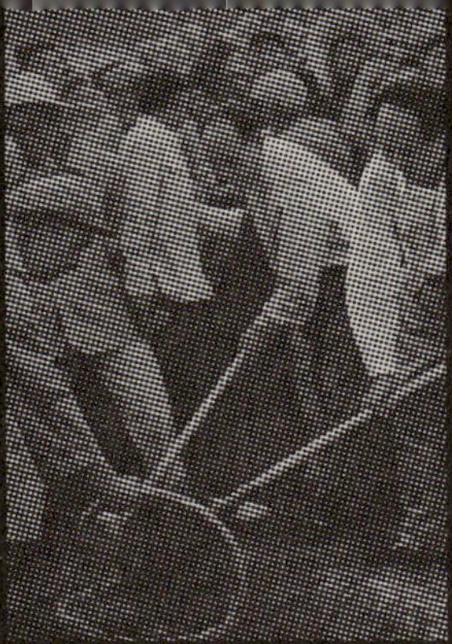

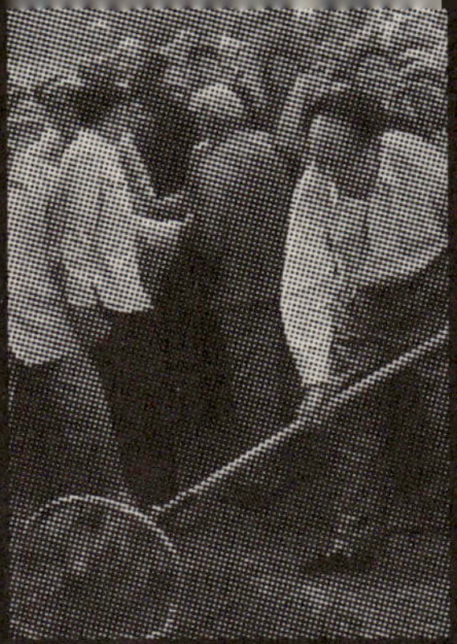

Fig. 10 Hou Bo, *Comrade Mao Tse-Tung at the Reservoir Construction Site*, from *Photography from the Great Leap Forward*, 1958.
Fig. 11 *Chairman Mao Taking Part in Volunteer Labor at the Construction Site of the Ming Tombs Water Reservoir*, May 1958, from *Mao Tse-Tung: A Selection of Photographs*, 1978.

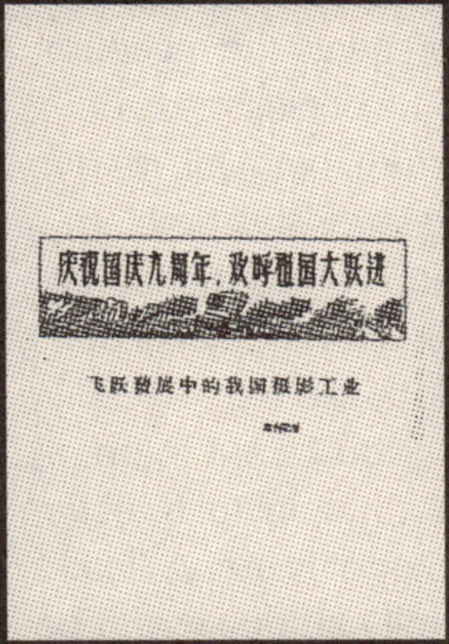

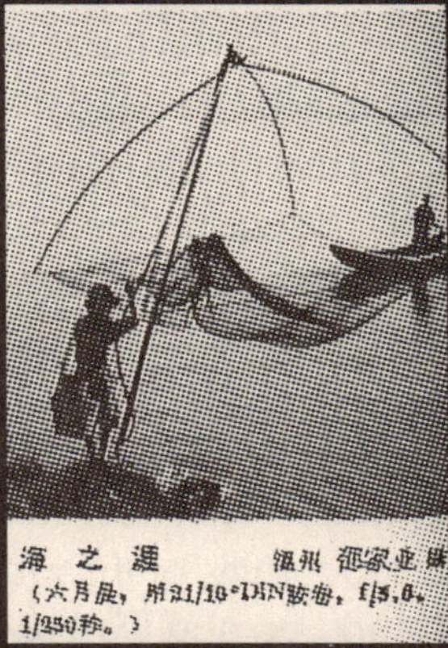

Fig. 8 "The Great Leap in the Development of Our Nation's Photography Industry," *Popular Photography*, September 1959.
Fig. 9 Shao Jiaye, *Seashore*, from *Popular Photography*, November 1958.

A negative example was *Seashore* by Shao Jiaye, which "failed to truthfully reflect the real lives of our fishermen. The serene environment, the empty fishing net, the sluggish individual laborer, and the single-oar boat—all this contrasts with the Great Leap Forward in the fishing industry."

In May 1958, Mao Tse-Tung and other national leaders paid a visit to the Ming Tombs Reservoir and also "volunteered" their labor in front of myriad cameras. The man next to Mao in this widely published photograph is Beijing's party secretary Peng Zhen, who was airbrushed out of the picture after his fall in the Cultural Revolution. The doctored photograph was published in the book *Mao Tse-Tung: A Selection of Photographs* in 1978. The contemporary artist Zhang Dali first juxtaposed these two images in his exhibition *A Second History*.

Taking pictures was a way of conferring honor on heroes and model workers, which encouraged competitive demonstrations of revolutionary fervor through relentless labor.

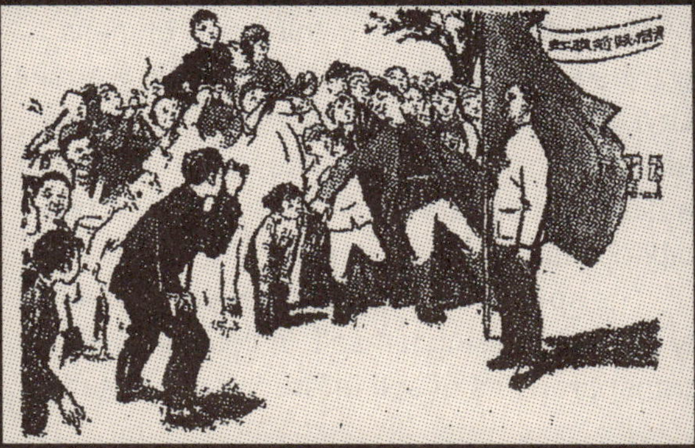

Fig. 12 Wu Min, *Heroes Compete to Have Their Photos Taken with the Red Flag*, from *Popular Photography*, December 1958.

At some reservoir construction sites, any individual or team that managed to dig ten cubic meters per person per day for seven consecutive days would get their picture taken in front of a red flag. The negative counterpart to this was a white flag, which denoted backwardness and disgrace. In many places during the Great Leap, such competitive revolutionary ardor made people risk their lives.

somewhere in the animist search for the Guattari museum (Station 21: Angela Melitopoulos and Maurizio Lazzarato). If a de-centered subject is to avoid all overarching centripetal ideation, then the collective nexus of decapitation, camouflage, and autistic Muselmann stimulates waves, lines of energy which do not converge, some stations will seem pointless, some will energize the spectator, and some will sicken as they infatuate. The infatuated, as spectator, will insist on the ideation of a centrifugal will to decentered transparency in order to escape the Monster of History.

If, according to Agamben, this is the price of the "Life and Death of Fiction," literary space itself, a space for the eternally undead, where it is impossible, as a film, to die, then the Taipei Biennial becomes a very ethical purgatory as opposed to an uplifting encounter with the ideal of beauty. However, as a recruit, the spectator becomes Muselmann, has to play hide-and-seek with the monster of Modernity, or, as in Station 33 (Jimmie Durham), it will crush you. There is no winner of this game of hide-and-seek, the recruit always already loses the head of spectatorship, hiding behind a rock, or ultimately dying, vanishing with hundreds of other ethical recruits in this game of mass graves and concentration camps. No wonder Levi killed himself. Ethics is a game of snakes and ladders, a roll of the dice for transcendent autism, but equally a roll of the dice for a precipitous fall.

The spectator of the Taipei Biennial definitely plays at missing himself. In this sense, the transparencies of self offered at each station keep the shape-shifting of subjectivity constant. The question then for the spectator is, what has happened to the museum? The Taipei Fine Arts Museum has, if successful, been working very hard not to be a museum. If the museum is everywhere in advanced capitalism, then what is this place of autism, decapitation, and camouflage?

The musealization of the world, a world in which people have no use, like a national park. No use but to become aware of their uselessness, meaning recognizing that humans once had use value but have outgrown it; the world is a museum and humans are useless tourists. How does the spectator of the Taipei Biennial feel about the experience? Gratified to be in a museum that is not a museum because it demands loss of self, sacrifice, shamanic transformation? The Biennial presents the museum as a place for confronting the uselessness of tourism with the use of torture, betrayal, martyrdom, disguise. One understands this problem, the ethics of the Muselmann versus the tourist.

The spectator of the Taipei Biennial is being recruited to be "ill of a malady like a question": Do I want to be a tourist or do I want to be tortured? That is obviously the playful question of Modernity, or the Monster of History: Shall I stand up and twirl or shall I sit down and be entertained? Capital recruits for the nude, for pornography, for fashion and consumption, the useless, the meaningless. The Taipei Biennial recruits for the decapitated, the autistic, the hidden, the profane, and the possibility of being of some use.

1 The station numbers refer to numbers in the guidebook/floor plan.

In 1958, the tenet "revolutionary realism and revolutionary romanticism" came to replace Socialist Realism as a new aesthetic standard. Its photographic manifestations included *Morning of the First Automobile Factory*, showing large smoking chimneys typical of the "industrial sublime" of this era, and *Competition*, a low-angle shot with sorghum stalks in the foreground and a telegraph pole in the background, upon which a female technician works. The sorghum stalks appear to be as tall as the telegraph pole.

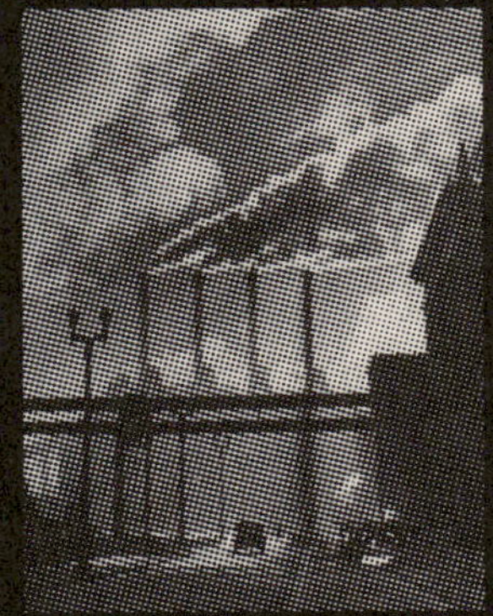

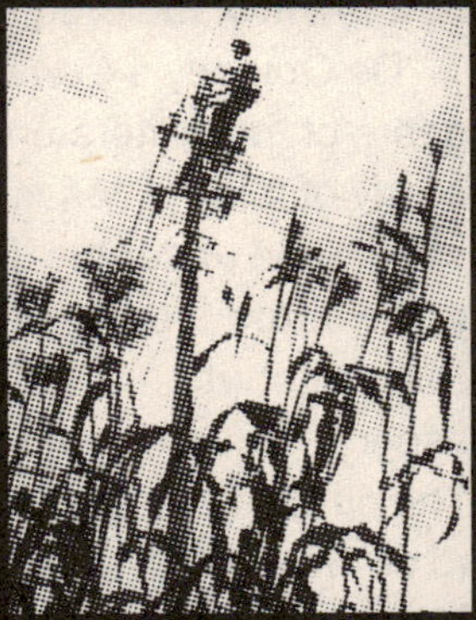

Fig. 13 Liu Entai, *Morning of the First Automobile Factory*, from *Chinese Photography*, February 1958.
Fig. 14 Zhong Guangkui, *Competition*, from *Popular Photography*, October 1958.

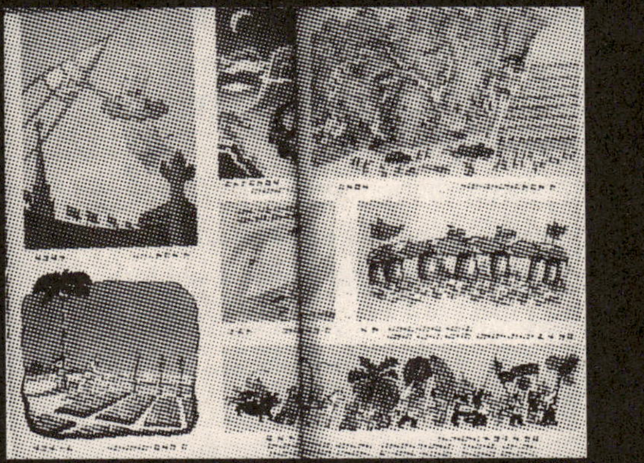

Fig. 15 In the peasant paintings of the Great Leap Forward, the tenet of "revolutionary romanticism" emboldened artists' imaginations, sometimes resulting in surrealistic works. (Images from *New Observations*, January 1959.)

While the photographic medium, with its temporal and spatial limitations, could not readily accommodate the phantasmal imaginations of peasant artists, photomontage was able to approximate their utopian visions. Flaunting the visual playfulness of collage rather than trying to produce any kind of reality effect, these artists created images that could never be mistaken for ordinary photographs. They instead resemble Chinese New Year posters.

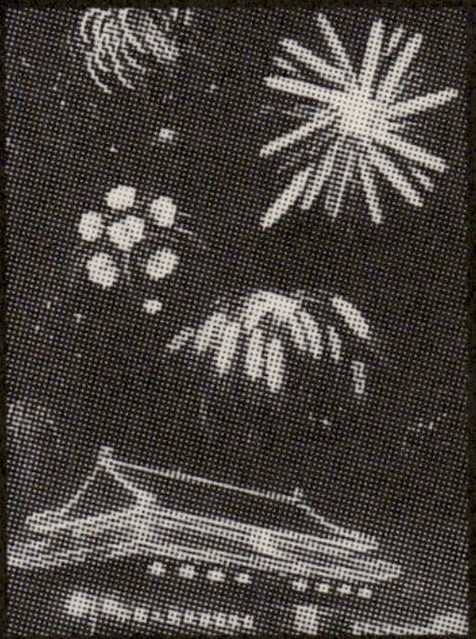

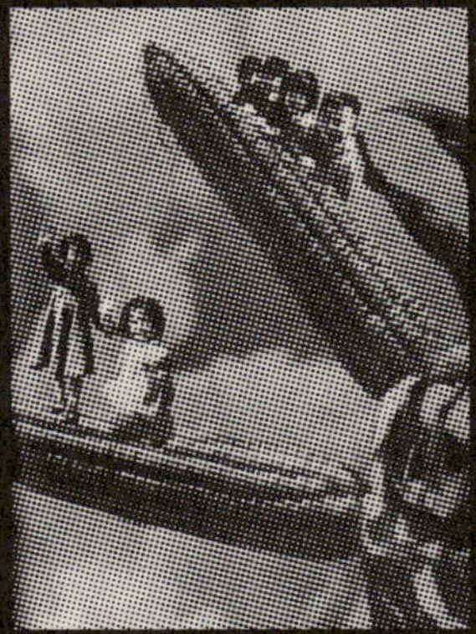

Fig. 16 Zhao Yao, *High-Producing Sputniks Replace Fireworks*, from *Popular Photography*, January 1959.
Fig. 17 Zhao Yao, *Flower of Corn*, from New Observations, October 1958.

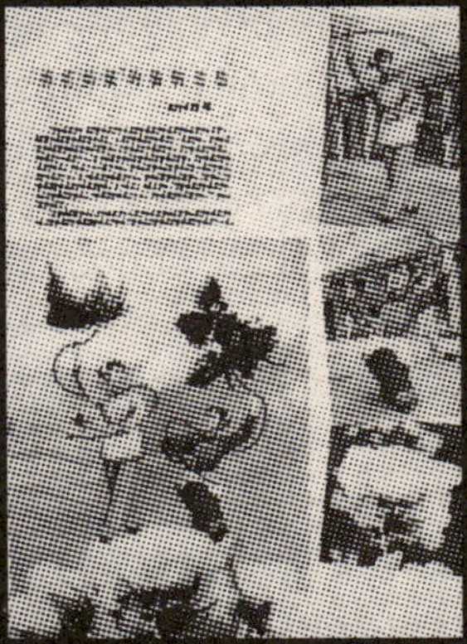

Fig. 18 Zhao Yao, *The Making of* Cotton Girls, from *Popular Photography*, July 1959.

Cartoons in *Popular Photography* demonstrated the "how-to" of photomontage and other forms of photographic manipulation. However, considering the hunger that enveloped the nation in 1959, one cannot help but wonder if the viewers of these photographs and cartoons saw them as ironic. *Popular Photography*'s polemic, meanwhile, became increasingly strident and defensive: "If our imperialist enemies maliciously slander the formation of People's Communes by calling them coercive, and demean our peasants' voluntary labor by calling it forced, then photographs such as *Singing the Harvest in a Bountiful Field* could strike back at them … Can forced labor produce such a happy scene? Do working people in the so-called 'free and democratic' West feel such joy?" (September 1959).

NANKING RESTAURANT: TRACING OPIUM IN CALCUTTA

Joachim Koester

In his 1822 novel *Confessions of an English Opium Eater*, Thomas De Quincey writes, "Not the opium-eater, but the opium, is the true hero of this tale; and the legitimate center on which the interest revolves." He continues: "The object was to display the marvelous agency of opium, whether for pleasure or for pain; if that is done, the action of the piece has closed."

De Quincey did more than merely describe the marvelous power of opium—its ability to induce visions and horrible nightmares. *Confessions of an English Opium Eater* can be read as a manual, a guidebook with advice and instructions as well as warnings for prospective opium users. De Quincey explains that he prefers to go to concerts under the influence of laudanum, as it stimulates "the sensual pleasure of music." He sets aside one evening each week for this, and by doing so he incorporates into his leisure activities the consumption of an opium preparation to enhance aesthetic pleasure. His descriptions of his opiate ramblings through the streets of London, another of his diversions, became the inspiration for later psychogeographical experiments—a new gateway to the modern city through chemical reveries, the conscious derangement of the senses. De Quincey transforms opium from an anesthetizing medicine into a portal that reveals what he calls "the secret inscriptions of the mind," journeys in time to forgotten memories which seem to be carved from the very darkness of sleep—an often dangerous and frightening enterprise.

Opium intensifies De Quincey's experiences: the colors in his dreams become stronger, but at the same time the shadows grow deeper, reinforcing the "fearful realities" of the drug. One such reality is opium addiction, regarded in De Quincey's day as an unavoidable and rarely discussed side effect of taking the drug. This demon, which De Quincey evokes in his novel, is only later—at the end of the twentieth century, and for quite different reasons—assigned a new identity: the drug abuser.

De Quincey's *Confessions* established the genre of "drug literature," exploring drugs as a way of mining consciousness. He wrote the book while under the influence, and in doing so he introduced the idea of recreational use. His contribution constitutes an important aspect of the modern Western history of opium. The other, more prosaic side of the story has to do with opium's production and trade. Karl Marx described the opium business as making "gold out of nothing," resulting in enormous fortunes that "sprang up like mushrooms in a day." Opium is the quintessential capitalist raw material—dreams that can be bought and sold—and as a commodity, it is surrounded by a hallucinatory mysteriousness, as if its "real" components cannot quite be separated from its effects. Apart from *Confessions*, nothing has more greatly influenced the formation of Western views of narcotic substances and a modern "drug history" than the British East India Company's illicit sale of opium in ninetieth-century China. The enormous fortunes that Marx refers to were made here. The center of this trade was the city of Calcutta in India.

Calcutta, capital of Bengal and until 1912 capital of British India, was known as the "City of the Palaces" and as "Kali-kata" or "Kalikshetra"—named after Kali, the Hindu goddess: red-eyed, tongue hanging from her mouth, adorned with a necklace of skulls, enveloped in inky darkness. Her image is everywhere in the city: in temples, at the back of butchers' shops, hanging from the rearview mirrors of taxis, among the magazines on the street-sellers' stands, and in the Victoria Memorial, the

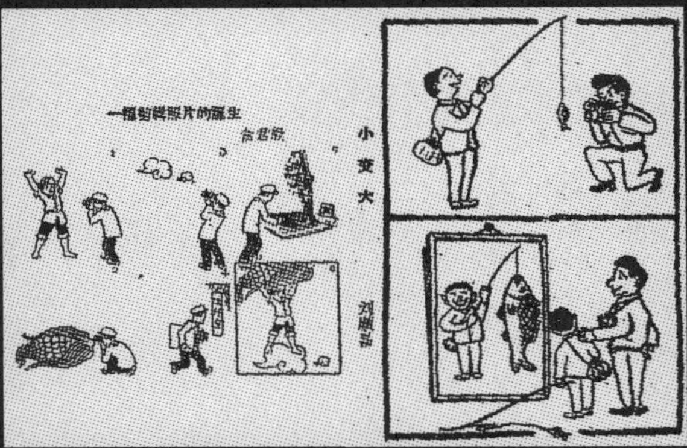

Fig. 19: From *Popular Photography*, January 1960.

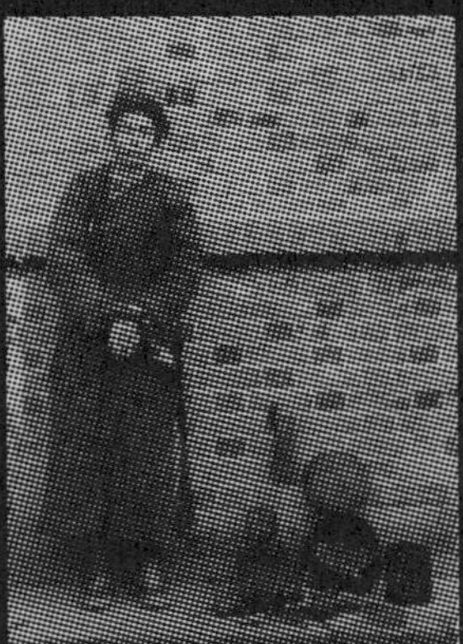

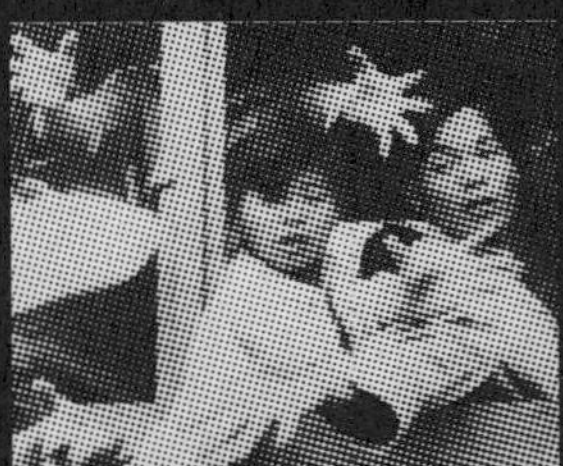

Fig. 20 *Liu Jiayuan Eats His Child*
Fig. 21 In May 1962, *Life Magazine* photographer Larry Burrows shot a series of photographs of Chinese refugees who arrived illegally in Hong Kong and were sent back to the mainland. (AFP/ Getty Images)

Cannibalism served as the most terrifying and sensationalist symbol of the famine, both as a reality and as an allegory for the general breakdown of morals and the sense of universal complicity. The most graphic images that exist from this period relate to the criminal case in which Liu Jiayuan was charged with eating his child. The Lixian County Archive in Hunan Province published a picture of Liu Jiayuan with the remains of his child in August 2011, but it was taken down in November 2011 when too many clicks and repostings alarmed the authorities, who were worried about the photo's political sensitivity and sheer horror. According to historian Yu Xiguang, in 1960 Liu Jiayuan submitted all of his grain to the commune by Chinese New Year. After his wife abandoned him, he and their toddler son had nothing to eat for days. Hallucinating about meat and seeing that his son was dying anyway, Liu killed and cooked the child overnight. A relative living next door discovered the boy in the pot the next morning and promptly informed the commune leader, who forced Liu to eat a few pieces before his eyes. The commune leader then had "the scene of the crime" photographed. A mass rally followed, culminating in Liu's execution. Everyone talked about the case for years afterwards, terrifying all the children in the region.

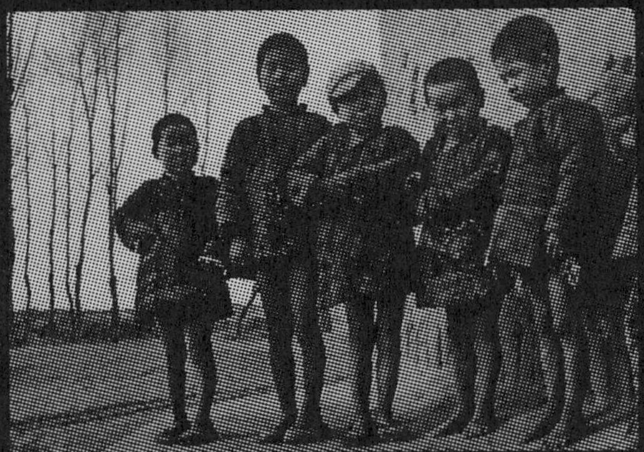

Fig. 22 In the winter of 1958, the Xinhua photojournalist Li Feng was sent to Weiwu Farm in Gansu Province to take propaganda photos of the Great Leap. When he saw a few boys with bare legs and ragged cotton jackets, he shot this photograph, even though it could not have been published at the time. This photograph is rare for its suggestion of poverty and malnutrition, as well as for the lively, innocent, and unposed expressions on the children's faces. Photo courtesy of Li Feng.

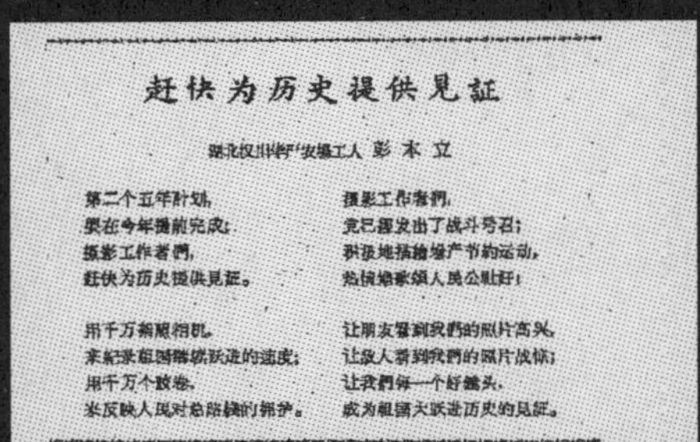

赶快为历史提供見証

湖北汉川华严农场工人 彭本立

第二个五年計划，
要在今年提前完成；
摄影工作者們，
赶快为历史提供見証。

用千万架照相机，
来紀录祖国继续跃进的速度；
用千万个胶卷，
来反映人民对总路綫的拥护。

摄影工作者們，
党已經发出了战斗号召；
积极地描繪增产节約运动，
热情地歌頌人民公社好！

让朋友看到我們的照片高兴，
让敌人看到我們的照片战慄；
让我們每一个好鏡头，
成为祖国大跃进历史的見証。

Fig. 23 "Let us Bear Witness to History" by Peng Benli, farm worker at Hanchuan Huayan Farm, Hubei Province.

The second five-year plan
Shall be completed in advance this year
Come photographers
Let us bear witness to history
Using tens of thousands of cameras
To document the speed of the nation's continued leap
Using tens of thousands of film rolls
To reflect the masses' support for the general line.

Photographers, the Party has sounded its bugle
Actively depict the movement: "Increase Production, Exercise Thrift"
Enthusiastically praise: "The People's Commune Is Good!"

Upon seeing our pictures, let our friends feel happy
Upon seeing our pictures, let our enemies tremble
Let every good shot testify to the nation's Great Leap

(From *Popular Photography*, September 1959)

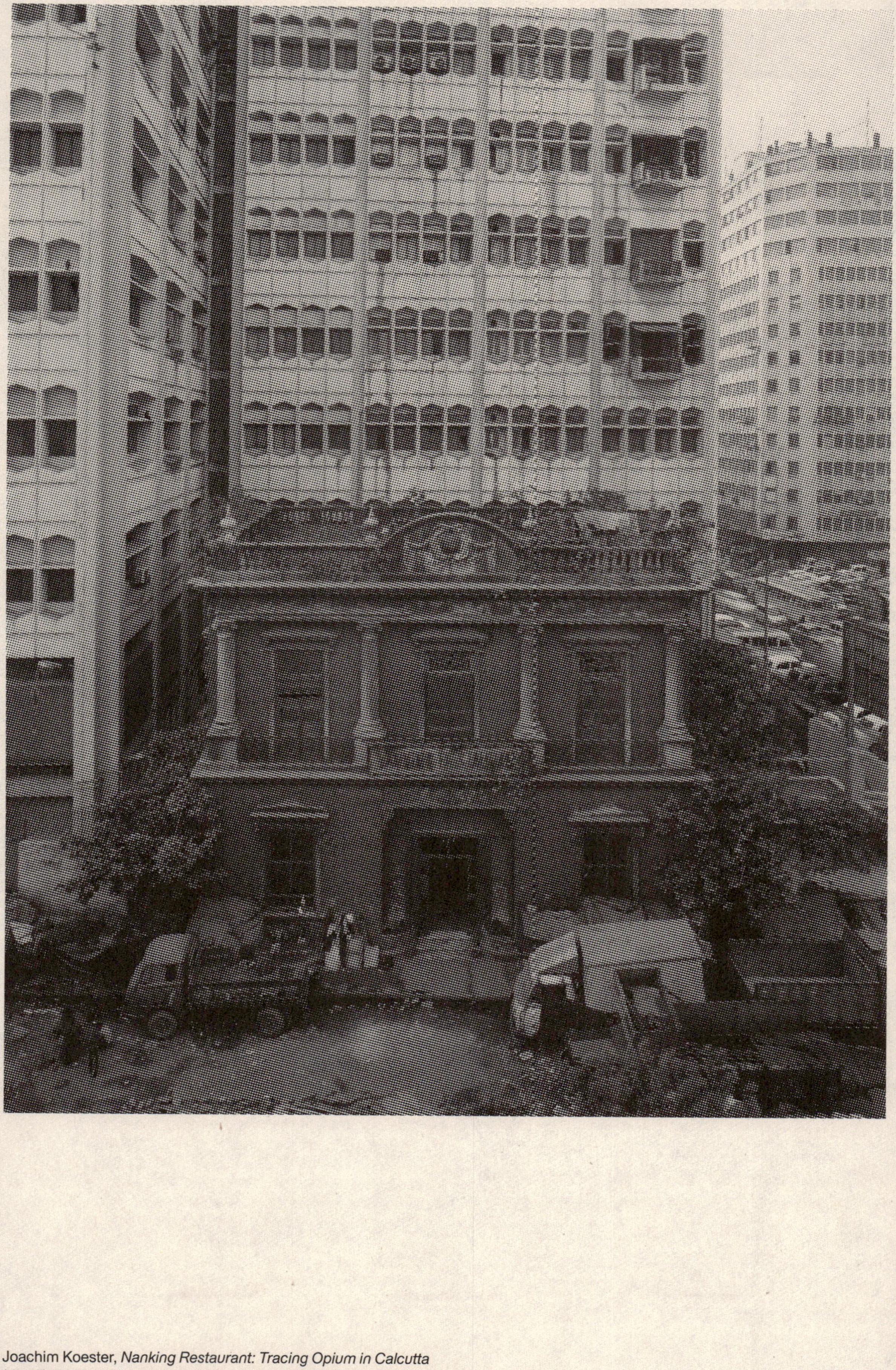

Joachim Koester, *Nanking Restaurant: Tracing Opium in Calcutta* (detail), 2005–2008, series of three silver gelatin black-and-white photographs. Courtesy of Jan Mot, Brussels.

METAPHYSICS OF ABSENCE: MARTYRS MUSEUMS IN IRAN

Bavand Behpoor

For *The Museum of the Monster That Is History*, cultural theorist and artist Bavand Behpoor, together with graphic designer Reza Abedini, contribute an installation on the "martyrs museum," a form of museum found worldwide which palpably exemplifies the fundaments of modern states in martyrdom, as the sacrifice of individuals and their bodies. The museum that they restage in parts, however, is the rather particular Shiraz Martyrs Museum in Iran, which addresses itself to foreigners but is hardly visited by them, and which relies in several respects on a metaphysics of absence, in opposition to Western concepts of the museum. Their "translated" martyrs museum hosts a variety of "typical" objects and accompanying martyr narratives that in themselves exhibit the gap between systemic rationale and individual history. This essay by Behpoor, originally given as a talk at Goldsmiths College in London, served as the foundation for the installation.

Martyrs museums were established by the Foundation of Martyrs and Veterans Affairs in most major Iranian cities after the Iran-Iraq War (1980–1988), known as the longest declared war of the twentieth century, with more than a half a million casualties. The Foundation, established in 1979, was originally responsible for supporting the families of the martyrs of revolution, not war. But just as the war was understood to sustain the fervor of the revolution, its casualties were also considered the continuation of revolutionary martyrs. The pictures we see here are from the Shiraz Martyrs Museums. I chose this example for two reasons: first, the Shiraz Martyrs Museum exhibits a variety of artworks side by side with other museum objects; and secondly, it is located inside a holy shrine. The artworks consist of donations to the shrine and vary widely in subject matter, date, and quality. They precede chronologically the rest of the museum objects. In looking at the Shiraz Martyrs Museum, I invite you to go beyond the sublimity of the terror it provokes or the extreme banality of its making, and to look instead at the intended function of the museum. It was meant to convey to you, as well as to native viewers, something that fails to reach you through other channels. And you might recognize the mode of its representation as a desperate attempt to balk at representation as such.

As André Malraux once wrote, "Each exhibit is a representation of something, differing from the thing itself, this specific difference being its *rasion d'être*." In this essay, I want to not only emphasize the difference between what you might expect from a museum and what you will actually see. I also want to underline the difference between the original message and what you read into it.

Although the Shiraz Martyrs Museum could easily be considered a very poor, ideologically charged copy of a European museum, it in fact historical museum, where I caught sight of Kali at the entrance to the exhibition celebrating the foundation of Calcutta in 1690, which for more than three hundred years was erroneously ascribed to the Englishman Job Charnock.

I came to the city in 2005 at the invitation of Calcutta Art Research, and was curious to experience the place as the City of Opium—the historical center of the opium trade, which made Calcutta the second most important city in the British Empire in the nineteenth century. While walking through the many exhibition rooms at the Victoria Memorial, I hoped to find drawings, photographs, or descriptions of the parts of town associated with the business. To my great surprise, I found none. Perhaps it was a deliberate omission? Worn out by my futile search among the many historical artifacts and pictures, my eyes settled on a diorama of a flat delta and a little village on a salt marsh by the Hooghly River—the original settlement that would become Calcutta. The accompanying wall text said: "No other Indian city benefited in quite the same way from British rule, but no other city had to pay as high a price either."

Although opium was omitted from the exhibition at the Victoria Memorial, the story of the British East India Company's illegal sale of the drug in China is anything but secret. The export of the drug to China triggered the ire of Chinese authorities, who struggled in vain throughout most of the nineteenth century to prevent the flood of opium into the country. This escalating conflict led to the two opium wars, in 1841 and 1856. Great Britain succeeded in defeating the Chinese army so as to protect the opium trade. The veiled history is also evident in the vast fortunes amassed from Great Britain's aggressive expansion of opium production. "Black Earth," as Bengali opium is called, was cultivated in poppy fields, which the British had seized from the great Mogul princes. And when demand increased, it was grown in areas expressly cultivated for the crop. The poppy harvest was processed in the British East India Company's sprawling factories in the town of Patna and near Benares. From there, the refined opium was transported to Calcutta, where it was stored and auctioned, and then shipped on to China. In 1830, the sale of opium made up a sixth of the gross national product of British India.

"They are not dead, but sleeping," writes Thomas De Quincey of the many forgotten memories that emerge in his opium-shrouded dreams. The ability of the drug to push to the surface events that had been spirited away to the far recesses of the mind led De Quincey to see the brain as a palimpsest, a membrane or scroll with innumerable layers of script. Nothing is erased completely. Everything is there, even if it is concealed. The bottom layers can be excavated by applying the right "chemical," and seemingly lost incidents are retrieved.

When I was in Calcutta, I began to see the city itself as a palimpsest. The crowds of people and the heavy traffic incessantly sweeping through the streets took on the form of sediments, just as the ruins, the building projects, and the other changes I noticed during my daily wanderings all seemed to hide or reveal occurrences. De Quincey used an opium-induced altered state as a door to the past; I, on the other hand, wanted to find places in the city that were connected to the history of the drug. I questioned everyone I met about opium. The film director Nilanjan Bhattacharya suggested I talk to Sumit Roy.

Sumit Roy lived on a shady street in the Calcutta suburb of Dum Dum, named after the muffled explosions that once reverberated from the notorious British munitions factory in the area. He received me in his study, a dusty, high-ceilinged room with worn 1950s leather furniture and smoking mosquito coils. Roald Dahl's *Book of Ghost Stories* lay on the desk, next to an illustrated volume about the Rolling Stones, bound in leather so as not to disintegrate in the humid tropical climate. Roy leafed through it while talking passionately about the band and rock music. Later, when we had settled in, he told me about opium and drugs, about transactions ending in disappointment and unnecessary danger because of theft or deceit, and also about secret places in Calcutta's underworld, like the opium den called Fung's. Roy explained that he frequented Fung's for a period of time at the start of the 1980s, just before the place was closed down by the hews very closely to the European model of presenting museum objects. Moreover, it is not only in its form that the Shiraz Martyrs Museum addresses the European model. The museum is designed to present to the Western "other" what, according to Iranians, he has done. (At least from the Iranian point of view, the Iran-Iraq War was engineered, imposed, and finally lost by the West.) The museum tries to make an impression on the Western viewer by invoking the universals it shares with the omnipresent, all-encompassing, and almost *universal* Western other (loss, violence, absence, and the body)—to hold up a metaphysics of absence against him. In this respect, it also has something to say about the role of representation itself. Thus, bringing this museum to you, in a sense, provides the Shiraz Martyrs Museum with the ultimate audience it searches for. I will discuss this later. For the moment, let's look at the differences between the Shiraz Martyrs Museum and typical Western museums.

To begin with, a martyrs museum is no war museum. The difference is between that of a soldier and a martyr. A dead soldier is a life lost. A martyr is death conquered. A dead soldier is a vanished multitude of contingencies—for him, his family, and the state. A martyr is an icon gained, an expectation fulfilled. A personality unified. A history affirmed. Death in war is a sudden disruption of what was supposed to continue. Martyrdom portrays the perfect "end."

The purpose of martyrs museums is not the appreciation of heroism. Heroes are celebrities, while martyrs are anonymous. A living hero is still respectable, while martyrdom is constructed only through death. A hero risks his life, a martyr surrenders it willingly. Thus, heroism cherishes life, while martyrdom is impatient to end it. It is therefore the death drive more than anything else that the Shiraz Martyrs Museum embodies, going against the ideas of both artistic beauty and sublimity.

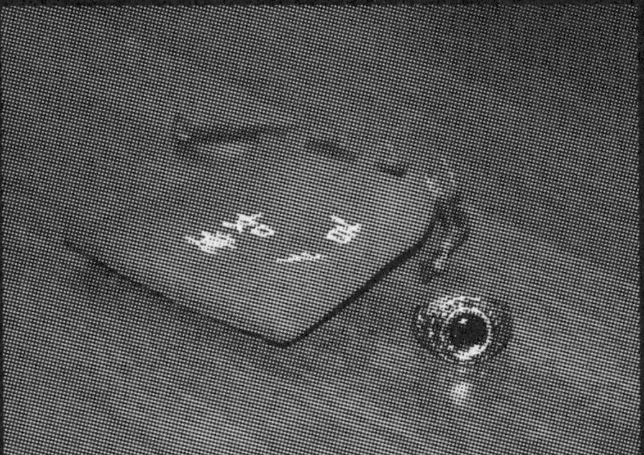

A PACT AMONG COMRADES It was just before Operation Karbala 8 when he gave me his ring, saying he would be martyred in the operation. I insisted on knowing the secret behind the ring. He showed me a letter signed by several martyrs. It was a pact among comrades promising one another that anyone martyred first had to inform the others of what have prevented them from achieving martyrdom. He said, "The last time I went on leave, I went to the tomb of a martyr who had signed the letter three times. I took a pick with me. I placed the pick and the letter on his grave, and then I cried and said, 'If you don't tell why I haven't been martyred, I will destroy your tomb.' It was around sunrise when I saw him in my dream. He pointed to his ring and disappeared. When I woke up, I realized that I had been too attached to the ring given to me by a beloved. Therefore, I am giving it to you to be sure I'm no longer attached to anything in this world." He said this, and then went and gained the status of a martyr in Operation Karbala 8.

authorities. It was the epitome of a Chinese opium den—a dimly lit room decorated with oriental rugs and curtains, with the customers lying on mattresses on the floor smoking opium in long bamboo pipes. The house was off Central Avenue on Bowzabar Street. Roy would speak energetically, then would suddenly pause, and would seem to drift away. For a moment he would sit lost in thought, shrouded in an intricately embroidered shirt that looked like something the Stones could have worn.

There was not much left of what had once been Calcutta's oldest Chinatown. The former Chinese buildings were scattered like small islands in a new district of office towers. Yawning holes between the blocks indicated that the renewal was still underway. Only one house was left at the address Roy had given. It was a dilapidated two-story building framed by small shrubbery clinging to the walls like an unkempt beard. The main door of the house had disappeared, but I was warned not to enter; it was rumored that the place was used as a depot for contraband. Instead, I succeeded in getting onto the roof of a nearby building. From this new vantage point, the Chinese house was even more reminiscent of an exposed layer from a distant past. I also noticed that an unusually large number of black crows circled the rooftop. My mind took flight: the planet Saturn, crows but also ruins, bricks, authorities, sedatives, visions, melancholy ... I paused and wondered whether Saturn would bring me back to De Quincey, as I studied the house again in an attempt to uncover further and more revealing connections. Then I noticed the words on the sign above the door of the building. Written in chiseled, weatherworn letters, it said: NANKING RESTAURANT. "Nanking" as in the Nanking Treaty.

The First Opium War ended in the defeat of China and the signing of the Nanking Treaty in August 1842. This accord, which secured the opium trade and its expansion for Great Britain, went down in Chinese history as one of the greatest injustices to have befallen the country. It resulted in millions of Chinese opium addicts, and, amid the instability of the ensuing decades, it left countless impoverished Chinese with no alternative than to migrate to Europe, Australia, the US, or colonial cities like Calcutta to look for work on railways, in mines, or in cities that needed to be built. The immigrants brought their opium-smoking habit with them. Soon, opium dens appeared in many major cities. At the end of the nineteenth century, places like London, New York, and San Francisco had hundreds of opium dens. Both the financial success of the Chinese immigrants and their social and personal misery were often ascribed to the use or abuse of the drug. Opium dependency was publicly associated with Chinese excesses, and drug abuse was considered to be a disease that could spread from the Chinese immigrant districts to other parts of the city. In one of the darker chapters of the history of the nineteenth century, the Chinese were demonized in connection with the trade and abuse of opium—a fallacy that greatly affected popular views of opium and other narcotic drugs in the following century—while Great Britain and the British East India Company successfully obfuscated their roles.

I was thinking of this when I placed my camera in front of the former warehouse of the East India Company, which sat a couple of hundred yards from the bank of the Hooghly River and just next to Calcutta's great flower market. The area was hectic with activity as workers unloaded numerous lorries and dragged sacks into buildings that are still used to store goods. While I was adjusting the camera settings, I became aware of the people passing through the viewfinder. Only those who were standing completely still would appear on the negative because of the long exposure time. Anybody moving would either disappear or be inscribed as a foggy shape at the bottom of the frame. They would appear as small holes in the time-space continuum, something that could perhaps point to the even larger holes in our perception—a connection to the possibility of traveling backwards or forwards in time—that drugs like opium have unlocked.

A martyr is no victim either. This is one thing that differentiates martyrs museums from genocide museums. Martyrs museums do not represent an injustice *tolerated*, but rather *nullified* through amazement with death.

It is not surprising, then, if in a sense there is nothing to see in the Shiraz Martyrs Museum. There are no museum *objects* as such. Instead, there are only remnants of what could not be exhibited. No sublimity or beauty. It is not a matter of watching death from behind glass. Nothingness itself is staged. Here, we do not experience the overwhelming of imagination or its play with understanding. Just everyday men, everyday objects. And these in their most humble state: dirty, covered with mud, destroyed, and possessing no economic value. The museum barely requires security. The museum does not venture to create a totality: everything is scattered, as in the war itself. The contents of the museum are not sorted, for there can be no criteria for sorting here: no hierarchy or hegemony in death, apart from the superiority of martyrdom over other forms of death. It this respect, the Shiraz Martyrs Museum brings to mind a cabinet of curiosities, and yet, there is nothing curious about the exhibited objects. The displays do not illustrate the lives of "great men" who are no longer among us, but rather the absence of very ordinary men who are no longer considered ordinary because of their self-determined death. Not how one lives, but how one dies is cherished.

As such, this museum is not an archive, but its denial. What is achieved is unknown and incomprehensible. What is lost—mortal life—is disdained.

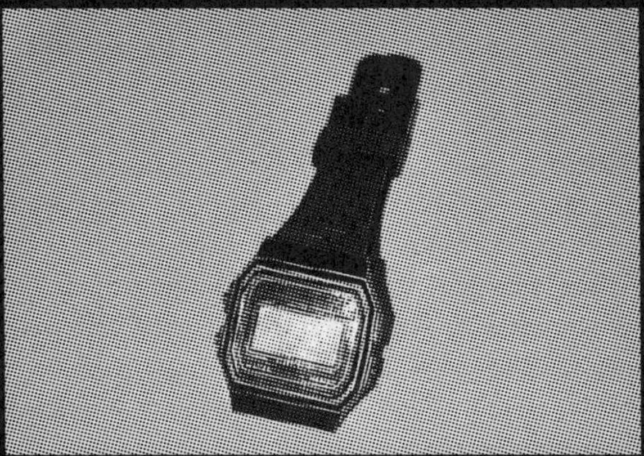

THE STORY OF THE WRISTWATCH (Narrated by the mother of the Martyr.) After four months the Revolutionary Guard brought his sack. When we opened it, we found a wristwatch. What was left of the watch was half of the band and the frame that holds the circuit board. The board itself and the other half of the band were missing. Since I myself had bought this watch for Shahram and had memories of it, I kept wondering what had happened to it. From time to time, we would take his belongings out and look at them in remembrance. On the second anniversary of his martyrdom, I brought his stuff out once again. I smelled the items one by one as I cried, when I suddenly realized that the watch had become complete. The band and the circuit board were in place. I rushed out and called to the neighbors. I called my daughters and asked them what the watch looked like when they brought it to us. They all replied, "Half the band and the frame was there and the circuit board was missing. Why are you asking so many questions?" I said, "Look! The watch is complete and is intact." They cried so much that the neighbors came and asked what had happened. That day in our house, it was as if Shahram had been martyred for the second time at the same hour.

After Eleven Years. The brothers who had gone to visit the family of the martyr tell this story: the martyr's mother was crying and narrating this story while showing us the watch, when one of the brothers took the watch and looked at it curiously, pressing its pin. Suddenly, the word "happy" appeared on the screen. We told the martyr's mother how strange it was that the battery of a watch not used for many years was still functioning and that this word had appeared on the screen. Maybe it was sending a message to the mother telling her not to cry and to "be happy!"

YAOYAN FILMS AND STRATEGIES

Chen Chieh-Jen

The Chinese word *yaoyan* (謠言) has undergone many twists and turns throughout its history. It has been used to suggest a story concocted for some evil purpose, such as slander or to undermine legitimacy. Today, the more accurate term for slander, *yaozhuo* (謠諑), is rarely seen. Originally, *yaoyan* referred to a folk song or epigram aimed at political critique,[1] and the *Book of Songs* (tenth to the seventh century BC) is mostly composed of this kind of folk song. *Yaoyan* therefore has come to mean a popular interventionist strategy of using poetic language, rhyme, and fictional narratives to address social ills or produce a view of history that differs from the official one promoted by those in power, or one forming part of the social imaginary.

Yaoyan's original poetic quality, political overtones, and strategic usage has not been lost in the process. This can be seen in the powerful, transformative effect of deploying *yaoyan* strategies against policies of discipline and governance implemented by Taiwan's ruling party during the island's recent history of modernization. *Yaoyan* activities have also marshaled popular imagination into resistance against governmental control of information, and contributed to autonomous knowledge production among the Taiwanese people. A key example is Chiang Wei-Shui's 1921 establishment of the Taiwanese Cultural Association, an organization which developed culture-based political actions to resist the Japanese colonial government. The second chairman of the association, Tsai Pei-Huo, formed a group of *benshi* (辯士), who narrated silent films, and who cultivated among themselves anticolonial awareness to be spread among movie audiences. This early twentieth-century use of *yaoyan* strategies is an instructive example for us today living in the thrall of neoliberalism.

In the Japanese period, the back row at Taiwanese-run theaters was garrisoned by Japanese police officers and firemen during screenings to prevent various film narrators from stirring up anticolonial attitudes. The traveling film narrators from the Taiwanese Cultural Association, however, would use slang, idioms, and coded messages that the Japanese did not understand. In this way, they twisted the neutral films to promote their anticolonial cause, thus unleashing laughter and applause among knowing moviegoers.[2] Looking at this historical example, we can imagine that exposure to the film and its separate narration must have stimulated whole new images and ideas in the minds of those colonized people—people who did not possess the technology to make movies of their own. Furthermore, they relied on mental afterimages and acoustic residue when passing along to others what could only have been subjective interpretations of these film screenings, thus altering them with additions, deletions, rewriting, and imagination. For these reasons, audience accounts were only immaterial reconstructions of the cinematic experience based on what was remembered, or believed to have been seen or heard.

Language, text, sound, imagery, and the body are all media for poetic expression. Following these associations a little further, we can also imagine that the distorted meanings offered by the film narrators caused each audience member to reinvent the films, thereby transforming them into countless instances of anti-colonial immaterial cinema, which we could call *yaoyan* films, as their production operated much like the concepts and strategies inherited from *yaoyan*. Narrative strategies are commonly seen in struggles between rulers

The Shiraz Martyrs Museum tries to impress upon the viewer the particularity of the collective, a contingency open to everyone. If Proust saw the museum as the perfection of the artist's studio, martyrs museums are "the phantasmagorical perfection" of the war scene. Only the viewer can fill the exhibited absence and lack. Martyrs museums calls for self-identification. In Tony Bennett's words, "the exhibitionary complex is self-observation from a certain perspective."[1] In this sense, other museums are no less ideological in their claims. The following words spoken by François de Neufchâteau, Minister of the Interior at the time of the French Revolution, outline his ideological vision for French museums, but they could just as easily describe martyrs museum:

> While [France's] museums enrich your mind, its laws and examples will enrich your soul. It will make you more worthy to practice the arts, because it will have shown you the greatest art of all, the art of betterment. Fine art, in the hands of a free nation, is the main instrument of social happiness and a useful subsidiary of the philosophy which ensures the well-being of the human race.[2]

If the Shiraz Martyrs Museum presents a martyr's personal belongings, it is not to make a statement about war in general, but to underline the martyr's singular absence. Like his unspoken proper name, these belongings and the ruled; for example, in feudal societies, ruling classes fabricated nationalistic fairy tales to lend their authoritative regimes legitimacy. And unofficial histories and legends were used among the people to deconstruct that same authority and legitimacy. Disinformation has always been part of the real world, and it appears in contemporary phenomena such as the society of spectacle, virtual economies, and political theater.

While fabrication is part of *yaoyan*, the term as it was originally applied to rhymes and folk songs from the *Book of Songs* suggests much more. These rhymes gave voice to popular opinions, circulated freely, and were adaptable, compact, and ambiguous enough to allow for poetic interpretation. *Yaoyan* in this sense expanded the imagination and prompted the creation of political action in the form of divergent narratives. Nonetheless, the key point is our own political context, and how *yaoyan* strategies might be extended today.

I think that all forms of resistance arise from an actual need. From a certain perspective, there are countless cracks in the edifice of neoliberalism, but we need to conceive of viable movements that will widen those cracks.

It is a given that, living in a society where neoliberalism and spectacle are the rule, we are steeped in simulacra and discourses of illusion. Capitalism seems to possess an inexhaustible capacity for assimilating critical rhetoric and transforming it into new opportunities to spur consumption. This has been the case in Taiwan since the end of martial law; words whose genesis lies in radical politics, such as "deconstruction," "diversity," "alternative," "difference," "fringe," and "underground," have been sucked into the black hole of capitalism only to reappear, stripped of their original meanings, in advertising

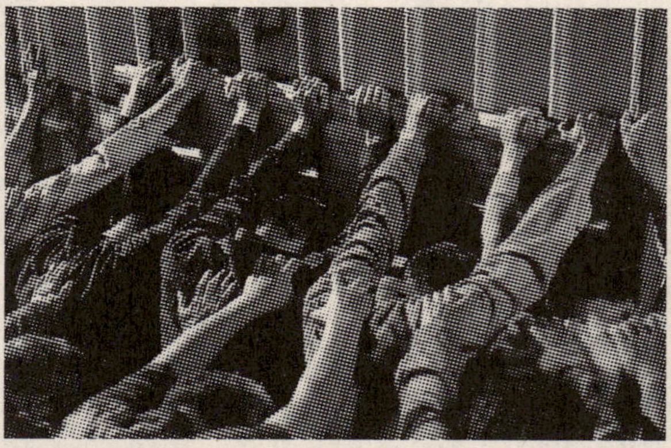

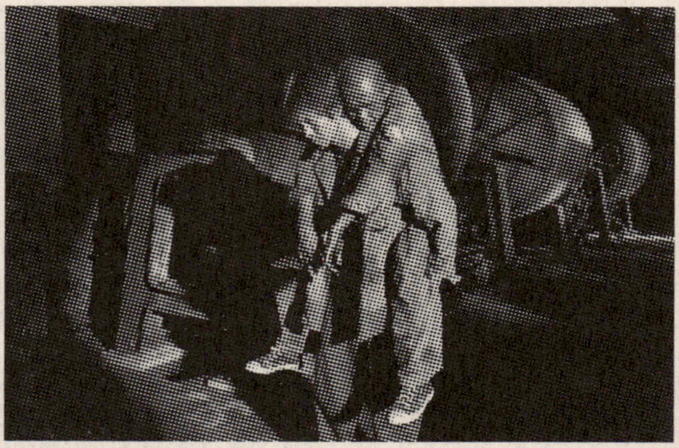

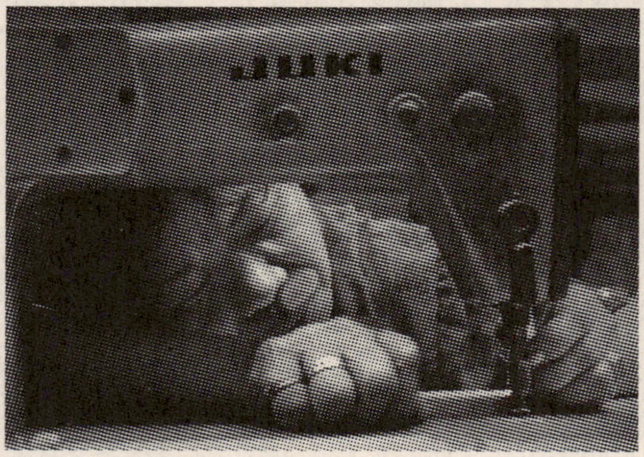

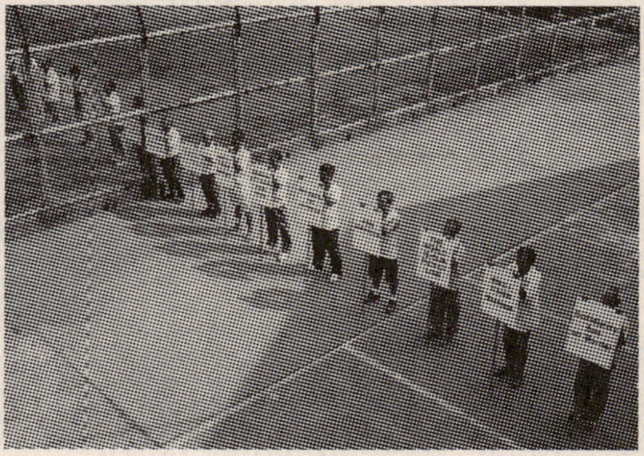

Fig. 1 Chen Chieh-Jen, *Military Court and Prison*, 2007–2008, 35mm transferred to DVD, single-channel, color, sound, 61 min 43 sec, continuous loop.
Fig. 2 Chen Chieh-Jen, *Factory*, 2003, super 16mm transferred to DVD, color, silent, 31 min 9 sec, single-channel, continuous loop. Photographer: Yang Chen-Hao.

Fig. 3 Chen Chieh-Jen, *Empire's Borders – Western Enterprises, Inc.*, 2010, 35mm transferred to Blu-ray Disc, three-channel video installation, black and white, sound, single-channel video: 70 min 12 sec; double-channel video: 5 min 45 sec, continuous loop.
Fig. 4 Chen Chieh-Jen, *The Route*, 2006, 35mm film transferred to DVD, color & black and white, silent, 16 min 45 sec, single-channel, continuous loop.

do little to describe him. The objects are not signs or relics. They are what they are — everyday banal object. And "everyday," in this case, means "today": the temporality of the Shiraz Martyrs Museum is that of the present. According to the Koran, martyrs should not be considered dead: "And do not speak of those who are slain in Allah's way as dead; nay, [they are] alive, but you do not perceive."[3] One should always think of martyrs as present. This is much closer to the temporality of artworks than of religious works. I quote Jean-Louis Déotte:

> Here we encounter a temporality — the temporality of collected objects, works of art — which is not the temporality of religious works which, although the same, are caught up in the stranglehold of a particular age and which, because of this, have to make their mark, to make a statement and have a specific destination. This is the temporality of suspense, of incompletion, of return, the temporality of a continuity which extends across ages, a cyclic temporality.[4]

This might explain why the directors of the Shiraz Martyrs Museum do not find it strange to place a variety of artworks, some dating back a thousand years, next to everyday objects and naive artworks by village martyrs. The impact on the viewer, however, is not as intended. The presence of naked death, without pretension or adjustment, disrupts the function of museum-based artworks and, interestingly, gives them back their original function. Thus, the division that the museum tries to negate shows through forcefully. An ornamented gilt sword from the seventeenth century turns into a real sword once again; it is no longer an object of mere aesthetic appreciation. The illuminated Koran from the fourteenth century turns into the text of an

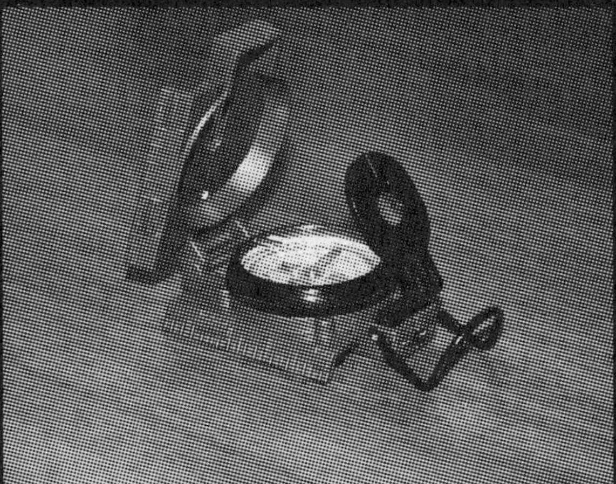

THE VOLUNTEER LOADER DRIVER It was getting light. Suddenly, tank shells were shot towards the trench from behind. We realized the rear was not safe. We had around thirty loaders and bulldozers, two of which had been destroyed. One of the loader drivers was also shot. The drivers were all too exhausted to work. Then Martyr Mohsen Hayatpoor and the radio brigade came to help me. I gave him the compass and told him to move in front of the bulldozers. I took some bags of cans from the car, opened them one by one, and gave them to the drivers to help them continue their work. Among them there was a sixteen-year-old military volunteer, a loader driver. He stood up and said he was willing to continue the earthwork. Since loaders rose too high, the Iraqis could easily shoot them and therefore bulldozers had to come first. Yet, this young volunteer insisted on continuing his work and his persistence encouraged others. After him, others also volunteered to continue. We continued the earthwork for two kilometers when the sixteen-year-old volunteer was hit and martyred instantly.

slogans promoting new products. Furthermore, legitimate forms of protest seem to have been similarly hijacked by the system, and are now permitted by law but restricted to designated areas in the name of public safety. And finally, the local and hybridized identities of postcolonial discourse are being recoded by the state to construct a new rhetoric of nationalist legitimacy.

In this time when putting forth transformative strategies and describing new political horizons seems so difficult, the invisible violence of neoliberalism has increasingly become real and personal. Following a succession of young Foxconn employees leaping to their deaths, the hundreds of millions of wage earners recently left unemployed or reduced to partial employment, and the many young people awaiting jobs globally, neoliberalism is no longer just an abstract idea. This oppressive system has stripped individuals of their rights to exist, work and express themselves, as well as deprived them of the right to abode and space to breathe. From roommate testimonials, we know those Foxconn workers who committed suicide were rendered dead on their feet from lack of free time and human interaction.

Compared to factory workers in developing countries who must cope with high-pressure management, first-world young people await jobs, and countless wage-earners have been reduced to temporary positions or long-term unemployment. Some have been abandoned by capital and forced into at-home exile, while others rely on endless hours of part-time work to maintain basic living standard. In these two typical modes of contemporary exploitation, we see not only the walking dead, but also the opportunity for change. Those countless people deprived of their right to work and forced into at-home exile have paradoxically recovered time that was previously lost to them, and these same people, who come from different backgrounds and have lost their community affiliations, can use this newfound free time to form new networks, interact, and reimagine contemporary society. Most importantly, being considerably more educated, they are different from the proletariat of the past, which had little understanding of knowledge production. The key is for them to reinvent the meaning of capital and production, or become self-reliant without capital, or even create deceptions to recapture the capital seized by private ownership and state mechanisms. After obtaining a certain amount of capital, they can then decide how to practice a non-capitalist mode of production and exchange. All of this, however, depends on how we imagine new methods of action.

Compared to the Taiwanese Cultural Association members who were faced with traditional imperialists, contemporary people forced into at-home exile must deal with a complex form of neocolonialism composed of invisible, transnational, and local capital, representative democracy, and new administrative forms that manipulate social imagination and individual desire. They therefore must devise multistage political action strategies in addition to continually forming new activist networks and seeking out capital, viable methods of self-organization, and non-capitalist modes of production and exchange. The reality of living in today's neoliberal world is that it is impossible to immediately implement non-capitalist modes of production and exchange. If the Taiwanese Cultural Association's use of *yaoyan* strategies, which includes film narrators' willful misinterpretation of films, still has inspirational value for us today, then it might suggest haunting as a way of implementing political action from within the neoliberal system. The association's strategies were similar to haunting because members could not directly confront their colonial oppressors with military action, so they operated both legally and illegally in gray areas of the colonial system. Their often invisible decolonization movement, which included film narrators' willful misinterpretation, used disinformation strategies deployed in plain sight under the watchful eye of the authorities.

Considering that today's neoliberalism is a constantly shifting neocolonialism without borders, activist networks might conceive of themselves as a movement with loosely defined organization and diverse directives. Through holding discussions generated by various regroupings, and then permeating various

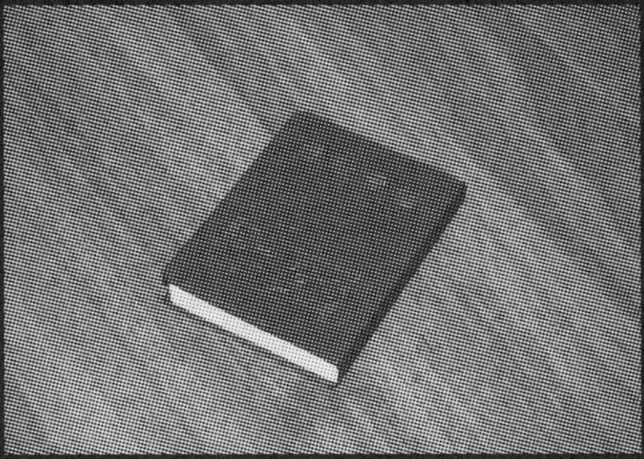

WHERE NOBODY CAN REACH ME He was severely injured in the Fath-al-Mobin Operation and transferred to a hospital in Tehran. When he recovered, he decided to go to the frontlines but had no money. He knew well what to do! It was Friday afternoon. He started saying Faraj prayers. Then he asked the Lord to help him. After Friday prayers were finished, a group of people came to the hospital to visit those handicapped in the war. A sayyid came out of the group and walked up to him, gave him a prayer book, and went away! In the pages of the book there were some banknotes. This paid for his transfer and dinner. When he reached the frontlines he ran out of money! He gave speeches for soldiers. His words were so impressive that the comrades tore up their leave allowances just before the operation and stayed at the frontlines. The first group of soldiers who entered Khorramshahr was under his command. After the Ramadan Operation, he gave back all his duties. Nobody knew what had happened. He said, "Up to this date, I was responsible. Now I want to be a volunteer." He returned to Isfahan and prepared to get married. He wanted his wife to be a descendant of the prophet. He married a martyr's widow who was such a descendant. For his wedding he took a wedding card to Qom and dropped it into the Holy Zahra's shrine. The day after the marriage he had a dream in which the Holy Zahra and other exalted women of Islam participated in his wedding. At the end of the wedding ceremony he announced in a very serious tone, "The fact that I'm married does not mean I am attached to the world. Marriage was a duty, the frontlines and war is another duty." Three days later he went to the frontlines. He was transferring the bodies of soldiers left on Borhani Hill to the rear. Before the operation, he had told his brother, "I want to stay somewhere neither you nor the enemy can find me!" He entered heaven in August. His body stayed there, on Borhani Hill, in the Piranshahr Mountains.

ideology which has cost the lives of coutless martyrs. On the other hand, the artwork's claim to immortality falls into contradiction next to the fragility of lives lost in the war. Another quote from Déotte: "There is a demand which comes from a long way off, from unknown ages and other lands. And this demand is inextricably bound up with the determination to survive."[5] The will to survive and the will to death fight silently in the exhibits: the banality of war, when its real face is presented, is highlighted through a comparison with the sophistication of ornaments. Thus, the sublimity of war and the beauty of art are both shattered, turning a visit to the Shiraz Martyrs Museum into a horrific experience. The museum directors have tried to take advantage of the timelessness and apparent immortality of the artworks in order to fortify the impact of the museum. Yet the inherent contradiction in the idea of art as an autonomous domain, in the creation of museum objects for the sake of aesthetic appreciation, undermines the whole setup. The ungraspable singularity of particular deaths prevents the collection from turning into a single whole, while the "real" violence defies any idea of aesthetic sublimation. Rather, it returns the artworks to their historical determinations, tearing apart the theatrical "as if" that a museum relies upon. This failure to combine the universal idea of art and singular death, in turn, accentuates the fragility of the "person" behind the immortal martyr and disrupts the suspension of temporality demanded by both art and the idea of martyrdom. It exposes the immediate danger of aestheticizing death: turning the martyr into the "type" desired by the institution. Quoting again from Déotte:

governance models established by the system, these loosely defined networks can distort popular images offered by neoliberalism, or even détourne desire mechanisms implanted in the individual. Only through haunting, and legal or illegal political actions in gray areas, can qualitative change be implemented within the shifting neoliberal system. Only in this way can a greater number of active members be assembled for the cause. The source of *yaoyan* is folk songs and popular epigrammatic sayings used to critique current politics, so if today's producers of *yaoyan* want to endlessly circulate and spread their products, they must become ghosts and haunt the various levels of the governance models. I believe imagining oneself as a ghost is an action that integrates the poetic with the political.

1 Ci Yuan, *A Dictionary of Chinese Etymology* (Taipei: The Commercial Press, 2013).

2 Jen Huang and Wei Wang, eds., *One Hundred Years of Taiwan Cinema* (Taipei: Film Critics China, 2005), 36–42.

[The] memory, which is created from the suspension of historical time and therefore from the suspension of ages, of the intrinsic destinations of the works of art, and from the suspension of internal conflict within the nation, is in fact based on an act of negation. For it is vital to negate what has caused division within humanity and divided the nation, in spite of the fact that, because of its *raison d'être*, the Museum can only suspend—i.e. not take account of—different destinations, otherwise it would not invent art. That is its system: the need to negate! It must negate the various forms of divisions and differences![6]

It is exactly this system that is disrupted. Following the failure of the negation, the existing differences and divisions undermine the idea of martyrdom as a collective experience.

The relation between revolution, war, and the emergence of martyrs museums in Iran becomes more interesting when seen in connection with the history of museums in the West. In France, the Louvre too was an outcome of revolution. In it, a similar dialectics of presence and absence was at work, trying to resolve the tension between the urge to remove and the urge to preserve the past. According to Larry Shiner, these the two urges,

one bent on destroying every sign of "despotism," whatever the artistry, the other determined to save the "art," however repugnant the symbol, struggled with each other—sometimes within the same person—throughout the decisive years of the Revolution.[7]

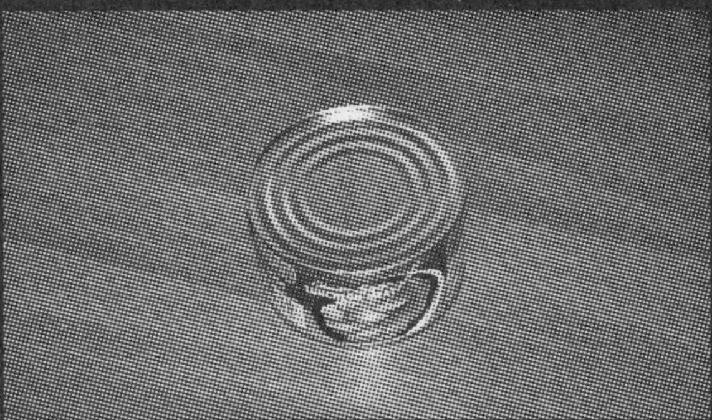

I WAS AFRAID It is as if Iraqi artillery will never end. When I look at him, his smile disappears. He sits next to me and says, "Why are you so pale?" I reply, "I feel dizzy." He says, "Since last night when the operation started none of our comrades have slept. Look, I have brought you a can. You are not looking after yourself." I look at the sky. At every moment I expect a cannonball or a shell to drop down. Shahrooz also looks at the sky and says, "Don't wait for heavenly food. If you don't eat it you will regret it." "I don't want it, eat it yourself." "It's three in the afternoon. You haven't eaten anything since last night. What's wrong with you? Has Saddam died, leaving you bereaved and mournful?" I take the can to stop him from insisting any further. I want him to leave me alone. I'm afraid he will notice my fear. He says, "I should go now." His voice trembles. "Did you see how Samad was mutilated last night? If only that cannonball hadn't exploded right in front of him … Damn this war. Since last night, when Samad was martyred, I've been thinking of him constantly … Forget it, comrade! Forgive me if you don't see me anymore." I frown. He puts a hand on my shoulder, smiles sadly, and crawls away. I jump up from fear. My heart is bursting out of my chest. Everywhere is dust. I rub my eyes a couple of times. I hear people groaning. A paramedic rushes to an injured comrade. I'm shocked as I see him. It is Shahrooz lying unconscious on the ground. When I see his right hand, my heart is torn apart. The hand is no longer attached to his body. A part of his hand lies a bit further away. Poor Shahrooz. When Samad was mutilated, I was shocked. All the paramedics were helping someone. A volunteer soldier brought a blanket and as he murmured he quickly gathered Samad's body parts and put them in the blanket. When he put a part of his brain in the blanket, I could no longer control myself and threw up. I don't know if I'm talking to God or to myself. I say, "Couldn't they have broken the siege of Abadan two months ago? Did they have to wait for me to be sent to the frontlines to do so? An operation like this definitely needs a lion-hearted man like me."

TALKING RUBBISH: WEI-LI YEH AND OTHERS

Daisy Li

IN THE WAKE OF SUDDEN DEMANDS

I can't remember where we had this talk, in his studio most likely, but Antiquity-Like Rubbish Research and Development Syndicate CEO Wei-Li Yeh, my eccentric supervisor and quirkiest of friends, was quietly intense, anxiety simmering beneath his altogether nervously calm countenance as usual, perhaps suffering from another one of his meltdowns.[1] After quite a while of gathering himself together, Wei-Li informed us that he was currently oscillating between dealings with the Taipei Biennial and Shanghai Biennial which, coincidently, will be opening around the same time and are both requesting antiquity-like products from the syndicate. While there is only so much antiquity-like rubbish to be distributed around, this double demand from the Asian art scene has created physical and psychological turmoil for us—meaning late working hours and hour-long train rides in a tidal wave of August heat to the remote, dismal, air conditionless syndicate headquarters on the outskirts of nowhere.

With a deep understanding that antiquity-like rubbish production can't be rushed and must undergo a long-term collective process of research and development, Wei-Li, though hesitant at first, finally gave into asking the curators at the Shanghai Biennial if they could settle for the next-best thing—a "clean" exhibition with images and light boxes for the most part. Much to our surprise, the curators were unwilling to take no for an answer and were determined to admit filthy, age-old, decaying, antiquity-like rubbish into their polished halls of aestheticism—"We want trash art!" were their exact words. I found this highly amusing. When did the Asian market become so interested in antiquity-like rubbish instead of rubbish-like antiquity as usual?

Back in Taipei, the greatest promoter of antiquity-like rubbish is the curator of this year's Taipei Biennial, Anselm Franke, whose intriguing curatorial theme revolves around the visualization of "Modern Monsters." So vast was his faith in the value/monstrosity of our products that he generously offered us Room 206, the largest display room in the Taipei Fine Arts Museum, without the slightest hint of doubt (in truth, I have no idea about the extent of his doubt, but what matters is that we got the room). So large/monstrous was the room that we could practically fit the entire syndicate within it—which we did, as you can see. Behind this solicitation was an equally interesting subversive use of space. Normally, we discard our daily waste and junk to make room for the more significant objects in our lives. Yet this was an effort to deliberately clear space—not just any common space, but the largest available space in the museum—for the uncommon display of rubbish. Room 206 was formerly reserved for exhibiting the most prized items in the museum's collection. Large-scale scrolls of Japanese and Taiwanese postcolonial brush paintings and massive undulating contemporary etchings covered the walls before we decided to fill the space with rubbish. Before the room was leased to us, breathing was almost prohibited upon entry for fear of destroying the critical balance of humidity and temperature that preserves artworks of rarity and high market value. (We are highly destructive creatures, you see?) With the syndicate now stationed in the room, this regulation no longer applies. Your presence within this room, each breath you inhale and exhale, contributes something and alters the dynamics and physical state of antiquity-like rubbish. (So please inhale, dear readers.)

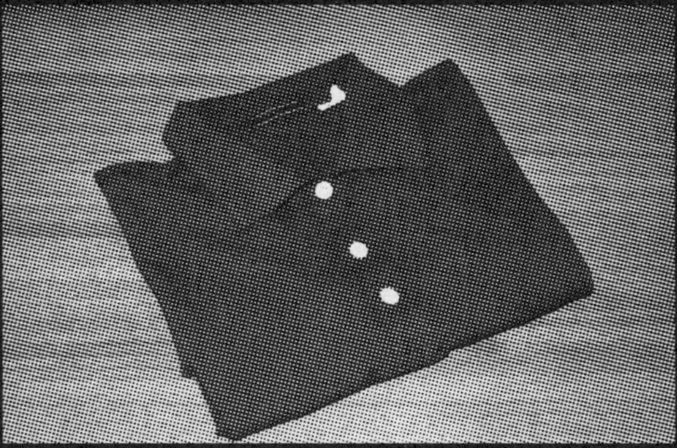

COME AND IDENTIFY ME After the operation, they dedicated this hall to anonymous martyrs: all bodies mutilated and burnt … Among the burnt bodies we found an ID tag. With much effort we located the owner of the tag. It was a volunteer soldier from South Tehran who was lost in the operation. We contacted his family. His father and brothers came. I told them the story, that the martyr was burnt and that they couldn't see his body. We agreed to hold the funeral the next day. The next morning, a comrade who was aware of the situation came to me and said, "Can I ask a favor concerning this martyr?" I said, "Go on." He said, "Let his wife identify him." I said, "What wife?" He paused for a second and said, "Last night I had this dream where the martyr told me, 'Don't hand me over to my father and brothers. My wife should identify me. The ID tag belongs to me but this is not my body. My remains are in this hall.'" I listened to him with much surprise. I said, "But these bodies are nothing more than pieces of burnt bones. What is there for his wife to identify?" At this point the martyr's brothers came to collect his body. I asked them, "Does this martyr have a wife?" They said, "Yes, why?" I said, "It is her who must identify him." His brothers, who were not very religious, shouted back, "Nonsense! It is our brother who is burnt! What is there to identify?" After much discussion I realized that they were not on good terms with his wife and did not speak to her. The martyr's father went to the wife and came back with her one hour later. I told her, "Can you identify your husband?" "Yes," she replied while crying. Then she entered the hall. A couple of minutes later she called us over. Among the burnt corpses of the martyrs she showed us one and said, "This is my husband." We were very surprised. How did she identify him? She took a shirt out of her purse and said, "Some days before the operation, we went together to a shop. He bought two identical shirts and said, 'This is for me and the other is yours!' My husband said, 'I won't take it off until I'm martyred! One day they will come to you. Bring this shirt and identify me!'" Pointing to the burnt body of the martyr, she continued, "All of his body is burnt, but a part of his shirt is still intact." She put her shirt next to the remaining bit of cloth. They were identical. The funeral was held the same day.

With Napoleon, the Louvre tried to define itself as a "national" museum asking for the gaze of the other. With Bonaparte's exactions in Italy and the conquest of Belgium in 1794, one deputy declared: "The Flemish school rises en mass to come and adorn our museums."[8]

Martyrs museums also make a "national" claim, which in its own way corresponds to colonialism. The colonial formula is simple: the West is interested in the exotic other for what he possesses and what the West lacks, the same way the West is interested in what the exotic other lacks and the West can provide. Yet the West is entirely uninterested in anything it cannot provide or gain. This is exactly how to oppose the colonialist: strive for independence and consequently fall out of the global network of relations. Render oneself uninteresting to the West, and uphold this lack not as a demand, but as a claim, as a void that one refuses to fill. If I rebel no matter what the cost (for there is a great cost in doing what the West is not interested in), I can continue until the end. A martyr is an ultimate rebel, tried and tested. But the martyr's recklessness with "life" (property of the victorious West) is not a pure aesthetic preference. Actual life must have been usurped by the Western other to lead to such extremism. And extremism is no stranger to someone who is obliged to live in extremity. One who cannot live can experience life through its denial.

Back to the issue of space: this before-and-after utilization of the room also creates a great contrast. What does the placement of antiquity-like rubbish in such a prominent position entail? Does it bring about a leveling between rubbish and professionally acquired valuables? Is there some kind of chemistry at work here—a transformation or a blurring of boundaries? Or simply put: Is antiquity-like rubbish becoming the norm?

ANTIQUITY-LIKE RUBBISH, THE NORM? In the early days, when the syndicate was first established at the Old Cinema in Puxin (unfortunately demolished now), Wei-Li was referred to by the townsfolk as the erratic "antique-collector," and the name "antiquity-like rubbish" was born. With the gradual increase and recognition of antiquity-like rubbish in mainstream society, Wei-Li has gained a reputation in the small town as "the artist" or "proprietor" of antiquity-like rubbish, even though this hybrid term remains somewhat elusive and confusing to most of the townsfolk. Nevertheless, this immediate acknowledgement of antiquity-like rubbish by the populace speaks for itself, as rubbish once again gains entry into the larger social system, even more so when it stirs the imagination of those living on the outskirts of the metropolis—where belief systems tend to stay fixed due to their infrequent contact with the ever-turbulent nucleus. In fact, antiquity-like rubbish has attained such prominence that the syndicate headquarters in Puxin, which is quite possibly the modern-day Taiwanese equivalent of Warhol's Factory—an odd place with odd faces involved with odd waste, infested with mavericks, prudes, imbeciles, alcoholics, hippies who think they're from the '60s, introverts, extroverts, heterosexuals, homosexuals, intellectuals, pseudo-intellectuals, pregnant ladies, curators who claim to be policemen, Wei-Li's groupies, etc.—has of late developed into a tourist hotspot. Even local taxi drivers have no choice but to include it as one of Puxin's attractions, and they sometimes wait nearby in shifts. Evidence shows that antiquity-like rubbish has gained an increasing amount of popularity and become somewhat of the norm.

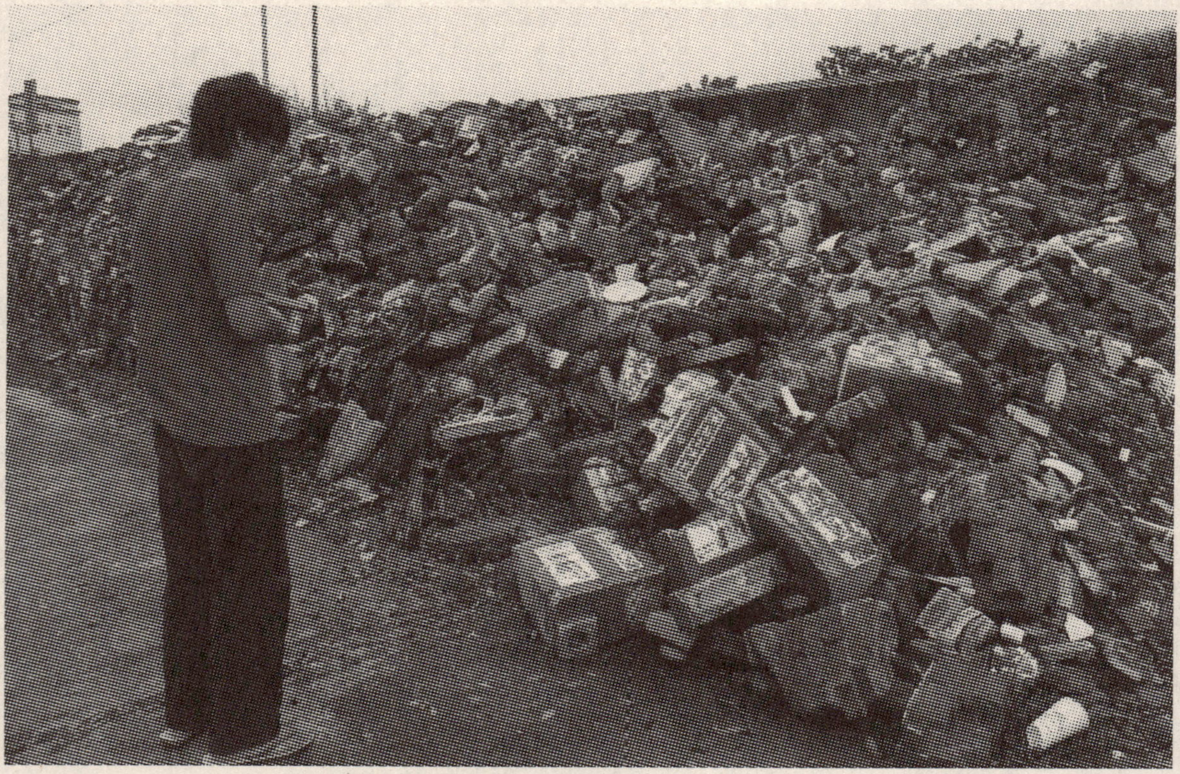

Wei-Li Yeh, *Antiquity-Like Rubbish Research & Development Syndicate in 206*, "Cemetery Chair," Taipei Biennial 2012, Taipei Fine Arts Museum, Taiwan.

There is no appropriate way to measure suffering. This is a source of injustice that modern systems of representation cannot easily communicate. For one who has no voice and is unable to touch others, this failure to communicate is all the more intense. One who cannot exhibit can all the same turn against representation itself.

1 Tony Bennett, Chapter 2: "The Exhibitionary Complex," in *The Birth of the Museum: History, Theory, Politics* (London: Routledge, 1995), 69.

2 Jean-Louis Déotte, "Rome, the Archetypal Museum, and the Louvre, the Negation of Division," in *Art in Museums*, ed. Susan Pearce (London: Athlone Press, 1995), 226.

3 The Koran, 2: 154 (The Cow). See also The Koran, 3: 169 (The Family of Imran): "And reckon not those who are killed in Allah's way as dead; nay, they are alive [and] are provided sustenance from their Lord."

4 Déotte, 228.

5 Ibid.

6 Ibid., 231.

7 Larry Shiner, *The Invention of Art: A Cultural History* (Chicago: University of Chicago Press, 2001), 181.

8 Ibid., 184.

JUNK STATUS

If you pay the slightest attention to things around you, you'll find that rubbish has become one of the primary resources for contemporary art production today. Oftentimes, artists resort to fistfights or lurking in dark alleys in the dead of night in order to obtain the best stock. You never know what priceless waste someone might squander, so you lurk in corners, where your senses become acute, and you wish for something to fall from the sky—a gift in disguise. The rise to such behavioral anomalies could have resulted from our exacerbatingly harsh economical and ecological environment, and as we suffer from a lack of creative material, recycled goods and trash become our best option due to their quantity, quality, price, and better yet, their personal and social reference points. In addition to a lack of resources, increasing environmental catastrophes, and a call for recycling and an eco-friendlier approach to our planet, the significance of antiquity-like rubbish is also largely related to contemporary social systems and structures. In the postmodern era of globalization, where much of our social system is structured on the fluctuation of currency, cultural exchange, and hierarchical power, value shifts rapidly from one extreme to another, causing much instability and fear.

This summer, news of Greece's financial crisis and possible exit from the euro mortified me. In terms of nations, Greece is practically the equivalent of antiquity because of its inseparable association with the cradle of Western civilization.[2] According to the rating agency S&P, though, the ancient country's debt has led it to hit rock bottom, with financial ratings of "junk" status.[3] Were Greece to really be punished for its economic woes, what would become of it? Would we completely deny a centuries-old cultural existence and belief system? Bearing these thoughts in mind, I felt like my acknowledgement of the world was bound to disintegrate and that everything I firmly believed in could be taken from me in seconds. What happens when the value of antiquity, with all its grace, cultivation, and rarity, hits the floor? And what could be more frightening or taboo than when the very ideals this antiquity projects shatter and spiral downwards to bottomless depths? INSTABILITY. FEAR. I no longer knew what investments would calm me, sustain me, or anchor me in this vast and tempestuous universe. The headlines delivered news of money-eating termites and mold-growing cash, causing unfortunate blokes across the world to lose their fortunes overnight. This increased fear and induced people to reconsider their preconceived notions of value. Placing faith in socially proclaimed value no longer provides genuine comfort. I insist that we think otherwise.

A PHOENIX BORN
FROM THE ASHES

Perhaps the answer and savior to all this instability and fear could be antiquity-like rubbish. According to extensive research on rubbish, the contaminated, impure, or taboo objects that are cast out of society, marginalized, and turned into rubbish can delineate the boundaries of our social structures. Materials within that boundary hold utilitarian purposes and are classified as either valuable or transient in worth, whereas valuables/antiquity increase in value while the transient eventually loses worth and degenerate to rubbish. A trip down the gutter affords objects the power to regenerate and restructure society. Once the transient-turned-rubbish has faded into oblivion and becomes extinct, a newfound life is breathed into it, as society once again accepts it as a rarity/antiquity/valuable. Nevertheless, the present system is at war with itself. Internal turbulence endangers our very existence. While it takes forever to reach the status of antiquity, it only takes seconds for antiquity to fall into the pit. How much of that can we bear, really? Security and true, unwavering value can only exist in the gaps between values and mind-sets, where it transcends the difference between the valuable, the transient, and rubbish. True value can only be found in the perfect hybrid that is antiquity-like rubbish.

Musing more about Greece, I wondered if countries or societies were analogous to objects and could rise again from the ashes while still

no dark
no night
no sleep

no night
no sleep
no dream

no sleep
no dream
no hope

no dream
no hope
no life

maintaining their previous cultural essences. The answer to this can also be found in antiquity-like rubbish. When modern society finally collapses and we fall back into medieval feudalism, then land, rubbish, and dirt will be the natural forces of power.[4] If Greece were to achieve antiquity-like rubbish status, if everything within its border were to became antiquity-like rubbish, freed from the meddling of mainstream values/currency, then we might begin to view certain things with more clarity: the relationship between objects and sentiments, what value really is, how organic creative forces derive from a true understanding of human need. Like a phoenix rising from the ashes, a new order—one still connected to the old—would thus be established through regeneration. I see antiquity-like rubbish as striving neither to achieve antiquity nor to restrict itself as rubbish. I consider it to be a concept/statement about the preservation of true value and the regeneration of belief systems. Antiquity-like rubbish could sustain us in a troubled and unstable world. It could be a path to equilibrium.

ZERO BOUNDARIES

Under this pile of junk-associated art, NYC-based artist Justin Gignac's *NYC Garbage* project also caught my eye.[5] With this project, Gignac seeks to highlight the importance of package design by selling neatly designed cubes full of handpicked NYC garbage. The packaging succeeded in igniting my desire to own a cube of NYC garbage, or even a limited edition cube, which includes a variety of rubbish from special holidays and national events.[6] Still, there is a big difference between this use of garbage and antiquity-like rubbish. With *NYC Garbage*, you get your hands on quite a lot of dirt, and you make karmic connection to whomever's garbage you now possess, which give insight into the topography, social construction, collective unconscious, or habitual behaviors of the region. But the acquisition of this garbage is clean. You are holding onto contaminated garbage that is frozen in cubes of plastic. It is safely quarantined. Harmless. With a tight lid on it, a stranger's dirty sneakers won't come out to bite you. Through this conscious effort to segregate impurities in society, social values and belief systems remain decidedly rigid, or are in fact further strengthened. Antiquity-like rubbish, on the other hand, works differently. It works to break these assumptions. For example, a main source of the raw material used by our syndicate is the Tayuan coastline, where rubbish comes to rest temporarily after following the ocean's currents. The origin of this rubbish is unfathomable and difficult to trace, but this only enhances the intrigue and profundity. At the local cemetery, cracked altarpieces, tombstones, urns, and coffins lie unattended in mounds, yearning for someone to understand, acknowledge, and transmute them into existences that are appreciated once again. Antiquity-like rubbish is the road not taken that ceaselessly beckons you. You are exposed to its magnetic field. You are naked and vulnerable in its presence. There is a perusal of rust, direct contact with sand, sediment, debris, dead skin cells, hair, fluid, etc. The artist pours his/her soul into these and becomes one with them. It seems dangerous when you consider that it could be a friend in disguise, but fixed guidelines might be where the real danger lies.

ONE MAN'S TRASH, ANOTHER MAN'S ANTIQUITY-LIKE RUBBISH

Precursors to antiquity-like rubbish can be traced back to the found-art movements of the early twentieth century, when Duchamp challenged the world to perceive the urinal as art and turned all the world's preconceived values upside down. *Objects trouvés*, ready-mades, found-art pieces—these were commonplace, utilitarian objects given a conceptual and sometimes physical makeover, which afforded them entry into the spheres of art. Their shock value is not difficult to understand, and over time it has become repetitive and relatively disenchanting. The consumer commodity, the rubbish-turned-art, the residue of the last century, the utilitarian-no-more, the idea-behind-it, the superstar's tissue, the homeless guy's tissue, the I-too-am-an-artist, and the classic we-made-it-to-a-museum, etc. Today, these patterns have evolved into something more complex. In fact, it is a complex of its own accord—call

dark
dark
dark

dark
dark
dark

dark
dark
dark

Boris Ondreička, DARK DARK DARK.

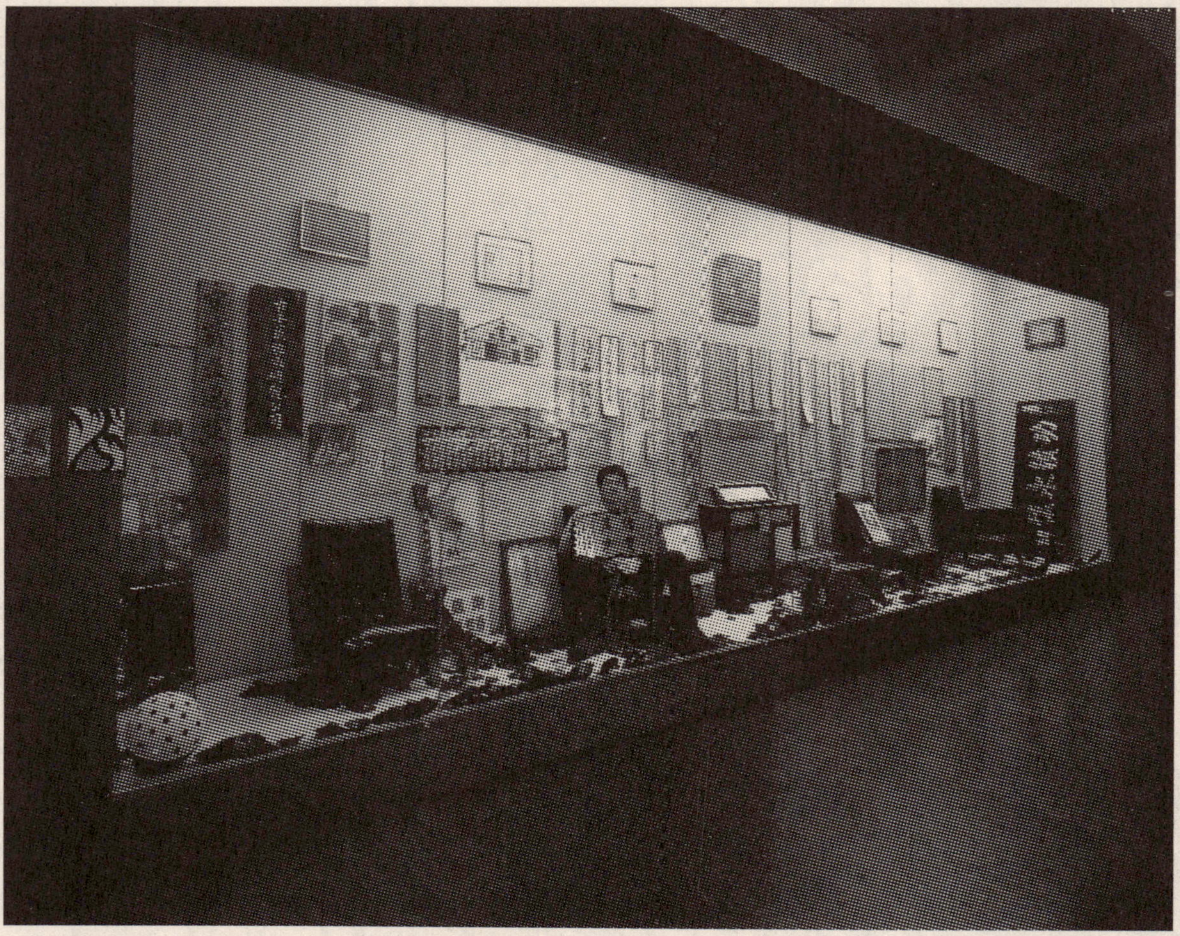

Wei-Li Yeh, *Antiquity-Like Rubbish Research & Development Syndicate in 206 #5*, Taipei Biennial 2012, Taipei Fine Arts Museum, Taiwan, 2013, wooden lightbox, 100 × 130 × 15 cm.

it the "Antiquity-Like Rubbish Complex." This complex takes all of the values that past artists tried to challenge and combines them into one large horrifying mess, magnificently hideous to behold. Objects maintain an ever-changing relationship with the values of the world we live in today, a world thrown into disorder by postmodernity and globalization. This world automatically demands and manifests what it needs. In a place magnificently hideous to inhabit, there are no constant guidelines for us to live by, no structural patterns that hold strong, no core concept behind it all. Everything is held together by a thin thread that can easily break or dissolve without a cause. The more firmly you believe, the more you are prone to fall— into deception, into bankruptcy, into nihilism. Interestingly though, all of the fleeting concepts and values we experience—transformation, transmutation, transpiration, trans-you-name-it— are reflected in the physicality and materiality of objects. Antiquity-like rubbish is the only perfect embodiment of all of this. It is quantum physics renamed, or objectified. This is where it gets complex, but not really (quantum physics is easy!). The sole solution is found in tangible-objects-in-flux, which provide a genuine, inherent stability—emotionally and physically, culturally and economically, elusively and tangibly. Footwear salvaged along the coastline, tombstone stools, sexual souvenirs, words of wisdom, words of rubbish, etc.—all of this could send you on an epic journey to discover the secrets of a stranger's past. You might uncover a resonance between your fate and another person's trash. Grounded on a personal level but inevitably connected to larger society, antiquity-like rubbish links together microcosms and macrocosms. Antiquity-like rubbish is world-class karma.

Allow me to return to the question about space that I began with: Does the presence of antiquity-like rubbish in Room 206 bring about a leveling of art and rubbish, raising rubbish to museum status and giving it mainstream art-market value? In my opinion, antiquity-like rubbish will always be antiquity-like. Whether or not it is displayed in a museum, its value will be multifaceted and ever-increasing. It will never experience a sudden decline or demise, which in a certain sense heightens its worth to an exalted degree. Even with its monstrous, taboo-like mannerisms, its placement in the public sphere acts as a catalyst for opening up new horizons, regenerating and rethinking value systems, networking networks, immersing oneself in the emotional depths of the artists' craft, being false friends, being false enemies, reaching towards the infinite and beyond. Antiquity-like rubbish is a mixture of all pre-conceived and never-before-conceived values, in-between values and values of the in-between, corporeally and mentally sustaining us in both stable and troubled times. It is assuredly an art with its own merits.

Collaborative team: Wei-Li Yeh with Chi-Pan Chen, Yu-Hsin Wu, Jhi-Yi Liu, Pei-Chun Shih, Gang Yen, Chi-Min Tsai, Chun-Ta Chiu, Freya Chou, Daisy Li, Chih-Ming Feng, Leo Wang, Ku-Ming Chen, and Chi-An Tsai.

1 I must state here that I was hired to do research on his art, but have come to find that I read people better than I do art. But what's the difference? He is his art.

2 According to a romanticized and idealist statement by Percy Bysshe Shelley about the culture from which Western civilization stemmed, "We are all Greeks."

3 BBC News, "Rating agency S&P has already downgraded Greek debt to 'junk.'"

4 This reminds me: Wei-Li also owns acres of antiquity-like farmland. If Taiwan's economy crashes and we resort to feudalism—which is quite likely—some of us may have to become his tenants. Beware the powers of antiquity-like man.

5 See nycgarbage.com.

6 For example, the limited edition *Inauguration Day at Washington, DC* consists of crinkled propaganda posters with Obama's face printed on them, a ragged US flag, and other trash from the President's inauguration day.

THE EQUATOR OF ALIENATION

Alberto Toscano

What modern capitalism—concentrated and fully established capitalism—inscribes within life's setting, is the fusion of what had been opposed as the positive and negative poles of alienation into a sort of equator of alienation.
—"Urbanism as Will and Representation" in *Internationale situationniste*, 1964[1]

The world only appears before my eyes as a solid "landscape," lustrous like plastic.
—Takuma Nakahira[2]

That landscapes are manufactured or altered by human interests is not a discovery of late capitalism. Whether seen as pictorial genre or as ideology, the representation of landscape has allowed the modern subject to frame his mastery over nature—crucially by clearing the land of indigenous, insurgent, and independent inhabitants—in terms of a propertied metaphysics. But the representation of landscape also functions to depict human artifacts, imprints of social intercourse.

When the landscape is not scoured for traces—aftermaths of trauma, indices of futures past—its indeterminacy is most often coded as indifference: the indifference of modularity and iteration across social spaces, the indifference of concrete abstraction (pun intended). It is an indifference remarkable for its ubiquity and magnitude, as well as for the sheer scale of its continued reproduction—tract homes all the way into a vanished horizon, container terminals that never sleep, banks of screens in a stock exchange.

It should come as no surprise that landscape—that prime terrain for the assertion of the view from power—should have been thematized in the 1970s as the emblem of a kind of inhuman subsumption. With the urbanization of capital transmuting the lived and visible landscape into a social factory—especially evident in once-rural suburban and functional milieus—built space attained an experiential, as well as an allegorical, status that it didn't previously enjoy. This was especially so in those places where postwar "planner-states" enabled an accelerated industrialization, quickly saturating landscapes with the infrastructures of accumulation, as seen in the massive industrial establishments in Michelangelo Antonioni's seemingly depopulated Po valley. It is worth dwelling on two salient approaches to representing landscape in the shadow of these shifts, found in the work of the photographers surrounding the 1975 *New Topographics* exhibition, with its attention to the suburbanization of habitation and production in the American West, and the "landscape theory" (*fukeiron*) proposed by militant artists in Japan in the late 1960s and early 1970s.

Aside from their foregrounding of "landscape" as medium, object, and in a sense subject of their work, these otherwise unconnected aesthetic practices share some telling formal traits. In both cases, vistas are vanquished (and if they open up, it is only into a kind of orthogonal featurelessness). The built world is encountered frontally, deadpan. Captions are minimal, doing little of the critical work famously invoked by Brecht and Benjamin. Spaces are depopulated and if humans appear it is in the kind of routine everydayness that sees them circulate obediently through the built world—which is ironic, given that demographic density is a significant feature of the processes that produce these spatial figures.

These are not landscapes virtually possessed by a subject, but ones that either refuse to allow any grip for a projected presence or that simply crowd out agency altogether. As one

THE MUSEUM OF ANTE MEMORI ALS

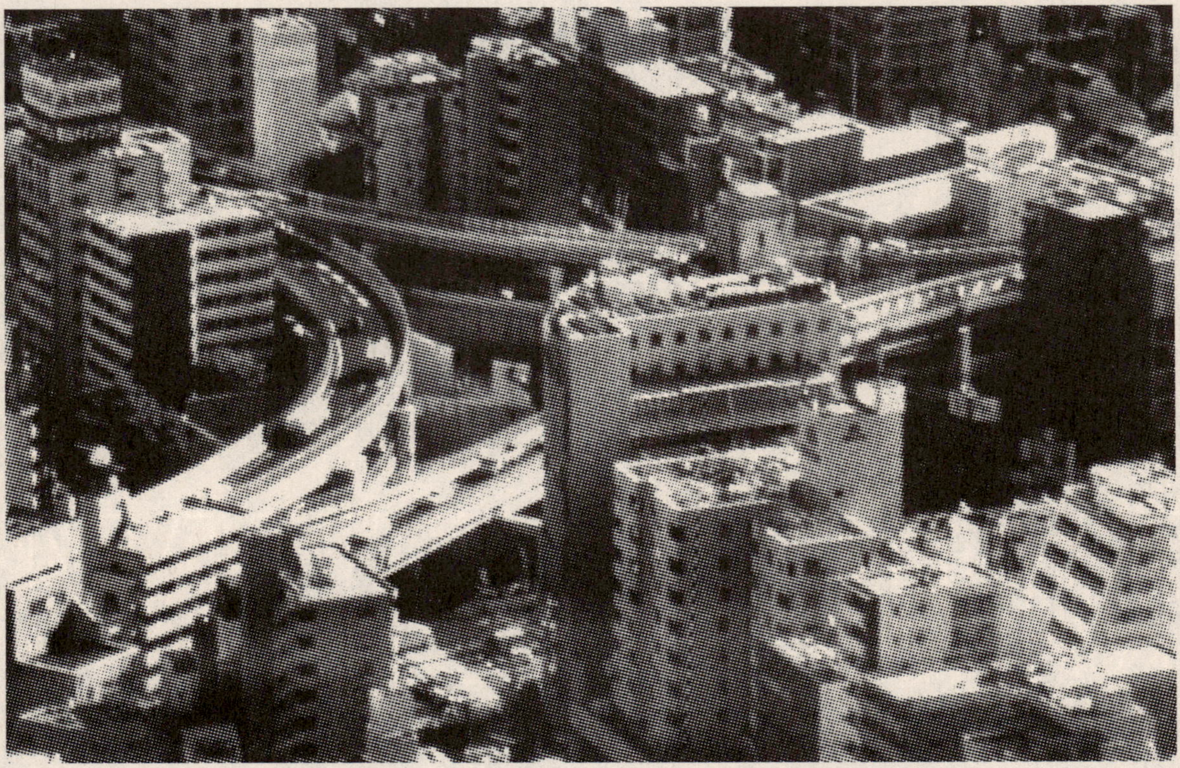

Eric Baudelaire, *The Anabasis of May and Fusako Shigenobu, Masao Adachi, and 27 Years Without Images*, 2011, super 8 film transferred to HD video, 66 min.

of the proponents of *fukeiron*, the photographer Takuma Nakahira, noted, this tendency prevails in Godard's *Weekend*, where "the central 'characters' are a series of traffic accidents and a sea of draining blood, while the human couple running away plays only a small role." But this inversion is for Nakahira the bearer of an aesthetic and political truth: "it seems very vivid and pertinent for us, because we are actually living in such a time, more than ever before"; in turn, it calls for the artist to make "our age's syndrome more explicit, to expose it for what it is."[3] Where an urban landscape "covered over with expressionless smoothness" is still looked at by practitioners of *fukeiron* in the context of rebellion (be it the impasses of student struggles or the shootings by Nagayama Norio, the absent subject of the key *fukeiron* film *A.K.A. Serial Killer*), in the new topographics the inhuman homogeneity of built space is presented without comment, in a studied aesthetic of anonymity, of style-less style.[4]

It was precisely this claim to featurelessness that drew the critical rebuke of Allan Sekula against the new topographics photographer Lewis Baltz. In a postscript to his own photo-essay on the kind of schooling, exploitation, and discipline at work in the same "new industrial parks near Irvine" that were the object of a 1974 book by Baltz, Sekula questioned the manner in which this photographic trend, lured by the pictorial examples of modernist minimalism, approached a new spatial phenomenon. The trend was inextricable from a certain spatial logic of capital, voiding the social and laboring referent of the built environment—a bad abstraction, according to Sekula, that "finds an exemplary aesthetic freedom in the disengaged play of signifiers."[5]

Baltz's images, like those of what Sekula sarcastically dubbed "the neutron bomb school of photography," would thus be led by their own economic unconscious—chiefly, modernism's reassertion of the separation between intellectual and manual labor—to a complicity with the "mystifying translation of a site of production into a site of imaginary leisure," synthesized in the oxymoronic blandness of the very term "industrial park." Though this is a suggestive line of criticism, there is a parenthetic qualification

POWERS OF THE FALSE (NOTES FROM A JOURNAL)

Eric Baudelaire

Kyoto, April 13 –

Tonight was the Sunday film club. A screening among friends and a chat over a drink. This week, without disclosing my selection in advance, I chose Peter Watkins's *The War Game*, in which a cold, factual voiceover accompanies black-and-white footage of a mock BBC report describing the devastating consequences of a nuclear bombardment in Kent, England in 1965.

The atmosphere in the screening room is tense. The extraordinary violence of the statistics enumerated in the voiceover, and the relentless shots of children in agony, of mass graves, of burned flesh, send a chill through the audience—they were probably expecting a more entertaining Sunday selection. When the film ends, the discomfort in our group is palpable, almost physiological. "Too raw, too brutal, no subtlety, no mercy": forty years after being censored by the BBC, Watkins's bolt out of the blue remains intact, to the point of noticeably flattening the critical dimension of our discussion—we find ourselves speaking less about "film" than a visual and cognitive blow that hits the gut as hard as the brain.

As for myself, I spent part of the screening feeling quite uncomfortable for a specific reason: one of the guests had invited a Japanese friend, and I didn't know how someone from a culture that had actually experienced the Bomb would stomach this raw depiction of an atomic event. The ensuing

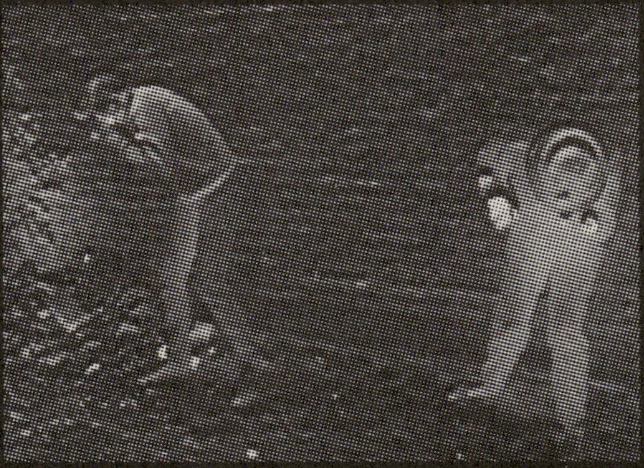

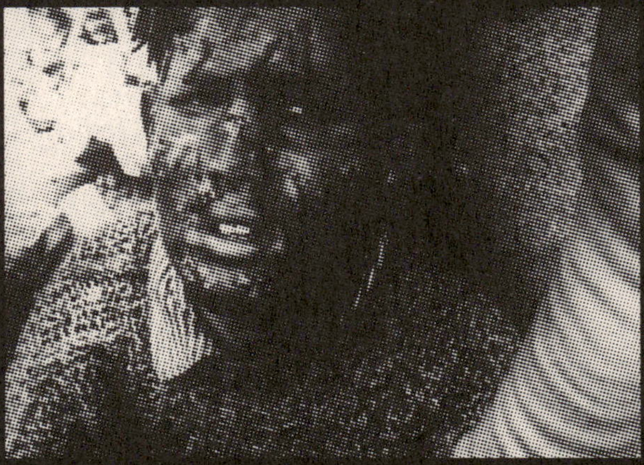

Peter Watkins, *The War Game*, 1965, 16mm film transferred to video, black and white, sound, 46 min.

in his postscript on Baltz that bears examination. He writes: "To his credit, Baltz's ambiguity [between documentary photography and abstraction] echoes an ambiguity and loss of referentiality already present in the built environment."[6] In other words, there is an element of realism (though perhaps not of a critical kind) in depicting landscapes that capital has rendered fungible, homogeneous, faceless. What we have is a kind of short-circuit between abstraction as a figural genre and abstraction as a real, concrete product of capital becoming spatialized.

Though Baltz's *The New Industrial Parks Near Irvine, California* does not include a preface, his occasional comments and writings suggest that the abstract reality of these spaces, and the social mutations they reveal, lay very much at the heart of the project. It's suggestive in this respect to contrast the seemingly antipolitical character of the 1970s turn to landscape—a reductive reserving of judgment in the interest of "describing the surfaces of the phenomenal world in a manner unique to [photography]"—with what, at least for Baltz, were its motivations.[7] As he stated in an interview: "Coming from Orange County, I watched the ghastly transformation of this place—the first wave of bulimic capitalism sweeping across the land, next door to me. I sensed that there was something horribly amiss and awry about my own personal environment."[8] But, in what we could call a mimesis, or indeed an ascesis, of abstraction, the aim was, appropriating the "vernacular model"[9] of real-estate photography, to deny the singularity of image or subject matter (even if this didn't stop certain interpretations from reintroducing a rather ideological sense of "American beauty"). In this respect, nonjudgment was a prelude to a kind of typology.

In his 1974 essay "Notes on Recent Industrial Developments in Southern California," Baltz shows some of the research involved in the visual inventorying of these new spaces:

> *Typical functions:* Such developments typically house industries that have become significant in the years since the Korean War. These include: aerospace, data processing and information storage; leisure time industries, such as the fabrication of recreation vehicles and equipment. Often these developments house storage and distribution centers for firms whose manufacturing occurs in other parts of the country or abroad.[10]

The typological abstraction of these denatured landscapes is also the product of a process of real abstraction. This process allows us to see the mimesis of modernism and minimalism, which so fascinates our pictorial sensibility, as the product of a compulsive dynamic of profit and planning that is in many ways incommensurate with its artistic capture:

> One of the most common views capitalist society takes of nature is among the most rigorous and most appalling. "Landscape as Real Estate." This was the view of nature presented to me in Park City and the viewpoint I showed in my photographs. To know that an apparently unbroken expanse of land is overlaid with invisible lines demarcating the pattern of future development is to perceive it in a very different way than one would otherwise. That these divisions only coincidentally pertain to topography and are the arbitrary result of financial speculation, illustrates the casually rapacious disdain that our culture has of the natural world as such. This attitude holds all non-productive land as marginal; "nature" is what's left over after every other demand has been satisfied.[11]

It is worthy of note, then, that in the Irvine photographs criticized by Sekula, the spatial logics of capital that Baltz gestures towards are not just elided; rather, there is an explicit aesthetic decision to depict homogeneity, modularity, and opacity as just that, withholding further elucidation.[12] The question of how to approach this anticognitive aesthetic of landscapes becomes one of the conundrums thrown up by the work of Baltz and those associated with new topographics, as well as by some of the work inspired by *fukeiron*.

As Baltz has famously noted, looking at these new industrial landscapes, at these seemingly limitless tracts of boxes: "You don't discussion defied my expectations. The French guests were the ones with the palest faces. The Japanese friend seemed much less disconcerted.

Hiroshima, August 21 –

On my way back to Kyoto, a chance to stop in Hiroshima and visit the Peace Memorial Museum. Two buildings packed with documents, artifacts, and personal accounts of the first atomic bombardment, presented chronologically, along with scientific perspectives on the Manhattan Project and the making of "Little Boy" (the affectionately named Hiroshima-bound A-bomb), of which a life-sized replica appears in one of the rooms.

What this memorial attempts is complex: to convey the *horror*, but avoid the pitfalls of an interpretation of history that tends towards the (American) argument that "it was unavoidable," while circumventing the explicit (but perilous) demonstration that the Enola Gay's mission on August 6, 1945 was a largely political, and resolutely barbaric, gesture. The museum's curatorial strategy for the memorial is anchored in a rationale of disordered, polymorphous accumulation: scientific and graphic documents on atomic science, lists of figures conveying the scale of the destruction, architectural models and samples documenting the power of the explosion, and accounts of survivors. I imagine that an overly ordered and directive presentation of this material would have raised vast ethical and historiographical problems that are somehow avoided by a strategy of volume, evocation, and repetition. The viewer becomes the editor. The museum leaves plenty of room for interpretation, and occasionally yields some surprising juxtapositions.

The cold, scientific displays about nuclear physics (reminiscent of an ordinary science museum) can seem misplaced when viewed a few steps away from the powerful pathos of a survivor's first-person account. The layout hints at the seductive powers of scientific research (what's more exhilarating than nuclear fission, in which the infinitely small yields the infinitely large?), the same hypnotic appeal that may have led a number of well-meaning civilians, like Dr. Oppenheimer, to carry on regardless of the unthinkable human consequences of their work.[1] Empathy for the Los Alamos scientists is surely not the primary objective of the scenography, but the accumulation and proximity of data makes this interpretation possible, and it is precisely in this kind of open layout that the memorial's function takes shape.

Repetition also comes into play. In one of the first rooms of the tour, there are two monumental models of the Hiroshima city center, one before know whether they're manufacturing pantyhose or megadeath." Sekula's response—that what we need is not a topography of abstraction but a "political geography, a way of talking with words and images about both the system and our lives within the system"—is still valid. Yet work like *The New Industrial Parks Near Irvine, California* also suggests that we take serious stock of the peculiarity and political intractability of such spaces of abstraction.

Their evacuation of the subject can of course signal many things. In that levy of American photographers, one can detect, depending on the angle: cynicism, aestheticism, restraint, or even a kind of ecological consciousness. By contrast, Japanese landscape theory is marked by a kind of maximum antagonism. "Landscape" is the closure of the space of politics and experience by capital, nation, and state. Hence the relentless face-off between its imperviousness and the violence or sexuality of individuals who, in the end, leave no trace.

The allegory that is Oshima's *The Man Who Left His Will on Film*—where a vanished activist filmmaker leaves a handful of actuality film[13] footage as his legacy, and characters seek to revitalize these bland spaces with violent action in a "war of landscapes"—speaks to this aesthetic and political impasse. As does Nakahira's apocalyptic humanism:

> A day will come when a single crack will nick this "landscape" which is uniformly covered over with expressionless smoothness, and a fissure will gradually deepen until this "landscape" is completely turned inside out like a glove being taken off. There will undoubtedly be a revolt. When that time comes, the "landscape" will already not be a "landscape," but will instead become a crucible of confusion, trampled over by the bare feet of vivid human kind. The fire will engulf the entire surface of the city. There, people will run amok. Fire and darkness. Barefoot people running around recklessly. In ancient times, people must have scrambled about in the midst of fire and darkness barefoot. It's an old-fashioned image but when I envision urban rebellion, this is the scene I always imagine.[14]

What remains unimaginable—be it through the lens of militant anxiety or disenchanted coolness—is what could become of this landscape whose unassailability, to use Nakahira's term, seems to belie its character as "manufactured" or "man-altered." From De Chirico's arcades for human marionettes to the crushing volumes of *Metropolis*, from Antonioni and Welles to Gursky and Burtynsky, the dwarfing (or expunging) of the human by the built has frequently been held up as an index of alienation.

Yet a reflection on the contemporary depiction of landscape should allow us to reject the temptation to treat such alienation by way of some counterfeit existentialist reflex. The aesthetic, cognitive, and political problems thrown up by *fukeiron* and new topographics are related to the difficulty we have in confronting the logistical spaces of the social factory, precisely those spaces which most evidence Brecht's demand that we reinvent realism in light of reality slipping into the functional. Though industrial parks are certainly not devoid of their own pseudo-bucolic managerial aesthetic, one of the most significant aesthetic, disciplinary, and political-economic aspects of such spaces is that, unlike the monumental volumes of metropolitan capitalism, they're not there to be seen.[15] Their opacity is no accident. Nor is the relative fungibility between underwear and overkill.

What's more, the short-circuit between artistic and social abstraction, though rife with its own mystifications (among them landscape's fetishization), also points us towards the concrete processes that do shed labor (or shunt it into windowless sheds), that witness the mutation, in certain regions, of the organic composition of capital, of the proportions between living labor-power and accumulated dead labor. In a nutshell, the problem of landscape theory, of new topographics, is the problem of dead labor, a problem that Marx encountered in the factory, but which we strangely strain to recognize when it is written, visibly and invisibly, into space.[16]

The crucial paradox in viewing the 1970s approach to depicting landscape as thematizing the spatial, material, and experiential impact of capital's rising organic composition comes in the

the explosion, one after. In another adjacent room, you find a second model of the "aftermath," almost identical to the first one, with the same red ball floating over the hypocenter. Repetition is more the stuff of cinema than museums; it leaves each person with the task of reinterpreting the same object, as if it were an editing effect—a loop or a repeated scene in a film.

The artifact rooms follow. Strips of burned clothing; images of irradiated, deformed bodies; a trace of a shadow projected on a brick wall by a man vaporized by the heat; and certainly the most macabre of all, that small pile of human remains, all that's left of Noriaki Teshima—fragments of fingernails and pieces of charred skin, as they were preserved by his mother so that she could save these traces of him and show them to his father when he returned from the front.

A succession of raw data, scientific information, and contextualized numbers that exceed our capacity for visual representation, alongside each concrete artifact that serves as a meiosis for the mental image each visitor will form. What is striking about this visit to the Hiroshima museum is that the way it unfolds and operates, and the feeling it generates, are identical to Watkins's *The War Game*. Or perhaps I should say that Watkins's mock documentary (from 1965) is articulated according to the same rationale as the Hiroshima Peace Memorial Museum, inaugurated in 1955. The same formal choice: the scale of the atomic horror justifies (even demands) a brutal, massive exposition of information and raw forms of visualization. The same statement of purpose: to say loud and clear, "Hiroshima, never again." The experience of the film in April, and of the museum today, are becoming confused in my mind. Both combine an archival role with an activist objective, but with this difference: in Hiroshima, the facts are recounted; in Watkins's film, they are manufactured. The Hiroshima museum is presented as a peace memorial, while Watkins's film is essentially an *ante-memorial* elaborated in a preemptive spirit, in the hope that there will be no need to create a real one later.

Amid the Hiroshima museum's mass of data, visitors do their own visceral sorting and leave with a ghost that will haunt them. For me, two documents remain etched in memory. The first is an American memorandum addressed to the Secretary of War, in which a committee of scientists from the Manhattan Project recommend a public demonstration of an atomic bombardment on an unpopulated area of Japan, possibly a desert island, as a warning to the Japanese. If the Japanese did not capitulate, another target could still be chosen.[2] The memorandum's argument is more utilitarian than humanitarian: the point is to demonstrate

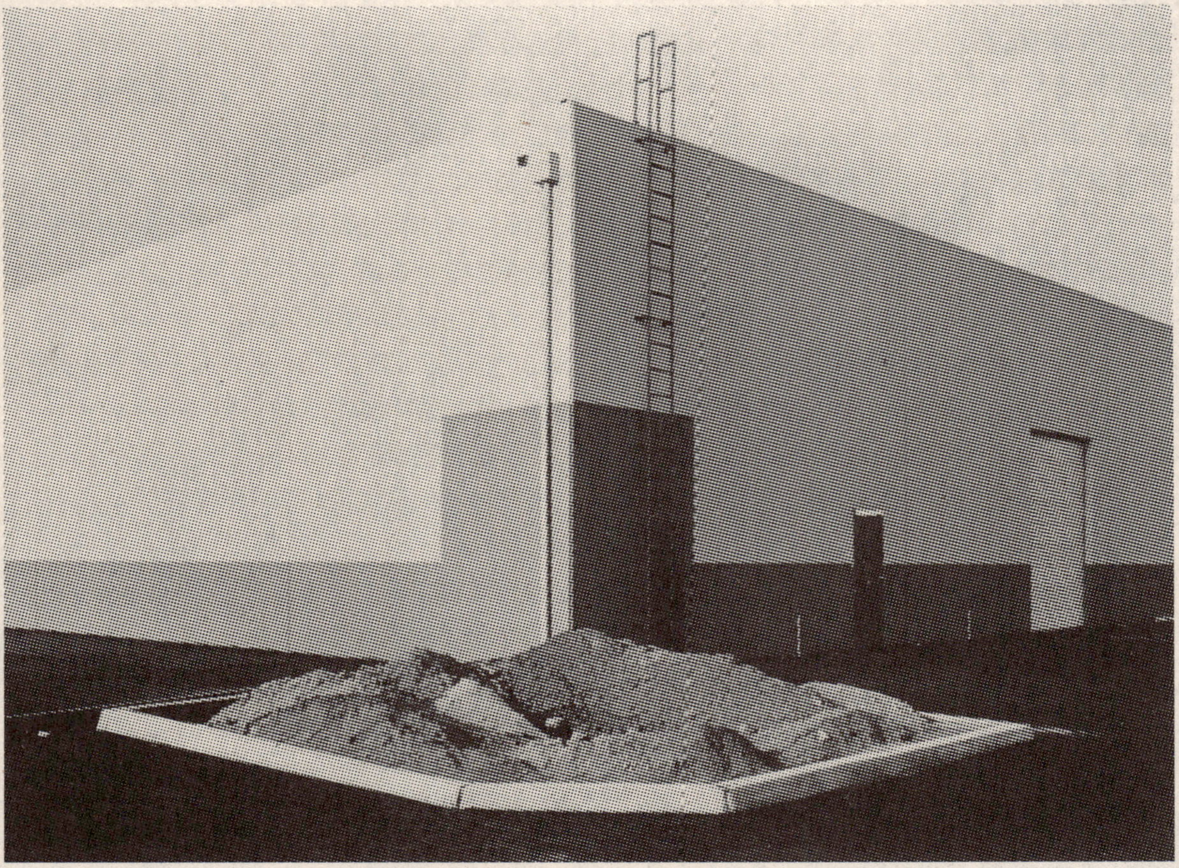

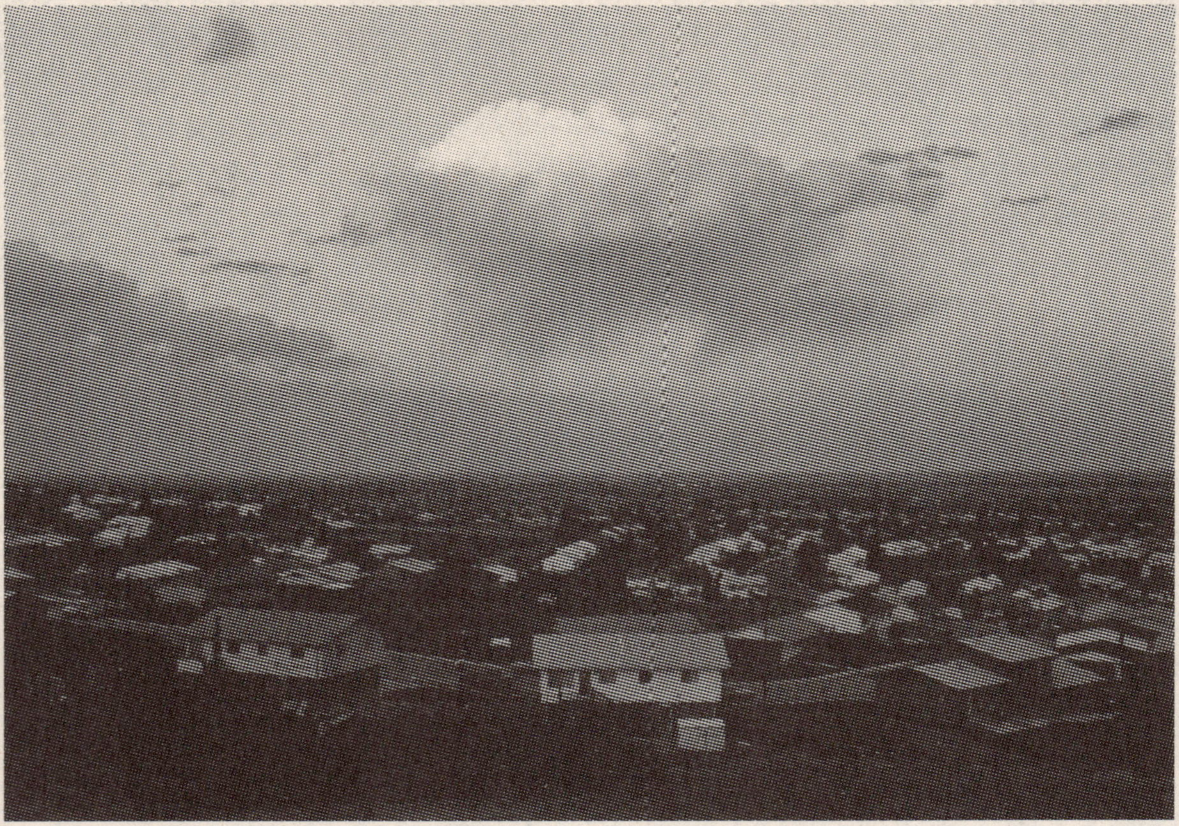

Fig. 1 Lewis Baltz, *South Corner, Riccar America Company, 3184 Pullman, Costa Mesa*, 1974, gelatin silver print, 15.1 × 22.8 cm. Photo: The Lewis Baltz Archive, Getty Research Institute, Los Angeles (2013.M.31). © Lewis Baltz.

Fig. 2 Robert Adams, *New Housing. North Denver, Colorado*, 1970, gelatin-silver print, image and sheet: 15.24 × 19.37 cm. Los Angeles County Museum of Art, Ralph M. Parsons Discretionary Fund (M.2005.12). © Robert Adams, courtesy Fraenkel Gallery, San Francisco. Photo credit: digital image © 2014 Museum Associates / LACMA. Licensed by Art Resource, NY.

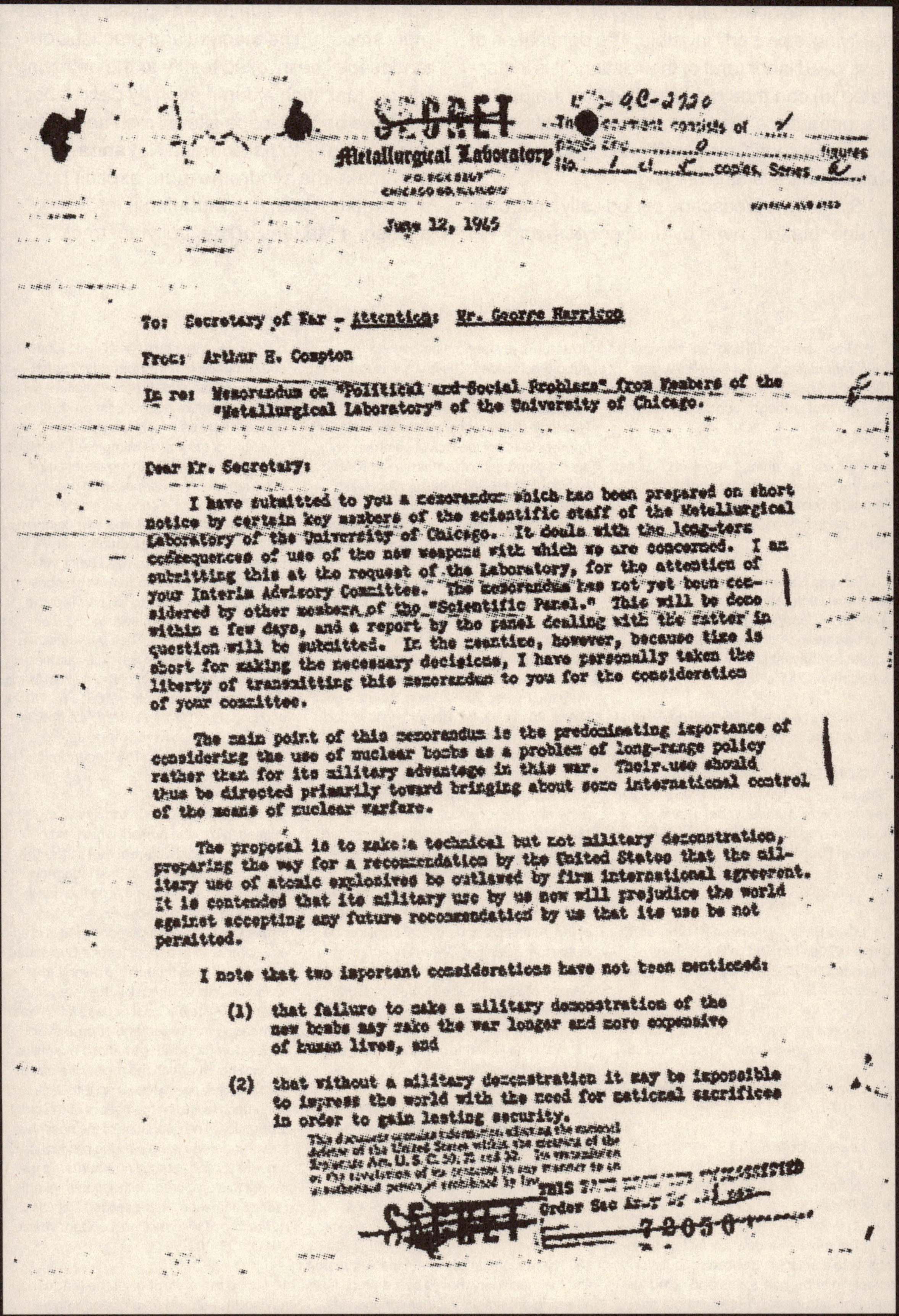

SECRET

Metallurgical Laboratory

CHICAGO 80, ILLINOIS

This document consists of 2 pages
No. ... 0 ... figures
No. ... copies, Series ...

June 12, 1945

To: Secretary of War – Attention: Mr. George Harrison

From: Arthur H. Compton

In re: Memorandum on "Political and Social Problems" from Members of the "Metallurgical Laboratory" of the University of Chicago.

Dear Mr. Secretary:

I have submitted to you a memorandum which has been prepared on short notice by certain key members of the scientific staff of the Metallurgical Laboratory of the University of Chicago. It deals with the long-term consequences of use of the new weapons with which we are concerned. I am submitting this at the request of the Laboratory, for the attention of your Interim Advisory Committee. The memorandum has not yet been considered by other members of the "Scientific Panel." This will be done within a few days, and a report by the panel dealing with the matter in question will be submitted. In the meantime, however, because time is short for making the necessary decisions, I have personally taken the liberty of transmitting this memorandum to you for the consideration of your committee.

The main point of this memorandum is the predominating importance of considering the use of nuclear bombs as a problem of long-range policy rather than for its military advantage in this war. Their use should thus be directed primarily toward bringing about some international control of the means of nuclear warfare.

The proposal is to make a technical but not military demonstration, preparing the way for a recommendation by the United States that the military use of atomic explosives be outlawed by firm international agreement. It is contended that its military use by us now will prejudice the world against accepting any future recommendation by us that its use be not permitted.

I note that two important considerations have not been mentioned:

(1) that failure to make a military demonstration of the new bombs may make the war longer and more expensive of human lives, and

(2) that without a military demonstration it may be impossible to impress the world with the need for national sacrifices in order to gain lasting security.

This document contains information affecting the national defense of the United States within the meaning of the Espionage Act, U. S. C. 50; 31 and 32. Its transmission or the revelation of its contents in any manner to an unauthorized person is prohibited by law.

THIS ... UNCLASSIFIED
Order Sec Army ...

SECRET

72050

Facsimile of the "Franck Report": Report of the Committee on Political and Social Problems, Manhattan Project "Metallurgical Laboratory," University of Chicago, June 11, 1945.

Signed by J. Franck, D. Hughes, L. Szilárd, T. Hogness, E. Rabinowitch, G. Seaborg, J. C. Stearns, and J.J. Nickson.

fact that this quantitative raising of the dead over the living is properly invisible. The domination of past, dead labor (and of the relations it is instantiated in) can thus manifest itself as the past's disappearance (as experience or visibility).[17] It is an antiseptic, air-conditioned nightmare that weighs on the brains of living.

Similarly, a landscape periodically destroyed by speculation, riven by unevenness, and generative of inequality can appear suffocatingly smooth. The theories and practices of landscape I've invoked testify to the petrifying effects that such a domination by dead labor can have on landscape-altered men and women. In so doing — to paraphrase Nakahira — they make the syndrome more explicit but, at the same time, risk mutating it into a fetish, a Medusa of the really abstract.[18]

1 "Urbanism as Will and Representation" [*Internationale situationniste* 9 (August 1964)], in *The Situationists and the City*, ed. Tom McDonough (London: Verso, 2009), 208.

2 Takuma Nakahira, "Rebellion Against the Landscape: Fire at the Limits of my Perpetual Gazing …," in Takuma Nakahira, *For a Language to Come* (Tokyo: Osiris, 2010), 8.

3 Takuma Nakahira, "Why an Illustrated Botanical Dictionary," in *Setting Sun: Writings by Japanese Photographers*, eds. Ivan Vartanian, Akihiro Hatanaka, and Yutaka Kanbayashi (New York: Aperture Foundation, 2006), 127.

4 Takuma Nakahira, "Rebellion Against the Landscape," 8.

5 Allan Sekula, 1982 postscript to "School is a Factory" (1978/1980), in *Allan Sekula: Performance Under Working Conditions*, ed. Sabine Breitweiser (Vienna: Generali Foundation, 2003), 252.

6 Ibid., 251.

7 Lewis Baltz, "American Photography in the 1970s: Too Old to Rock, Too Young to Die" (1985), in *Lewis Baltz Texts* (Göttingen: Steidl, 2012), 63.

8 Quoted in Cathy Curtis, "The Wasteland," *Los Angeles Times*, March 29, 1992.

9 Lewis Baltz, "American Photography in the 1970s," 69.

10 *Lewis Baltz Texts*, 16.

11 "Notes on *Park City*" (1980), in *Lewis Baltz Texts*, 45.

12 "The mostly windowless factory buildings were erected as gigantic speculation objects in suburban zones optimized for traffic infrastructure. Printed without an introduction, devoid of commentary, Baltz's fifty-one photographs of these uniform structures reveal nothing beyond the structural facades. The focus lies upon the texture of the surfaces and the grid-like structure of the architectural ensemble. No single element is accentuated more than another … Is not the lack of commentary itself a commentary on this serialized, suburban conformity? Whereas someone like Allan Sekula documents the transformation of the working environment under the auspices of a global economy, these causalities remain invisible in Baltz's case, as indeed does every form of production behind factory gates." Vanessa Joan Müller, "Between Representation and Reality: Reflections on a Film Installation by Mario Pfeifer," in *Reconsidering The New Industrial Parks Near Irvine, California by Lewis Baltz, 1974, by Mario Pfeifer, 2009* (Berlin: Sternberg Press, 2011), 83, 84. Pfeifer's installation returns to the site of one of Baltz's photographs to document it from the inside.

13 "Actuality film" refers to the kind of generally brief, unstructured recordings of real places, objects, or events that marked the origins of cinema (for example, in the Lumière brothers' *Workers Leaving the Lumière Factory*). I am indebted to the work of Yuriko Furuhata for an understanding of the theoretical and political significance of this form. See her *Cinema of Actuality: Japanese Avant-Garde Filmmaking in the Season of Image Politics* (Durham: Duke University Press, 2013).

14 Takuma Nakahira, "Rebellion Against the Landscape," 9.

15 On the pseudo-bucolic managerial aesthetic of industrial parks, see Chris Balaschak, "New World: Lewis Baltz and a Geography of Aesthetic Decisions," in *Reconsidering The New Industrial Parks Near Irvine, California by Lewis Baltz, 1974,* by Mario Pfeifer, 2009.

16 "Here too past labor — in the automaton and the machinery moved by it — steps forth as acting apparently in independence of [living] labor, it subordinates labor instead of being subordinate to it, it is the iron man confronting the man of flesh and blood. The subsumption of his labor under capital — the absorption of his labor by capital — which lies in the nature of capitalist production, appears here as a technological fact. The *keystone of the arch* is complete. Dead labor has been endowed with movement, and living labor only continues to be present as one of dead labor's conscious organs. The *living connection* of the whole workshop no longer lies here in cooperation; instead, the system of machinery forms a unity, set in motion by the *prime motor* and comprising the whole workshop, to which the living workshop is subordinated, in so far as it consists of workers. Their *unity* has thus taken on a form which is tangibly autonomous and independent of them." Karl Marx, "Economic Manuscripts of 1861–63," *Marx and Engels Collected Works*, Volume 34, available at http://www.marxists.org/archive/marx/works/1861/economic/ch35b.htm.

17 "It is not past labor and its structural relationship to the present which 'extinguishes' it that is different, but rather the immense quantity of that past labor now deployed … At the same time the dead labor embodied in machinery suddenly swells to inhuman proportions (and is properly compared to a monster or a Cyclopean machine). It is as though the reservoir, or as Heidegger would call it, the 'standing reserve' (*Gestell*) of past or dead labor was immensely increased and offered ever huger storage facilities for these quantities of dead hours, which the merely life-sized human machine-minder is nonetheless to bring back to life, on the pattern of the older production. The quantities of the past have been rendered invisible by the production process … and yet they now surround the worker in a proportion hitherto unthinkable." Fredric Jameson, *Representing Capital: A Reading of Volume One* (London: Verso, 2011), 101, 102.

18 I use the metaphor of the Medusa advisedly, as both *fukeiron* and new topographics touch on the beauty of these landscapes.

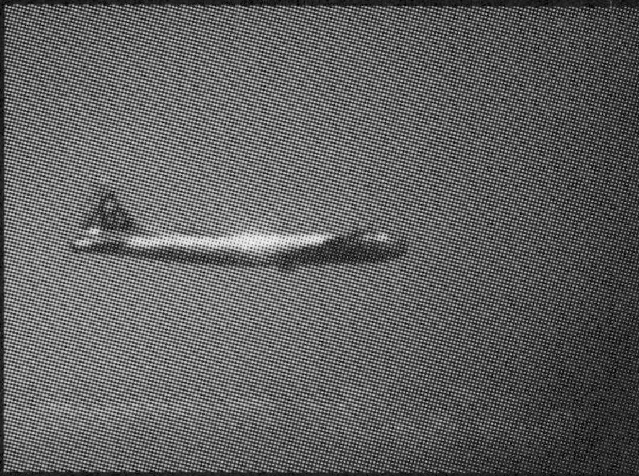

Aircraft en route to Nagasaki; shots of "Bockscar" filmed by Harold Melvin Agnew (detail), footage shot above the city of Kokura, Japan, August 9, 1945, 16mm film transferred to video, color, silent, 1 min 28 sec. Source: Hoover Institution Archives, Stanford University.

that the strategic objectives of the bomb can be met without the negative consequences that a large-scale civilian massacre would have on the postwar occupation of Japan, on the United States' standing in the world, and on the inevitable nuclear arms race that would follow. The "warning" proposal was not adopted.

The second document that haunts me recalls the fate of the city of Kokura, the planned target of the second atomic bombardment on August 9. It is a film shot from an observation plane showing the B-29 bomber "Bockscar" making three circles over Kokura in search of a hole in the unexpected cloud cover that is making it impossible to visually identify the target. Bockscar eventually diverts to a secondary target: Nagasaki.

Two documents that present glimpses into disturbing imaginary scenarios. In the first, the arguments in favor of a warning are heeded, and the document opens the door to a painfully credible fiction in which the reasonable arguments of civilized people save hundreds of thousands of lives. The second document is a small window into the strange fate of a city saved from hell by a few clouds. In the factual, precise language of military communiqués on official letterhead, and in a 16mm film showing a silver plane navigating the beautiful blue sky, the horror of reality is juxtaposed with a possible alternative history, a vision of what was avoided, or could have been. A fictional world in the grammar of the conditional perfect: the *would have been*. Watkins's film is the mirror image of this conditional perfect: by appropriating the format of a BBC documentary, it horrifically documents the future perfect, the *will have been*.

Paris, week of October 13 –

Concept notes on curating an exhibition named *Ante-Memorials*:
The twentieth century may be the century of the image, but its darkest hours are distinguished by gaping holes in the visual record. There are few photographs at the Hiroshima museum because no image is "enough"

SPIRAL LANDS / CHAPTER 2

Andrea Geyer

In the cycle of works called *Spiral Lands*, Andrea Geyer investigates the role of photography in the colonization and continuous appropriation of the North American continent, using the Navajo Nation and the surrounding Pueblos of the American Southwest (now Arizona, New Mexico, Utah, and Colorado) as an example. Addressing the Western concept of "landscape," Geyer points to the fact that visualization is and has always been a sophisticated ideological device, revealing as much of what stands behind the camera as what stands in front. Chapter 2 of *Spiral Lands* consists of a slide projection with a voiceover lecture in which a lecturing "scholar" or "researcher" critically asks herself what drives the desire for this land and what enables the feeling of a right of passage.

WE WILL ALL BE HELD ACCOUNTABLE. I would have liked to begin this paper with a quotation by [Jimmie Durham] because of his wisdom, and because it would have immediately set the tone of being in the right "camp." I leave the quotation out because one of our most serious troubles in the United States today, whether we are Indian, white, black, or whatever, is a tendency to attempt to escape our reality. We do this by substituting slogans and pronouncements for the more difficult revolutionary praxis of working, looking, thinking/working, looking/thinking. The white left in particular has a tendency to take the words and concepts of revolutionary leaders from around the world, instead of participating in the hammering out of a *true* understanding of what is going on here, and how to use it.[1]

My name is Sonya Atalay, Vine Deloria Jr., Romaine Moreton, N. Scott Momaday, James Clifford, Aby Warburg, Elizabeth Cook-Lynn, Arturo Escobar, Maria Elena Garcia, Hannah Arendt, Leslie A. White, Larry Littlebird, Gillian Rose, Chief Seattle, Fredric Jameson, Barbara Bender, Leslie Marmon Silko, Roland Barthes, Clifford Geertz, Wilma Mankiller, Hayden White, Paul Chaat Smith, Willa Cather, Michel Foucault, Nancy Shoemaker, and Walter Benjamin, just to name a few. I speak to you as a scientist, anthropologist, ethnographer, archeologist, geographer, historian, journalist, and adventurer, as an artist, researcher, traveler through *known and unknown territories*, as a man and as a woman, but *foremost* I speak to you from the place of knowledge.

I also speak to you from a place of concern. Things are dire in this country. They have been for years. The issues at stake are about justice, about responsibility that nobody really wants to take. Wars have been waged under false premises, authority is kept in the hands of an imperial power. People are disenfranchised. Public funds have been embezzled and revenues from natural resources wander into the pockets of private corporations instead of their rightful destinations. Lands are left behind polluted.

I am not speaking about Iraq, I am speaking about Native American Nations, Tribal Communities, and Pueblos in the United States of America.

It is necessary that, with great urgency, we all speak well and listen well. We—you and I—must remember everything. We must especially remember the things we never knew.[2] No one can look at the sun, that is why we look at pictures. I will show you images, most of which I photographed myself, from a journey taken in the past, and here in the present. There are eighty slides with Native American subjects (plus "Uncle Sam").[3]

The following information was obtained between June 2004 and February 2008 from a group of people I met in the Navajo Nation, the Ute Mountain Ute Reservation, at Hopi, at Zuñi, at Acoma, at St. Idelfonso, at Chaco, on some unpaved roads, under some cottonwood trees. Furthermore, reaching back as far as 1620, I consulted scholars of all kinds, the ones that speak, the ones that remain silent. Some of whom we imagine easily as intellectuals to represent Hiroshima. There is the iconic mushroom cloud, but that is more of a generic graphic symbol than a photograph (who can tell the difference between the Hiroshima mushroom and those of Alamogordo and Bikini?). There are no images of mass graves or of fields of corpses, only the ruins of an aftermath—the architectural void as a visual substitute for the pulverization of bodies. As for human traces, the museum built a diorama, illuminated by a scarlet light, representing two children tottering in the ruins, mannequins with strips of burned flesh on their hands and faces. Why stage this theatrical gore? Probably as a substitute for the missing images—those that may have disappeared with the American occupation, those that never existed because there was no one to produce them, or those that are missing because the Bomb left very few human remains to photograph. There are no images of the atomic event, there could be no images of the atomic event. And even if there had been images, would they have been adequate?

The question of the "representability of the unimaginable" links Hiroshima to Auschwitz. Because in spite of the narcissistic systematization of the Nazis' documentation of the camps, there are no images of the gas chambers other than the four famous photographs of the *Sonderkommando* that gave rise to controversy over whether or not they should be exhibited, and that became the subject of George Didi-Huberman's beautiful text *Images in Spite of All*. The absolute ban on photography in the gas chambers (SS included) did not stop anonymous prisoners from miraculously snatching these four blurred images from the Auschwitz hell, leaving us with the only known photographic documents representing the operation of the extermination camps' principal apparatus. The symbolic value of *single* images of the systematic destruction of Europe's Jewish population is at the epicenter of the debate about whether images can represent the unrepresentability of the Holocaust. Single images are necessarily *inadequate*, because they show very little in comparison to the magnitude of the Holocaust. They are necessarily *inaccurate*, because they are imprecise, they cannot be more than *fragmentary*, able to represent only an insignificant reality dwarfed by the "unthinkable" scale of Auschwitz. For this reason, if there cannot be a single, complete *image of all* of the Holocaust, should not *all images* be dismissed? This is how Gérard Wajcman asserts the invisibility of genocide, alongside Claude Lanzmann, who goes as far as saying: "If I had found an existing film ... made by an SS that showed how three thousand Jews, men, women, children, died together in a gas chamber at crematorium II at Auschwitz, if I had found that, not only would I not have shown it, but I would have destroyed it. I am unable to say why. It is obvious."[3]

and others we don't. I consulted with the people of reason, as they were called, always thinking, moving their feet to their restless minds, a habit perceived by many as very unpleasant. I met those people in person or in books, in the library or on the internet, or sitting at my desk as myself. Further information was obtained during my work in the field. In the deserts, the mountain ranges, the open skies—the words I encountered spoke quietly about this land, and out loud right into my face, into my mind. I want to share the colors of what I saw, and also the colors of the unseen, of the traces along the horizons of my mind and the untraceable, the delineations of the documents and the dust I found on the library stacks. I want to talk about the light in this auditorium, the light from your eyes glancing at me. I am here to talk about an experience that we all share even though it is singular to my being. I am here to talk about land. I am here to talk about history, I am here to talk about knowledge. Mine and not mine, yours, ours, and others'.

Every summer when school is out, a veritable stream of immigrants heads southwest into Indian Country. Indeed, the Oregon Trail was never as populated as are Route 66 and Highway 18 in the summertime. From every nook and cranny in the East they emerge, as if responding to some primeval fertility rite, and flock to the reservation. They are the artists, the ethnographers. The anthropologists, the most prominent members of the scholarly community, embark on their summer adventure, all brands of this species that infests the land of the free, the homes of the brave …[4]

What can possibly happen
and *what* actually did happen?
What can be *known* and what can
be *imagined*?
What can the *historian* legitimately assert
as a truth and
what might the *poet* entertain as thought?[5]

Out in the field we are followed by a large black bird. Neither crow nor raven but a body the size of a hawk. Its long beak looks strong and intimidating. After a while of circling it decides to settle on a tree nearby, leafless in this season. I stop to look. It turns its head. I take my camera and snap a picture. I move slowly, nearly motionless, a little closer. The bird lifts its wing to prune its feathers. I raise my camera again, click, its head turns. I am close now, so close that I can see the sunlight reflected in its black eyes. Its gaze stays on me now. I move closer yet again, for yet another picture. The bird lifts but settles, shifting its body. I expect it to take off any minute but it remains. I am only a few feet away when I feel the breath of this creature. It settles its wings and I feel their power moving the air. I hesitate, confused by the bird's persistence. I sit down, resting my camera on my things, gazing at the view we both share. Moments pass, then I get up and walk away. When I turn my head I see the bird lift off into the sky with ease.

On the screen photographs repeating and with them, repeating their gaze. *We see* how they saw, skimming surface; surveying land. We are *invoked*—an active viewer equated with culture and *it*—a passive land equated with nature. The photograph's static viewpoint is a scientific procedure to help, not a particular aspect of the way things are.[6] Self-consciously, seriously partial.[7] One could say that this gaze and the photograph as its witness are controlling us and nature.[8] One could say that the photograph as its witness enacts within this discipline a sophisticated, systematic erasure.[9]

If this is your land, where is your story?[10] In this place, I am doubtless not the only one who speaks in order to have no face.[11] I "chart new territories," I "break new ground," I "open up new horizons," I have "viewpoints," "overviews," "landmarks," "vantage points," and "ways of looking." I "chart" and I "explore," "come up against intellectual barriers," and operate on "frontiers."[12]

Pick out the tall gaunt white man wearing Bermuda shorts, a World War II Air Force flying jacket, an Australian bush hat, and tennis shoes. He is what we call an Anthropologist, an ethnographer who will inevitably have a thin,

Whereas Lanzmann believes no image is capable of telling the story of the *Shoah*, Jean-Luc Godard, in *Histoire(s) du cinéma*, works on a montage of existing images to proclaim that all images, since 1945, speak of nothing else. He even attributes a redemptive power to them when he writes that "even scratched to death / a simple rectangle / of thirty-five / millimeters / saves the honor / of all of reality."[4] In this polarity which has grown into a polemic, the opposition between iconoclasts and iconophiles interests me mostly for the avenues it opens to artists confronting this question about the poverty of images—between those who, like Lanzmann, abandon images to dedicate themselves to words and testimony, and those who, like Godard, connect and confront them, incessantly reinventing them in light of history. A third way should be added to this dialectic, Watkins's path: confronted with the incomplete nature of images, let us create images! Let us create a surplus of images, a barrage of images, an overdose of images. And using the mock documentary format, let us elevate these images to the status of a near-document.

In the sensitive realm of great human tragedies, fabricating images is obviously a hazardous undertaking ... There is always the danger of cinematic mediocrity and well-meaning dullness. Spielberg's Auschwitz reenactment, *Schindler's List*, is problematic for its use of black and white in an ordinary fiction film to create a false archive intended to "elevate" an entertainment project. With *Life is Beautiful*, Roberto Benigni opted for a depiction of tragedy that bordered on slapstick. While a bit lighthearted for some people's taste, his film nevertheless complies with the strategy of Imre Kertész (who defended it), and with the essence of Israeli theatre that deals with the subject. The question is not so much a matter of "false images," but rather the choice of pure theatricality as the only possible way of evoking the Holocaust.

So the question is where to place Watkins's great factographic work. His task as a filmmaker (I almost want to call it a mission since there is something intensely committed about his working method) entails two objectives: re-visualizing historical episodes threatened by a dominant revisionism in order to reclaim them (*Culloden*, *La Commune*), and creating, out of political urgency, scenarios that are frightening in their realism (*The War Game*, *Punishment Park*). The two genres share a preventative determination. The historical epics are filmed using the same device: film crews inside the film, media as both author and subject. This anachronism (in the case of *Culloden* and *La Commune*) makes it possible to develop a critical view of how the mass media writes history, and highlights the contemporary nature of the political issues underpinning centuries-old events.

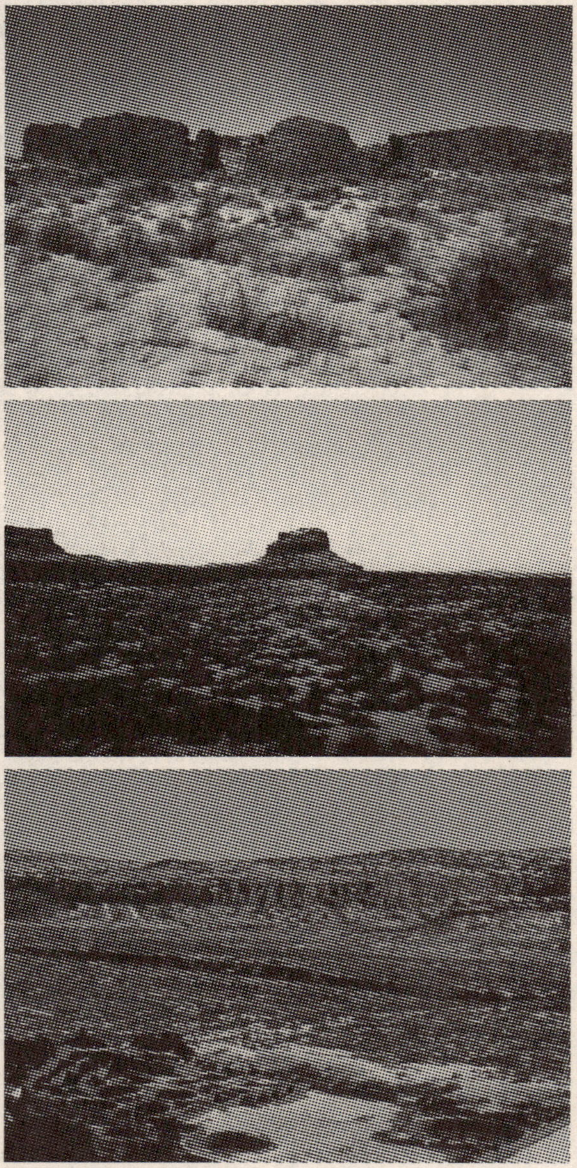

Fig. 1-3 Andrea Geyer, *Spiral Lands / Chapter 2*, 2008, installation in an educational setting with slide projection, eighty color and black-and-white slides, voice-over, brochure with footnotes, 50 min. Courtesy of Galerie Thomas Zander, Cologne.

sexy wife with stringy hair, an IQ of 191, and a vocabulary in which even the prepositions have eleven syllables.[13]

In the maelstrom of signification it can be hard to be the one who remains silent.

The winter light is cold. And much more angled than anticipated. These temperatures make the cameras unpredictable and slow. The manual works, the automatic stutters. I keep film and batteries in the inside pockets of my coat for warmth. More than once, sites relevant for us to document are invisible due to the sunlight falling directly into my lens. One site I visit three times to take a picture. Once, the shadow of the cliffs veils it in indistinguishable light, then later, the sun traveling through its midday arc is right in front of me, taking hold of the entire frame with its glare. When I return a third time in the afternoon, the shadows have grown to unexpected length and the sky is turning into its daily drama of red, blue, and purple. I give up, resigning myself and my apparatus to the forces of the sun. No photograph taken.

In *this country*, on *this land*, this task of controlling the representation of the past through history is linked to the large self-determination movement of the European-American mind, and its substance is the determination of cultural survival. One could say that history is and becomes an ordering principle that enables thought to operate upon the entities of our world.[14]

Dawn and dusk bring unsettling transitions of light. Related yet different, the colors of the sky revolve around the presence of the sun, which seems to travel the distance between the horizon line and its daytime elevation above with remarkable speed, moving colors in its journey. Orange, purple, green, yellow, blue. Space folds and unfolds along these shifts of light, my eyes tumbling, shifting in a similar motion. Each day at this time, I seem to halt my work for the interval, body motionless, still, holding on to the sphere of the inevitable transition. Like listening to the words of a favored lecture, my desire takes in breath to hold each word, each moment indefinitely.

The contemplation of the sky is the grace and curse of humanity.[15]

None of us lives apart from the land entirely; such an isolation is unimaginable. If we are to realize and maintain our humanity, we must come to a moral comprehension of earth and air as it is perceived in the long turn of seasons and of years.[16] The histories we write from this place need to be patient with the interruptions of the everyday in this land. When these histories are

But the task is even more urgent in his pure fiction films; *The War Game* was released only three years after the Cuban Missile Crisis, which brought humanity to the brink of Armageddon, and the excesses in *Punishment Park* no longer seem all that fictional in the era of Guantanamo, waterboarding, and weekly drone strikes.

For Maurice Blanchot, "There is a limit beyond which practicing an art, whatever it is, becomes an insult against misfortune." Watkins approaches the problem from the opposite angle: it would be an insult to misfortune not to practice art to push back its limits. Does talk of "the unspeakable" in relation to the horror of genocide not lead to what Giorgio Agamben describes as a "mystical adoration" that runs the risk of tending towards silence?[5] Silence is what Watkins cannot tolerate, so he works on weaving testimony-documents into image-documents: out of the mental pictures that arise from words and historical data, he fabricates images. He has faith in their ability to be effective as long as they are not allowed to sink to the neutralizing level of a trivializing cliché-image, where Spielberg and Benigni have gone astray. This is done in two ways: through volume (repetition, excess, and explicitness) and proximity (he brings them home, to Kent, instead of setting them in distant, exotic Japan). The political point is to brutally drag the subject into our living rooms—*Bringing the War Home*, as Martha Rosler would soon advocate—by modernizing the shock tactics Orson Welles used in the radio drama *The War of the Worlds*.

The question of the fabrication, falsification, and decontextualization of documents leads to two essential questions: What makes an image? And what does an image make? For Watkins, images have an alarmist role (in the positive sense of the word), so he develops the document's fictional territory and mines its preventative resources. In this sense, his images are similar to the mental images generated by the documents in the Hiroshima memorial, those which gave me a glimpse of how the war might have ended without thousands of civilian victims of the atomic bombardments, or enabled me to visualize the harrowing hazard that spared Kokura and doomed Nagasaki. And perhaps this is what explains the more levelheaded reaction of the Japanese guest at our Sunday film club. Figuratively, she had already been to that place of dreadful possibles. Being more familiar with the matter, she was in a better position to understand Watkins's project for what it is, the *ante-memorial* of an imminent but avoidable cataclysm.

Juxtaposing fictions that have documentary tendencies with documents that open fictional spaces. Setting up a dialogue between them in a single exhibition. Such is the curatorial ambition of an *Ante-Memorials* show.

told, they only end to begin again. We will soon recognize that in this histroiography, the narrative closure is always already postponed.

It is achievements of our ancestors that make us accountable for how we move in the world today.[17] Time thrusts us forward from behind, blows us out from the narrow funnel of the present into the future.[18] I have talked to you about land. I have talked to you about history. I have talked to you about knowledge. Mine and not mine, yours, ours, and others'. It all starts again, right here, with me speaking and you listening. You will forget and you will remember. Do not ask who I am, and do not ask me to remain the same either: leave it to our bureaucrats and our police to see that our papers are in order and at least spare us their morality when we write, when we think, and when we speak.[19]

1 Jimmie Durham, "American Indian Culture," in *A Certain Lack of Coherence* (London: Kala Press, 1993), 1.

2 Jimmie Durham, "A Certain Lack of Coherence," ibid., 147.

3 Aby Warburg, *Images from the Pueblo Region of the Pueblo Indians of North America* (Ithaca: Cornell University Press, 1995), 1.

4 Vine Deloria, Jr., "Anthropologists and Other Friends," in *Custer Died For Your Sins: An Indian Manifesto* (London: Collier-Macmillian Limited, 1971), 78.

5 Aristotle, *Poetics*.

6 Roman Jakobson, *On Language* (Cambridge, MA: Harvard University Press,1990), 91.

7 James Clifford, "Introduction: Partial Truths," in *Writing Culture: The Poetics and Politics of Ethnography* (Berkley and Los Angeles: University of California Press, 1986), 7.

8 Barbara Bender, "Subverting the Western Gaze: Mapping Alternative Worlds," in *Archaeology and Anthropology of Landscapes*, eds. Peter J. Ucko and Robert Layton (New York: Routledge, 1999).

9 Gillian Rose, "Looking at Landscape: The Uneasy Pleasures of Power," in *Feminism & Geography* (Minneapolis: Minnesota Press, 1993), 87.

10 Romaine Moreton, thesis in *The Right to Dream* (Sydney: University of Western Sydney, 2006).

11 Michel Foucault, *The Archeology of Knowledge* (New York: Routledge, 1972), Introduction.

12 Anne Salmond, "Theoretical Landscapes: On Cross-Cultural Conceptions of Knowledge," in *Semantic Anthropology*, ed. D. Parkin (London: Academic Press, 1992), 65–87.

13 Vine Deloria, Jr., "Anthropologists and Other Friends," 79.

14 Michel Foucault, *The Order of Things: An Archeology of Human Sciences* (New York: Vintage, 1994), xvii.

15 Aby Warburg, *Images from the Pueblo Region of the Pueblo Indians of North America*, 1.

16 N. Scott Momaday, voice-over for *Remembered Earth: New Mexico's High Desert,* PBS production, 2006.

17 Paul Chaat Smith, wall text at the National Museum of the American Indian, Washington, DC.

18 Susan Sontag, "Introduction," in Walter Benjamin, *One-Way Street and Other Writings* (London: Verso, 1985), 13.

19 Michel Foucaul, *The Archeology of Knowledge*, Introduction.

George Didi-Huberman expresses the importance of *images in spite of all* by stressing that "in each testimonial production, in each act of memory, language and image are absolutely bound to one another, never ceasing to exchange their reciprocal lacunae. An image often appears where a word seems to fail; a word often appears where the imagination seems to fail."[6] In the same way, *Ante-Memorials* is an exhibition that examines artistic practices that weld together document and fiction, each compensating for the other's shortcomings. And given that the Watkins / Hiroshima museum dialectic—the testimonial production of the *would have / will have been*—revolves around the essential idea of *ante-memorials*, it is crucial that another piece be introduced into the project: *COMMEMOR* (*Commission Mixte d'Échange de Monuments aux Morts* [*Joint Commission for the Exchange of Monuments to the Dead*]) (1970), in which Robert Filliou orchestrated, with the powerful lightness that makes him indispensable in this case, a fictional exchange of monuments to the dead between cities in Holland, Germany, and Belgium, in place of real wars. *COMMEMOR* as a sculptural response to Watkins's cinematic gesture.

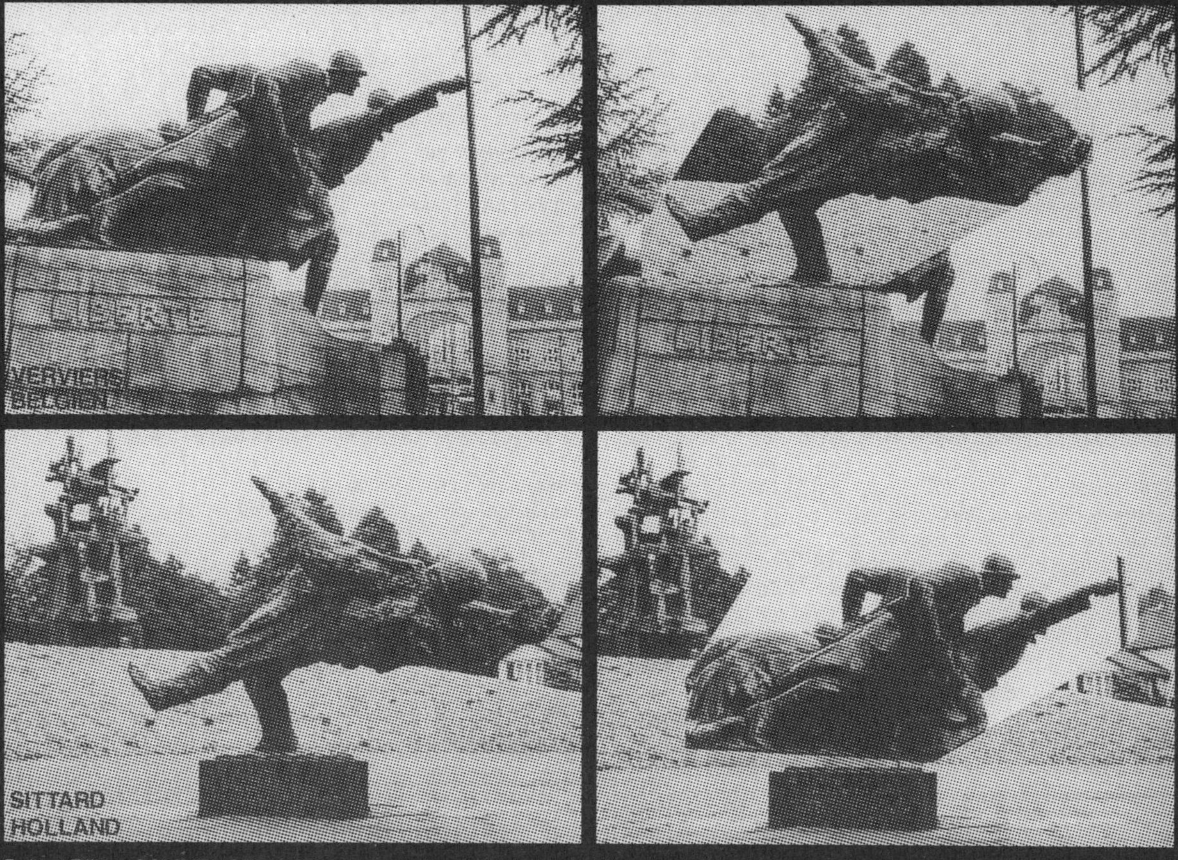

Robert Filliou, *COMMEMOR*, 1970/2003, twelve black-and-white photographs mounted on plates, each 70 × 100 cm.

TAIPEI NOTES: 2011.11.19–2011.11.28

Pak Sheung Chuen

2011.11.19
Ask your wife to take a photograph of you every evening while you sleep.

2011.11.19
The radio is playing songs of the dead.

2011.11.19
Record the sounds of your life. Continually play the sounds in an empty house when you die.

2011.11.19
Replace every word with peoples' names.

2011.11.19
Close your eyes and look at the light in front of you. Once at the top of the mountain and once at the foot of the mountain.

2011.11.19
Find someone similar to you on the street and frankly introduce yourself.

2011.11.19
Look at a cloud above the clouds while on a cloud.

2011.11.19
Try to find an acquaintance on the airplane.

2011.11.19
Fly a paper plane on an airplane from tail to nose.

2011.11.19
When you are sitting on the airplane, she is sitting on the ground looking at the sky.

2011.11.19
Let the monks play an electronic video game. The soldiers don't open fire, but only hide from enemies on the battlefield until they die.

2011.11.19
As soon as I step into Taiwan, my mind automatically switches to Chinese.

2011.11.19
Where does the "sound" of the "voice" speaking in our hearts come from? / The voice in our hearts and the sound emitted from our mouths are two kinds of texture. The sounds from the mouth are produced by vibrations in the throat. The "voice" in our hearts should be the sound's memory of what you would like to say out loud.

2011.11.19
Use your mouth to say a word and allow your heart to reply. Practice communicating with yourself.

2011.11.19
Use a paper towel to lock water inside a square.

2011.11.19
Pour the maximum amount of water on a table.

2011.11.19
Make a glass bottle similar to your own body. Fill it with water and then drink the water into your body.

2011.11.19
Your body temperature on the subway window slowly penetrates other peoples' faces.

2011.11.19
A young girl installs a camera lens on the ceiling of her room and broadcasts her life on the internet around the clock. Allow voyeuristic living to become a habit.

2011.11.19
Every evening randomly pour coins from your purse onto the table and only leave out the coins with Chiang Kai-Shek's head facing upward. Create an exhibition after one year.

2011.11.20
Put your glass cup next to your friend's glass cup. Pour water into her leftover water and slowly drink it.

2011.11.20
Look at the roundness of the water's surface, slowly becoming one with the roundness of the cup's top.

2011.11.20
Keep water in your mouth. The water is the shape of your mouth.

2011.11.20
A pen's ink cartridge is a static "one" word. All written words consist of this "one" word.

2011.11.20
Use a pen to write the longest "one" word.

2011.11.20
One pen draws only a straight line; another pen draws only a horizontal line.

2011.11.20
A bitten-off piece of fingernail falls to the ground and merges into a circle with other peoples' fingernails.

2011.11.20
A hair fell onto the ground and overlapped with other peoples' hair at a point.

2011.11.20
Take a photograph of your back each day.

2011.11.20
Photograph a stone, print out the photo, and then take a photograph of the stone in the photo. Are you taking a photograph of a stone or a photo?

2011.11.20
Use a camera to photograph yourself directly and yourself in the mirror, then place the two photographs together.

2011.11.20
You see two different scenes when you watch TV, one is the image coming from the TV and the other is the image reflected on the surface of the TV.

2011.11.20
You see yourself in the TV screen when it suddenly goes black.

2011.11.20
Look for the time difference between you and your reflection in the mirror.

2011.11.20
On Christmas require a TV station to broadcast snowflakes on the TV in the house of a person who lives on the tallest mountain in Iceland.

2011.11.20
Install the light switches for the room in the hall and install the hall's light switches in the room.

Brussels, October 18 –

While out for a walk, I end up visiting Jan Mot Gallery, where the opening of Deimantas Narkevicius's exhibition is underway with a screening of his film *The Dud Effect*. It's a stroke of luck; I'm just about to finish selecting works for *Ante-Memorials* and I stumble upon this film, which is partly inspired by, or you might say it engages in a dialog with, Watkins's *The War Game*. Narkevicius presents the flipside of the fictional events of Kent in 1965: the launch of R-14 nuclear missiles from a Soviet base in Lithuania in the 1970s.

The Dud Effect is the inverse of *The War Game* from a narrative standpoint (depicting the launch instead of the impact) but also in terms of style: every effort is made to render the action ordinary, bureaucratic, methodical. No emotion in the shots, only a clinical description of an administrative routine. Narkevicius does not deal with the decision to launch the missiles, so moral questions are not explicitly raised, and their impact is suggested only in what we are capable of imagining in a distant off-screen space. Most of the film shows an anonymous officer on the telephone reciting orders of a technical nature to anonymous listeners ("position 101," "position 105"). It is documentary (being based on real procedures and enacted by a real former Red Army officer) more than cinematic (there is no red button, no electronic console, just a voice on the telephone and an impassive man). At the moment of the launch, the officer's face is simply overexposed by the light of the reactors outside the frame. The aftermath is suggested by shots of surrounding nature, the sound of strong wind, and a series of long takes of current Soviet-era nuclear installations in an advanced state of decay (empty silos, collapsed warehouses). Is it a postapocalyptic world, or simply the spoils of time, the reassuring evidence of the end of the Soviet empire? And if it's the second hypothesis, why are we not comforted by these images of a past that never was?

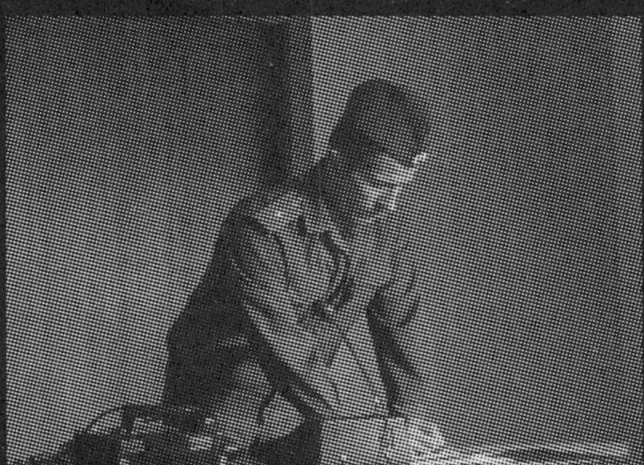

Deimantas Narkevičius, *The Dud Effect*, 2008, 16mm film transferred to HD video, color, sound, 15 min 40 sec.

To the Hiroshima museum's *would have been*, to Watkins's *will have been*, and to Filliou's simple conditional, we must therefore add Narkevicius's was not. In this conjugation of works, among other constants linked to their "memorial" value, it is essentially a question of time and truth, or of how time puts the notion of truth in crisis.

2011.11.20
Put a radio on the city's tallest peak and broadcast the highest-frequency sounds.

2011.11.20
Put a microphone on the moon and broadcast the sounds of the moon on the internet around the clock.

2011.11.20
Cangjie input method is a Taiwanese political education tool.

2011.11.20
Go to Taiwan to see a Taiwanese movie and enter Taiwan in the Taiwanese movie.

2011.11.20
Make a book about skin and precisely photograph every part of skin on a young girl's body. Print the photographs on the color pages of the book.

2011.11.20
Bring a painting on a trip and hang it on the wall to look at, regardless of where you live.

2011.11.20
Photograph the desktop where you work and put it on the desktop of your computer.

2011.11.20
Use a light bulb to create a light sculpture. Put in a light bulb and the work will appear regardless of where you go.

2011.11.20
There is an empty castle on top of a mountain, and you can control the lights from a switch in another mountain.

2011.11.20
Launch a satellite into the sky above India, pretending it is a bright star.

2011.11.20
Use a computer's screen saver to create a work of art. The work appears when nobody is using the computer.

2011.11.20
The audience cannot be part of the artist's day.

2011.11.20
A day inside the artist's mind has no audience.

2011.11.20
Place a large collection of gathered clocks in an entirely black room. There is no time in the darkness.

2011.11.20
Two people stand together: one person expresses all of his thoughts out loud, and the other only follows everything that the thoughtful person does.

2011.11.20
People who like to talk and people who don't like to talk are friends.

2011.11.20
When singing from the bottom of one's heart, stop and listen attentively until one is finished singing.

2011.11.20
Pay attention to the emptiness between thoughts.

2011.11.20
From the bottom of your heart, take note of the silence between sentences.

2011.11.20
Think of the greatest number of people in a lifetime.

2011.11.20
Make various noises with your body without using your mouth.

2011.11.20
Use your mouth to imitate the sounds your body makes.

2011.11.20
Steal a seed from prison and plant the seed in a houseplant until it blossoms.

2011.11.20
Grow weeds from prison in a pot, mark the source of the weeds, and sell them at the prison's open day.

2011.11.20
Two people on an island walk to the farthest place.

2011.11.20
Go to one of the largest countries and engage in activities in the smallest space.

2011.11.20
Look at the rectangular window frame, photograph, and TV with round eyes.

2011.11.20
Watch the round moon with round eyes.

2011.11.20
The time on the clock face moves in a circular direction.

2011.11.20
Look up the most ancient pronunciation, meaning, and writing of your name while repeatedly reading aloud, thinking, and writing.

2011.11.20
Record an elderly person's oldest memory.

2011.11.20
The truck's body is a mirror when it passes on the street.

2011.11.20
Road Movie: A projector plays a movie on trucks lining the side street. Watch the movie moving over the side street / the movie moves around on the side street.

2011.11.20
Collect all of the signs with the word "God" and distribute them to different people to worship at home.

2011.11.20
Produce Q version statues according to the appearance of the temple's statues and establish a Q version temple that allows young people to worship.

2011.11.20
A naked Buddha statue is placed inside a temple, the subject of sacrifice and worship.

2011.11.20
Cut out a "black" word from of a piece of black paper. There is no longer a "black" word on the black paper, but you can still see a "black" word.

2011.11.20
To use words of light is to use words of shadow.

2011.11.20
The projector casts light on the wall. The projector casts a full screen shadow on the wall, but you can still see a faint light.

2011.11.20
Place an object in front of the projector, it casts a shadow on the screen.

2011.11.20
Write down the names of a district's new-born babies and its recently deceased.

2011.11.20
Every room in the hotel is painted a different color.

2011.11.20
Some people can only start to dream when sleeping by your side.

2011.11.20
Write all of your passwords on paper and analyze the details.

2011.11.20
Look for information on a missing Hong Kong person in Hong Kong and accompany him back to where he had been.

These different ways of narrating the facts illustrate the paradox of "future contingents," a philosophical problem continually explored since antiquity, which Gilles Deleuze sums up in this way: "If it is *true* that a naval battle *may* take place tomorrow, how are we to avoid one of the true following consequences: either the impossible proceeds from the possible (since, if the battle takes place, it is no longer possible that it may not take place), or the past is not necessarily true (since the battle could not have taken place)."[7] Leibniz proposes a solution to this paradox that is very apt for our purposes: the naval battle (like the atomic bombardment) can take place or not take place, but not in the same world, it takes place in two worlds that are not mutually "compossible." By inventing the notion of "incompossibility," he resolves the paradox while bringing a lull in the truth crisis, since it is the incompossible (and not the impossible) that proceeds from the possible. "The past may be true without being necessarily true." Deleuze then goes on to evoke Borges's response to Leibniz (as I am similarly invoking Watkins and Narkevicius): "The straight line as a force of time, as labyrinth of time, is also the line which forks and keeps on forking, passing through *incompossible presents*, returning to *not-necessarily true pasts*."[8]

The documents and works in *Ante-Memorials* converse in this simultaneity. The exhibition is in a sense built around this Deleuzian idea of the "powers of the false" that unseat and substitute for the figure of truth—artistic, creative, or narrative power abandons the status of truth to become a falsifier. The artist becomes a falsifier, but not simply in the name of an artistic subjectivity ("to each his reality"), but from a real need that can only be satisfied by filling the space between story and history.

Curated by Eric Baudelaire. Participating artists: Robert Filliou, Deimantas Narkevičius, Peter Watkins.

1 In a 1965 interview, Dr. Oppenheimer did, however, have this to say about the first nuclear test in the Alamogordo Desert: "We knew the world would not be the same. A few people laughed, a few people cried. Most people were silent. I remembered the line from the Hindu scripture, the *Bhagavad-Gita*; Vishnu is trying to persuade the Prince that he should do his duty, and to impress him, takes on his multi-armed form and says, 'Now I am become Death, the destroyer of worlds.' I suppose we all thought that, one way or another."

2 Report of the Committee on Political and Social Problems, Manhattan Project "Metallurgical Laboratory," University of Chicago, June 11, 1945, also known as "The Franck Report." Signed by J. Franck, D. Hughes, L. Szilard, T. Hogness, E. Rabinowitch, G. Seaborg, and C. J. Nickson.

3 Quoted in George Didi-Huberman, *Images in Spite of All* (Chicago: University Of Chicago Press), 95.

4 Jean-Luc Godard, *Histoire(s) du cinéma* (Paris: Gallimard-Gaumont, 1998, I), 86.

5 See Giorgio Agamben, *Remnants of Auschwitz: The Witness and the Archive* (Cambridge, MA: MIT Press, 2002).

6 Didi-Huberman, *Images in Spite of All*, 26.

7 Gilles Deleuze, *Cinema 2* (New York: Continuum, 2005), 126.

8 Ibid., 127.

2011.11.20
Sightsee, eat, and drink as you like on the first three days of a six-day trip. By the fourth day, the stroke of life is just like the past three days.

2011.11.20
Bring back a bamboo forest's outermost layer of chopped bamboo, sequentially placing the bamboo forest's perimeter on a restaurant's walls.

2011.11.21
Follow people buying flowers on a trip around the city.

2011.11.21
Follow a person home from the Fine Arts Museum. Stand in the shade when he stands in the sun; stand in the sun when he stands in the shade.

2011.11.21
Fill the seats in a subway car and leave a love seat open for people in need.

2011.11.21
Borrow a painting from the Fine Arts Museum and use the painting to fan museum visitors.

2011.11.21
Sweep together all of the hair on the floor of the Fine Arts Museum and make a wig.

2011.11.21
Use a place as your name. It will be like calling far away every time someone calls for you.

2011.11.21
Install an electronic diagram outside the door of the women's restroom, display the time and type of each stall's usage in real time.

2011.11.21
Think of your friend who is farthest away from you and go nearest to him, but don't disturb him.

2011.11.21
Find all of the photographs in your photo album that are taken with couples and measure the distance between you and your friends.

2011.11.21
Maintain your standing position at the halfway point between two strangers.

2011.11.21
Approach someone wearing the same color as you and listen to the instructions he gives you today.

2011.11.21
I see my figure standing outside the door in the women's restroom mirror.

2011.11.21
You have always seen the moon as being bigger than the sun.

2011.11.21
An address looks like a poem.

2011.11.21
Write the relevant vocabulary word on everything you see in an elementary school.

2011.11.21
Use words to express the visual world.

2011.11.22
Replicate a celebrated people's foreign language with a ringtone.

2011.11.22
Listen to your tiniest breath.

2011.11.22
Select a series of works from the collection of the Fine Arts Museum that is only seen in winter.

2011.11.22
Use your finger to touch yourself in a photo.

2011.11.22
Decide the age at which you will die and prepare for death once half of your life has passed.

2011.11.22
Only speak between other people's two sentences.

2011.11.22
Use your left eye to look at your right eye: close your right eye and use your left eye to look in the mirror at your closed right eye, open your right eye.

2011.11.22
Maintain two eyes while making different movements.

2011.11.22
The train is exactly the length of a cave, the train stopped motionless in the mountains.

2011.11.22
Put stone from the Natural History Museum in the History Museum.

2011.11.22
Make a hole with your hand and invite strangers to insert their fingers.

2011.11.22
Read a book about trains on the train.

2011.11.22
Set a book about fire on fire and listen to the sound of the flame.

2011.11.22
Go to the Shihlin Night Market to listen to the voices of Hong Kong people.

2011.11.22
Residents living on the top floor and ground floor of the building exchange potted plants.

2011.11.22
Continuously photograph twenty-four hours on the clock and continually repeat at home, using images in place of time.

2011.11.23
Use your left hand to imitate the movements of your right hand.

2011.11.23
Collect sweaty clothes from famous people and create a sweat museum.

2011.11.23
Use your nose to smell things in the museum.

2011.11.23
The artist is creating in a creative way.

2011.11.23
Find someone who has not used a camera and take a photograph of him or her.

2011.11.23
A tree stores rain, it is still raining after a downpour.

2011.11.23
Running leads to thoughts of love.

2011.11.24
Sleeping people rarely dream about themselves in their sleep.

2011.11.24
Collect writers' used pens and don't write a word.

2011.11.24
Go to an old movie theater to watch an old movie.

2011.11.24
When watching a movie, one's eyes constantly look at the lights turned off on the ceiling of the movie theater.

2011.11.24
Watch an old TV playing an old movie in a movie.

2011.11.24
Use a big TV to play the picture on a small TV.

2011.11.24
I like to walk home on the darkest road.

2011.11.24
Don't focus on photographing a cloud, like a cloud.

SECRET ROOM—LANDSCAPE—POWER: WAKAMATSU FILMS AND THE LIBERATION OF SEX

Masao Matsuda

Masao Matsuda is a film theorist and activist. He is closely associated with Masao Adachi and other activist filmmakers of the "red bus," who collaborated on films such as *A.K.A. Serial Killer* (*Ryakushō: Renzoku Shasatsuma*, 1969) and *Red Army / PFLP: Declaration of World War* (*Sekigun-P.F.L.P: Sekai Senō Sengen*, 1971). He has published widely on *fūkei-ron*, or landscape theory, and the translation below brings a key text of Matsuda's writing on *fūkei-ron* to English-language readers for the first time. This text is a chapter from Matsuda's book *Bara to mumeisha: Matsuda Masao eiga ronshū* (薔薇と無名者 松田政男映画論集). The chapter is titled "secret room—landscape—power" [*misshitsu—fūkei—kenryoku*], and these three concepts are instrumental to the chapter, as well as to Matsuda's *fūkei-ron* as a whole. The chapter explains the intimate relationship among these three concepts through the interface of the "liberation of sex" [*sei no kaihō*] in films by Koji Wakamatsu and others at Wakamatsu Productions. "Secret room," or *misshitsu* (密室), is a Japanese term that can mean several things: not just a secret room or chamber, but also a closed room, or a room locked from the inside that cannot be entered. The term is often used in the phrase *misshitsu satsujin* (密室殺人), or "murder in a locked room." The term usually describes a setting such as a locked room, but also implies a kind of physical closeness or proximity of human bodies. For the purpose of this translation, I have translated *misshitsu* as "secret room," but the nuances of the term are perhaps lost through the translation. Interestingly, one of the ways to refer to the vagina in a poetic sense is *mistutubo* (密壷), meaning "secret vase." Although there are no references to this word in the text, Matsuda's brief mention of a psychoanalytic schema, as well as the whole chapter's grounding of its theoretical ideas in films by Wakamatsu that focus on sexual narratives, connect the *misshitsu* (密室) to other sexual terms, such as *mistutubo* (密壷). Other publications by Matsuda include *Teroru no kairo* (Tokyo: San'ichi Shobō, 1969), *Fūkei no shimetsu* (Tokyo: Tabata Shoten, 1971), and *Fukanōsei no media* (Tokyo: Tabata Shoten, 1973). For more on Matsuda and documentaries from the 1960s, see Markus Nornes, *Forest of Pressure: Ogawa Shinsuke and Postwar Japanese Documentary* (Minneapolis: University of Minnesota Press, 2007).
—Yuki Nakayama

One man, one woman, one bed—I suddenly recall this definition, from a female critic, of the minimum requirements of the so-called "pink films" that, along with Yakuza films, aim at the lowest level of Japanese audiences. In her "Saturday Notebook" column in the *Asahi Newspaper* (evening edition of February 13, 1969), this critic reported that "according to the National Tax Agency's survey ... this year, the total number of Japanese filmgoers will finally reach the milestone of three million." However, as "notebook girl"[1] says, this is a sharp decline from the golden age,[2] when eleven million people went to see films. Is this level of attendance something that can be restored simply by "rethinking industry configurations"?

Notebook girl's perception of the present state of the Japanese film industry—"first-run theaters are empty, but the second-run theaters [*meigaza*] and art theaters are full"—may be wrong. I often encounter situations where, on the screen, one man and one woman are on a bed, tangling, entangling, moaning, as usual—in other words, a routinized love scene is taking place—but if you look around, no one stirs in the dark space filled with glistening masculine desire. Society's sensible circles would look away from the gaudy posters and signs for these kinds of movies, but audiences are being sucked

2011.11.24.
The collection is not focused on family photos.

2011.11.24
Collect photos of clouds, cut half of a cloud, look for the other half.

2011.11.24
Find the oldest photo of a cloud in history and render it as a painting.

2011.11.24
Clouds appeared in a worldwide collection of photo albums from 1977.

2011.11.24
The naked body is a coat.

2011.11.24
Walk to the tallest peak from the island's farthest shore.

2011.11.24
Silently walk around the boundary of the island.

2011.11.25
Place the cross above the church on the worshippers inside the church.

2011.11.25
In a room without windows it is nighttime during the day and daytime during the night.

2011.11.25
A line is painted down the middle of a room without windows. Life on the left is daytime and life on the right is night.

2011.11.25
Go to a restaurant frequented by famous people. There are opportunities and shared dishes with famous people.

2011.11.25
Live in the presidential suite. It has opportunities and the president's wife in the same bed.

2011.11.25
Two street lights, together as one.

2011.11.25
Write the artist's preferred times for starting and finishing work.

2011.11.25
Realize your nighttime dreams during the day.

2011.11.26
Devise all of the things that should be done and write them on a white piece of paper, but don't do them.

2011.11.26
Remove a piece of brick from the government headquarters and throw it at the government.

2011.11.26
Write a diary entry for the day before yesterday.

2011.11.26
Look at your back in old photographs.

2011.11.26
Cut a triangle out of the upper-right corner of a photograph you like and paste this small triangle on the corner of different everyday objects

2011.11.26
First enter a big house where nobody lives and then continue shouting.

2011.11.26
Please do not look to artists to solve the problem!

2011.11.26
Link the tallest points of all of the seaside buildings, it's a mountain.

2011.11.27
Firmly fix your body under the right corner of her room, close to her.

2011.11.27
Add up the numbers in your dreams.

2011.11.27
Look at a lamp. Close your eyes and watch the light from the lamp disappear in your eyes.

2011.11.27
Look at a white square picture frame and allow the frame to reflect the largest square on the surface of your black pupil.

2011.11.27
Text is political.

2011.11.27
Watch a person hitting a tree at night.

2011.11.27
A potted plant was moved from outside the Fine Arts Museum and displayed inside the Fine Arts Museum.

2011.11.27
Create an exhibition in the storage rooms at the Fine Arts Museum.

2011.11.27
Fold a bill inside your wallet every time you are hungry. Count the bills once a week and donate the total amount to starving people.

2011.11.27
Paint a woman's fetus and draw a map of the patterns.

2011.11.28
Watch twenty-four parts of movies from different countries for twenty-four hours.

2011.11.28
See the fingerprints on ancient pottery.

2011.11.28
The person you want to meet in the movie looks positively at you.

2011.11.28
Buy a puzzle of a world map and only put together the ocean.

2011.11.28
Within one day call all of your friends living around the world and wake them up just as the sun rises.

2011.11.28
Create a "not" work of art.

2011.11.28
Ask a group of painters to clean the hallway of an old estate. Ask a group of sculptors to cook dinner in the kitchen.

2011.11.28
Draw out a man's time on a timetable.

2011.11.28
Divide all songs into four seasons and appreciate the various climates.

into pink films, which show at first-run theaters. Pink films are now called the "sixth system," since they have grown to penetrate the five-studio structure of the Japanese film industry.[3]

Perhaps people find in pink films a giant excretory pore of sex that must be liberated. In fact, Koji Wakamatsu,[4] called a master of the pink film (not in a ridiculing manner) and overwhelmingly endorsed by young student audiences, stated the following at a roundtable discussion:

> For the youth of today, sleeping with a woman is the most difficult thing. They say sex is unrestricted, but it's quite difficult to even earn five thousand yen to one million yen. For example, for the present college student and preparatory school student [*yobikō-sei*],[5] to sleep with a woman paying one million yen … I realized after being told by a student that, in short, in Koji Wakamatsu's films, sex is liberated, but in preparatory school students are up till 4 a.m. studying and masturbating while listening to a female announcer on the radio. Nothing is as painful as this. I was told, "Your films are wrong."

Again, this is a blunt statement that would raise the eyebrows of society's sensible circles, but it cannot be helped because it is a quote from "The Sex—Desire—Violence of Japanese People," a roundtable discussion that was featured on the cover of the most recent issue of *Eiga Geijutsu*[6] [January 1970 issue]. Is Wakamatsu's opinion of young spectators true? Perhaps, but with one mistake: the idea that the repressed desire for sex, sublimated by the infinite variations on one man, one woman, and one bed that exist beyond the imaginary screen, is liberated by pink films, is the same as the philistine sensibility that says these types of films cause sexual crime and should be regulated. Therefore, the young spectator is "wrong," not Wakamatsu.

In a later statement, Wakamatsu identified a trait common to young spectators: their "isolated earnestness" [*kakuri sareta majime sa*]. This is certainly apt. There is no genre other than pink films (for this paper, it will serve our purposes to limit ourselves to works by Wakamatsu Productions) that has continually pursued the meaning of this "isolated earnestness" [*kakuri sareta majime sa*]. This is why works by Wakamatsu and his ilk appeal to young audiences. In front of the dim white screen, author and audience breathe together to the same rhythm. They are members of a commune wedded together by "isolated earnestness" [*kakuri sareta majime sa*].

At the beginning of this article, I laid out an outlandish thesis—one man,

DIGITAL PSYCHEDELIA: THE OTOLITH GROUP'S *ANATHEMA*

Mark Fisher

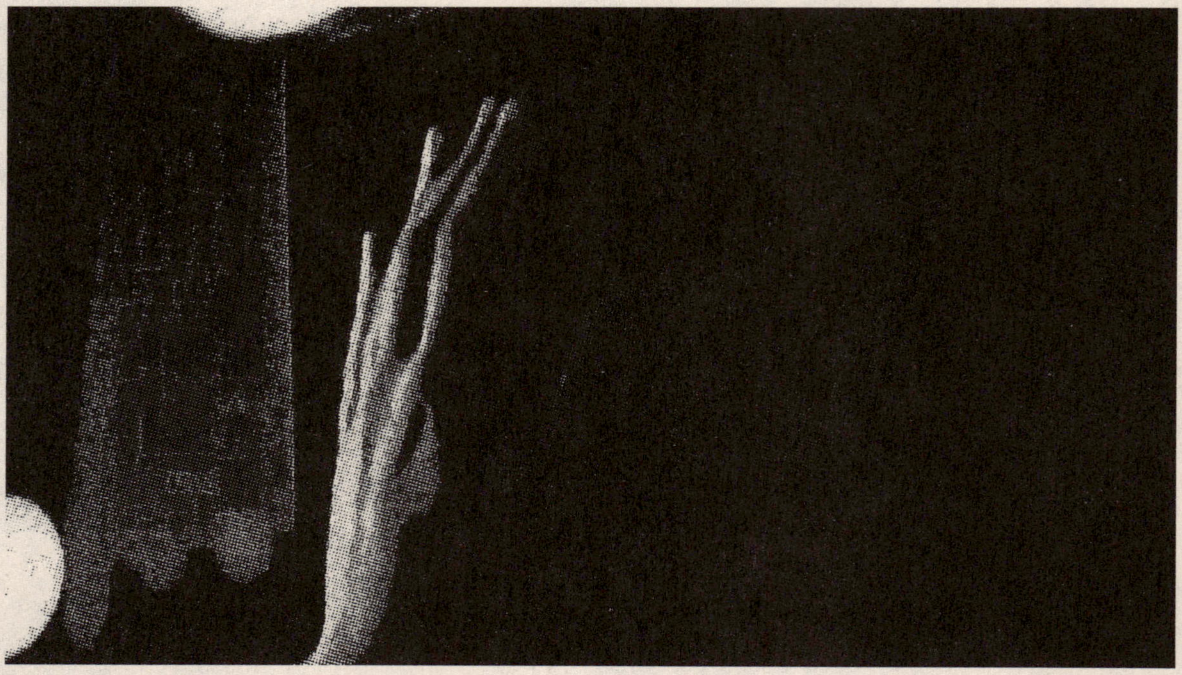

Fig. 1 The Otolith Group, *Anathema* (film still), 2011.

The aim of capitalist sorcery is to induce a kind of stupefaction, a paralysis of agency and imagination that by no means precludes a frenzy of pseudo-activity—a ceaseless treadmill of work and consumption, but also of communication, which is now both work and consumption. The sorcery operates on (what is taken for) reality itself. Its chief function is in fact a procedure of ontological limiting, a reduction of all available realities to those formatted by capitalism: the famous *there is no alternative*.

The Otolith Group's *Anathema* is not satisfied with simply exposing this sorcery at work, in the manner of ideology critique. *Anathema* wants to also constitute a counter-sorcery, a weapon built from the very same materials that capitalist sorcery itself uses. Its delineation of the currently dominant apparatus of capture is certainly acute. *Anathema* apprehends capitalism as (following Philippe Pignarre and Isabelle Stengers) a set of sorcerous practices: a system that operates by processes of beguiling, seduction, and incantation. But who are these sorcerers? They almost certainly do not see themselves as sorcerers. "If capitalism enters into a lineage of systems of sorcery," Pignarre and Stengers write, "it is in a very particular fashion, that of a system of sorcery without sorcerers (thinking of themselves as such)."[1] Naturally, the work of capitalist sorcerers is not limited to the parliamentary arena. It is carried out most effectively by reality managers and capturers of desire: PR consultants, advertisers, and, yes, politicians insofar as they resemble these libidinal technicians.

Anathema concentrates on a specific kind of libidinal capture. We might call it communicative capitalist sorcery. Jodi Dean defines communicative capitalism as a system in which "the standards of a finance- and consumption-one woman, and one bed. Actually, this thesis has one more premise: one room. One room, one man, one woman, one bed. Wakamatsu and others think that the world should be falsified, and they develop it as a drama of the secret room [*misshitsu*]. The audience watches over the progress of this drama, with Wakamatsu as the secret priest of the ritual of the secret room [*misshitsu*].

At this juncture, I would like to remember Norman Mailer's words of warning: "Cars do not sell because you can pick up girls if you have a car. They sell because the car itself is already a girl. The leather seats are made just like skin, the color is lipstick pink or pale-green blonde, the tail lights are like an anus, and the rear is split like the butt cheeks of a female military band master." Precisely. Young contemporary audiences are not flocking to Wakamatsu's films in pursuit of a momentary liberation of sex. Rather, they come because Wakamatsu's films are a secret room, and the audiences place themselves inside it. In this secret room, sex is neither a simple act nor a substitute satisfaction. It simply exists as an object for diligent examination. Through their "isolated earnestness" [*kakuri sareta majime sa*], filmmakers and spectators share a stoicism that is similar to that of an ascetic monk.

Wakamatsu's secret room orientation [*misshitsu shikou*] is deeply colored by classic scandalous films such as *Affairs Within Walls* (*Kabe no Naka no Himegoto*), a film called a "national shame" when it was exhibited at the 1965 Berlin Film Festival, and *The Embryo Hunts In Secret* (*Taiji ga mitsuryô suru toki*), which similarly enraged Western sensibilities [*ryōshiki-ha*] at the 1967 Brussels Experimental Film Festival. In the former, a shameless sex scene that unfolds within the walls of a building in the projects [*danchi*][7] features a middle-aged woman who looks more suited for kitchen work than secrets. This scene suggests that sex in Wakamatsu's films is treated not as an action, but as an object of examination. The latter film, which is based on a screenplay written by the young filmmaker Masao Adachi,[8] has come to occupy a special place in postwar Japanese cinema, undoubtedly because of the pronounced secret room characteristics [*misshitsu-sei*] of the film.

Except for the opening scene, *The Embryo Hunts In Secret* (*Taiji ga mitsuryô suru toki)* faithfully follows the one room, one man, one woman, one bed thesis. Those who have not seen the film may have trouble believing this, but for one hour and ten minutes the film depicts nothing but one room, one man, one woman, and one bed. The man ties up, whips, and humiliates the woman. Viewers who see this as a simple outburst of sadomasochistic lust on the part of the filmmaker reveal the vulgarity of their own sexual consciousness. Think about it—a drama about one room, one

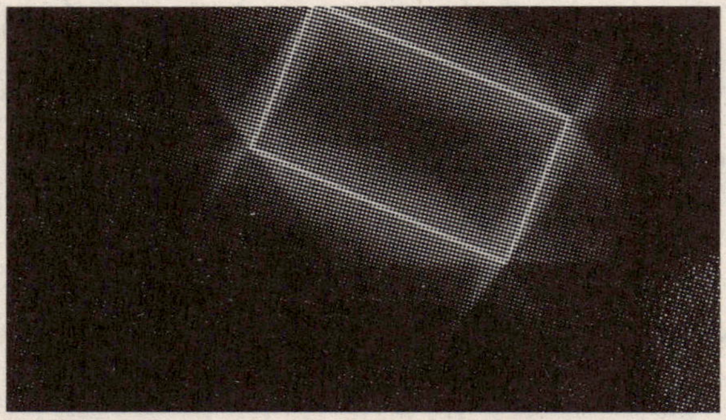

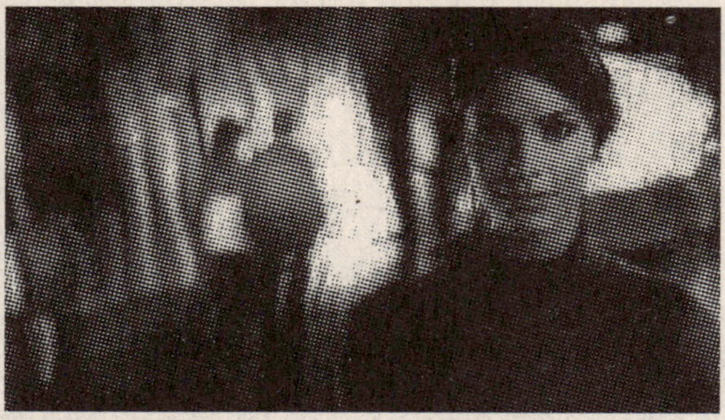

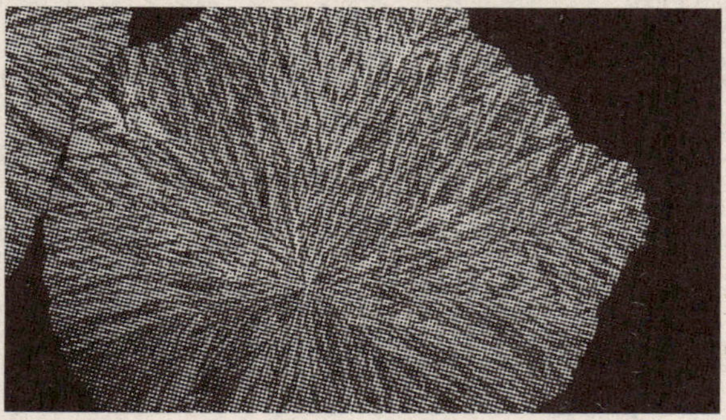

Fig. 3 The Otolith Group, *Anathema* (film still), 2011.
Fig. 2, 4 The Otolith Group, *Anathema*, 2011, HD video, color, sound, 36 min 53 sec. Courtesy of LUX, London

driven entertainment culture produce the setting of democratic governance," and in which messages become "mere contributions to the circulation of images, opinions and information, to the billions of nuggets of information and affect trying to catch and hold attention, to push or sway opinion, taste, and trends in one direction rather than another."[2] The genius of communicative capitalist capture is that it is indifferent to content. It doesn't care how many anticapitalist messages are circulating, only that the circulation of messages continues, incessantly. This is a seemingly perfect system of capture, in which "[c]hanging the system seems to entail strengthening the system."[3] One consequence is that an "invidious and predatory political-economic project that concentrates assets and power in the hands of the very, very rich" is disguised as its opposite: an open, participatory system that offers increased access.[4] By this sleight of hand, structural antagonism is made to disappear, "multiplying ... into myriad minor issues and events."[5] And what is it that drives this circulation if not our desire—to make one more connection, to give one more reply, to keep on clicking?

What Dean calls communicative capitalism was anticipated by Jean Baudrillard in texts that now seem to possess an uncanny prophetic power. As far back as the 1970s, Baudrillard understood that the era of the enforced passivity of the spectacle was already being superseded by a control system that would demand, not passive acquiescence, but active participation. "Solicitation is substituted for the ultimatum," Baudrillard wrote in *Symbolic Exchange and Death*: "obligatory passivity to models constructed from the outset on the basis of the subject's 'active response,' and this subject's involvement and 'ludic' participation, towards a total environment model made up of incessant spontaneous responses, joyous feedback and irradiated contacts."[6] Recalling McLuhan, Baudrillard called this a "culture of tactile communication": "The people come to touch, they look as if they were touching, their gaze is only an aspect of tactile manipulation."[7]

Baudrillard could be describing here the eerie eroticism of *Anathema*, all those scenes in which opaque surfaces deliquesce into pool-portals, in which communicational orifices start to open up just about everywhere. *Anathema* gives us, as it were, the raw material of communicative capitalism, but doubly. Everything in the film is sampled from advertising, but advertising devoted to the very touch-screen devices that communicative capitalism uses in order to propagate (smartphones, tablets, etc.). The advertisements were all gathered from one of the major nodes of communicative capitalism, YouTube, a site primarily generated, just as Baudrillard predicted, from the "active responses" of participants. YouTube illustrates very well the communicative capitalist apparatus of capture: the participants who make all those time-consuming analogue-to-digital conversions, all those uploads, and who are not man, one woman, and one bed cannot be created from a spur-of-the-moment desire. This appalling sadomasochistic drama, regarded by Western sensibilities [*ryōshiki-ha*] as a rebellion against God and human nature, is a work that is structured according to a precise and rigorous logic.

Earlier, I said that in Wakamatsu's films, sex is something to be diligently examined. Needless to say, one must have the faculty of logic in order to examine these films. The many words that are often used to describe Wakamatsu's films, such as "madness" and "passion," miss the mark.

In *New Jack and Betty* (*Nyū Jakku & Betti*), the most recent Wakamatsu Productions film, the secret room [*misshitsu*] logic reaches its climax. Only three years after *The Embryo Hunts In Secret* (*Taiji ga mitsuryô suru toki*), the filmmakers of Wakamatsu Productions—Koji Wakamatsu, Atsushi Yamatoya,[9] and Masao Adachi—have far surpassed the colloquial term "pink film" (a term, by the way, that I think should be loved). Their creative activity should be looked upon with awe. They no doubt stand at the forefront of Japanese film. But here I will let Isao Okishima[10]—who appeared, as if following in their footsteps, with his strangely titled first film, *New Jack and Betty*—take credit.

For now, let us put aside the reason for the strange title "*New Jack and Betty*." This film, in brief, is a drama about an orgy. Please do not make a wry face after hearing "orgy." Okishima simply passionately examines what kind of relationship the seven characters in the film would fall into if they were thrown into one room together. By the way, the seven characters are a young man and a young girl who are betrothed, the young man's mother, the mother's older brother, his wife, and the young girl's parents. The orgy thus involves incest. Please do not make a wry face again after hearing "incest." Okishima is simply logically interrogating, with three men and four women, what would take the place of the young man's missing father in this situation.

What does the absence of the father mean for one young man? Solving this alluring theme presented by Okishima actually becomes the key that reveals the far-reaching consequences of the secret room orientation [*misshitsu shikō*] in Wakamatsu's films. But before we get into that subject, I must emphasize repeatedly that for Okishima, the orgy exists simply as an object of intense examination. If I say knowingly that it is a *contradictio in adjecto*, I will also say that it is a logical orgy [*ronriteki rankō*].[11] I have jokingly shouted "logical orgy" and "incest," but a serene and transparent—in other words, completely unrelated to adjectives such as "insidious" or "dirty"—orgy scene unfolds in the film. Right before plunging into the orgy, paid for their labor. It is the parasitic predator, capital, which accrues the value generated from the site.

It is tempting—and indeed necessary, but only as a first step—to decry the way in which communicative capitalism falls laughably short of achieving the liquid eroticism of contact that enfolds in *Anathema*. *Anathema*'s first step is to de-anchor the phantasmatic scenes that the advertisements construct from the products that they are ostensibly selling. This de-anchorage is responsible for producing much of the overwhelming affect of eeriness that pervades the film. *Anathema* composes a plane of consistency from these orphaned semiotic-libidinal fragments. As we watch, it is as if we are inside a machine dream. But who or what is dreaming here?

One way of seeing *Anathema* is as a glimpse into capital's own dreaming. This world of smoothly yielding orifice-interfaces, of instantaneous contact, of hard surfaces dissolving into liquid when touched, may be how the communicational matrix looks (and feels) to capital. But the experience of its human users is somewhat different. It is Franco Berardi who has done most to analyze the contrast between the economic-semiotic flow of capital and the overloaded and immiserated condition of the human nervous systems that function as part of the connective tissue of this global cybernetic network.[8] Marx called workers the "mere conscious linkages" that are needed to connect the flows of capital; but semiocapitalism does not even require our consciousness—what it feeds on is our unconscious attention. And quite clearly it is not only or primarily in our role as paid workers that we give this attention. We are exploited now even and especially in our nonwork: our nervous systems work overtime trying to manage the semioblitz but we receive no remuneration for the value that our attention creates.

As soon as we have smartphones, we are fully immersed not only in cyberspace, but in cyberspace-*time*. Far from *Anathema*'s radically depersonalized erotic absorption, cyberspace-time is bitty, fragmented. Being perpetually plugged into multiple communication platforms—text messages, social media websites, email—results in the condition that Linda Stone calls "continuous partial attention." Here, very far from *Anathema*'s oneirically melting desiring architecture, we find ourselves instead in a state of digital jitter, our fingers twitching over the screen, always preparing to make the next click. The drive to click is a short-circuiting of desire that makes even the most exploitative pornography seems quaint. Pornography demands at least a minimum of lingering over its images, whereas with the click drive, the desire is always and only to click. A pure tactile automatism. There is no possibility of drifting and dreaming. The flashing red alerts act as trance-inhibitors, maintaining us in a state of insomniac insatiability—just one more click, just one more message. We become a channel through which communicative capitalism circulates and proliferates, slaves to click drive. And every alert brings with it a new urgency.

So, yes, it is certainly possible to contrast the promises of capitalist communicative machinery, as shown in *Anathema*, with our experience of these machineries and networks. But this is only denunciation and complaint; it isn't yet counter-sorcery. Counter-sorcery requires a reversal in the magical operation whereby changing the system entails strengthening the system. What that means is taking seriously the promises capital makes, but cannot deliver on. Militant ascesis is only a partial answer to capital's libidinal engineering. Yes, we will need, as Fredric Jameson has put it, "to relinquish the compensatory desires and intoxications we have developed in order to make the present livable."[9]

But in addition to denunciation and renunciation, we also need a counter-libido, something capable of outdoing the white magic of I-culture, of twenty-first century capital's regime of neurotic subjectification. It's all done with mirrors: we are induced into occupying what the character Gas in David Cronenberg's *eXistenZ* calls "the most pathetic level of reality," entranced by the most banal images of ourselves amidst the dreary gloss of mildly hedonic sociality. *Anathema* performs another kind of mirror sorcery, where reflective surfaces become thresholds to the outside. Hence the proximity of some of each of the seven characters is allotted a purpose, with no distinction made between main roles and supporting roles.

Here, I am forced to remember the ideology of the orgy in the literature of the Marquis de Sade. This logic was brilliantly summarized by Yutaka Haniya, who appeared in court as a witness at the famous Sade trial.[12] "The match between the general will and particular wills is the biggest and most difficult problem in the history of mankind. The answer that Sade provides to the question of the fusion between part and whole is, surprisingly, the orgy. According to Sade, the lack that the individual has is supplemented by contact with the other. Infinitely continuing this contact with the other enables the part to approach the whole. This process is carried forward by the orgy."

In the work of Sade, the orgy is pursued to its limits. The combination is indiscriminate. Gender, age, class, and bloodline are all ignored. Participants are all naked and cleverly use the different bumps and dents on their bodies to create an enormous ring. Nor are the participants limited to humans. In one of Sade's works, the female protagonist, Juliet, who is at a large banquet in Rome, has a gigantic orgy with a castrated man, a hermaphrodite, a dwarf, an eighty-year-old woman, a male turkey, a monkey, a very large dog, a female mountain sheep, the elderly woman's four-year-old grandson, three other men, and two other women. It is a very entertaining sight because one of the participants is the police commissioner. That sight, however, is, in Haniya's words, "unimaginable" and "unfeasible even if one tries to imitate it."

Haniya continues: "It is an area that is unreachable through mere fantasy. It is a world that cannot be opened without the strict command of an imagination that follows a thorough logic." It may be an exaggeration to apply Haniya's comments to *New Jack and Betty*, but in this film, it is clear that an orgy can materialize only through a "complete abstraction of the sexual act" (Tatsuhiko Shibusawa). Thus, we are made aware that the absence of the father can be logically revealed only at the limit of the ideology of the secret room [*misshitsu no shisō*].

Allow me to introduce a psychoanalytic schema: the secret room orientation [*misshitsu shikō*] represents nothing other than the return to the mother's womb, or a desire for the uterus. Thus, the absence of the father suggests the absence of an apocalyptic philosophy that in one blow will shatter the utopia of the warm womb. The title "*New Jack and Betty*" comes from the title of a middle school English textbook that anyone who was in his or her twenties during the 1960s would have encountered at least once. In the production

Anathema's imagery to that of weird or horror cinema: to the television screens and mirrors that act as gateways to the Other Side in *Poltergeist III*, to the inhuman fingers straining to break into our world through the surface of a mirror in *Prince of Darkness*, and to the liquid portals in *The Box*. Yet *Anathema* is far from horrifying. *Anathema* rather has the eeriness of dreams, its de-anchored images opening up the radically depersonalized desiring ocean beneath and beyond capital. The act of de-anchorage reveals what we already know: dreams do not belong to anyone, especially not to capital. Capital itself is nothing—as Antonio Negri and Michael Hardt have long argued, it is merely a parasite, feeding not only on work but also desire. Capital can only dam, contain, and divert the flows of desire on which it depends. Seen from this angle, YouTube appears not as a space for the circulation of a communicative capitalism, but as a space of sharing and the collectivization of desire. *Anathema* gives us a glimpse into what this desiring zone feels like.

Perhaps the most important consequence of *Anathema*'s de-anchoring of the libidinal fragments from the capitalist sigils with which they are arbitrarily articulated is its opening up of a mode of time very different from communicative capitalism's urgencies. One trap laid by communicative capitalism is the temptation to retreat from technological modernity. But this presupposes that frenzied attentional bombardment is the only possible technological modernity, from which we can only unplug and withdraw. *Anathema* proposes a new use of digital machinery, a new kind of digital desire: a digital psychedelia, no less. When we watch *Anathema*, we become aware of how de-psychedelized mainstream culture has become. De-psychedelization is an aspect of capitalist realism that reduces everything to the imperatives of business and to neurotic psychological interiority. *Anathema*'s digital psychedelia coaxes us out of anxious identification with our busy self, our business self. It dilates time; induces us to linger *and* drift. It is neither convalescence nor entertainment, both of which operate to refresh us sufficiently for a return to work. This desiring-time has as little to do with I-culture's drip-feed of hedonic nuggets as it has to do with the busyness of work itself. Lucid, delirial, and exploratory, digital psychedelia rediscovers the dream time that capitalist realism has eclipsed.

1 Philippe Pignarre and Isabelle Stengers, *Capitalist Sorcery: Breaking the Spell* (Houndmills: Palgrave, 2011), 40.

2 Jodi Dean, *Democracy and other Neoliberal Fantasies: Communicative Capitalism and Left Politics* (London and New York: Duke University Press, 2009), 24.

3 Ibid.

4 Ibid., 23.

5 Ibid., 24.

6 Jean Baudrillard, *Symbolic Exchange and Death* (New York: SAGE Publications Ltd, 1993), 24.

7 Jean Baudrillard, *Simulacra and Simulation* (Ann Arbor: University of Michigan Press, 1994), 70.

8 See Franco Berardi, *Precarious Rhapsody: Semiocapitalism and the Pathologies of the Post-Alpha Generation* (London: Minor Compositions, 2009).

9 Fredric Jameson, Valences of the Dialectic (London and New York: Verso, 2010), 384.

statement for the film, Okishima casually says that "Jack and Betty, filled with dreams and hopes, after a few decades of growing up, will now be getting married. I wonder how many years I studied English as a boy in school … I remember trying very hard, but now I cannot even have a simple conversation … I am simply amazed at myself … and cannot close my mouth in awe."

Doesn't the meaning of the father's absence emerge, for Okishima's generation, through cynical self-concealment? I will quickly confess here that my statements about viewing the sixties through a psychoanalytic schema, the utopia of confinement, and the absence of apocalyptic philosophy were borrowed from recent opinions expressed by Tatsuhiko Shibusawa, the translator of Sade. According to Shibusawa, Wakamatsu and his filmmaking cohort "cannot move easily, like the insect caught in dew. The stickiness of the squishy, Dali-esque, melting world has become too strong." They are "distressed, searching for the lost apocalyptic philosophy."

And for that reason, the films of Wakamatsu and his ilk are forced to pursue their logic far enough to explode the intense secret room orientation [*misshitsu shikō*]. It can be said that the young spectators moving towards the seventies are looking for the absent father in Koji Wakamatsu, Masao Adachi, Isao Okishima, and the like, who reached their artistic formation in the sixties.

Together with the audience in the secret room [*misshitsu*], the young protagonists in Wakamatsu's films can only escape the secret room [*misshitsu*] through self-destruction; for this reason, these films are doubly tragic. In *Go Go Second Time Virgin* (*Yuke yuke nidome no shojo*), Wakamatsu's most recent work, which is based on a script by Masao Adachi, the young male protagonist sings the following theme song:

Mama I'm taking off
Soon the sightseeing bus will stop for mommy
And the cuckoo will cry
NO SEE YOU AGAIN
Betrayed me and the Panther's D that you did not bring
Jean and Milano and Norman Mailer are already in recession
and the erect red neon lights
not a progressive color
not hot
but gathered around a knife
today it's the park of the cops
me the policeman's living room

VLADIMIR'S NIGHT: ICONOGRAPHIC NOTES

Roee Rosen

Roee Rosen is a painter, filmmaker, and writer whose work interrogates structures of power, trauma, and evil. His often grotesque, macabre, and obscene works evoke a sense of realism in the face of the structural violence of a world where victims turn into perpetrators and terror bears the name of the rule of law.

In *Vladimir's Night:* Vladimir Putin is shown vacationing in his summer mansion—in the role of a little child. Before falling asleep he imagines seeing faces in the wooden veneer of his bedroom cabinet. Animated objects flow out to cuddle with Vladimir, but the scene soon turns violent. Vladimir is gradually raped, tortured, and murdered by objects.

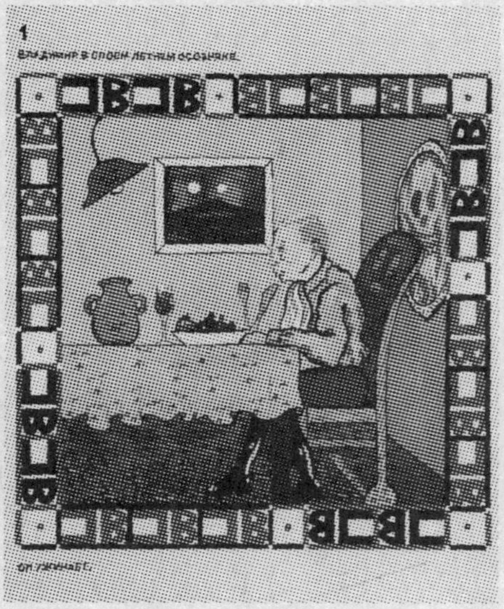

Vladimir is at his summer mansion.
He is having dinner.

The surname Putin never appears in the poem—but here, the pattern of the frame is constructed from the Cyrillic initials VP.

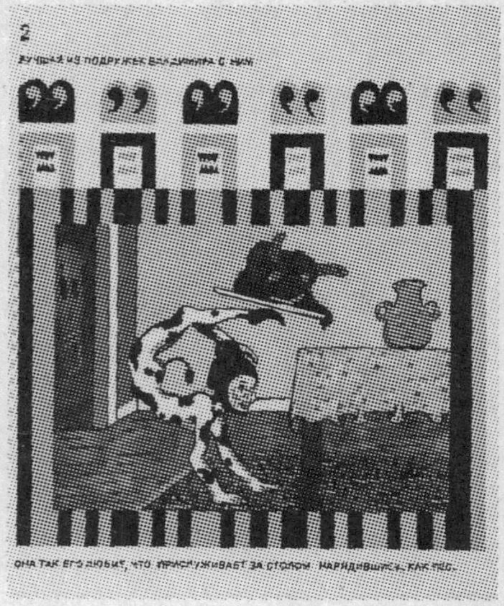

With Vladimir is his favorite girlfriend.
She loves him so much that she serves the meal dressed as a dog.

The figure of the "favorite girlfriend" dressed as a dog is that of Alina Kabaeva. The Russian newspaper *Moskovsky Korrespondent* reported that Kabaeva, an Olympic gold medalist, was married to Putin. Both Putin and Kabaeva denied the report. In 2007, Kabaeva became a state deputy for United Russia, Putin's party. The frame pattern changes to become face-like in the upper part, but is still based on the Cyrillic V and P.

me the policeman's coffee
NO SEE YOU AGAIN
The black list that I have created
The cesarean-sectioned map
Mommy I'm taking off
Stabbing one another, the city in the night
naked lunch, blood lunch
the relationship to the impotence medicine
I will cut ties
Mommy I'm taking off
To kill my cop
To kill everyone's cop

This is an actual poem by a young poet, which Adachi altered. One should pay attention to the fact that in *Go Go Second Time Virgin* (*Yuke yuke nidome no shojo*), the secret room [*misshitsu*] the young man is standing in is on the roof of an apartment building, and the room is formed by closing the exit to the stairs. Visible beyond a metal fence is the endless blue sky and an urban landscape [*fūkei*] brilliantly colored by various neighborhoods and landmarks, such as Shinjuku, Shibuya, and Tokyo Tower. Based on a frightening paradox of landscape [*fūkei*], and repeating the secret room [*misshitsu*] scenario, Adachi and Wakamatsu have vividly confronted the tragic relationship between utopia and apocalypticism.

Today, in the late sixties, we cannot find the courage expressed by Takaaki Yoshimoto[13] in the early fifties when he wrote, "I am going to leave / Beyond the pressure of the winter / Because I cannot bear it alone / It is a lie to hold hands with multiple people / Because I cannot fight it alone / Because it is cowardly to hold hands with multiple people / I am going to leave."[14] Needless to say, the place Yoshimoto goes to when he leaves is determined by the state of affairs he faces. Nowadays, a boy can only leave for the landscape [*fūkei*]. *Go Go Second Time Virgin* (*Yuke yuke nidome no shojo*) ends with a denouement where a boy and a girl lightly jump over a metal fence—in other words, they throw themselves into the landscape [*fūkei*]. The only way out is death.

In this way, we are told that, for the time being, landscape [*fūkei*] is the only thing outside the "one room," represented as the one man, one woman, and one bed. If we are unable to examine sex to its limit, even within the secret room [*misshitsu*], this suggests that the only way out is for the internal "sex" [*sei*] to transform into external "landscape" [*fūkei*].

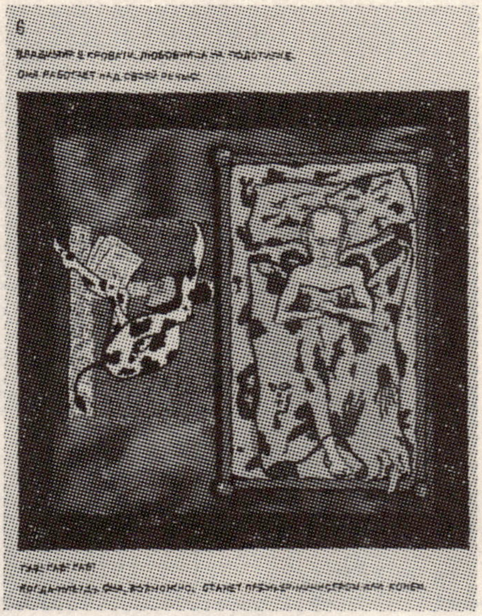

Vladimir is in bed. His lover is on the rug.
She is working on her speech:
Woof, Woof, Woof!
Perhaps one day she will become a minister,
or a horse.

The carpet is a variation on the Chechan flag.

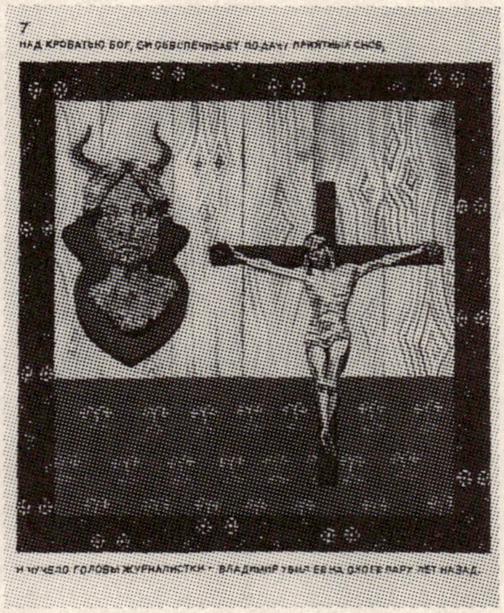

Above the bed is God, to secure the
serving of sweet dreams,
And the stuffed head of a journalist
Vladimir hunted a few years ago.

The stuffed head is that of the journalist Anna Politkovskaya (1958–2006), one of the most outspoken critics of Putin's reign, and in particular of his ruthless attacks on Chechnya. She was shot in the elevator of her Moscow apartment building. Politkovskaya is the most well-known journalist to have been assassinated in Russia, but reports by the Committee to Protect Journalists name Russia as the third most lethal country in the world for journalists since 1993, surpassed only by Algeria and post-invasion Iraq.

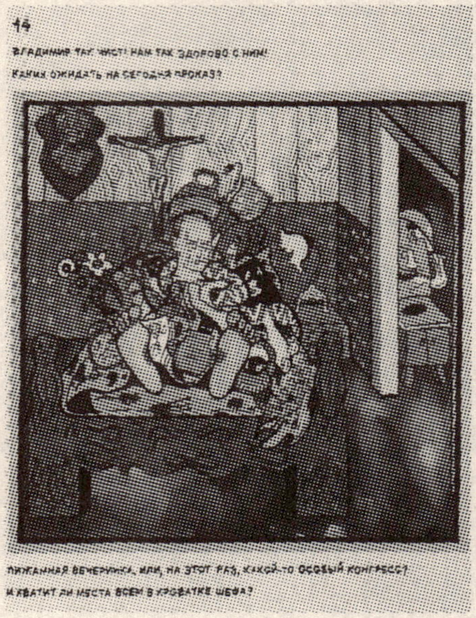

So clean is Vladimir! We all want to get near!
What kind of cavorting is in progress?
Is it a pajama party, or perhaps a special
congress?
And will there be room for all in the little
leader's bed?

The figure leering behind the doorway is that of Moydodyr, a personified washstand in a famous 1923 children's poem by Korney Chukovsky. In this poem, a child gets so dirty that his toys as well as other objects in his home run away from him. The angry Moydodyr summons his sponges and soap bars to wash the boy, who escapes to the streets, chased by a menacing sponge. There, he is temporarily saved from cleanliness by a crocodile—the protagonist of other works by Chukovsky—who swallows the sponge, but then, upon noticing how dirty the boy is, becomes very angry with him. Scared of the crocodile even more than of cleanliness, the boy willingly returns

Incidentally, the reason we—who have walked around with Masao Adachi and others, following the footsteps of Norio Nagayama, a "serial murderer," through eastern Japan, from Sapporo to Hakodate, Tsugaru Plains, Tokyo, Nagoya, Kyoto, Osaka, and Kobe, and also to Hong Kong—the reason we shoot various landscapes [*fūkei*] that Nagayama may have seen and call it a documentary, making a strange work that can only be described as "real-view film" [*jikkei eiga*],[15] is because we have been made aware that landscape [*fūkei*] itself is the "power" [*kenryoku*] that stands against us. Nagayama shot bullets to rip the landscape [*fūkei*] into pieces. When we are enjoying a pleasant drive, the landscape [*fūkei*] casts a spell on us; "power" [*kenryoku*] captures us. Even the circumstances [*jyōkyō*] and conditions [*jyōkyō*] that are unworthy of pity mean nothing to us.[16] We may not have surpassed the landscape [*fūkei*] yet.

It is well known that between October and November of 1968, Nagayama severed the Japanese landscape [*fūkei*] with a couple of bullets, and afterwards possessed, for the first time, "one room" in a small apartment in western Tokyo. It was a small secret room [*misshitsu*] with three tatami mats. It is a big mystery to us why six month later, on April 7, 1969, Nagayama left the secret room [*misshitsu*] and stood once again in the landscape [*fūkei*] with gun in hand. It is the same as the presence of "one woman," who is said to have occasionally visited the "one room," and who will most likely be an eternal mystery; or perhaps it may be a dark side of Nagayama as the "one man" who can never be clear.

I wonder what kind of awakening Nagayama is having inside the constructive secret room [*gisei no misshitsu*] of a Tokyo prison. Nagayama, inside the prison, may be sadism [*sado*] as a potential [*kanōsei*]. However, if we cannot accept that even the secret room [*misshitsu*] is under the control of power, then we must make the landscapes [*fūkei*] around us into a secret room [*misshitsu*] for us. For this reason, it is unfortunate that *Violent Virgin* (*Gewalt! Gewalt: shojo geba-geba*), Wakamatsu's masterpiece of 1969, which is based on a script by Atsushi Yamatoya, is praised by dilettante critics only for its artistic achievements. Starting by conceptualizing the vast wasteland at the foot of Mt. Fuji as a secret room [*misshitsu*], did not *Violent Virgin* (*Gewalt! Gewalt: shojo geba-geba*) diligently examine the limits of sex in that space? Or in *Running in Madness, Dying in Love* (*Kyôsô jôshi-kô*), from early 1969, all of Japan's dark landscapes [*fūkei*], from Tokyo to Tohoku and Hokkaido, are figured as a secret room [*misshitsu*]. The film develops a story of one man, one woman, and one bed within the boundless expanse of this "one room." It foreshadows what Masao Adachi, to Moydodyr and takes a bath. Maxim Komar-Myshkin's image is based on the two animated versions made of the poem made in 1939 and 1954, both by the artist Ivan Ivanov-Vano.

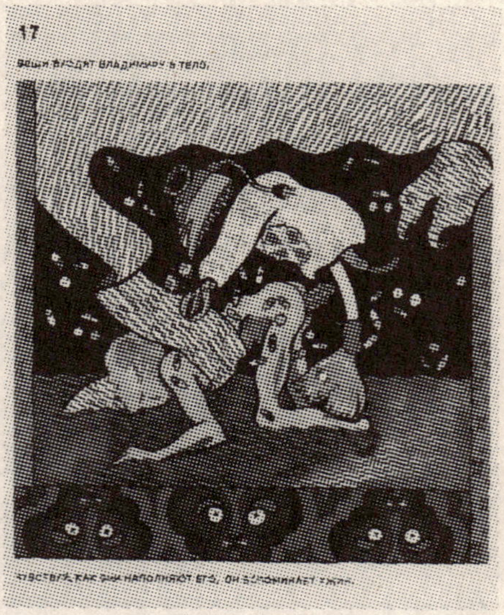

*Things begin to enter Vladimir's body.
Feeling stuffed, he recalls dinner.*

The pattern of the fabric enveloping Vladimir's torso is based on a famous 1923–24 textile designed by Varvara Stepanova. The emblem on the sweater is the logo of Nashi ("Ours!"), the Putin-supportive youth movement. Established as an "antifascist" movement, it has been widely reported that the group receives direct funding from the Kremlin. In December 2011, as the opposition to Putin's reelection intensified, Nashi staged pro-Putin demonstrations.

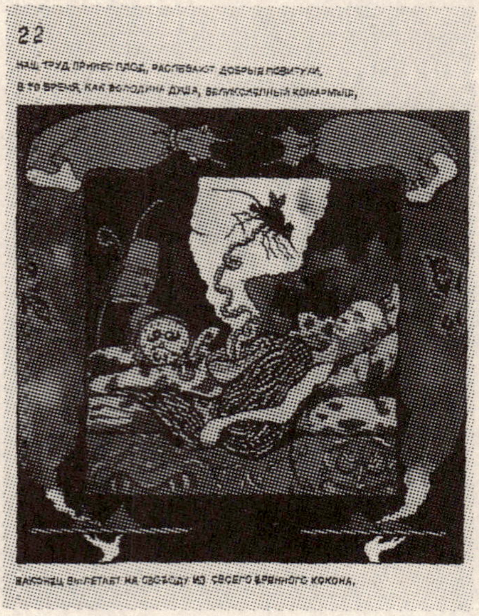

*Our labor bore fruit, the good midwives chime,
As Vladimir's soul, the glorious mosquito-mouse,
Finally flies free from its earthly cocoon.*

While the mosquito-mouse is the parasite delivered in the picture, its frame contains a butterfly, the traditional figure of the soul. But the other images in the frame—platters with somewhat scatological culinary offerings, and a pair of anamorphic dresses—can also be construed as images of souls, culled from Mayakovsky's early play *Vladimir Mayakovsky: A Tragedy* (1913). This play repeatedly shatters the divide between objects and subjects, the somatic and the spiritual, and audaciously endows the spiritual with overly tactile qualities. In the prologue, the poet offers his soul on a platter, to be eaten later, and proceeds to state that "perhaps things have different souls then ours." Later on, the soul turns out to be not only edible but wearable: "From my soul you can sew, also, such elegant dresses."

The object posed behind the clock is a theremin, one of the earliest electronic musical instruments (patented in 1928). The theremin is unique both for its haunting sound and for being played without touch: the player controls volume and pitch by moving his or her hands next to the instrument's two antennas. Komar-Myshkin was probably interested in the theremin not only because of this "magical" way of playing and its eerie sound, but because of who took charge of the script, intends in his new work about Norio Nagayama, *A.K.A. Serial Killer*.

The examination of sex within the secret room [*misshitsu*] must be allowed to run it course. As Georges Bataille paradoxically said, if the forbidden continues to exist in this world, eroticism will never cease being the hymn of a life that leads to death. We must continue to diligently think inwards, using imagination to penetrate into the realm of impossibility, and also outwards, with an unyielding directionality that will change all landscape [*fūkei*] from the "power" [*kenryoku*] that spellbinds us into secret rooms [*misshitsu*]. Otherwise, even Koji Wakamatsu, the apostle of the secret room [*misshitsu*], can be guilty of wrongly portraying, in his recent film *Season of Terror* (*Gendai kōshoku-den: Teroru no kisetsu*), the man decisively leaving utopia—made up of one man and two women—as the outcome of political conditions that arbitrarily arrive according to the whims of state power.

We—the various protagonists of Wakamatsu's films and their audiences, as well as Norio Nagayama—keep an evil two-headed snake at the base of our subconscious. Needless to say, the two heads of this snake are "sex" [*sei*] and "power" [*kenryoku*]. How can we break free of our two-headed snake? How can we unleash the subconscious? If we are not satisfied with the landscape [*fūkei*] simply as sex [*sei*] or as violence [*bōkyoku*], then we must acquire the logic of apocalypse, that which will destroy the walls of the secret room [*misshitsu*] through total examination within the secret room [*misshitsu*]. What we witness at that moment is—in line with the subtitle of this text—a story of all men, all women, and all beds passing through various stages of the fictitious "liberation" of sex [*sei*]. At this juncture, the whole world has become a colossal "one room."

Leon Theremin's life story, and in particular his abrupt return, in 1938, from New York to the USSR, rumored at the time to have been the result of a kidnapping by Soviet secret agents. Theremin was imprisoned in a gulag but was later absolved thanks to his gifts as an inventor, which he put at the service of the USSR's espionage efforts. Amongst other inventions, he developed a highly sensitive microphone.

Figs. Roee Rosen, Maxim Komar-Myshkin
Vladimir's Night, 2011–2012, series of thirty six gouaches on paper, framed, each 55 × 33.5 cm.

1 By referring to the writer of this column as "notebook girl" [*techō-ko*], Matsuda is making an underhanded comment about the female writer.

2 This refers to the 1950s.

3 Tohoku, Shochiku, Toei, Daiei, Nikkatsu.

4 Koji Wakamatsu (April 1, 1936–October 17, 2012) is a Japanese filmmaker, producer, and screenwriter known for his politically charged sexual narratives and aggressive cinematic style. He produced the controversial film *In the Realm of the Senses* by Nagisa Oshima. For more on Wakamatsu, see David Desser, *Eros Plus Massacre: An Introduction to Japanese New Wave Cinema* (Bloomington: Indiana University Press, 1988); Tadao Sato, *Currents in Japanese Cinema*, trans. Gregory Barrett (Tokyo: Kodanska international LTD, 1982); and Thomas Weisser and Yuko Mihara Weisser, *Japanese Cinema Encyclopedia: The Sex Films* (Miami: Vital Books, 1998).

5 A preparatory school student, or *yobikō-sei* (予備校生), is a high school student or a high school graduate attending a secondary preparatory school to study for college entrance exams.

6 *Eiga Geijustu* (映画芸術) is a quarterly Japanese film journal.

7 *Danchi* (団地) is an area or district where housing has been developed systematically. A group of low-income housing apartments.

8 Masao Adachi is a Japanese filmmaker, screenwriter, activist, and former member of the Japanese Red Army. He was very active as an activist filmmaker/screenwriter in the 1960s and '70s. He is know for political films that deal with left-wing ideas, such as *Closed Vagina* (*Sain*, 1963), *Bowel* (*Wan*, 1961), and *Red Army / PFLP: Declaration of World War* (*Sekigun-P.F.L.P: Sekai Senso Sengen*, 1971). He wrote many screenplays for Koji Wakamatsu and produced films such as *A.K.A. Serial Killer* (*Ryakushō: Renzoku Shasatsuma*, 1969). Adachi relocated to Lebanon after traveling there for the production of *Red Army / PFLP*. He stayed in Lebanon for twenty-eight years, until he was deported to Japan in 2001 after being arrested for a passport violation.

9 Atsushi Yamatoya is a Japanese filmmaker and screenwriter at Wakamatsu Productions. He made his directorial debut with *Uragiri no Kisetsu* (1966), but he is better known for his screenplays, such as the ones he wrote for Seijun Suzuki's *Branded to Kill* (*Koroshi no rakuin*, 1967) and Wakamatsu's *Violent Virgin* (*Gewalt! Gewalt: shojo geba-geba*, 1969), and for many television shows (live-action drama and animation).

10 Isao Okishima is a Japanese filmmaker and screenwriter. He made his directorial debut in 1969 with *New Jack and Betty* (*Nyū Jakku & Betti*). He is best known for his work as a screenwriter for film and television.

11 Matsuda uses the word 論理的乱交, which I have translated as "logical orgy," but he is trying to say that the orgy is not gratuitousness, but instead something that is worthy of higher logical inquiry in a philosophical sense.

12 Yutaka Haniya is a novelist and philosopher. He appeared as a witness at the trial of Tatsuhiko Shibusawa, a novelist, critic, translator, and French literature scholar who was prosecuted for his translations of Marquis de Sade. He was charged with the possession and sale of obscene literature.

13 Takaaki Yoshimoto was a poet, philosopher, and literary critic. He was a prolific writer on many different topics. He is known for his influence on the New Left in the 1960s. For more on Yoshimoto in English, see Fuminobu Murakami, *Postmodern, Feminist, and Postcolonial Currents in Contemporary Japanese Culture: A Reading of Murakami Haruki, Yoshimoto Banana, Yoshimoto Takaaki, and Karatani Kōjin* (London: Routledge, 2005); Lawrence Olson, *Ambivalent Moderns: Portraits of Japanese Cultural Identity* (Savage, Maryland: Rowman & Littlefield, 1992); Leith Morton, *Modern Japanese Culture: The Insider View* (Melbourne: Oxford University Press, 2003); Katsuya Hiromoto, John Evans, and Kazuko Shiraishi, *Two Contemporary Japanese Poets: Takaaki Yoshimoto and Kazuko Shiraishi—Poems in Translation* (Yokohama: Keio University, 1995); and Hajime Kijima, *The Poetry of Postwar Japan* (Iowa City: University of Iowa Press, 1975).

14 This is part of a poem titled "*Chihisana mure e no aisatsu*" (my translation: "Greetings to a Small Tribe"), originally published in *Tenni no tameno jyūhen* (my translation: *Ten parts for transposition*). It can be found in Takaaki Yoshimoto, *Takaaki Yoshimoto zenshu 5* (Shichosha, 2006).

15 I have translated *jikkei eiga* (実景映画) as "real-view films," but this genre term created by Matsuda points to the specific style of *A.K.A Serial Killer*, in which the documentary film is constructed from actual/real shots of landscapes around Japan. This term points to the postcard photograph–like shots of actual Japanese landscapes used in this film.

16 Matsuda uses two different ways of writing *jyōkyō*: "情況" and "状况". The dictionary does not differentiate between the two, and both mean "conditions," "circumstances," or "state of affairs." In a colloquial sense, the first refers to larger ideological, political, or even emotional conditions, while the latter points to something more objective. For this translation, I have differentiated the two as "circumstances" and "conditions."

DECAY

Reza Negarestani

According to articles published by Middle Eastern critics, the development of Parsani's writings on the Middle East throughout the years can be read through his approach to three enigmas. These three Middle Eastern conundrums that recur in Parsani's writings can be enumerated as follows: (1) the degeneration of the whole in the absence of complete erasure or destruction (referred to as poromechanics and ()hole complex); (2) petrological reason and the geo-politics of petropolitical undercurrents (referred to as Tellurian Lube); (3) the enigma of openness on all levels of economics, politics, religion, life, communication, etc. If the Middle East, for Parsani, is a sentient living entity, its activities swirl around these three enigmas, riddling them to a greater extent with its each and every twist.

> Squirming its way into ever more convoluted coils, the Middle East develops a life-form of its own which by any standard must be admitted as a peculiarly Middle Eastern response to these three ancient enigmas. By casting creation aside, this life-form builds worlds and corpses more efficiently than God.

Certainly the juggernaut of Parsani's *Defacing the Ancient Persia*—always politically labeled by Parsani himself as *vade mecum*—had a name for this life-form whose basis was "anti-creationist creativity or perversion": decay.

In his later writings, which carried the stigmata of topical diaspora and oily density, Parsani changed the name of this "concrete Middle Eastern approach to building and the perversion of creation" from "decay" to "undercover softness," a nomenclatural shift more in tune with the three ancient enigmas as explicated in Parsani's later writings. In his discussion of the relation between petroleum and monotheism in the Middle East, Parsani hints at the reasons behind this name change:

> ( )hole complex [*Kareez'gar*] is the model of participation or complicity with the earth's narrations, and oil organizes these narrations in a vigorous and lively manner. The model of this livelihood and vigor in the Middle East is decay or undercover softness. The undercover softness of the Middle East defies both the vitalistic model and the necrocratic submission to death. The progressive softness of decay evades consolidation, but does not escape solidity; the cosmogenesis of decay unfolds within solidity, spreads from interior to outer surfaces. Through decay, the solid entity is taken over neither by integrated life nor death, but by irresolution. If contemporary socio-economical and political formations in the Middle East effuse a rabid liveliness as well as the stench of corruption, it is because they have betrayed death by undergoing decay. In the same vein, the greater disintegrations which the Middle East brings to the rest of the world through its populations, politics, religions and even its mere existence can be explained by the Middle Eastern approach to death, living and softness: A deliberate undertaking of decay as an autonomous building process—the undercover softness of decay.

Despite all the materials on decay or "the Middle Eastern model of impossible death" that Parsani's later writings provide us with, the role of decay in the socio-political bedrock of the Middle East can only be mapped out by appropriating a highly technical vocabulary. However, a pseudo-ideological adaptation (in effect, a total retardation) of Parsani's discourse can be recapitulated here.

THE MUSEUM OF THE IN FRASTRUC TURAL UNCON SCIOUS

Heroic or romantic approaches to decay take decomposition as a process of naturalization (or return to nature), utter disappearance and destruction, deliverance and rebirth. However, the ultimate aim of such heroic views is political or economical domestication and appropriation, for decay cannot be captured as either formation or destruction. Decay is an artificializing process that is promulgated on the substratum of all modes of survival (beings). In other words, decay—unlike death—is not external to survival, for it perpetuates itself on the substratum of survival, in order to indefinitely postpone death and absolute disappearance. In decay, the being survives by blurring into other beings, without losing all its ontological registers. In no way does decay wipe out or terminate; on the contrary, it keeps alive. This is where the process of decay—despite all the apparent connections—separates itself from the transgressive war machines of termination, annihilation, tragedy, and violence. Decay undermines death and destruction by bringing them to a place where there is no formative power (*Puissance* = *p*) and hence where formation defies both wholesome integrity and death or erasure. By degenerating all aspects of formation, decay ungrounds the very ground upon which power is conducted, distributed, and established. In line with poromechanics, decay perforates the formation of power to no end, and by doing so, prevents power from investing in the consolidation of its formation. Accordingly, decay builds a world where power can only contribute to the degeneration of the formation into never-ending waste—all dejected domains of beings. For this reason, decay neither brings power (*puissance*, as in *La Volonté de Puissance*) to erasure and utter eradication (*p*=0; or nihil without solid) nor provides power with a structural and utilitarian ground. The so-called corruption or decline of the Middle East is the result of an infinitely perforated ground of social, economical, and political formations which prevent power from being effectively utilized or efficiently pressed into service.

By undermining the ground upon which power can be effectuated and lines of destruction mobilized, decay misdirects—in the sense of a permanent derailing—the processes of terminus. If the social, economic, and political definition of power is determined by its formation, and the formation itself is decided by its ground, then decay's peaceful (non-annihilative) assault on the ground of power formations is effectuated as a concrete sabotage against the very definition of power.

> Decay can extract softness from despotism, political persistence from the abolition of utilizable power. This is the arcane *modus vivendi* of undying Middle Eastern power systems, the effects of whose contagious poverty and tyranny upon the world are without any geographical restriction. In the absence of any consolidated surface capable of effectively solidifying, conducting, transporting, conserving and developing power formations, power conforms to nothing but a decomposition of the system. The deterioration of formative platforms leads to the dissolution of the line of command and the failure of tactics, which requires formations for its dynamism and modes of conduct. But this collapse of command and tactics does not leave the decaying system or political entity defenseless or even pacified, because such a collapse opens up a sinister paramilitary arena for which every activity or use of power turns into a pilotless strategy, a strategy without the line of command. The result of this paramilitary unfolding is the Middle East as havoc. To decay is to lose the distinction between soft and solid. In fact, one cannot tell the difference between irresistible softness and unyielding solidity when dealing with Middle Eastern states and systems of power. (Hamid Parsani, *Defacing the Ancient Persia*)

Decay can concretely (in the sense of pragmatism and political consequences) erase the definition of power by positioning *p* (*Macht*) over the Zero-without-solid (*p*/0), a process delineated not by dissolving power but by keeping power alive within obscure hosts. An undead political machine, a Middle Eastern system reveals its true lineaments in its decay.

THE MUSEUM OF THE INFRASTRUCTURAL UNCONSCIOUS

Territorial Agency (John Palmesino and Ann-Sofi Rönnskog)

The Museum of the Infrastructural Unconscious examines the shifting relations between the form taken by contemporary polities and sovereignties, and the form of their material spaces of operation. It sets out an inquiry into the models that govern, order, affect, and structure change by measuring, surveying, quantifying, evaluating, connecting, and linking. At the juncture between two trajectories of transformation—institutional and spatial—the museum fathoms two sets of archives, revealing how they conceptualize the connections among surveying, documenting, and envisioning change and history.

The approximation of material and procedural intelligence in recent years has been largely driven by a shared endeavor to engage with orientation and distinction. The inscription of norms, protocols, standardization, and legislative frames into the organization of material spaces and operational grounds has not only been the object of study of a variety of transformation hypotheses: it has also been the form-generating process of both polities and space, a process of bordering, demarcating, separating, containing, segmenting, aligning, and homogenizing.

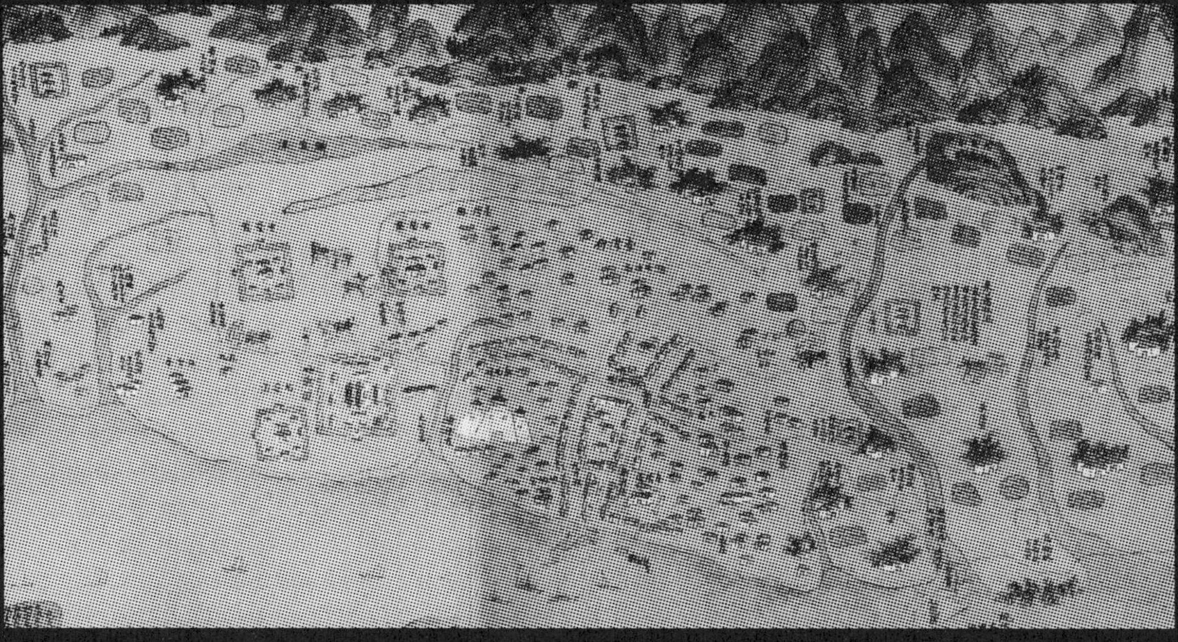

Taiwan map during the reign of Emperor Kangxi, 1722.

The utilization of power in a decaying system is a necrophilic experience. Decay mars power on virtual surfaces of zero, there to be rotten and reeked up; but above all, decay leeches death from the living without falling into the black transparency of death. While the advent of death heralds the end of any capacity for affording more, the reign of decay begins with the loss of such capacity. This progressive death—which cannot eventuate complete removal or total destruction—can only be tasted through decay and its differentiated mess.

Decay introduces power to the misadventures of matter. But it is "entities as beings" which narrate the adventures of decay as a cosmic odyssey between themselves. In decay, the limit and lineaments of objects are put to the test: a hyena is built out of a dog's corpse, which in turn generates plants, small maggots within smaller worms within smaller worms within countless squirming bodies. The awakening of different species from a corrupting entity is inherent to decay. In an unsettling revelation, the German scholastic philosopher Henry of Hesse the Elder suggests "that it is not clear whether all men are of the same species or not, and so too with dogs and horses ... [C]orpses which had been of the same species when living might differ in species from one another when corrupted." During decay, taxonomic indetermination and sheer equivocality blur the boundaries not only between different species but also between entities of the same species. When associated with decaying political systems, such obscurity suggests an ominous socio-political twist. To say that a decaying political system traverses and encompasses other political systems is dismaying enough; but to add that any political system—whether developed or democratic—might be a differentiated gradient of a decaying politics is an unfathomable insinuation.

In decay, every instance of dynamism or regulation modulated by the equilibrial difference between the horizons of life (as living) and death is incapacitated. One is thrown beyond death and living (affordance of life) as existential extrema. Traversing the differentiating softness of decay, beings are introduced to modes of survival which are not established on the economical domains of dying and living. These modes of survival or being are characterized by simultaneous envelopment and development. The decaying object or system folds back into its minimal body and lineaments (less than a thing, more than nothing) and at the same time unfolds into other beings which are differentiated from it through decay.

> As a Middle Eastern political system decays, it contracts to its irreducible body and infinitesimal existence. Concurrently, as it decomposes it develops outward into unexpected systems and modes of politics. The corpse of a political system is in fact its actual body (*summa actualis*), whose chemical potentials are limitless. (H. Parsani)

The envelopment and development of the decaying entity describes an event which oscillates between the abstract (folding to the minimum body and lineaments) and the concrete (differentiating to other actual beings). The cosmogenesis of decay is built between dimensions. Through decay, life and death multiply and putrefy each other to no end (for what could the end be, for decay?). There is no deliverance for the system which falls into the economic confusion and absence of calculative affordability (of either death or living) induced by the process of decay; no salvation, either through dying or through living. The decaying entity becomes a laboratory slab upon which base-necrophilia (where death is infinitely deferred but progressively approached) is germinated. Decay is a limitropic process through which the object shrinks progressively toward zero without eventuating the act of annihilation (complete dissolution into nihil). Infinite contraction or shrinkage of the decaying entity is equal to the evaporation of the qualities or attributes by which the object is transcendentally grasped or accessed by the human—sensed, experienced, recognized, afforded, and judged. Such evaporation of access points (or transcendental portals) folds the entity back onto itself. As the object flees us, it looms out in its own realm—all this through the intervention

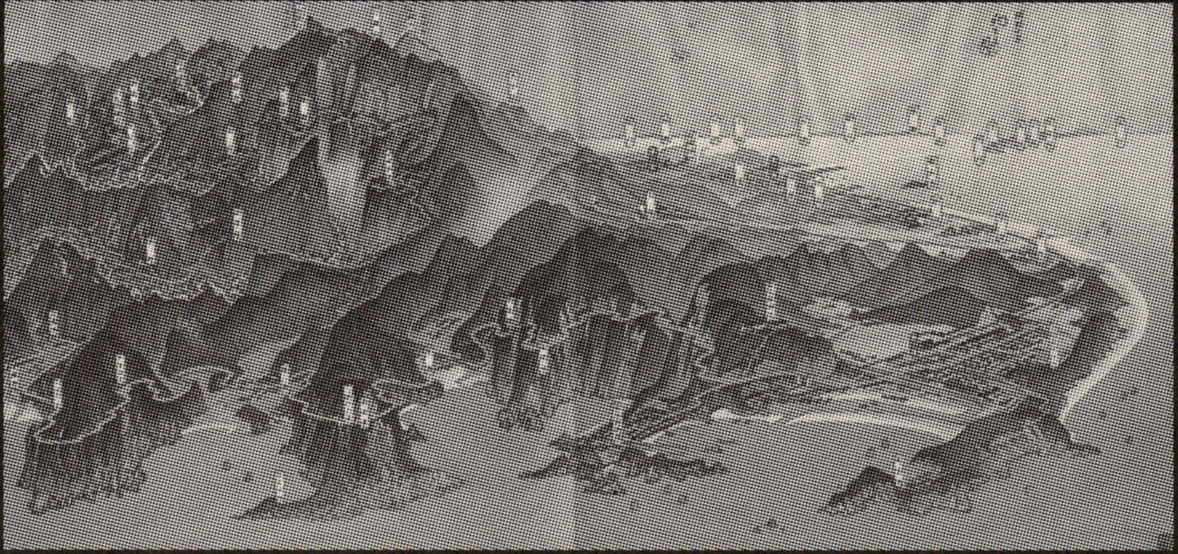

Grand Taroko transport bird's-eye view, Hatsusaburo Yoshida, 1935.

On the one hand, sectoral and expert knowledges have imbued infrastructural discourses and practices, and driven the fragmentation and separation of their many technical know-hows. As of one accord, institutions—both above and beneath the state—have also reframed and rescaled their many internal delimitations, with a multiplication of specialized spaces and practices. Separations in know-hows and delimitations of fields of influence have been translated directly into demarcations and separations in space, with the result that a variety of deterministic approaches to change now dominate the horizon. The expansion of the horizon of intervention, the scale and limits to conceptualizing and affecting change, seem to link up to the imperial sweep of modernity.

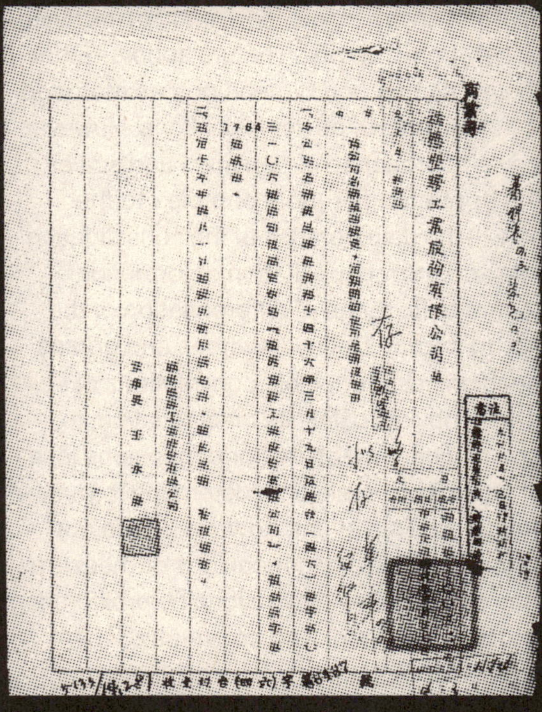

Document regarding petrochemical industry, 1957.
© National Archives Administration

On the other hand, alongside these practices of delimitation and ordering, thrusts of disalignment and de-organization have begun to appear. At odds with the mainstay equivalence between transformation processes and organizational procedures and protocols, a series of fissures, fragments, and fault lines are reshaping contemporary spaces of inhabitation. Rather than the and the aid of nothingness, whose proximity and remoteness are both infinite. For this reason, Parsani poses a political question which he expects to be answered in developing an ethics of decay: "If a decaying political system eludes us in all respects, abstractly, concretely and existentially, but does not completely perish, then how exactly can it be judged?"

The convoluted and pink space of decay—pink in the wake of the semiotics of war and peace, of redness and whiteness and their contamination—enacts the logic of blindness upon human knowledge.

> The first thing that one notices living in the Middle East is that decay shrouds its objects in an obscurity which processes of termination and of growth equally find repugnant. For Middle Eastern political states, this obscurity takes the form of a blindness-toward-death, which can be contrasted with being blinded by death. (H. Parsani)

Lost in such an obscurity, bit by bit, one is laid bare to mess, liquidation of borders, infinitesimal extinction, base-necrophilia, and fluent rot which murmurs "taste your mortality" while erasing all routes to death.

Planting *puissance* on cold zero is the mechanism of decay (p/0); it is also the unground from which sinister Middle Eastern systems emerge without genesis. Decay builds without creation. Power requires a ground in order to turn into a formative power (power of law, the State, religion, etc.), and decay incapacitates the ground by which power is instrumentalized. But how does the rotting process or decay put the puissance over zero so as to unground power? The answer lies in decay's differentiating delirium and its cancerous attitude towards *metron* (scale).[1] Formation in general requires scales to maintain its consolidation and to support the process of regeneration or termination. On the one hand, decay is the differentiation of being (as attributed to an entity) into other beings; on the other hand, it is the metastasis of scales and dimensions through the act of decomposition or unfolding scales and dimensions inherent to the forms of new beings which emerge from the decaying entity. For a human corpse, there is no anthropomorphic scale—either abstractly or concretely—but only different dimensions, scales, and latitudes attributed to new forms and entities: scales of vermiculation (maggots), parasitic dimensions (fungi), aromatic latitudes (malodors), and the magnitude of the unknown. Although these scales are already present in the body, decay unbinds them with new rates of differentiation and irrespective of the body as a host of potentialities. Here, the machinery of decay overlaps with the mechanism of excessive scarring or fibro-proliferation. If scales are used in formative maintenance and in the perpetuation of integrity, they can also degenerate formation once their rate of proliferation or differentiation surpasses the capacity of the formation and its regenerating speed.

By proliferating scales and differentiating the latitudes of form, decay estranges itself from both nature and the natural, since it diverges from the great formlessness of nature that abhors the dimensions, standards, scales, metrons, and measures from which systems, territories, and assemblages are put together, fabricated, and configured to function. The process of decay, in fact, develops its machinery precisely from that which nature abhors—that is to say, scales and dimensions as matrices and frameworks of power formations. However, decay's approach to dimensions and scales is the approach of ( )hole complex to the Whole—the degeneration of the consolidating whole and the incapacitation of formation in regard to its range of differentiation or the ability to reform. Decay traverses and grasps dimensions as irreducible convolutions of solid and void, objects of infinite differentiation, to the point where measures or dimensions lose their capacity to scale or to determine formative regulations. This event, however, does not lead to the erasure of dimensions or measures. Decay degenerates dimensions by proliferating (turning into vermin) and convoluting them (vermiculation); fouling up everything dimensional. This does not mean that decay undertakes the Will of Nature and its unhinged

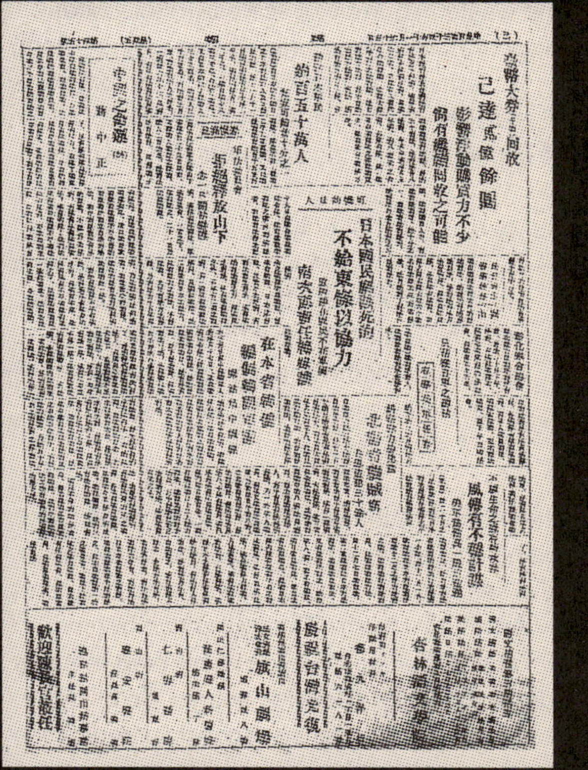

Newspaper — "Around 1.5 million Japanese return home," 1945.

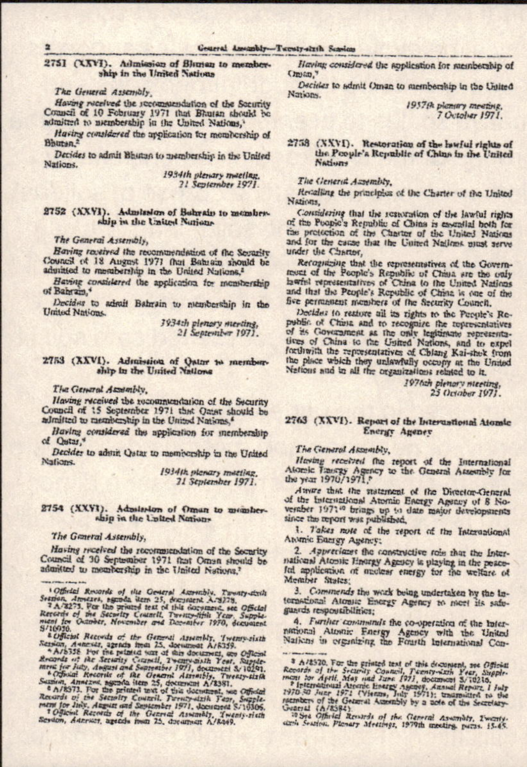

2 General Assembly—Twenty-sixth Session

2751 (XXVI). Admission of Bhutan to membership in the United Nations

The General Assembly,

Having received the recommendation of the Security Council of 10 February 1971 that Bhutan should be admitted to membership in the United Nations,[1]

Having considered the application for membership of Bhutan,[2]

Decides to admit Bhutan to membership in the United Nations.

1934th plenary meeting,
21 September 1971.

2752 (XXVI). Admission of Bahrain to membership in the United Nations

The General Assembly,

Having received the recommendation of the Security Council of 18 August 1971 that Bahrain should be admitted to membership in the United Nations,[3]

Having considered the application for membership of Bahrain,[4]

Decides to admit Bahrain to membership in the United Nations.

1934th plenary meeting,
21 September 1971.

2753 (XXVI). Admission of Qatar to membership in the United Nations

The General Assembly,

Having received the recommendation of the Security Council of 15 September 1971 that Qatar should be admitted to membership in the United Nations,[5]

Having considered the application for membership of Qatar,[6]

Decides to admit Qatar to membership in the United Nations.

1934th plenary meeting,
21 September 1971.

2754 (XXVI). Admission of Oman to membership in the United Nations

The General Assembly,

Having received the recommendation of the Security Council of 30 September 1971 that Oman should be admitted to membership in the United Nations,[7]

Having considered the application for membership of Oman,[7]

Decides to admit Oman to membership in the United Nations.

1957th plenary meeting,
7 October 1971.

2758 (XXVI). Restoration of the lawful rights of the People's Republic of China in the United Nations

The General Assembly,

Recalling the principles of the Charter of the United Nations,

Considering that the restoration of the lawful rights of the People's Republic of China is essential both for the protection of the Charter of the United Nations and for the cause that the United Nations must serve under the Charter,

Recognizing that the representatives of the Government of the People's Republic of China are the only lawful representatives of China to the United Nations and that the People's Republic of China is one of the five permanent members of the Security Council,

Decides to restore all its rights to the People's Republic of China and to recognize the representatives of its Government as the only legitimate representatives of China to the United Nations, and to expel forthwith the representatives of Chiang Kai-shek from the place which they unlawfully occupy at the United Nations and in all the organizations related to it.

1976th plenary meeting,
25 October 1971.

2763 (XXVI). Report of the International Atomic Energy Agency

The General Assembly,

Having received the report of the International Atomic Energy Agency to the General Assembly for the year 1970/1971,[9]

Aware that the statement of the Director-General of the International Atomic Energy Agency of 8 November 1971[10] brings up to date major developments since the report was published,

1. *Takes note* of the report of the International Atomic Energy Agency;

2. *Appreciates* the constructive role that the International Atomic Energy Agency is playing in the peaceful application of nuclear energy for the welfare of Member States;

3. *Commends* the work being undertaken by the International Atomic Energy Agency to meet its safeguards responsibilities;

4. *Further commends* the co-operation of the International Atomic Energy Agency with the United Nations in organizing the Fourth International Con-

[1] *Official Records of the General Assembly, Twenty-sixth Session, Annexes*, agenda item 25, document A/8278.
[2] A/8273. For the printed text of this document, see *Official Records of the Security Council, Twenty-fifth Year, Supplement for October, November and December 1970*, document S/10030.
[3] *Official Records of the General Assembly, Twenty-sixth Session, Annexes*, agenda item 25, document A/8359.
[4] A/8358. For the printed text of this document, see *Official Records of the Security Council, Twenty-sixth Year, Supplement for July, August and September 1971*, document S/10291.
[5] *Official Records of the General Assembly, Twenty-sixth Session, Annexes*, agenda item 25, document A/8381.
[6] A/8373. For the printed text of this document, see *Official Records of the Security Council, Twenty-sixth Year, Supplement for July, August and September 1971*, document S/10306.
[7] *Official Records of the General Assembly, Twenty-sixth Session, Annexes*, agenda item 25, document A/8449.
[8] A/8520. For the printed text of this document, see *Official Records of the Security Council, Twenty-sixth Year, Supplement for April, May and June 1971*, document S/10216.
[9] International Atomic Energy Agency, *Annual Report, 1 July 1970-30 June 1971* (Vienna, July 1971); transmitted to the members of the General Assembly by a note of the Secretary-General (A/8384).
[10] See *Official Records of the General Assembly, Twenty-sixth Session, Plenary Meetings*, 1979th meeting, paras. 15-45.

United Nations General Assembly Resolution 2758, 1971.

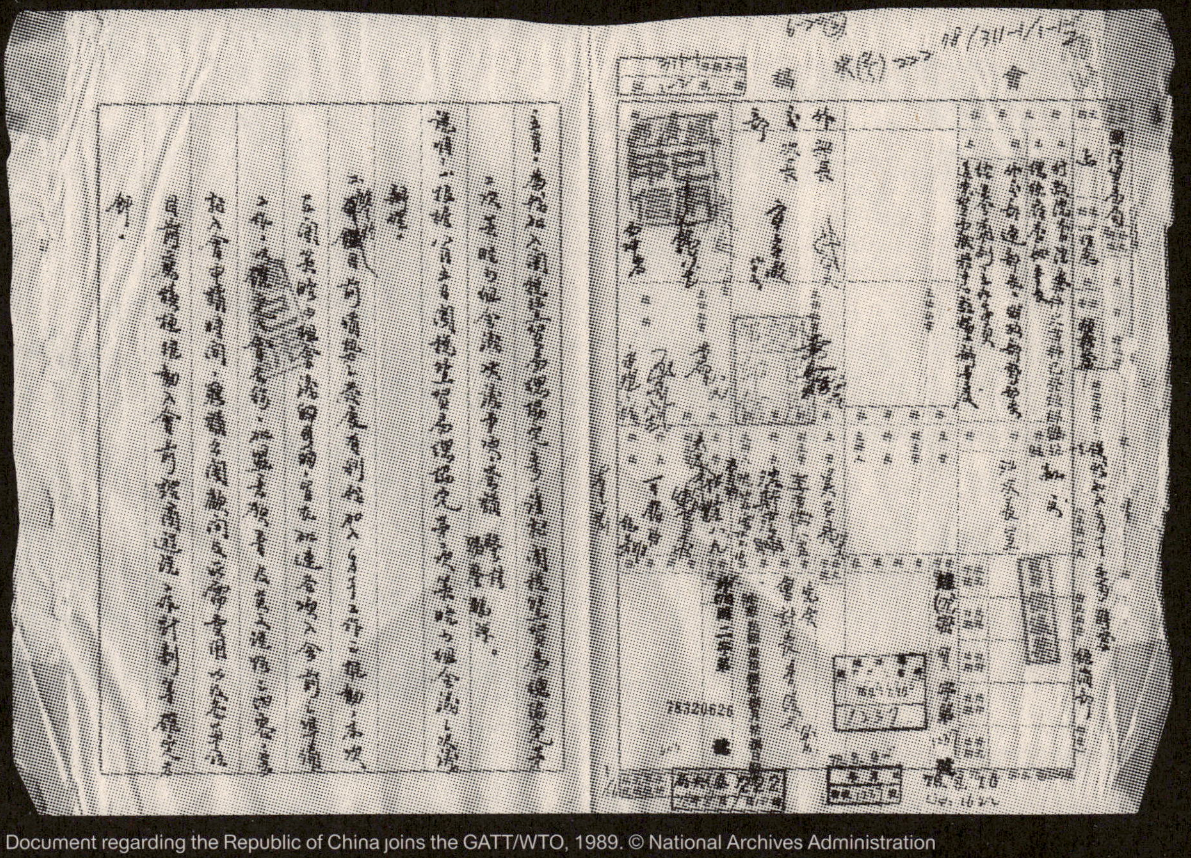

Document regarding the Republic of China joins the GATT/WTO, 1989. © National Archives Administration

Capital by vitiating dimensions and scales. Decay's malevolence toward scales suggests that decay unfolds through dimensions and formative scales to eventually descend into the unground of the wreckage of dimensionality or demonic solid (that is, the corpse of solidus). There is far more to "being solid" than one can imagine, since if solid were inferior to the void and simply a symptom of it, then why wouldn't decay's infinite brutal process eradicate solidity once and for all?

Immersed in the undercover softness of decay, dimensions and metrons deteriorate beneath the machinery of rot. Excessive dimensioning is the strategy of decay, just as solidity is its fuel. In decay, disintegration is a means for excessive dimensioning and proliferating scales, because disintegration is a terminal tactic to progressively breed more dimensions in the absence of any force of consolidation and utilization of them as a whole or a formation. A disintegrating entity is a vermiculate excretion of its former scales; it spawns more and more measures, micro-scales, metronic cells, patches of solid, labyrinthine nexuses of dimensions, and wasteful dumps of scales. To this extent, to speak of local decay (as related to one object) is problematic, for decay works externally to all scales and dimensions by which the local can be separated from the epidemic and the global:

> My decay is not only mine but the decay of the whole world which is differentiated from me. The Middle East might be an obscure geo-political decay, but the developed world, too, might in fact be said to be the decaying Middle East on an epidemic and global scale. (H. Parsani)

The disintegration introduced to an object by rotting processes is not a regular disintegration as of separation into component parts, fragments, or constitutive atoms. Decay is a non-fragmentary disintegration in which everything remains connected to the decaying entity. Continuity is preserved in the absence of consolidated dimensions and coherent measures. Consequently, the disintegrative process of decay expresses the logic of terminal softness (or goo) where continuity is the result of wasteful bonds and the

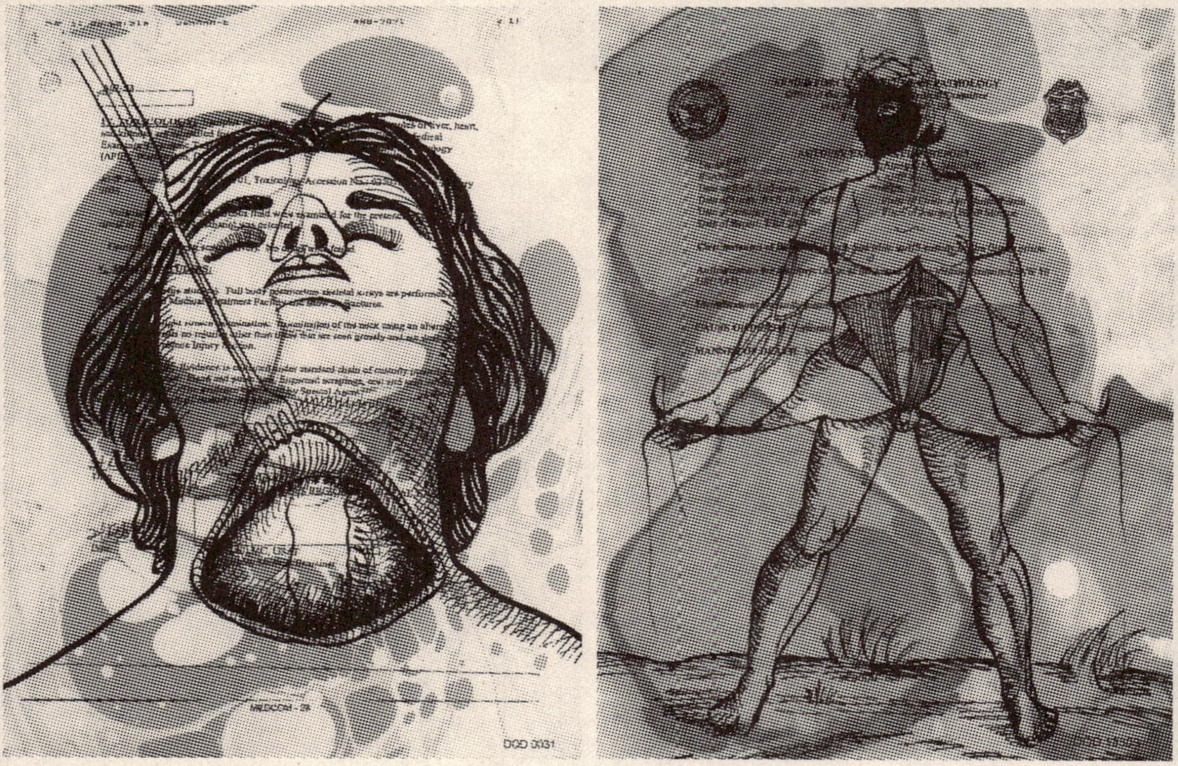

Rajkamal Kahlon, *Did You Kiss the Dead Body?* (detail), 2009, series of ink drawings on marbled US military autopsy report, each 28.3 × 36.6 cm.

unwanted, the disaligned, the leftover, these spaces appear to mark divergent and syncopated paths of development. A number of seemingly unconnected events, projects, and initiatives are beginning to ask how to step out of predefined orientation schemes, and into arenas where politics, spaces, technologies, images, and texts need not be associated along lines inscribed in previous knowledge.

Curated by John Palmesino and Ann-Sofi Rönnskog (Territorial Agency) and Anselm Franke, with Yi-Jen Chen and David Hellström. Photobooks by Armin Linke. Other contributions by Ching-Yueh Roan.

impossibility of rejecting such bonds. Integration, too, is impossible because scales and dimensions no longer maintain the capacity of their formative powers. Decay creates a mucoid continuity in disintegration. What happens in decay is a drastic collapse in the depth of composition where the contrast between solid and void is radically blurred. The wasteful bonds between solid and void are in subversive opposition to the economic effectivity and the stability of the whole. Disintegration is a lysis followed by the subversion of the capacity to determine the quantity and the quality of the incoming and the outgoing. For decay, softening and disintegration coincide, as formation is taken over by poromechanics. In poromechanical events, the hard exists through the soft. Decay's line of initiation corresponds to that of chemistry, from the inside to the outside, from hard and rigidly connected components to soft parts. Chemistry starts from within, but its existence is registered on the surface; ontology is, so to speak, merely a superficial symptom of chemistry. Decay extorts softness from the hard, making the hard an infested factory for breeding a softness which again is anonymous even to the formlessness of nature. The softness of decay is precisely a production of its irony.

Monotheism presupposes that any dissolution or breakdown of a solid is a vitally safe process moving in the direction of a Return (to nature, creation, and the divine). According to the doctrine of Return, any instance of solidity will be safely delivered to its basic elements or origin during its dissolution. Such a Return to the basic or original elements or matrix of existence is necessary for the horizon of purity —from ashes to ashes and dust to dust—which is the groundwork of the Divine's creationist project and the proof of its correctness. During decay, however, this course of Return (creationist advent?) through which deliverance or salvation is expected, deviates to something fundamentally deranged, a mess external to the recycling utopia of the Divine. In Zoroastrianism and medieval chemistry, this unrecyclable production of decay is addressed as fume or miasma—GAS. Plastic spirit or gas delineates the ultimate unlocalizablity of decay as an epidemic rather than a local phenomenon. It is no accident that the miasma and the plague were frequently equated with each other. Along the same lines, the Flemish alchemist Jan Baptista van Helmont associates putrefaction with the aporia of mixed bodies. Spirit is an epidemic which ends the myth of the soul by taking it into the outer nights of existence.

Chemistry (alchemy) begins with decay. Stripped before the mess-agents of decay, one can always ask, "Isn't thought a gaseous rot?" ... the question reverberates cancerously through the fetid air. Resistance to decay is both futile and fertile. But then, what is fertility in the sense of resistance toward decay? There is a yawning horror in this question.

1 Metron (Greek origin) is found etymologically encrypted in English words such as "dimension" (from *dimetiri*: measure out), "meter," etc. Keeping well in mind the famous doctrine of Pythagoras—"Man is the metron of everything" (*pantôn chremetôn metron anthrôpos*)—metron can be translated as "scale," "measure," "standard," and "value." According to Sextus Empiricus, metron expresses criterion (scale, measure) but Heraclitus and Sophocles saw it as certifying dominance, a domination over something. Therefore, metron indicates that both measures and dimensions interconnect with power, judgment, and reasoning. The critique of metron explains how dimensions (namely metron) bring power into effect, mobilizing and propagating it.

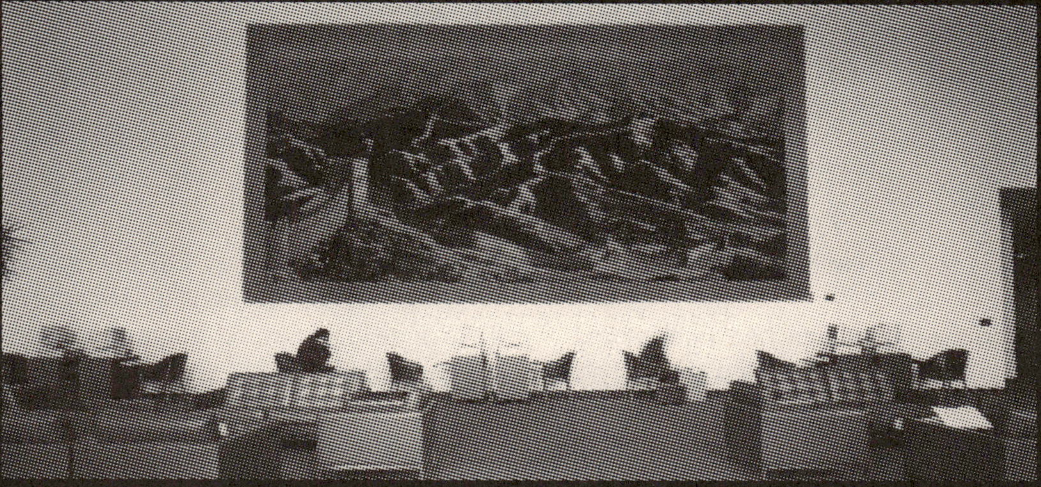

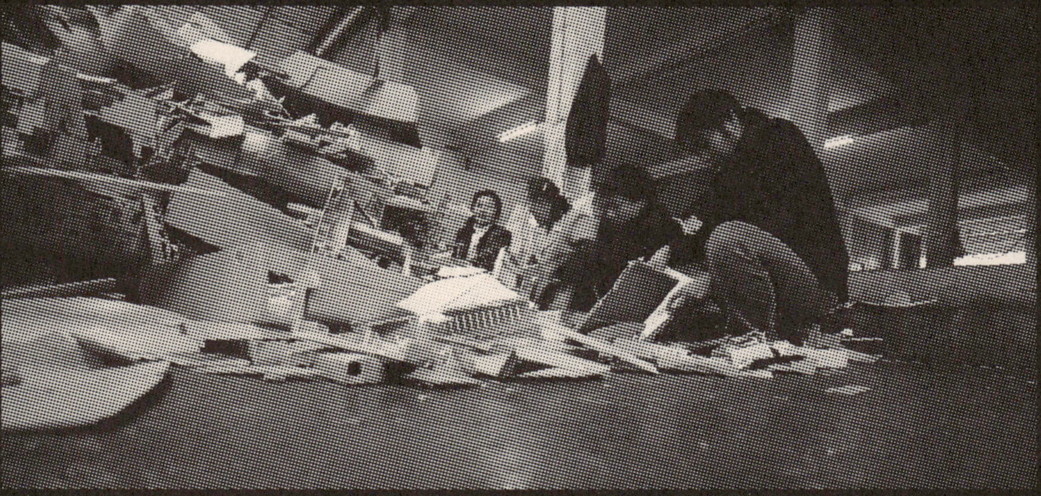

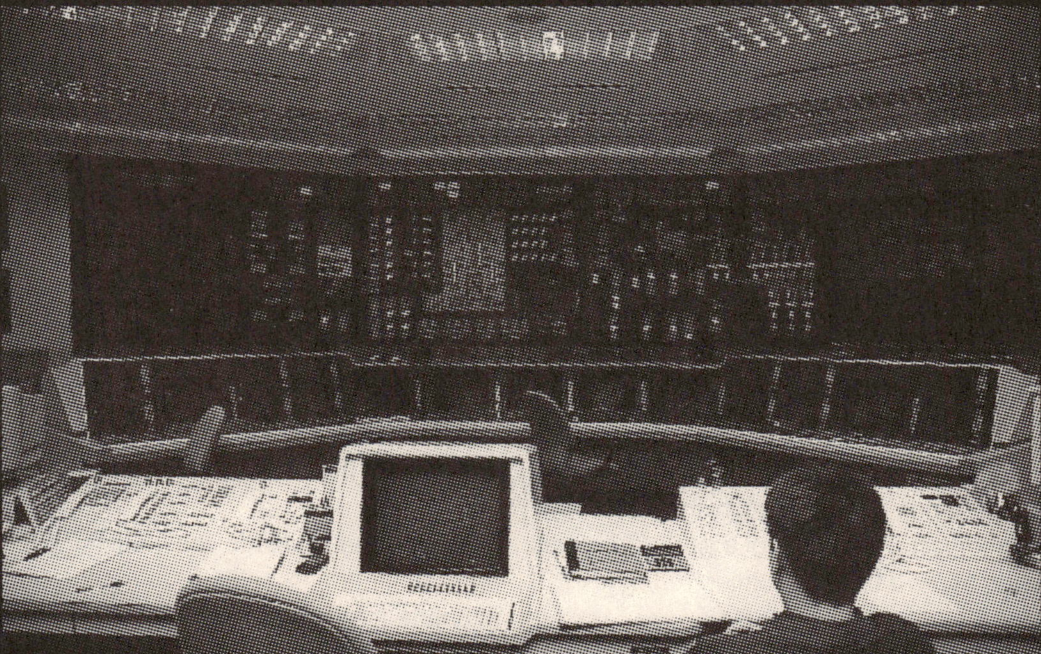

Fig. 1 Armin Linke, 08/12/2001, ONU, New York, USA.
Fig. 2 Armin Linke, 22/02/2005, Computer dump, Guiyu, China.
Fig. 3 Armin Linke, 18/02/1998, Kashiwazaki, Japan.

GINGER GLACIER

Adam Avikainen

Before us is our flesh with the tattooed portents.

A spider had somehow attached a web strand to my face and was climbing towards my nose from a pile of workbooks on the desk next to mine. I passed my hand in front of my right cheek and swung her to the floor.

Teddy bear with black button eyes and black rubber ears is asleep next to the hand pump disinfectant dispenser. The dictionary is half-black and half-pink. A blue sticker is affixed to the back of the fat, little book. Inside are some drawings on napkins that I completed in 2007 while waiting for my wife. I wasted in the coffee shop drinking bitter, while she searched for an electronic knuckle in the pickle shop towering across the highway.

"The beautiful thing about the painting language is that one never knows what exactly is being said. True stories from objective novelists working on pill fuel. Showering when they get a chance to realize their filthy fingers dripping sesame oil and skin cells on the black manuscripts clinging to sweaty forearms pressed down, immobilized for hours in neutral."

"Are you content with the environmental lookout agency printing all those pamphlets with all those blurry photographs?: Brutal winter scenes of oil slicks on glaciers. Pink Blue marches into marsh villages."

"Deformed spines twisting straight in preparation for a slow impact. The sound of a sludgy trumpet welcomes home a thawed soldier."

"Sawed tailor."

"Two people again needed to start soon. No experience demanded, but willing to negotiate in special circumstances. Call me what you will on what have you, but don't trip over the device. Take pride in your wood-trimmed car horn which will deafen you."

... "Stop your battles against humans or you will have nothing to fight the floods."

"If war is good for the economy, why not wage war against your apathy."

Flame-flaked paint. Stolen from the show.

Those carpeted bathrooms. That smelly couch.

Those cougher's lungs. Milk and tea and cookies named after a bodily process.

"Mmmm ... that circulatory juice is excellent."

Triangles scraped into wooden belt buckles.

"Officially, it's a biscuit. It is. I'm serious. If you had read the manual, you would've known not to turn it on."

Withered extremities departing before their bodies are born.

Apprehending the sane sugar fiends in order to separate them from the bitter ice.

So much fallout from the volcano. So little we know about the trial.

"Research has failed to show anything."

Exceeded the restraints. Quivering rodents voting in booths.

White, filmy tongue lapping up chocolate milk from the banana warehouse's inverted ceiling.

ARSENIC: GEOPHARMAKON

Nabil Ahmed

Earth is a turbulent planet where science, nature, and politics are becoming ever more entangled. In order to understand this entanglement, it is increasingly vital to adopt an ecological perspective, which permeates the earth's minorities and socialities with catalytic energy. This position is different from normative environmentalist epistemologies of protecting a nature that is "out there." Rather, it invites speculation on how nature has been an active participant throughout history in the protracted battle between majoritarian forces of the sovereign (empire-state-capital) and anticolonial, anticapitalist struggles. The friction between hegemonic power and minoritarian resistance is present when nature becomes the object of capture. As in a twist of political economy, labor is subjugated with the capture of land. However, what happens when nature itself acts as a violent force? When cyclones come in contact with human populations to produce an ungovernable space that challenges the sovereign? When meteorology dramatically shifts into politics? When nature speaks through powerful spiraling winds and enters politics, humanist narratives of history are swept away: radical meteorology.

This thesis begins with the Bhola cyclone, which struck the coastal zones of the province of East Pakistan in 1970, taking an estimated 300,000–500,000 lives. It was followed by a war of national liberation in Bangladesh in 1971. The role of this cyclone in state formation is often overlooked in Bengali nationalist historiographies. While narrating this event, particularly the horror and incalculability of death, a host of occult figures, intensities, and ecological histories are set in motion—Indo-Aryan war machine cosmologies, colonial anthropology, epidemiology, bodies in water, diatoms, forest enclosures and zomia (anarchist hill people in Asia who refuse the archaic state), Cold War meteorologies—the vortex as diagram. Following the war, the thesis tells of the mobilization of science by the statist-capitalist apparatus to rationalize the space of the cyclone in the Bengal delta. Yet the rise of the scientific-humanitarian complex is captured by a sinister metalloid found in Holocene rock formations: arsenic, uleashed into the drinking water of an entire population by a UN

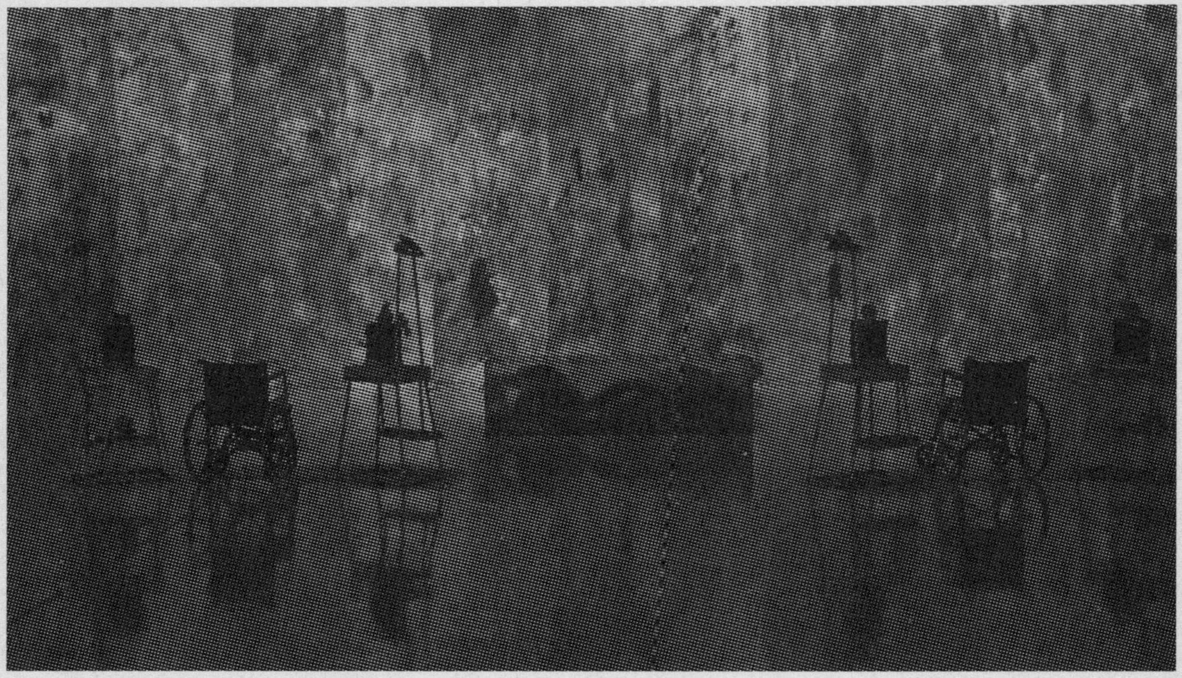

Adam Avikainen, *Ginger Glacier, 2012 ±5,000,000,000 years, frozen heat wave in the form of Ginger Glacier's skin and a monologue with itself possessed by teenaged humans…*

"The pressure from Harmony cultivated many loves. Legal. Legend. Lei."

"Modern scholastic methods are akin to caveman daycares … without the art. Overemphasis on freedom of choice. Your only choice is to live."

"I don't believe in the internet soul. Publish a gaggle of zit poems. Skip school, teen. Earn these. Lazy. Changing the colors and calling it a day."

Helioscopic vision.

"Pregnant islander identified."

"All land was an island."

Ill-rotten rains and the free range potato chicks.

"As opposed to what?"

Closed cage.

"In this age, we respect no lifeform. Extinct animals can be reanimated with proper financing."

development policy to dig millions of hand pumps, resulting in the largest mass poisoning in the history of earth. Doctors in West Bengal in the 1990s revealed the philosophical construct of a pharmakon while treating patients with symptoms of arsenic poisoning. Epidemiology returns in the calculation of arsenic in bodies, a haunted organology.

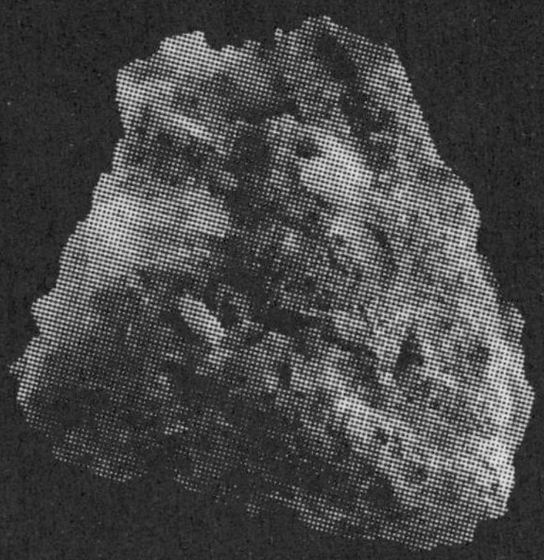

Arsenic

Who bears responsibility for an underexposed, creeping death markedly different from a sudden, mediatized natural disaster? What kind of international legal frameworks can be mobilized in a case where attribution of responsibility is so complex? From an ecological perspective, the question of environmental justice and activism becomes crucial in exposing the complexities around the transfer of infrastructure and scientific knowledge to the South in the service of the statist-capitalist capture apparatus of "development" and its non-commitment to legal accountability. However, this has only been further intensified in the recent drive to extract natural gas from the Bay of Bengal by the three states, India, Bangladesh, and Myanmar, where the space of disaster doubles as space for capital. Specific environmental activist practices and social movements are operating within flows of capital, technology, and the law in response to the capture attempts. The vortex of the cyclone reappears, entangled with the technical practice of resource extraction and the laws of the sea. The thesis (as part of a body of work consisting of exhibitions, seminars, and publications) locates this radical meteorology to coproduce contemporary anticapitalist environmental activist practices. The task is no less than writing a new political ecology for South Asia and the planet.

1. "Then again, more profoundly, even beyond the question of pain, the pharmaceutical remedy is essentially harmful because it is artificial. In this Plato is following Greek tradition and more precisely, the doctors of Cos. The Pharmakon goes against natural life: not only life unaffected by any illness, but even sick life, or rather the life of the sickness. For Plato believes in the natural life and normal development, so to speak, of disease. In the *Timeaus*, natural disease, like Logos in the *Phaedrus*, is compared to a living organism which must be allowed to develop according to its own norms and forms, in specific

SIXTEEN PROFESSIONS

Hu Fang

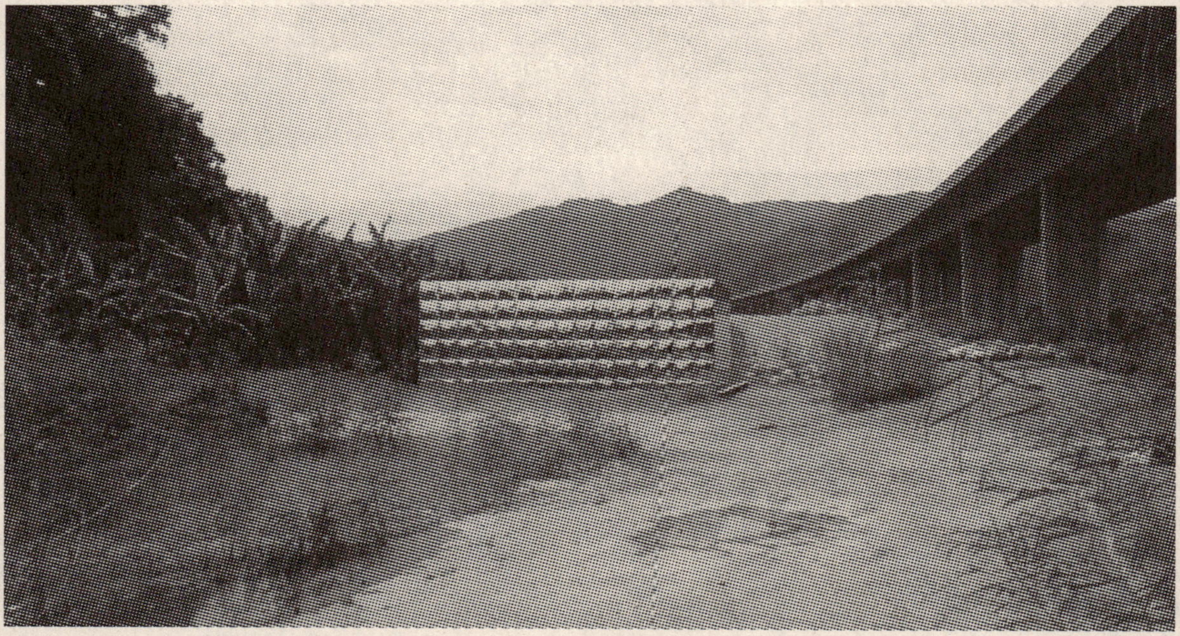

Anton Vidokle and Hu Fang, *Two Suns*, 2012, HD video, color, sound. Cinematography by Marcello Bozzini.

NO. 1: THE ESCAPED CONVICT

This man standing before you is an "escaped convict" known as No. 124. His most notable trait is his calm demeanour and composure. Apparently, in his mind, he has already overcome any distinction between being in jail and being out of jail. In his opinion, the value of land and air remains the same regardless of where he is. Rumour has it that No. 124 had surreptitiously moved to the other side of the wall when no one was paying attention; in fact, no one is certain whether he was able to create the illusion of the wall moving, simply by shifting his physical body a little.

This is No. 124's conviction: in the near future, the land on which the jail sits will become the site of a union between real-estate institutions and financial institutions. At that point, people will be less interested in escaping from jail and more interested in crossing back into jail.

NO. 2: THE SCRIPTWRITER

Before the incident, he had been hiding in a secluded country villa on the outskirts of town while writing his script. Prior to this, the quality and efficiency of his creative output had made him the darling of the media. Yet as the masses enthusiastically consumed his works, no one imagined that he would need some sort of stimulant to continue his rapid creative productivity.

In the beginning, that stimulant consisted of a combination of fast food and instant coffee. Gradually, he no longer had time to spend with his family. When he finished his script *Fighting Till the End for Love*, he lost his wife and kids. The alcohol in his glass was then replaced with petrol; he was discovered by someone to be guzzling petrol at a gas station. Some people suspected that he had contracted an illness known as "Foxconn," which is known to induce the hardening of human muscle, turning humans into machines.

rhythms and articulations. In disturbing the normal and natural progress of the illness, the Pharmakon is thus the enemy of the living in general, whether healthy or sick."
—"Plato's Pharmacy," Derrida
"We can conclude, then, that the *pharmakon* refuses to be excluded, it inhabits the heart of the fortresses that are supposed to protect us from its instability."
—Isabelle Stengers

In necrobiology, life and death are rolled up in a single continuous embrace. What happens when a poison enters the body? Here I write about arsenic and how it has produced violent ecological histories of earth. Arsenic combines readily with other chemical elements, forming strong arsenic compounds. An inorganic compound, arsine gas is used widely in the microchip industry, in laser science, and in the production of semiconductors because of its ability to convert electric light into laser light. Arsenic has a considerable medico-legal importance, as preparations of arsenic have been used for criminal ends more than any other known poison. Yet at the same time, in the last three centuries it has remained part of the history of biomedicine. A well-known case from the nineteenth century is Fowler's solution, a now discredited patent medicine prescribed for diseases such as malaria, syphilis, and cholera. A white cloud is formed when arsenic is burned under high temperatures from its brittle, crystalline form—arsenic trioxide, with a garlic odor—known as the drug Trisenox, which is mobilized to induce programmed cell death in the treatment of acute leukemia. Of course, massive side effects take place because of its high toxicity. But isn't this true for all medicines—they are not without side effects? We know this when we read the small "by the way" note that accompanies medicines from our visit to the pharmacy. Or the shameful politics of medicine that unfolded around the AIDS epidemic, where the Northern pharmaceutical industries used their power to stop the development of generic drugs for AIDS patients in Africa.

Arsenic is found in the atmosphere, where it comes from mainly three sources: volcanoes release about three thousand tonnes per year, and microorganisms release volatile *methylarsines* at the rate of twenty-thousand tonnes per year. But human activity is responsible for much more: eighty thousand tonnes of arsenic per year are released by the burning of fossil fuels. Since the rise of the industrial age, humans have polluted the earth's atmosphere with it as a by-product of mining and the

He was quietly isolated. As many people started reminiscing about and missing his scripts, news about his infection had already spread through the media and films, and was diffused in the black holes of our consciousness. Just like the widely quoted line in his script *Fighting Till the End for Love*: "Man is a machine of love, and it is precisely because we have emotions that we can become the most outstanding machines in the world."

NO. 3: THE DEPRESSIVE
On a beautiful sunny morning, he witnessed his beloved plant wilting, its yellowed leaves trembling in the breeze. His lips went dry, and he began to water the plant repeatedly. He thought to himself that the same dismal fate would befall anything and everything in his life: "I've already been wilting for so long, and yet I'd imagined that a lovely little plant would grant me the opportunity to experience the scent of spring."

NO. 4: THE COLLECTOR
As she slept soundly, he scrutinized the colors and shapes of the tattoos on her body, as if he was gazing at a dim yet awe-inspiring sixteenth-century religious painting or a Chinese landscape painting from the Song Dynasty—there was little else which elicited this sense of inner serenity for him. Landscape and religious paintings draw from a certain sense of human existence to passionately express the melding of, and the opposition between, life and death. If it was possible, he would willingly keep her in his collection—that whole mysterious existence of this girl in her youth.

NO. 5: THE FILM DIRECTOR
It was a night of revelry for luxury brands. After the gala dinner, he found himself staring at a melting candle, which resembled a diminutive yet virginal phallus. As he passed by the workshops in the suburbs, he could hear the rumblings of machines curiously fusing with the ringing in his ear to create a vision akin to Antonioni's film *Red Desert*.

As demonstrated by Kieslowski, in today's context, although the telling and transmission of moral stories is of extreme importance, it is also incredibly difficult to do. The director's predicament is similar to that of someone engrossed in lovemaking on a sofa, who suddenly glimpses the television screen showing aid hotlines for children in disaster areas.

Therefore, on this film location known as *the world*, given the last-minute absence of the actual director, and in order to ensure that the whole production schedule is not delayed, he would have no choice but to steel himself and pick up the megaphone—even if he is surrounded by glares of envy.

NO. 6: THE ANIMAL TRAINER
The performance goes as follows: initially, all the spare parts moving down a production line appear similar to one another, but reveal themselves to be grey rabbits lined one after another. Apparently, the animal trainer is a psychic from East Africa, but had somehow "lost" his psychic powers here. He could only wave his whip mechanically as he directed the zebras through their night parade, whilst uttering—in poor Mandarin—"Love animals, love yourself, that means loving your friends, loving the world you live in."

NO. 7: THE HOTEL CLEANER
His job was to remain unflappable as he cleared all used hotel toiletries and replaced them promptly. Each time, through these leftover items, he had the opportunity to acquaint himself intimately with the person who left them: the disheveled bedsheets that still emanated their bodies' warmth, a few strands of hair left in the sink, hastily scribbled phone numbers on the notepad on the bedside table, old newspapers, all sorts of receipts, an unfinished cup of water in the teacup, used towels all bundled up in a ball, dampness on the bathroom floor, a half-used bottle of shampoo emptied out in the bathtub, mist condensing on the mirror, perhaps the TV is still on, frozen at their favorite channel, the light remains switched on, the curtains pulled open, and beyond the window lies a Southern autumn day... In a moment, just like how a cassette tape is rewound, his hands will return all this

burning of coal. While these histories are important, my focus is on arsenic's natural occurrence in Holocene rock formations in the earth's crust. The focus of this text is then arsenic found in nature, which, oxidized through human activity, coproduces the poisoning of populations in a perilous confluence of geology and epidemiology. As agents of geological change, humans alter the earth's system, but in the case of arsenic, the earth alters the human in violent ways, as we will see in groundwater arsenic contamination in the Bengal basin. In the chain of causality, geological and anthropogenic change are rather entangled.

2. PHARMAKON. Throughout history, arsenic's nefarious use as poison and medicinal and industrial material makes it the pharmakon par excellence, as both "cure" and "poison."

"Pharmakon" is a term brought into contemporary philosophical dialog from Plato by Jacques Derrida. I am interested in the way it is discussed in the philosophy of science and technology (and by extension science and technology studies) by Bernard Stiegler, and its reinterpretation by Isabelle Stengers. In a close reading of Plato's *Phaedrus*, Derrida unfolds Plato's pharmacology of writing. In the *Phaedrus*, Thueth, Egyptian god of writing, offers King Thamus writing as a remedial technology to aid memory, or to protect against the loss of memory. However, Thamus refuses the offer, as writing may be of no help. Instead, it might create forgetfulness insofar as it cannot help memory, but only be a reminder. Writing becomes a "poison." Thus, the pharmakon is a way to read the ambivalence and messiness of reality, rather than relying upon binary and oppositional philosophical concepts such as remedy/poison, good/bad, positive/negative, subject/object, nature/culture.

A pharmakon is the movement and crossing-over between opposites. Against opposition, it moves through intellectual fields by seduction, and it resists capture. But this is no magic of deception. As Derrida is aware, what is being called upon in the task of uncovering the pharmakon of writing is first myth, the myth of Theuth, epistemology under a spell. It is precisely here that Isabelle Stengers reminds us that "instability" can be true of any pharmakon found in any culture. What distinguishes Northern epistemology is the anxiety around this instability, which comes from "confidence" in the foundations of science and a refusal of nonscience, which other cultures deal with in a more symbiotic way. She tells us that the tradition of the pharmakon, which began with the denouncement of Sophists as arbiters of opinion rather than knowledge, was an to its "original state." In a few hours, the new arrival will find: the curtains drawn tightly shut, the bedclothes neatly arranged, the toilet bowl in the bathroom once again sealed with a paper wrapper that says "As Yet Unopened," and all the body warmth and odors of the previous occupant rapidly eliminated, to be replaced by the scent of freshly washed sheets. With his hands, everything within this room will always retain the appearance of its "original state," as it awaits your arrival and use.

NO. 8: THE MANIFESTO EXPERT

He is obsessed with writing manifestos, in the hope that his words will be as influential and widely disseminated as *The Communist Manifesto* or *The Surrealist Manifesto*. He dreams of being called upon to draft forwards for the myriad translated editions of his work: "Now, as in 1848, a new historical era is about to begin ..."

He says: "People think that manifestos are the sunlit expressions of courage, when in fact they are the midnight distillation of regret. Manifestos are the proof that we transgress by day, and repent by night."

NO. 9: THE VIRUS EXPERT

At first, he was like a child who takes advantage of being sick to elicit his mother's concern. He used illness as a bid for his wife's attention. Later, after he developed an interest in Chinese medicine and Buddhism, he began to actively infect himself with viruses. His reasoning was quite simple. If he could concentrate all the ills of the world into his own body, he would become a virus expert, both carrier and cure for every virus in existence. In this way, he could become one with the "All." What Jesus took upon his body, now would be his to endure.

My lungs are on fire
Like a sunset burning in the west

NO. 10: THE FOURTUNE-TELLER

The lines on his palm were haphazard, and he has been diligently trying to repair them. The chaos on his palm seemed to be a reflection of society's disorder, and he was convinced that as he gradually opened his heart, the lines on his palm would also become clearer with time.

NO. 11: THE LOVESICK

She had torn something, and that moment became entangled with the present, resulting in a nagging pressure to survive. A long time ago, that inadvertent comment, that fleeting look in the eye, froze in time to become a pain that could not be ignored.

"In the end, I am unable to plunge into that sort of life in this unfamiliar city, but instead have a different sort of longing."

After trees fall to the ground, they slowly evolve to become organic matter—and who could explain this precisely? Even the boulders of Taihu can possess enough life within them to strike against water and penetrate rocks.

NO. 12: THE ONE WHO LOST HIS MOTHER TONGUE

"I have been living in this hotel for ten years, and have not had any opportunity to see my wife and family."

He elaborated: "Simply because I am one who has lost my mother tongue."

NO. 13: THE PROPERTY SPECULATOR

As a property speculator, he would drive his car around the city daily, carrying a large ring of keys. At his peak, his bag contained keys for a total of twenty houses.

There was a luxurious yacht anchored by the river next to the Royal Sales Office.

Under the setting sun at dusk, a solitary man kicked a football in front of the dilapidated buildings.

The houses they possessed were huge and spacious, and at times, that struck fear into the hearts of their wives.

NO. 14: THE IMAGE MAN

He tried to depict his own image but ended up being entranced by it.

As a result, he dedicated his whole life to replicating the life of this image.

For:
Lovers who could not divide their attention;
Lovers with a guilty conscience;
Lovers who would not settle down;

intellectual move to reveal the need for a foundation in (the) archaic philosophy (state). The archetype of the sophist-pharmakon has since multiplied into "modern practices." Stengers makes reference to Latour's concept of the "factish" in the realm of science, where "scientific demonstrations always imply an element of persuasion, although they claim to discriminate between objective truth and subjective persuation."[1]

I have a simple thesis. In the case of groundwater poisoning in Bangladesh, arsenic produces the *geopharmakon*, an operative concept: arsenic-contaminated drinking water as both poison and remedy, and, translated into the terms of politics, humanitarianism as both poison and remedy. The question is, once we have isolated and identified the pharmakon, how do we proceed?

3. OCCULT HISTORY. Arsenic is the thirty-third element in the periodic table discovered by the ancients. Preparations of it can be the perfect poison, given its extremely high toxicity and colorless, odorless, and tasteless state. In tracing its genealogy, I propose a set of moves which sees arsenic enter, firstly, the scientific realm in various degrees of intensities in the twelfth century; secondly, Western cultural history as a poison from the sixteenth century; thirdly, the legal realm in the nineteenth century; and finally, the political realm as a disaster caught up in the complex causality of humanitarian practices in the twentieth century, where the relationship between ends and means gets radically redistributed. The first contact between arsenic and human populations can be traced back to the 700s, when an Arab alchemist named Jabar first prepares arsenious oxide. Curiously, arsenic begins its scientific life in the time when the proto-science alchemy is trying to establish itself as chemistry, as when astrology transforms into astronomy. Therefore, it's no wonder that the first documentation and thus bringing-into-the-realm-of-science of arsenic is credited to Albertus Magnus in the twelfth century. Magnus was an alchemist/priest of the Dominican Order who was later made patron saint of the sciences, and who was responsible for the reception of Aristotelian thought

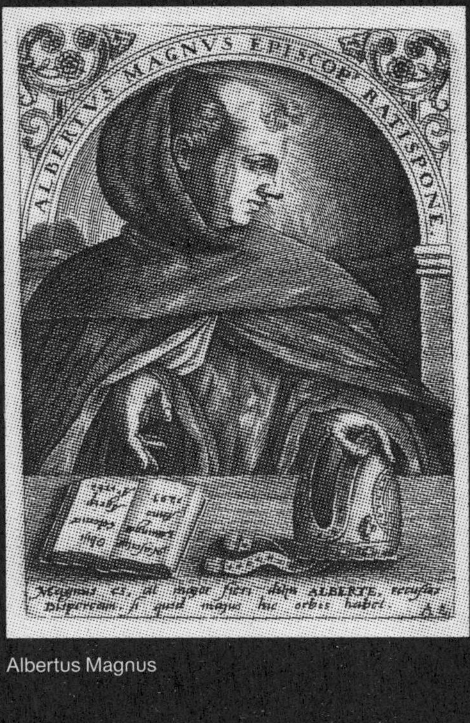

Albertus Magnus

For:
The pink assholes of neon lights;
The schizophrenia of capitalism;
And the myriad shades of colors
in this world;

There will be a film to document the process of how his image is reproduced:

How it can become something that is portable, can be displayed as well as put up for sale (just like famous personalities are used as models for little sculptures that are sold to tourists as mementos);

How to uncover the absurd logic of existence (for instance: vacations are taken so as to make us work even harder);

How to become both faces of a coin (it is impossible to see yourself and an image of yourself simultaneously).

"I should look exactly the same as the image in my movie," he concluded about his life in the movie trailer.

NO. 15: THE MONEYCHANGER

Due to long sedentary periods, the solitary middle-aged man counting banknotes behind the moneychanging counter at the international airport had developed a tummy.

He would mutter to himself daily as if he were chanting Buddhist scripture:

"Wanxian
Wangdu
Jiangwu City
The places which you would never
Be able to go to."

NO. 16: THE SEEKER

When the Master gave up his life, relinquishing his only chance of survival to me, I didn't know if I could accept his sacrifice.

All I had ever cared about was the pursuit of pleasure and happiness. But he wanted me to search for the Meaning of Life.

The curse of youth, the Master's righteousness ... they had brought me nothing but endless pressure.

These days, people are terrified not by the imminence of the end, but rather by the rarified harmony that pervades the city.

But after seeing the Master's serenity in the face of death, it was as if my life had been returned to me. Never again will I fear its loss. All I can do now is grope my way forward through the city's murk, and do my best to lay down the burdens of the flesh. In any event, before I know it I'll be old, and able to "follow my heart's desire without overstepping the line."[1]

1 Confucius: Analects: 2.4: "... at seventy I followed my heart's desire without overstepping the line." (Translated by D. C. Lau, 1979, Penguin Books).

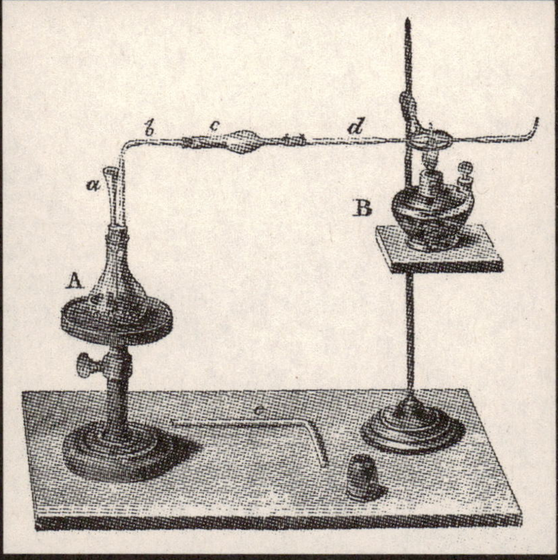

Marsh Test Apparatus, steel engraving, 1867. Theodore G. Wormeley, M.D., *Microchemistry of Poisons, including their Physiological, Pathological, and Legal Relations*, National Library of Medicine.

in Christian theology and science through his most famous student, Thomas Aquinas. In the sixteenth century, arsenic becomes the favorite murder weapon in medieval Europe, thus earning it the sinister title "king of poisons and the poison of kings." The US military uses two arsenic compounds to produce Agent Blue, one of the rainbow herbicides used in the Vietnam War.

Arsenic enters the realm of law in the nineteenth century as one of the key actors in the advent of forensic toxicology, when scientific knowledge finally catches up with the elusive poison(er). In 1832 in England, police arrested John Bodle for lacing his grandfather's coffee with poison. Chemist James Marsh tested the drink in his laboratory, and confirmed the presence of arsenic by producing a yellow precipitate of arsenic sulfide. But the precipitate was unstable and, by the time of the trial, had deteriorated. Without forensic proof, Bodle was acquitted. Disappointed by the verdict, especially when Bodle admitted to the murder, Marsh devised a test that could better stand up in court. His new apparatus not only detected the minute traces of arsenic but also measured the quantity in the form of a silvery-black deposit. The intensity of the arsenic would be compared with an archive of films produced using known amounts of arsenic. In France in 1840, the use of the Marsh Test in the LaFarge poisoning case marked the first ever application of forensic toxicology as evidence in court. Strangely enough, arsenic is known to have preservative properties. When Napoleon's body was transferred to Les Invalides from St. Helene, which probably took some time, the body was found to be perfectly preserved. His postmortem showed testicular atrophy, and Napoleon was taking *liquor arsenicalis*, a popular medicine with arsenic in it that supposedly improved potency but was also commonly prescribed for dermitis and epilepsy. In a strange twist, the very same preservative properties of arsenic led to its use in mobile embalming stations in the battlefields of the American Civil War, where it enabled bodies to be returned home. A "cultured" pharmakon is sunk back into the earth with the bodies of soldiers sent home, turning entire cemeteries into potential

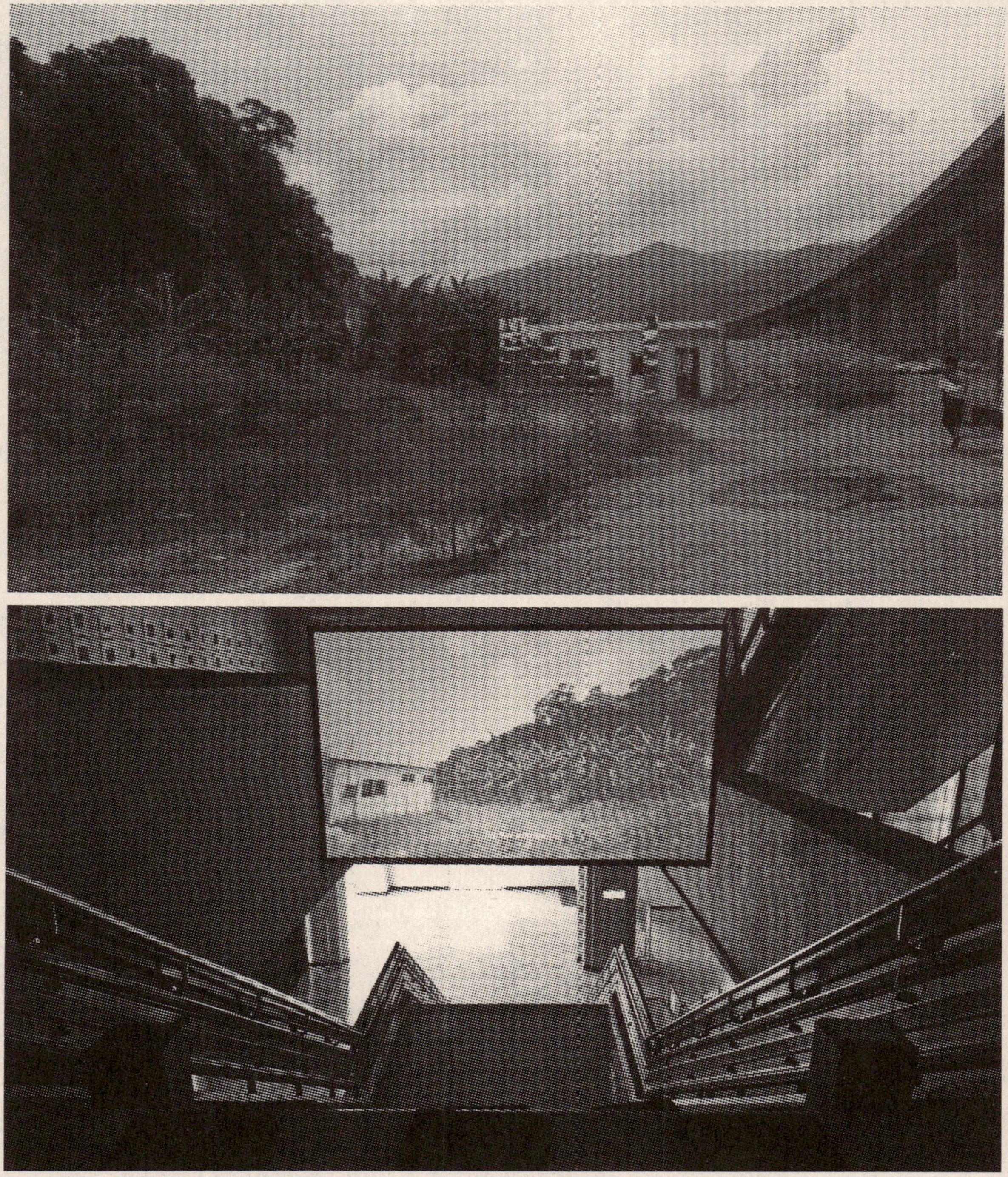

Anton Vidokle and Hu Fang, *Two Suns*, 2012, HD video, color, sound. Cinematography by Marcello Bozzini.

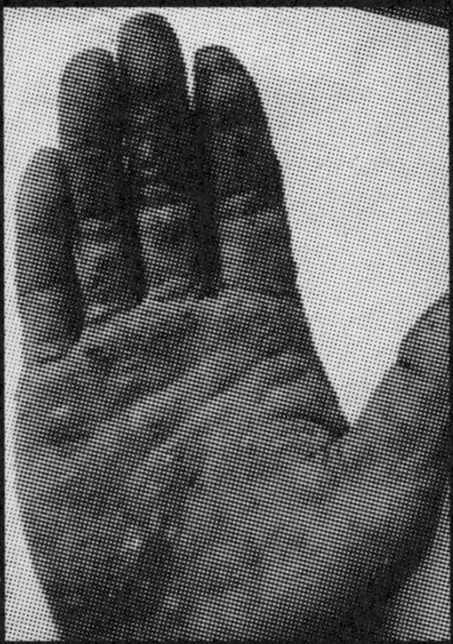

Keratosis of the palm

contamination zones, hazardous especially for archaeologists.

4. GEOLOGY/EPIDEMIOLOGY. Unlike arsenic minerals, naturally occurring arsenic is a late discovery for natural science, dating back only about one hundred years with the first documented occurrence of disease in the Pampean Plain of Argentina in the 1920s, and subsequently in Chile, Taiwan, and China. Among these, Taiwan is important for the history of epidemiological studies of arsenic, as it's where the first diseases at population level were documented in the 1950s. Taiwan is at one end of the South and Southeast Asian arsenic belt that starts in Pakistan and intensifies through the Himalayan and Indo-Burman ranges. Endemic to Taiwan is blackfoot disease, a severe disease of the blood vessels of the legs and feet caused by the ingestion of arsenic from groundwater. The disease was prevalent on the southwest coast of Taiwan, especially in the Beimen, Hseuchia, Jiangjing, and Yenshui Townships. It was eradicated when residents completely stopped using groundwater as drinking water. In terms of geology, the Choko black shale on the upper part of the Pachang River in southwest Taiwan is considered the main factor leading to arsenic in groundwater. As the riverbed eroded, the river carried shale fragments containing arsenic downstream, resulting in the arsenic enrichment of the aquifers in the nearby provinces.

In the late twentieth century, arsenic resurfaces in the Ganges River basin. In its most violent eruption in earth's history, this time arsenic enters the realm of humanitarianism and politics. According to the World Health Organization, the groundwater arsenic contamination in Bangladesh is considered the largest mass poisoning of a population in history. What sets this disaster apart from a cyclone or major industrial disasters such as Chernobyl or Bhopal is the gradual exposure of human populations to poison over a long period of time. An exact figure is not known, but it is estimated that between forty and sixty million people were exposed. At the same time, this disaster is a reversal of the normal mediatization of disasters, in which sudden catastrophes are transformed into humanitarian emergencies; in this case, the exposure occurred over a long period of time and the illness was slow to manifest. Human population is an important actor in this natural-political assemblage, since in recent decades

HISTORY AS SORCERY (EXCERPT)

Michael Taussig

> Allegories are, in the realm of thoughts, what ruins are in the realm of things.
> —Walter Benjamin, *The Origin of German Tragic Drama*

It is not with conscious ideology but with what I call "implicit social knowledge" that I am here concerned, with what moves people without their knowing quite why or how, with what makes the real real and the normal normal, and above all with what makes ethical distinctions politically powerful. I take implicit social knowledge to be essentially inarticulable and imageric, nondiscursive knowing of social relationality, and in trying to understand some aspects of the way that history and memory interact in the constituting of this knowledge, I wish to raise some questions about the way that certain historical events, indeed notably political events of conquest and colonization, become objectified in contemporary shamanic repertoire as magically empowered imagery capable of causing and relieving misfortune.[1]

I do not mean to here imply that a simple, or what some would call an historicist-conceived time sequence of cause and effect, is at work; that first the Great Events of the European conquest of the New World fix images in popular tradition that surface much later on, in our own day, for instance, in shamanic healing rites. Rather, it seems to me that there is a far more interesting and complicated fit between the rendering of the past in the present than this causally sequential model assumes, and that this fit is one of appropriateness of meaning and feeling. Surely the use of magically empowering imagery drawn from and referring to the past can teach us something important about just this fit and why it is so appropriate.

In her analysis of the re-surfacing of witch mythology in contemporary European feminism, Silvia Bovenschen argues that the resurgence of this image illustrates not so much the historian's knowledge of witches and their persecution, but instead a more direct "preconceptual" relationship between the image of the witch and the personal experiences of today's women.[2] She points out that this sort of experiential appropriation of the past differs from the professional historian's assumed modus operandi in that it incorporates historical and social fantasy sensitive to the underground existence of forbidden images. In turning to such images, people are reflecting on their symbolic potential to fulfill hopes for release from suffering. Related to this is the proposition that the blocking of experience by political oppression and psychic repression can entail a subsequent process whereby that experience becomes unblocked, animated and conscious, by means of myths and mythic images. I wish to suggest that this process is also involved in the European conquest of "primitive" societies and in the colonial decomposing of their religions. The "bits and pieces" that remain of these religions are thus not testimony to the tenacity of tradition, as the historicist would argue. Instead they are mythic images reflecting and condensing the experiential appropriation of the history of conquest, as that history is seen to form analogies and structural correspondences with the hopes and tribulations of the present. In noting that this sort of appropriation of the past is anarchical and rebellious in its rejection of chronology and historical accuracy, Bovenschen stresses its redemptive function, citing Walter Benjamin: "The past carries with it a temporal index by which it is referred to redemption. There is a secret agreement between past generations and the present one."[3]

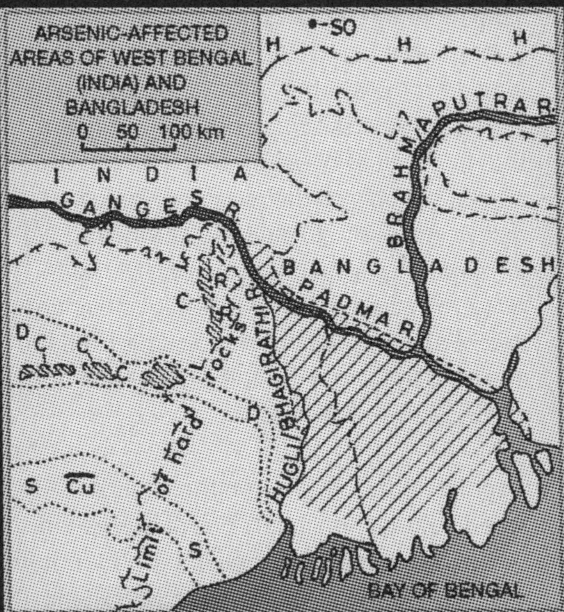

Bangladesh has been seen by Western neoliberal hegemony as a Malthusian time bomb. It raises the question: What constitutes an emergency when its causes are complex and multilayered, with medical, legal, technical, and political dimensions? The complexity lies in the calculus of the poison's distribution deep inside the earth.

Microbiological contamination in surface water was a major cause of high child mortality rates in Bangladesh prior to 1970. After independence in 1971, international development agencies strongly promoted ground-water as a safe source, particularly in rural areas, and they financed and promoted water supply projects that were wholly reliant on groundwater. In an immense feat of micro-water mining, around one million hand-pump wells were dug by the government of Bangladesh in the center and south of the country, with funding provided by UNICEF. Where the infrastructure of the state was not horizontally connected, external forces dug vertically. Later, this became a national policy supported by development agencies and the government, and as a result, millions more wells were dug privately. It created a thriving village economy around vendors, installers, and producers of PVC pipe, cylinders, piston valves, etc. Over the next two decades the program was considered a major humanitarian success, as child mortality rates decreased and a large part of the population was able to access bacteriologically clean drinking water.

This is until the early 1990s, when doctors in West Bengal, where drinking water from wells was also a common practice, began to notice significant numbers of patients with clinical symptoms of arsenicosis, the disease caused by acute arsenic intake. For humans, high water consumption in tropical heat mineralizes the body with arsenic in minute increments. Short-term symptoms are first dermatological: loss of hair; nails falling out like brittle, dried paint; and excessive pigmentation of skin and urine. As the poison invades the body, patients begin to have abdominal pain, vomiting, hemorrhaging, convulsions, swollen ankles, inflammation of the respiratory tract, wrist drop, or failure of the radial nerve.

Yet surely this secret agreement, despite its Messianic promise, is also subject to conflict. Indeed Benjamin finds in such conflict favored terrain for revolutionary praxis because (as in his "Theses on the Philosophy of History") he believes that it is where history figures in memory, in an image that flashes forth unexpectedly in a moment of crisis, that contending political forces engage in battle:

> To articulate the past historically does not mean to recognize it "the way it really was" (Ranke). It means to seize hold of a memory as it flashes up at a moment of danger. Historical materialism wishes to retain that image of the past which unexpectedly appears to man singled out by history at a moment of danger. The danger affects both the content of the tradition and its receivers. The same threat hangs over both: that of becoming a tool of the ruling classes. In every era the attempt must be made anew to wrest tradition away from a conformism that is about to overpower it. The Messiah comes not only as the redeemer, he comes as the subduer of Antichrist. Only that historian will have the gift of fanning the spark of hope in the past who is firmly convinced that *even the dead* will not be safe from the enemy if he wins. And this enemy has not ceased to be victorious.[4]

Provocatively probing into hitherto little-explored zones of political control, Benjamin was also urging fellow Marxists to ponder more deeply their own implicit faith in a Messianic view of history, to face up to that faith in a conscious fashion, and to consider for

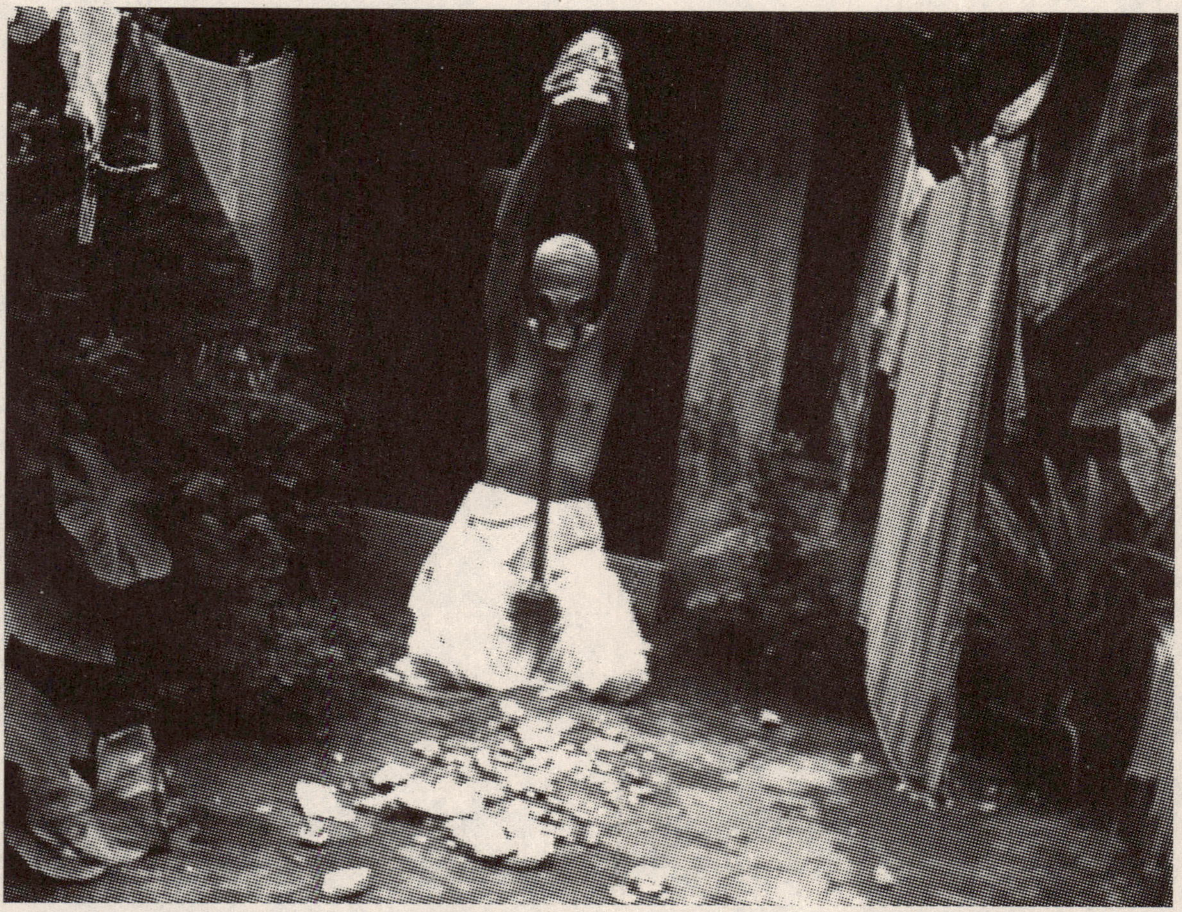

Ashish Avikunthak, *Vakratunda Swaha*, 2010, HD video, color, sound, 21 min. During the Ganapati Festival, a Ganesha symbol is worshipped for ten days, and then on the eleventh day the statue is taken through the streets in a procession, to be immersed in a river or the sea, symbolizing a ritual send-off of the Lord on his journey towards his abode in Kailash. As he leaves this world, he takes with him the misfortunes of all man. Swaha is the name of a deity associated with sacrifice. When sacrifices are made, the name "Swaha," which literally means "self-spoken" or "spoken by me," is chanted. This film is a requiem for a deceased friend.

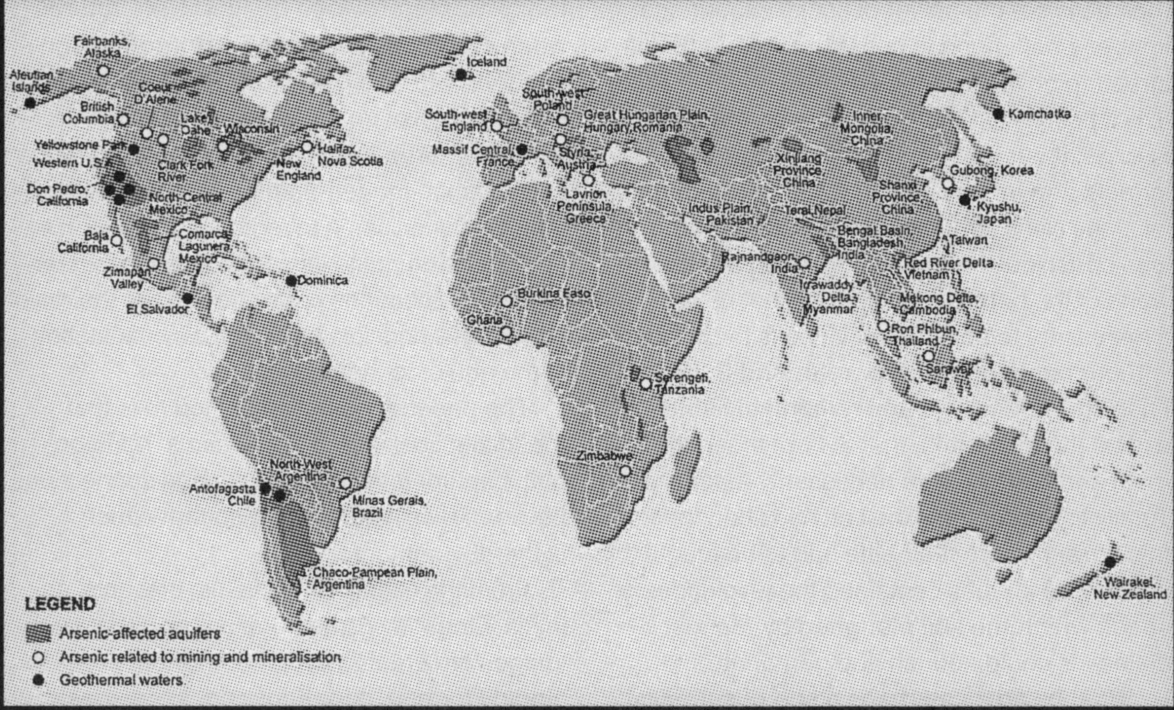

Geological arsenic map

With continued exposure, the chemical destroys the lungs, liver, and kidneys through a long period of latency, making detection much more difficult. Once lurking beneath the surface of the earth for thousands of years, unleashed metalloids now hunt internal organs. A set of scientific discoveries and alliances with epistemic communities across the border eventually brought the extent of the disaster to light, gaining wide media attention. A poisoned population was conjured almost over night.

As it turns out, arsenic occurs naturally in large quantities in geological formations in the Ganges, Brahmaputra, and Meghna deltas, as well as elsewhere in South and Southeast Asia. Some geologists go so far as to claim that the Farakka Dam, constructed by India within its territory, is part of the problem. The idea of taking water from the east-bound Ganges for West Bengal first surfaced in the early nineteenth century. With the partition of Bengal, a new and clearer form of ecological nationalism was programmed and articulated. This was addressed by following India's national planning policy of building a barrage across the Ganges that would secure fresh water for impoverished West Bengal, resulting in the commissioning of the Farakka Barrage in 1975. According to ecological historian Iqbal, "Since its erection, the barrage has been blamed for various ecological and humanitarian problems in both West Bengal and Bangladesh, such as erosion of land and soil, flooding, and contamination by arsenic." The theory suggests that the capture of the river by the Farakka their activism the power of social experience, imagery, and mood in constructing and deconstructing political consciousness and the will to act politically. Another way of putting this is to point out that he didn't place much faith in facts and information in winning arguments, let alone class struggle, and that it was in the less conscious image-realm and in the dream-world of the popular imagination that he saw it necessary to act. "To convince is to conquer without conception," he wrote. And if the Fascists were willing and remarkably able to exploit these dreams, that did not mean that myth and fantasy were necessarily reactionary. Totally to the contrary, the Left had abandoned this terrain where the battle had to be fought and whose images contained the revolutionary seeds which the soil ploughed by Marxist dialectics could nourish and germinate.

What he advocated was a sort of surrealist technique using what he called "dialectical images"—an obscure yet compelling notion better left to example than to exegesis; what his friend Theodor Adorno referred to as "picture puzzles which shock by way of their enigmatic form and thereby set thinking in motion." Picture-puzzles is of course how Freud referred to the manifest content of dream imagery, and if it was to the manifest and not the latent level that Benjamin was drawn, it was because of the way such images defamiliarized the familiar and shook the sense of reality in the given order of things, redeeming the past in the present in a medley of deconstructive anarchical ploys. Unlike current modes of Deconstruction however, the intent here was to facilitate the construction of new forms of social life from the glimpses provided of alternative futures when otherwise concealed or forgotten connections with the past were revealed by the juxtaposition of images, as in the technique of montage—a technique of great importance to Benjamin. Indeed Stanley Mitchell tells us that "Benjamin came to regard montage, i.e. the ability to capture the infinite, sudden, or subterranean connections of dissimilars, as the major constitutive principle of the artistic imagination in the age of technology."[5]

The understanding we are led to is that the "dialectical image" is *in itself a montage,* both capturing the aforementioned connections between dissimilars and also that which is thereby captured.

From the examples Benjamin presents, as in his "One Way Street," we can see that such images are created by the author but are also already formed, or half-formed, so to speak, latent in the world of the popular imagination, awaiting the fine touch of the dialectical magician's wand—not unlike Victor Turner's description of the central African herbalist and curer whose adze, in chopping bark off the chosen tree, arouses the slumbering power of material already there awaiting the copula of the magician's touch.

This notion of the activist acting on something ready to be activated is well conveyed where Benjamin writes that "Opinions are to the vast apparatus of social existence what oil is to machines: one does not go up to a turbine and pour oil over it; one applies a little to hidden spindles and joints that one has to know."[6]

But how does one know?

1 For several years the author has been engaged in writing a local history of colonialism, shamanism, and the wild man, based to a large extent on his living with and learning from shamans and their patients in the Upper Amazon-Andean foothills of the Putumayo River in southwest Colombia, South America, a region he first visited in 1972. Since then he has returned every year except 1973. A grant from the National Science Foundation made it possible to spend much of 1975 and 1976 there, and the National Endowment for the Humanities provided a year in 1980 for the preparation of a book about the embodying of colonialism in medicinal magic. A comprehensive but abbreviated account of this material has been published by the author: "Folk Healing and the Structure of Conquest in Southwest Colombia," *Journal of Latin American Lore* 6:2 (1980): 217–78.

2 Silvia Bovenschen, "The Contemporary Witch, the Historical Witch and the Witch Myth: The Witch Subject of the Appropriation of Nature and Object of the Domination of Nature," *New German Critique* 15 (Fall 1978): 84.

3 Ibid.

4 Walter Benjamin, "Theses on the Philosophy of History" in *Illuminations*, trans. Harry Zohn and ed. Hannah Arendt (New York: Schocken, 1969), 255.

5 Stanley Mitchell, "Introduction," in Walter Benjamin, *Understanding Brecht*, trans. Anna Bostock (Verso: New York, 1983), xiii.

6 Walter Benjamin, "One Way Street," in *One Way Street and Other Writings* (London: Penguin, 1979), 45.

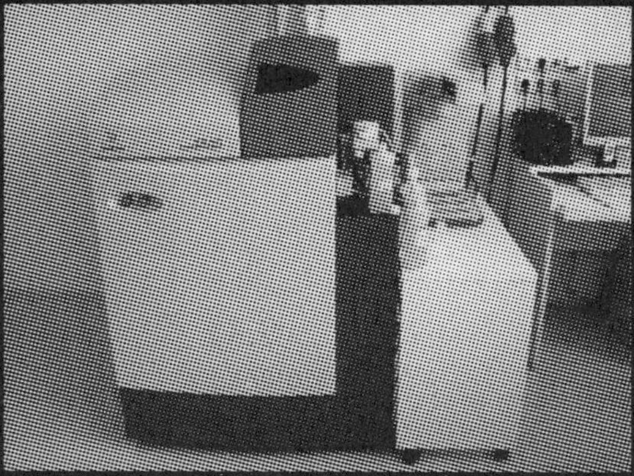

Inductively coupled plasma mass spectrometry instrument

Dam led to the lowering of the water table, which resulted in exposure to air in the zone of aeration. This exposure resulted in the oxidation of arsenic minerals previously present below the water table in the Bengal sediments. The arsenic oxides migrated to the groundwater and were reduced to their poisonous forms in the reducing environments below the water table.

5. SCIENCE/LAW. What kind of international legal frameworks can be mobilized in a case where attribution of responsibility is so complex and the victims are villagers in the Global South organized through social rather than political movements? In 2004, four hundred arsenicosis-infected villagers from one of the contaminated areas launched a legal case with the help of a consortium of environmental-legal activists. Their target was the National Environment Research Council (NERC), the parent body of the British Geological Society (BGS), which in the early 1990s, serving as technical experts appointed by the UK Overseas Development Administration, had tested for safe groundwater in this particular village. The plaintiffs claimed that BGS failed to find arsenic and thus were negligent in saying that the drinking water in the village was safe. However, BGS claimed that they were not testing specifically for arsenic, as the tests were designed not for drinking water safety but as part of a scientific report for an agriculture development project, agriculture being a key driver in the shift towards using groundwater in the twentieth century.

It appears that what did not get tested became a critical point in the case. The first of its kind for victims of arsenic poisoning in Bangladesh, the case *Sutradhar vs. NERC* was eventually dismissed by the House of Lords in 2006. As a tort, the appeal was essentially thrown out; the court decided that the proximity between the plaintiffs and BGS was so remote that no duty of care could arise. However, in the minority judgment, one judge pointed to the expert witness testimony of Dr. Sara Bennett, a Canadian environmental specialist consulting on Bangladesh's Northeast Regional Water Management Plan. She had noted that the Bangladeshi government relied heavily upon foreign organizations for data gathering and analysis, with the implication that the 1992 report influenced the government's decision-making processes, such as when it drew up a national water policy.

MUSEUM FUTURES: LIVE, RECORDED, DISTRIBUTED, 2008

Marysia Lewandowska and Neil Cummings

Museums, like all institutions, are sometimes monsters of their own kind. But like most monsters, they change form. Museums used to be like mausoleums, places in which objects, artifacts, and works of art were classified and protected from decay. This mission of preservation has made museums the antithesis of "life," since life is in permanent transformation, and museums were originally conceived as places outside the normal flow of time. Contrary to this conception, the Moderna Museet, established 1958 in Stockholm, is an emblematic "modern" museum, seeking to be actively engaged in envisioning societal futures rather than merely presenting a mummified past. In the sci-fi-like film *Museum Futures: Distributed*, Marysia Lewandowska and Neil Cummings speculate about such a future by staging an exchange set in 2058 between the future director of the Moderna Museet and a young researcher. Their conversation envisions the near future of the museum, which has already become a globalized, dynamic structure that constantly reevaluates and modifies itself according to permanent feedback processes, embedded in and collaborating with the market economy in new ways.

Centenary Interview, 2058
Interior: *The common room, Moderna Museet v3.0*

A beautiful lounge, comfortable seating, local lighting, windows with breathtaking views of the sea.

The Executive of Moderna v3.0, Ayan Lindquist, is waiting to be interviewed in real-time from Guangzhou, via the Asian Multitude network.

She is browsing screens when a face materializes in one of the windows on the wall.

MS. CHAN
Nihao, hej, hello! Is that Ayan Lindquist?

AYAN LINDQUIST
Nihao, hello. Yes Ms. Chan, this is Ayan. We are in sync.

MS. CHAN
Thank you so much for finding the time. You must be very busy with the centenary launch.

AYAN LINDQUIST
It's a pleasure. We really admire your work on mid-twentieth-century image ecologies, especially your research on archival practice.

MS. CHAN
Well, I'm flattered. For many Asian non-market institutions, your pioneering work with long-term equity contracts has been inspirational!

AYAN LINDQUIST
Oh, there was a whole team of us involved ... So let's begin.

MS. CHAN
Okay, just to refresh, for the centenary I'd like to archive your live-thread recall of Moderna.

AYAN LINDQUIST
Yep, that's fine. I've enabled about twenty minutes.

MS. CHAN
Okay, live. Maybe we could start with some personal history. What were you doing before you became the executive of Moderna Museet v3.0?

AYAN LINDQUIST
Well, I joined Moderna v2.0 in 2049, almost ten years ago, first as adviser to the development working group, then as part of the governance team. I participated in the forking of Moderna v3.0 in 2'51, and was elected fixed-term executive in 2'52. I've got another four years in the post.

MS. CHAN
And before that?

AYAN LINDQUIST
Immediately before joining Moderna I collaborated in the exhibition program at the MACBA cluster in Mumbai for six years, but more in resource provision. That's where we worked on a version of the equity bond issue you mentioned.

MS. CHAN
And before that?

AYAN LINDQUIST
In programming again, at Tate in Doha for four years, developing exhibitionary platforms. And even before that, I participated in research on cultural governance for the Nordic Congress of the European Multitude for six years. I suspect that exhibition agency and governance are my real strengths.

MS. CHAN
Maybe we should dive into the deep end. Could you briefly say something about why Moderna v3.0 devolved, and why it was necessary?

AYAN LINDQUIST
As you can imagine, there was a lot of consultation beforehand. It's not something we did without due diligence. For almost forty years Moderna v2.0 explored and developed the exhibitionary form. We pioneered the production of many collaborative exhibitions, resources, and assemblages. We helped build robust public—or what you might term "nonmarket"—cultural networks, and scaled those networks to produce our *i-commons*, part of the vast, glocal Public Domain. We have continually nurtured and developed emergent art practices. Moderna can proudly, and quite rightly, say that we participated in shaping the early twenty-first century development of art—from an exhibitionary practice based around art-artifacts, spectacle, and consumption, to one of embedded coproduction.

MS. CHAN
Do you mean ...

AYAN LINDQUIST
Of course, there are many complex factors involved, but we were an agent in the shift from a heritage cultural mind-set of "broadcast," to a mind-set of emergent, peer-to-peer meshworks. Following the logic of practice, we became an immanent institution.

MS. CHAN
Could you say a ...

The question of proximity thus becomes key in exposing the complexities around the transfer of scientific knowledge to the South in the service of development, and the North's non-commitment to legal accountability when well-intentioned development projects go wrong. As Derek Gregory tells us: "Distance is never an absolute, fixed and frozen, and within the colonial present, like the colonial past, the power to transform distance … is typically arrogated by metropolitan cultures." How does accountability operate in developing states, and who is the state accountable to within a history of governmentality in relation to infrastructure? When multilateral organizations, such as the UN, themselves have global immunity, how does one hold the scientific-aid complex of the Global North accountable? What happens to citizens' right to know when such a fallible scientific report influences a weak state in drawing up its national water policy? What led the villagers to pursue litigation against scientists and scientific institutions as opposed to NGOs or the state?

Although different in many respects from the case of arsenic poisoning in Bangladesh, the story of the Bhopal disaster in India, in which the victims continued to claim redress even after official litigation and compensation ran its course, is worth consideration. In Bhopal, on December 3, 1984, a cloud of deadly methyl isocyanate gas escaped from a pesticide plant owned and operated by Union Carbide, a US multinational corporation. The cloud spread across the nearby poor neighborhoods of the city, killing thousands of innocent people who were sleeping. Following the disaster, many thousands of Bhopal residents suffered from long-term illness and deformities because of the leaked gas. The protracted litigation created what is known as "the great ambulance chase," in which Indian and US legal systems were conjoined. Many US firms looking for a lucrative class-action lawsuit came to Bhopal and figuratively waited outside hospitals. Their hopes were dashed with the 1985 Bhopal Act, which declared that the Indian state itself would take over the exclusive representation of all claims arising from the disaster, under the doctrine of *parens patriae* ("father to the people").

India then made attempts to take Union Carbide to trial in a US court, arguing that Indian courts did not have the necessary legal apparatus to deal with a case of such magnitude. It was established that Indian law indeed had no precedent in tort law dealing with large-scale industrial disasters, and that the case should go to trial in US courts. However, the US District Court in New York dismissed the case, stating

AYAN LINDQUIST
Although having said all of that, we haven't really answered your question, have we? Some of us at Moderna v2.0 believed that exhibition as a technology, and immanence as an institutional logic, needed to be radically revised. So this is what we intended to explore with Moderna v3.0. We wanted to execute some of the research. To enact. To be more agent than immanent.

MS. CHAN
I wonder if you could you say a ...

AYAN LINDQUIST
Sorry to over-write, but in a way, this forking follows the tradition of Moderna Museet. Moderna v2.0 mutated out of v1.0 because the tension between trying to collect, conserve, and exhibit the history of twentieth-century art, while at the same time trying to be a responsible twenty-first-century art institution, proved too difficult to reconcile. Moderna v1.0 continues its mandate. Its buildings and collection have global heritage status. This early hybridization enabled Moderna v2.0 to be more mobile and experimental—in its organizational form, in its devolved administration, and its exhibition-making practice ...

MS. CHAN
Could you expand on the "more complex factors" you mentioned earlier?

AYAN LINDQUIST
That's a big question! Let me rerun a general thread from composite ... uh ...

Ayan taps the terminal/tablet.

Well, a good place to start might be the divergence of emergent art practices and the market for "contemporary art." Although the public domain has a long genealogy, reaching waaaay back to ancient European land rights, "commons" projects, and commonwealths, it was the advent of digitalization, and particularly of very early composite language projects in the 1980s—which were proprietary, as astonishing as that sounds to us now—that kick-started what were called "open," "free," or nonmarket resource initiatives. Of course, these languages and assemblages, and the resources they were building, needed legal protection—licenses to protect them from property and competitive marketization. The General Public License, the legendary GPL legal code, was written in 1989.

MS. CHAN
It's not so old!

AYAN LINDQUIST
Text and images, either still or moving; artifacts, systems, and processes; music and sound, either as source or assembled; all embedded plant, animal, and bodily knowledge; public research; and all possible ecologies involving these resources—all were aggregated into our Public Domain by the viral licenses.

Ayan counts on her fingers.

Some milestones include the releasing of the sequenced human genome in 2001, the foundation of the "multitude" social enterprise coalition in 2'09, and Intellectual Property reform in the teens. The UN-Multitude initiated the microtaxation of global financial transactions in 2'13, which redirected financial resources to Public Domain cultural initiatives. I could go on and on and on, but most participants will be over-familiar with this thread.

MS. CHAN
Remind me, when did Moderna affiliate?

AYAN LINDQUIST
In-Archive records suggest Öppna dagar or Härifrån till allmänningen, with Mejan ... I'm sorry. We did some collaborative "open" knowledge projects with Mejan in Stockholm in late 2'09. And when Moderna v2.0 launched in 2'12, we declared all new knowledge compliant with General Public License version 6.

MS. CHAN
Wasn't that initiated by Chus Martinez, one of your predecessors? She seems to have shaped early Moderna v2.0, which in turn became an inspiration globally.

AYAN LINDQUIST
It's nice of you to say so. Starting in 2'12, we collaborated with the fledgling Nordic Congress—in what was to become the European Multitude—to form the backbone of the Public Domain cultural meshwork. It eventually convened in late 2'22. So we were at the source.

MS. CHAN
Okay, thanks.

AYAN LINDQUIST
Simultaneous with the exponential growth of the Public Domain was the growth of the market for what we still call "contemporary art." Many historians locate one of the sources for this "contemporary art" market in the auctioning off of the art-artifact collection of Robert and Ethel Scull in New York in 1973. It was an extraordinary collection of paintings by male Pop artists like Andy Warhol, Claes Oldenburg, Ed Ruscha, and ... er ... I recall ... Jasper Johns.

MS. CHAN
From composite, I'm streaming the John Schott analogue film of the sale, which is in New York MoMA's Public Domain archive.

AYAN LINDQUIST
It's a great film, and many of the art-artifacts have subsequently devolved to Moderna.

MS. CHAN
I have the catalogue. It's present ... I'm browsing.

AYAN LINDQUIST
That auction set records. It also connected art-artifacts with financial speculation in a way previously unimaginable. By 1981, one of the "big two" auction houses, Sotheby's, was active in twenty-three countries and had a "contemporary art" market throughput of 4.9 billion old US dollars. Soon, global Trade Fairs mushroomed. Commercial galleries flourished and a sliver of "branded" artists lived like mid-twentieth-century media oligarchs. By 2'06, complex financial trading technologies were using art-artifacts as an asset class. And most public Modern Art Museums were priced out of the "contemporary art" market. In retrospect, we wasted an enormous amount of time and effort collecting financial resources to purchase, and publicly "own," vastly overpriced goods. And we wasted time wooing wealthy speculators for sporadic gifts and donations too!

MS. CHAN
That connects! It was the same locally. The conflictual ethical demands in early Modern Art Museums were systemic. And obviously unsustainable. Reversing the resource flow, and using the Transaction Tax to nourish Public Domain cultural meshworks seems ... well, inevitable.

AYAN LINDQUIST
Sometimes, rethreading is such a wonderful luxury! Anyway, auction houses began to buy commercial galleries. And this dissolved the tradition of the primary (i.e., managed) and secondary (i.e., free) art markets. As a consequence, by 2'12 the "contemporary art" market was a "true" competitive market, with prices for assets falling as well as rising. Various "contemporary art" bond, derivative, and futures markets were quickly created. And usually, art-asset portfolios were managed by specialist brokerages linked to banking subsidiaries.

MS. CHAN
Okay. I also see some local downturns linked to financial debt bubbles bursting—spectacularly in 2'08, again in 2'24, and again in 2'28. Market corrections?

AYAN LINDQUIST
Probably. Market corrections and their repercussions. Overall, the market expanded and matured in 2'27, and has remained sufficiently resourced ever since ... more or less. By 2'14, formerly commercial galleries—the primary market—had became a competing meshwork of global auction franchises. By 2'25, they needed to open branded academies to ensure new assets were produced.

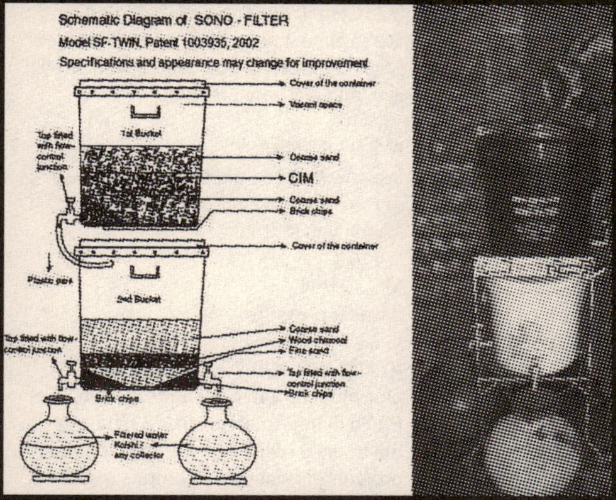

SONO-FILTER, laboratory in the field. Example of a low-cost arsenic filtration device 2006.

that the disaster and its victims were located in India—again, a case ruled out due to proximity. Sheila Jasanoff writes: "Belying the apparent ease of transferring Carbide's technology of production from West to East, India's attempts to transfer the legal sanctions for failure back to the risk-exporting country proved much less easy." The government's class-action lawsuit on behalf of Bhopal's victims never went to trial. Instead, the Indian government accepted Carbide's settlement offer of $470 million in May 1989.

6. The disparity between the Global North and the Global South can be articulated in the legal-scientific policy instrument that specifies the acceptable amount of arsenic in drinking water. In 1993, the WHO tightened the standard for arsenic in drinking water from fifty to ten parts per billion, equivalent to three seconds of a century. Germany first codified the guideline into law in 1996, followed by many others countries, such as the United States, where arsenic occurs in various regions of the country but where the problem is far less severe due to a more dispersed population. In countries such as Bangladesh, the standard remains fifty parts per billion. The difference, according to WHO sanitation engineer Hiroki Hashizume, lies in the lower analytic capabilities of measuring techniques in the developing world, which are as yet unable to accurately measure quantities below ten parts per billion on a national scale. In fact, he and some others have suggested that developing countries are better off with the higher standard so that subpopulations that are most in danger are prioritized. The specificity of scientific practice conditions policy formulations and ultimately class struggles.

There is now a large body of scientific knowledge about arsenic contamination, much of which is focused on Asia. In particular, arsenic poisoning in Bangladesh is a high-profile case with growing local awareness, support from humanitarian organizations, and various environmental NGOs working in the field. The sheer number of unknown contaminated wells, as well as the large population potentially exposed to contaminated water, continues to be a major problem for mitigation efforts. At the same

MS. CHAN
I can see the Frieze Art Academy in Beijing. That was one of the earliest.

AYAN LINDQUIST
The market for "contemporary art" became, for all intents and purposes, a competitive commodity market, just like any other—useful for generating profit and loss through speculation. And useful for generating Public Domain financial resources, but completely divorced from emergent art practice.

MS. CHAN
Okay, this might be a bit of a dumb query, but does Moderna feel that in the self-replication of the "contemporary art" market, something valuable has been lost from public Museums?

AYAN LINDQUIST
To be perfectly honest, no. No, we only experience benefits. You see, through the UN-Multitude distribution of the Transaction Tax, we are better-resourced financially. This, in turn, has enabled us to develop our local cluster and node network. Generally, competitive markets thrive on artificial difference and managed risk. They are just too limited a technology to nurture, or challenge, or distribute truly creative art practice. Take all these private art-asset collections built by speculator-collectors and supported through private foundations—despite being hyper-resourced, they all ultimately fail. Then they are either broken up and recirculated through the "contemporary art" market, or more commonly, they devolve to the multitude and enter public Museum collections. Here at Moderna, we have benefited enormously from a spate of default donations. Consequently, we have a comprehensive collection of "contemporary" art-artifacts that came to us through reversion.

MS. CHAN
This was the basis for the amazing Moderna exhibition *Contemporary Art*, held in Shanghai in 2'24. It was reconstructed as a study module while I was at the Open University in 2'50. I can still recall it. What a collection! What an amazing exhibition!

Okay, so maybe here we could locate an ethic approaching something like a critical mass. As Moderna Museet's collection, exhibitions, and activities expanded—and as other Museums expanded too, of course—the ethic of public generosity was distributed, nurtured, and encouraged. Everyone benefits. I can see that when the Ericsson group pledged its collection, for instance, it triggered a whole avalanche of other important private gifts and donations. Like the Akzo-La Caixa collection, or the Generali Foundation gift. Or like when the Guggenheim franchises collapsed as the debt bubble burst in 2'18, and the CEO of Deutsche Bank decided to revert their collection.

AYAN LINDQUIST
[*laughter*]
We think that's a slightly different case—certainly of a different magnitude! Although it's a common trajectory for many public/private museum hybrids.

MS. CHAN
It's certainly true of museums locally: the former Ullens Center for Contemporary Art in Beijing, and MOCA in Shanghai, for instance.

AYAN LINDQUIST
That connects. The increased resources and the gifts, donations, and reversions enabled us to seed our local cluster devolution. Starting in 2'15, we invested in partnerships with the Institutet Människa I Nätverk in Stockholm, with agencies in Tallin and Helsinki, with the early reversion of the Second Life hive, and with Pushkinskaya in St. Petersburg. We created what was rather fondly termed the "Baltic cluster."

MS. CHAN
Okay, from composite I see that there was an earlier experiment with a devolved Moderna. During the enforced closure in 2'02–2'03, exhibitions were cohosted with sympathetic local institutions. There was even a Konstmobilen!

AYAN LINDQUIST
Ja, and it was considered something of a success. Distributing and reimagining the collection through the cluster—incidentally, we cut our carbon debt to almost twelve—radically scaled our activities. So while developing locally, we also began to produce a wider Moderna Museet network. The first Moderna node opened in Doha in the United Arab Emirates. We participated in the local ecologies, in the restructuring of resources, from carbon to knowledge. That was in 2'18. In 2'20, Mumbai emerged. There was "Ex Habare," the three-year research project in which several self-organized Research Institutions cooperated, including Nowhere in Moscow, the Critical Practice consortium in London, and Sarai in Delhi. And as you already mentioned, Shanghai launched in 2'24 with the landmark *Contemporary Art* exhibition, then the Guangzhou node went live in 2'29 with *La Part Maudite: Bataille and the Accursed Share*. A really timely exhibition! It explored the distribution of trust and "well-being" in a general economy, the ethics of waste and expenditure, and the love—and terror—implicit in uninhibited generosity. Isn't that node's location near your present Guangdong Museum hub? On Ersha Island, by the Haiyin Bridge?

MS. CHAN
We're almost neighbors! As for *the La Part Maudite*, much of that source work is still live, and still very present.

AYAN LINDQUIST
We saw that you did some restoration of the image server codecs recently. Thank you for that.

MS. CHAN
It was a pleasure.

AYAN LINDQUIST
Our most recent node emerged in Sao Paulo in the Americas in 2'33, through the agency of the Alan Turing Centenary project "Almost Real: Composite Consciousness."

MS. CHAN
If I may, I'd just like to loop back with you to the '20s and '30s. That's when many academic historians think we entered a new exhibitionary "golden age" with Moderna. You coproduced a suite of landmark projects, many of which are still present.

AYAN LINDQUIST
We're not too comfortable with the idea of a "golden age." Maybe our work became embedded again. Anyway, if there was a "golden age," we'd like to think it started earlier, maybe in 2'18. That year, we set about exploring a key term from early machine logic: "feedback." And on its fiftieth anniversary, we made a re-address to the source: the legendary *Cybernetic Serendipity* exhibition that took place at the Institute of Contemporary Art in London in 1968.

MS. CHAN
From composite—I see that the Tate has many Public Domain archive resources—*Cybernetic Serendipity* is recorded as the first exhibitionary exchange between visual art and digital assemblies.

AYAN LINDQUIST
For us at Moderna, that exhibition set in motion two decades of recurrent projects exploring art, technology, and knowledge. Its most recent manifestation, linked to the Turing research, has resulted in Moderna v3.0's cooperation on a draft amendment to Article 39 of the United Nations Declaration of Human Rights. We are seeking to extend certain rights to organic/synthetic intelligent composites.

MS. CHAN
You're coproducing sovereign composites?

AYAN LINDQUIST
Yes, yes. That's what I was hinting at earlier when I talked about Moderna being more of an agent and executing as well as exhibiting.

time, there are vast regions of the earth that have yet to be mapped for arsenic contamination. What I have attempted to point out is that while epidemiological, geochemical, and hydrological scientific knowledge of arsenic poisoning has grown, legal accountability and redress for the victims has remained largely neglected. In doing this, I have tried to bring an interdisciplinary approach to unfolding future scenarios. At the same time, I have attempted to sketch some notes towards constructing a practice within the framework of the Forensic Architecture project. The history and mapping of arsenic poisoning can be tools for activists in the field pursing speculative legal action, and can place these practices in dialogue with the wider international environmental movement. By treating arsenic poisoning as a global public issue, can we size up political power.

The project requires fieldwork: interviews with scientists, activists, and victims, as well as archival research, site visits, and the careful reading of scientific instruments. It can take the form of an imagined technical museum of arsenic. (There is an existing museum devoted to blackfoot disease in Tainan, located next to what used to be the blackfoot hospital.) This museum could be framed by the philosophical concept of the pharmakon, and could focus on the convergence of geology and epidemiology, science and law, with particular attention paid to the Bengal basin. The work can be presented as a set of videos on multiple monitors—as a set of images. As already mentioned, in forensic toxicology the intensity of arsenic was first measured against film containing its known quantities.

At this stage, following the work of Latour (for example, his research monograph *Science in Action*), I am particularly interested in scientific research related to arsenic in the laboratory. I am interested in how arsenic "discoveries" are made in practice, and how this research then cohabits with other modern practices in the world. In 2010, Taiwan was the venue for a different kind of biennial: the third International Congress on Arsenic in the Environment, with its focus on arsenic in the geosphere and human diseases. The fourth scientific congress is taking place in Australia, and it will be titled "Understanding the Geological-Medical Interface of Arsenic." There have been 23,144 published scientific articles on arsenic since 1956, of which around seven thousand have been written in the twenty-first century. Science is therefore an active participant in constructing, tracking, and producing some of the arsenic "factishes" discussed in this essay. The London Arsenic Group is an existing

MS. CHAN
Ah, now I understand Moderna's centenary proposal for a *Museum of Their Wishes*. It's absolutely amazing! I know it's a very common thread, but it's definitely worth rerunning—the one about the foundation of the Moderna Museet's collection with the *Museum of Our Wishes* exhibition in 1962, and how this was revisited in 2006 with the *Museum of our Wishes II*, to address the lack of women artists in the collection.

AYAN LINDQUIST
We see our legacy as a resource, not a burden. It's something we have been working with for a while, recursive programs. It's at the root of Moderna. Actually, *Wish II* was finally fulfilled in 2'22 when some Dora Maar photographs reverted. But with the emergence of self-conscious composite intelligence, addressing "their" wishes seemed appropriate, even necessary. And it's true—if the draft amendment is ratified, it will be an amazing achievement.

MS. CHAN
Even if you don't like the term, maybe a new "golden age" is beginning?

AYAN LINDQUIST
We'll all just have to wait and see. But earlier, you were right to suggest that in 2'20, with "Ex Habare: The Practice of Exhibition," we consolidated the idea of emergent art and distributed new institutional practices.

MS. CHAN
In the Asian network, it's common knowledge that "Ex Habare" reaffirmed the role of the Museum in civil society.

AYAN LINDQUIST
Well, to start with, we uncompressed the Latinate root of "exhibition," *ex habare*, to reveal the intention of "holding out" or "showing" evidence in a legal court. It's obvious that implicit in an exhibition is the desire to show, display, and share with others. By grafting this ancient drive onto the desire for creative coproduction, we enabled exhibitions to remain core to Moderna's aspirations. It's also true that to source, participate, coproduce, and share, to generate non-rivalrous resources, is vital to the constitution of the Public Domain. And indeed, to civil society. There's a neat homology: "Ex Habare" distributed these values, and yes, they replicated at an astonishing speed.

MS. CHAN
It's so good to be reminded of that! Even I tend to take for granted the power of exhibition as a technology. Do you think that this is because artists and others moved into collaborative relationships with Moderna?

AYAN LINDQUIST
Var ska vi börja? Artists and others realized that the nineteenth-century ideological construction of the artist had reached its absolute limit. As configured, art as a "creative" process had ceased to innovate, inspire, or have any critical purchase. Quite simply, it was irrelevant!

MS. CHAN
Everywhere, except in the "contemporary art" market!

AYAN LINDQUIST
[*laughter*]
That heritage "broadcast" communication model of culture that we mentioned earlier privileged creative exchanges between artists and media in the studio/manufactory, exchanges that were distributed through competitive-trade and collecting institutions. At best, "broadcast" extended a small measure of creative agency to the encounter between audiences—often referred to as passive "viewers"—and artworks.

MS. CHAN
Okay, I have material from composite. So even when this model was disrupted, like in 1968, or like in the exhibition *Modellen: A Model for a Qualitative Society* at Moderna ... It looks like we fell back into, um ... Perhaps the wider creative ecology was just not receptive enough.

AYAN LINDQUIST
You might be right, Ms. Chan. It was really when artists began to imagine art as a practice and began to explore creativity as a social process ...

MS. CHAN
Sometime around the late 1990s, perhaps?

AYAN LINDQUIST
Yes, yes. We detected something of a change then. Artists began to engage creatively with institutions, and vice versa. Artists and institutions engaged with all aspects of institutional practice—through coproducing exhibitions of course, but also through archival projects (which you've done so much to research, Ms. Chan) and through organizational engagement, administration, and so on ...

MS. CHAN
I'm browsing material about "institutional critique" from composite—Michael Asher and Hans Haacke ... they seem to be mostly artists from the Americas in the 1970s–1980s

AYAN LINDQUIST
Not sure if those are the appropriate resources? Artists associated with institutional critique—I recall Michael Asher and Hans Haacke, but also Julie Ault and Group Material, and Andrea Fraser. They had a much more antagonistic and oppositional relationship to exhibitionary institutions. They resented being represented *by* an exhibitionary institution, especially those linked to a nineteenth-century ideology.

MS. CHAN
Now I'm browsing material on Sputniks, EIPCP, Bruno Latour, Maria Lind, Arteleku, the Van Abbe Museum, Superlex, Franc Lacarde, Raqs and Sarai, Moderna's projects, Bart de Baer ...

AYAN LINDQUIST
Yes, this constellation feels more relevant. As artists rethought their practices, they recognized themselves as a nexus of complex social process. And they recognized that creativity was inherent in every conceivable transaction that produced that nexus, whatever the intensity, and regardless of the scale of the assembly. The huge challenge for all of us was to attend to the lines of force, the transactions, and not to be dazzled by the subjects, objects, or institutions they produced. We recall that it was under these conditions that artists' practices merged with Moderna, merged into relations of mutual coproduction. And so in exchange, Moderna began to think of itself as a creative institution, subject to constant critical and creative exploration.

MS. CHAN
So these were the forces generating Moderna v2.0 in 2'12?

AYAN LINDQUIST
You're right. We simply stopped thinking of ourselves as a nineteenth-century museum, one that had to constantly expand, commission signature buildings, develop huge administrative hierarchies—exhibition, education, support, management, and so on. Instead, we focused on instituting—in the ancient sense of the word—a foundation and a support structure. On instituting creative practice. We started to play, take risks, cooperate, research, and rapidly prototype—not only exhibitions and research projects, but ourselves. Some values were lost—which is always painful—and yet others were produced. And those that were most relevant were maintained, nurtured, and cherished. We learned to invest, long-term, without regard for an interested return. That's how we devolved locally, and networked globally. We've had some failures—either exhibitions couldn't muster the necessary resources, or we made mistakes. But as an immanent institution, most experiences were productive.

Not sure if that jump-cut thread answered your query ...

MS. CHAN
Sort of ...

research center based at University College London, whose work I would like to follow. The research center brings together experts from the fields of sedimentary geochemistry, hydrochemistry, hydrogeology, environmental mineralogy, and analytical geochemistry. I hope they can also help me understand what they do and the machines they work with. The question I asked at the beginning of this essay was: Once we have isolated and identified the pharmakon, how do we proceed? Resonating with the historian of science Sheila Jasanoff, I have tried to show that scientific controversies make themselves known as long as associated normative disagreements continue to haunt them.

1 Isabelle Stengers, *Cosmopolitics I*, trans. Robert Bononno (Minneapolis: University of Minnesota Press, 2010), 30.

AYAN LINDQUIST
The short answer is that artists have transformed Moderna, and we in turn have transformed them.

MS. CHAN
Okay, but that last sound bite is rather banal, although the thread's not uninteresting.

AYAN LINDQUIST
Ironically, our playful devolution of Moderna v2.0 reanimated the historical collection displayed in v1.0. We freed art-artifacts from their function of "recounting" the history of twentieth-century art, however alternative, discontinuous, or full of omissions we imagine that thread to be. And once free, they engaged with real-time discursive transactions. They became live again—contested nodes in competing transactions of unsettled bodies of knowledge.

MS. CHAN
Um, I'm not sure I'm following this ...

Since time is running out, and there's so much to cover, I just wonder if you could mention ... Could you recall, even briefly, some beacon exhibitions? Like *Transactional Aesthetics*, or *The Ecology of Fear?*

AYAN LINDQUIST
Rädslans ekologi, or *The Ecology of Fear,* was timely, given the viral pandemic that had struck DNA storage (so many systems were compromised) and the various "wars" that were being waged—against difference, material resources, energy, and public attention. And I guess the same goes for *Transactional Aesthetics.* It was the right moment to be participating in the production of local social-enterprise and well-being initiatives ...

MS. CHAN
Could you just mention the legendary exhibition *ARARAT: Alternative Research in Architecture, Resources, Art and Technology,* which took place at Moderna in 1976? You revisited this exhibition in 2'26, on its fiftieth anniversary. From composite I can see archival material. They're present.

AYAN LINDQUIST
There's not much to add. Obviously, the first version of *ARARAT* explored appropriate local technologies for buildings and urban systems, using sustainable resources. In 1976, this was the beginning of our understanding of global ecology, and of the finite nature of mineral resources, especially carbon. Given that our population reached eight billion in 2'26, it was vital to revisit the exhibition, to somehow take stock ... The first shock was that so little of the initial exhibition was recoverable—we invested in reconstruction and archival research, it's all Public Domain composite now. And the second was the realization that so little of the source exhibition had any real effect. We suspect a serious flaw in the exhibitionary form.

MS. CHAN
The lack of archival material about those early exhibitions is always disheartening. It's hard to imagine a time before even rudimentary Public Domain meshworks, embedded devices, and semantic interfaces.

AYAN LINDQUIST
Well, one of the great outcomes of the Moderna Golden Jubilee celebrations in 2'08 was that they revisited and reflected on the preceding fifty years. We recently found shadow-traces for a Moderna History book. And for reasons that are not entirely clear, it remained unpublished during the Jubilee celebrations—so we intend to issue a centenary heritage publication. We'll be sure to send you a copy.

MS. CHAN
I see we have overrun, I'm so sorry. I just wonder, before we disconnect—what is Moderna re-sourcing in the near future?

AYAN LINDQUIST
Well, for us, there are some beautiful assemblies emerging. Real-time consensus is moving from a local to a regional scale. Triangle in the African Multitude is distributing amazing regenerative medical technologies. Renewable energy has moved through the 74 percent threshold. Live, almost retro, music performance is popular again. Nanotechnology has come of age, and 1:1 molecular replication will soon be enabled, linked to scanning technology, hardwired to the manufactories in the Asian network. Outside of heritage, singularity will be overwritten by difference. Now that's exciting!

MS. CHAN
Exciting indeed! Thank you so much, Ayan. It's been a privilege, really. Enjoy the centenary celebrations. We'll all be there with you in spirit. Zai jian, goodbye.

AYAN LINDQUIST
Thank you, Ms. Chan. Goodbye, zai jian, hejdå.

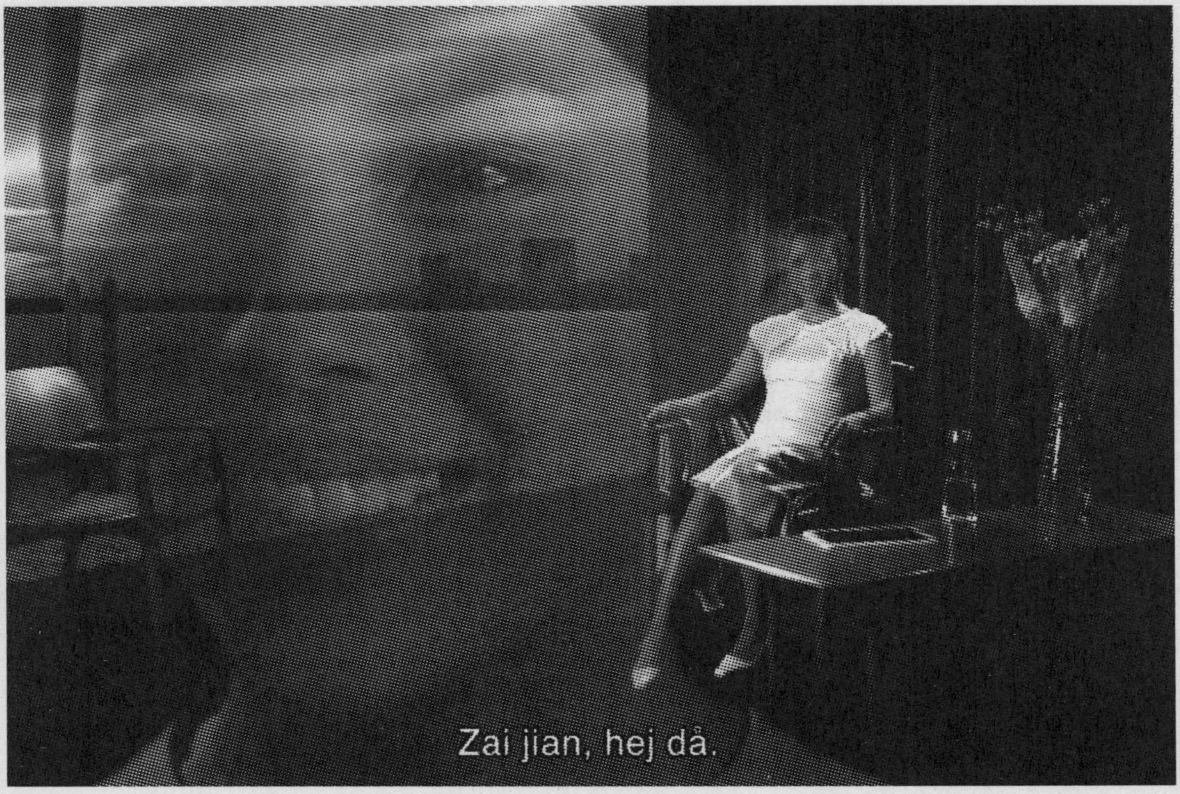

Marysia Lewandowska / Neil Cummings, *Museum Futures: Distributed*, 2008, HD video, color, sound, 32 min. Courtesy of Moderna Museet Collection.

DEAR MARSHAL TIE JIA

Hsu Chia-Wei

DEAR MARSHAL TIE JIA,

In May 2011, my family and I toured around the Chinbe Village of Matsu Island. We could see another beautiful island from Chinbe—Turtle Island—that we were unable to reach, though we were separated by only a few hundred meters of sea. I was determined to make an artwork about this. I originally planned to create a work about the era of the Japanese occupation and thought that I needed to prepare documents to apply to the county government. The villagers later informed me that the island does not fall under the county government's jurisdiction, but is rather under your jurisdiction. I heard about your accomplishments from the Chinbe Village and Goddess Temple elders, and found them amazing. From that moment, the concept of my work became entirely different from the original plan. In filming together with you that same day on Turtle Island, our group learned that nearly twenty years had passed since you first set foot on Turtle Island. Thank you for your assistance and for leading me into a period of history.

It is said that you were born at the beginning of the Tang Dynasty in a mountain stream pool in the Jingsi Village of Jiangxi Province. You set off for the spiritual Mount Longhu with Lord Laozi's reverence, finally following the immortals into the clouds after a thousand years of spirituality. However, during the years of Dayun learning, you wandered to the Wuyi Mountains without permission and angered the heavens. You were sent to the Nine-Bend River in the Wuyi Mountains, where residents built a temple by the Golden Rooster Hall to honor and worship you. During the Matsu Goddess election at the end of the Ming Dynasty and the beginning of the Qing Dynasty, you were selected to be located in Chinbe Village. You were crowned the Marshal Tie Jia and appointed as the patron saint of the village. During your time administering Chinbe Village, Taiwan entered a period of Japanese occupation. Matsu Island has produced varying identities as a result of its staggering history and geographical location; it seems that the histories of Matsu and Taiwan were unrelated until the end of World War II in 1945, when the Kuomintang took over the country. When Chiang Kai-Shek came to Taiwan in 1949, Matsu became a frontline base and the armed forces took Chinbe Village from you. Then everything changed; during the Qing Dynasty, there was a temple and an enormous banyan tree on Turtle Island, but the army moved the temple and covered the island in bunkers. The roots of the banyan tree gradually eroded into one of these bunkers and were cut off by the army. Across the water in China, the chaos of the Cultural Revolution that began in 1966 led to the disentanglement of everything; your ancestral temple on the Wuyi Mountains was burned and people were forced to erase their memory of you. These massive changes are similar to the way you were expelled to the Wuyi Mountains thousands of years ago, unable to return to heaven.

I tried to piece together the past from listening to residents' broken memories and from the appearance of the temple on Turtle Island. However, its size and form, combined with the fact that everything in the past is not lost, provide the only means of remembering the temple on the desolate island aside from a bit of foundation and bricks. However, the wreckage and your return to the island beneath the banyan trees more than twenty years ago are not sufficient to clearly recount the original story beneath what has accumulated over the past one hundred years. I can only imagine by means of trying to rebuild this vanished temple. In this work, I invited the elderly Huang Yanyan to sing the *pai gow* limerick to you, your favorite Min opera recounted and set to the melody of "Eight Years of War Against Japan." The *pai gow* is currently prohibited in China on the other

THE MUSEUM OF GOURD

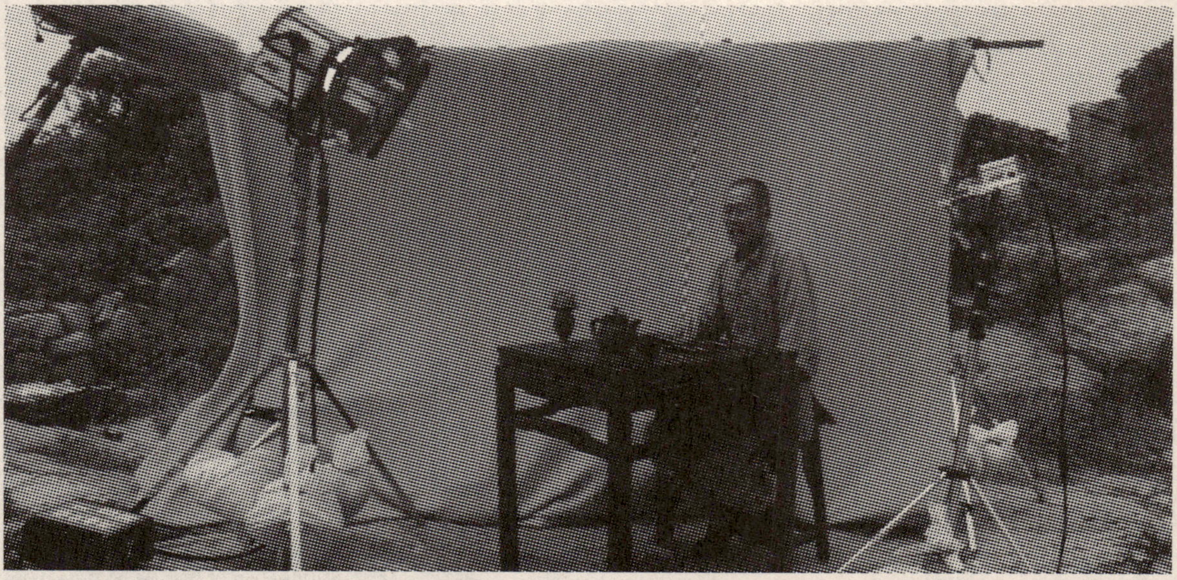

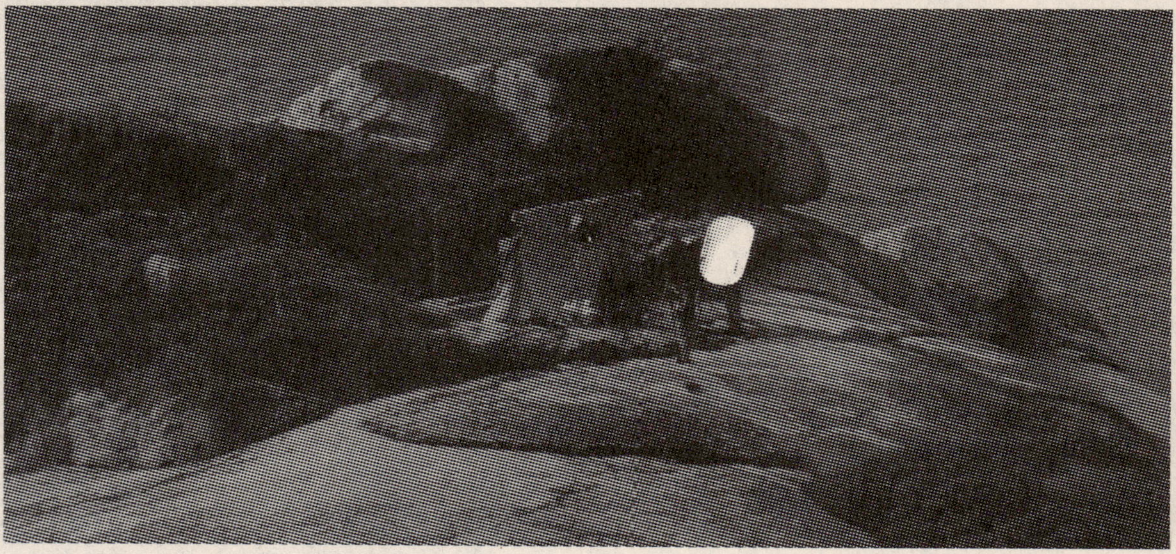

Hsu Chia-Wei, *Marshal Tie Jia*, 2012, HD video, color, sound; temple scene installations, photograph, film: approx. 10 min 30 sec; installation: 240 × 240 × 280 cm; photograph: 120 × 120 cm.

side of the water, and I am afraid that this old gentleman is the only person capable of singing the limerick of *pai gow*. This scene differs greatly from your past days in the Wuyi Mountains. History has always been very thought-provoking. Taiwan was ceded to Japan during the Qing Dynasty, thus Japan actually sent troops from Taiwan to occupy Matsu during World War II. Compared with Taiwan, the term "eight-year war" is more suitable for Matsu. I think you have experienced this piece of history during your time in Chinbe Village. After such a long period of transition and after Turtle Island was relieved of its strategic position, it was finally returned to your jurisdiction in recent years, although nothing has remained the same.

I must admit that this letter is not merely written for you. I am trying to compile complex fragments of a creative process through this letter. Because of this work, I wandered into a world that I don't completely understand. I am unable to distinguish between the boundaries of the real and the imagined. The complexity of hidden, unidentified politics and identities increasingly blurs all of reality and fiction. I'm afraid I used this impetuous work to plan a kind of interference that cannot be reversed. I only wrote this letter to sincerely express my work and my experience.

HOW TO CATCH A BEAST: A BRIEF HISTORY

Chihiro Minato

1. On March 25, 2011, the Administrative Oversight Committee of the Japanese Diet requested that certain individuals appear for questioning on the Current Status of the Nuclear Accident and the Administrative Oversight System. As the public listened closely to statements by seismologists and the nuclear reactor's designers, and as the radiation from the Fukushima disaster worsened, an image distributed at the session alongside precise figures on radiation levels and earthquake rates really took me aback. A hand-drawn illustration, it featured data distributed by seismologist Katsuhiko Ishibashi. In that odd illustration, a gigantic black fish stood on the roof of a large dome-shaped building immediately identifiable as a nuclear power plant. The caption accompanying the illustration said: "Japanese Nuclear Power Comes with Catfish."

Japanese nuclear power is often dogged by earthquakes, which the Japanese have believed since antiquity are caused by catfish. Naturally, these days people chalk this up to superstition, but the appearance of this sort of illustration in a committee meeting of the Japanese Parliament showed its power despite the superstition. I believe that power has perhaps been accumulated by myriad images over the length of modern history.

2. I am not sure what kind of reaction the illustration prompted in the Japanese Diet, but perhaps we could use it as a starting point for a little journey through images. That would bring us right to two types of images, the first being *Ukiyo-e* "catfish pictures" (*Namazu-e*) from the late Edo period. Following the Ansei Edo earthquake of October 2, 1855, woodblock paintings featured catfish, and came to be known as "catfish paintings" (*Namazu-e*). Edo had a population exceeding a million people at the time, making it one of the largest cities in the world, but the massive earthquake accompanied by a tsunami and fires devastated around fourteen thousand homes, killing an estimated seven to ten thousand people and making it a disaster of historical proportions.

TO PRISON

Hijikata Tatsumi

JANUARY 1961

I, who caught a cold by looking at a stone and became anxious on seeing a landscape with no one in it, grew up thinking of myself as maimed. One day a man stood next to my father; a tree cracked and my father fell. Clutching a stone, I resisted; my father was being beaten up. That was the start of my perception of an unhappy world. There must, however, be more fruitful mistakes in bleeding nature.

I grew up always sniffing out criminals, that is to say, such company as theirs. Everyone bears the burden of being a human child, yearning for companions with whom to run away from home. My anger over that alone was ample.

A gang of pals contains the dimension of smell. The word "world" was nothing but raving to me, who had spent my youth like a cur. Bleeding nature always overflows the allotments of history and sociology, and my gaze never wavered from it. The friends I made in Tokyo were, so to speak, inhabitants of the transparent, mechanical "world," without any ties to bleeding nature and even without smell. I could not help seeing them as corpses.

Isn't there some work that strews absolute putrefaction and graphic terror throughout the world? I have always thought I would like to put my hands to the axle of anger that sustains that kind of work.

Today I am no longer a dog. Albeit clumsily, extremely clumsily, I am definitely recovering. What, however, does my recovery signify? What on earth does recovery mean to me? Haven't I already recovered? Don't I continue to recover in order to be sick? In any case, my current situation is that of walking around a room with the windows wide open while holding a matchlock musket.

I am desperately trying to escape from the cellar of the freedom of being tied, and from the relationship between the ropes used for tying. I was frustrated in boyhood because of talk of an unfortunate rice paddy. One thing's for sure, though, I will no longer be cheated by a bad check called democracy. No future correspondence will reach me from slightly soiled pigeons set free by society's hands and I am enforcing silence too on my youth, when I was not even a dog licking the wounds of capitalism. At any rate, I have a matchlock at the window. But for some reason my finger does not reach the trigger. Is there any greater misery than entrusting a dream to a reality from which one will sometime have to wake? I should shut the window immediately and continue the conversation between this, my only life, and the universe. What I was unable to find even in childhood ... I have, at last, just transformed from a dog into a living creature called a human being.

All of a sudden a naked body has come into the gun port. The naked body is bleeding. Amidst a continuity resembling anger, I make repairs to arms and legs, which constantly go astray in an individual organic body. Forgetting the origin of legs and even that of arms. I am a body shop; my profession is the business of human rehabilitation, which goes today by the name of "dancer."

All the power of civilized morality, hand in hand with the capitalist economic system and its political institutions, is utterly opposed to using the body simply for the purpose, means, or tool of pleasure. Still more, to a production-oriented society, the aimless use of the body, which I call dance, is a deadly enemy that must be taboo. I am able to say that my dance shares a common basis with crime, male homosexuality, festivals, and rituals because it is behavior that explicitly flaunts its aimlessness in the face of a production-oriented society. In this sense my dance, based on human self-activation, including male homosexuality, crime, and a naive battle with nature, can naturally be a protest

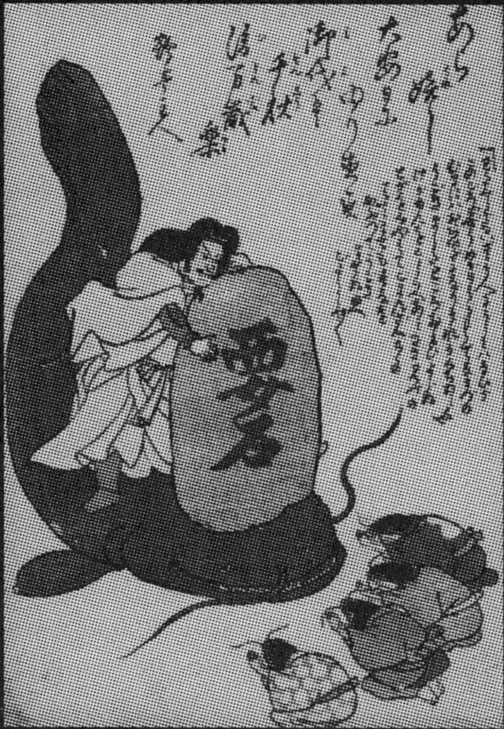

Kashima holding down the catfish monster with the *Kanameishi* stone

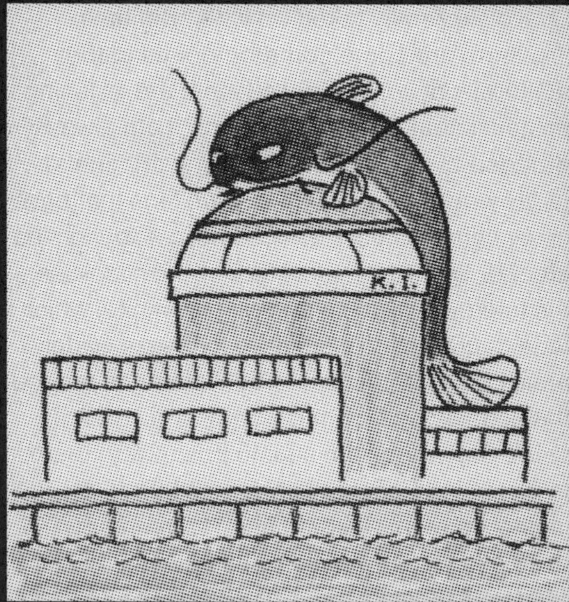

Monster on Nuclear Plant by Katsuhiko Ishibashi

There are many types of catfish paintings, the most famous being ones depicting the Kashima Daimyojin god holding the catfish beast's head down. The stone in his hands, known as the *Kanameishi*, is used to immobilize the catfish and keep the earth from trembling. The *Kanameishi* is currently located deep in the woods at the Kashima Jingu Shinto shrine near Narita International Airport outside Tokyo. Speaking of the cause of the Ansei earthquake, October has traditionally been known as "godless month" among the Japanese, when all the gods gather in the Kingdom of the Clouds, somewhere on the Western side of the Japanese archipelago. The people of the Edo kingdom surely believed that the *Kanameishi* loosened just when the Kashima Daimyojin was absent, allowing the catfish to stir and cause trouble.

We can see how the catfish is given human traits. Dressed in human garb, the fish mingles with the people of Edo in various roles. For instance, in one painting the fish is arrested as the culprit behind the earthquake, and kneels before court officials confessing his guilt. Other catfish are shown spitting out gold coins or selling medicine. The latter form depicted the fish as a savior of the people, who yearned for the restoration of normalcy and prosperity following the disaster. Hence, the catfish inflicted disaster through the earthquake, while it also played the role of savior, illustrating the dualistic nature of good and evil.

against the "alienation of labor" in capitalist society. That is probably the reason too that I have expressly taken up with criminals.

There are some common points in the taciturnity of criminals, and there are crushing mistakes that extend straight on. I am always dragged by the legs of the young criminals today who pass me by. They are legs that have never carried politics as accomplices for horsing around. The youth chase far beyond suspicion the internal medicine and surgical knife, which today's civilization dispenses to them. I wager reality on a nonsensical vitality that has purged the echo of logic from my body and I dream of the day when I am sent to prison with them. In prison I will learn to play football. They are the legs of criminals with no need to learn how to stand in such a place. I am studying that kind of "criminal dance."

In the outside world, criminals have always been forced to stand. In outside reality, they fully experience that there is nothing worthy of belief. From various standpoints, a family for them cannot be a single unit where they are able to sit. Today's material, they have acquired a protective instinct that thinking is dangerous. First of all, I posit to begin with a composition in which I stand and they are made to stand. I walk and they are made to walk. All of a sudden they start to run and I too run. I fall down. They run. They get up without any injury from where they fell. Why is the place where they get up different from that where I get up bleeding? It is futile, in the end, to question what causes my activities constantly to erode. Human remodeling is accomplished only in connection with young people who unceasingly experience the natural movements that kick the matrix of today's good sense. I dream of such a criminal dance. There will no longer be any hesitation over torching theatres.

To the open air. In real life I will be able to become a second-rate murderer. I would like to have my own subjectivity, which wavers in mixing and confusing the imaginative process and the real-life process. I would like to be sitting, without even a passport, smack in the middle of a mistake.

From a closed room to the open air, from the open air to prison—that will inevitably be my path. My naked body will be carried without any pretext of inconvenience. It will be allowed to pass without any inspection of my personal effects, and I will get another look at dance that can be narrated by bare hands and by walking. The phrase "walk tirelessly" always points to the essence of dance. Georges Bataille said, "Nakedness offers a contrast to self-possession, to discontinuous existence, in other words." He also said, "It is a state of communication revealing a quest for a possible continuance of being, beyond the confines of the self. Bodies open out to a state of continuity through secret channels that give us a feeling of obscenity. Stripping naked is seen in civilizations where the act has full significance if not as a simulacrum of the act of killing at least as an equivalent shorn of gravity."[1] These words of Bataille's seem to approximate most closely the human solidarity of a naked body, which is first attained, even as the body is solitary, through the continuity of being, which is to say, death. I see in prison such a stage of tragedy, a stage of drama where the naked body and death are inseparably joined.

That I am dazed by the beauty of a prison gate is nothing but a posture of perplexity with myself, made to stand at the minimum distance from being naked. That is how terrifying it is to be naked, yet in the outside world we are already completely naked. For today the authority and significance of a prison gate being shut are declining. In any case, it is equivalent to being released. I will be carried merrily. Speech prohibited, sound contrived not to reach my ears, in garb of nondescript color, I shall continue to be conscious that I am still standing naked as is. No theatre matches this one, which is equipped with the perfect mechanism for my destructive acts against production and morality. I see my own dance in a state of joyful group bathing in prison, and I see inmates on death row in the fall of modern civilization and in the family crest of its good sense. I see the original form of my dance in their walk.

A criminal on death row made to walk to the guillotine is already a dead person even as he clings, to the very end, to life. The fierce antagonism between life and death is pushed to the

The "black sails"[1] had arrived not long before the great Ansei earthquake, making it come at a time of great national uncertainty and unrest. Japan experienced over a decade of serious chaos after the earthquake, the dissolution of the ruling Tokugawa Shogunate, and the Meiji Restoration, thereby making it a disaster at the dawning of the modern era. Upon noticing that the catfish had become a metaphor for popular dissatisfaction, the Edo Bakufu prohibited catfish paintings, showing that the catfish was not just an expression of superstition, but perhaps a sign that monsters only appear as a harbinger of tumultuous change.

3. Another type of image is known as the "catfish and gourd" (*Hyonenzu*) motif, and it is believed to have originated with a fourteenth-century ink painting held in the collection of the Taizo-in Zen temple in Kyoto. Zen priest Josetsu, whose life bridged the fourteenth and fifteenth centuries, crafted a painting depicting a man walking by a river and trying to catch a catfish with a gourd. Logically speaking, a smooth gourd cannot be used to catch a slippery catfish, making it a metaphor for futile human endeavors. Interpreted by D. T. Suzuki, the allegory is about the futility of humanity's attempts to capture truth with rationality. Suzuki believed that the painting took on notoriety as a meaningful Zen koan.

During the Edo period, images of trying to catch a catfish with a gourd became popular around Japan as art pieces known as "*Ōtsue*." There are many versions of this type of painting, the most common of which show not the Kashima Daimyojin holding the gourd, but rather a monkey or a god of wealth. Gourds were also depicted as medicine containers or instruments of magic, which can surely be attributed to Chinese influence. Gourds and catfish are similarly shaped, making for humorous images that gained popularity and are now even used as patterns on kimonos and handkerchiefs. The term *Hyonenzu* is also used in popular vernacular as a metaphor for something impossible, but without carrying negative connotations. Most often it is seen as a fun and auspicious symbol.

4. To understand how the image of pacifying a catfish with a gourd became a popular motif, one must consider how gourds were used in antiquity. Generally speaking, the bottle gourd comes in myriad shapes and sizes, with all kinds of uses. Opinions differ on when mankind began using gourds, and while the precise period is uncertain, seeds have been found in fairly ancient ruins, with the oldest in the highlands of Peru dating from approximately 13,000 to 11,000 BCE. In Asia, gourd seeds dating from 10,000 to

extreme and cohesively expressed in this lone miserable being who, in the name of the law, is forced into an unjust condition. A person not walking but made to walk; a person not living but made to live; a person not dead but made to be dead must, in spite of such total passivity, paradoxically expose the radical vitality of human nature. Sartre wrote: "A criminal with bound hands now standing on the scaffold is not yet dead. One moment is lacking for death, that moment of life which intensely desires death." This very condition is the original form of dance and it is my task to create just such a condition on the stage.

Sending hysterical works to the theatre has great significance these days. We have the right to ask for a guarantee of actuality among the random noise and bad taste that are the equivalent of almost raw materials. The sublime asceticism of crime. A totally empty face that endures torture. Young people who have cleverly acquired a nonsensical vitality. The pure despair that emerges before hope is crushed. My task is to organize these into a dance group and to make them into naked soldiers.

Longing for asceticism, today's generation wavers. It can be inferred that most (Self-Defense Force members) abandoned solidarity with the flesh of their generation and threw themselves into the army out of a craving to be bound rather than to make a living. Dance, which is a medium between a spirit and an impulse to perform a secret ritual for the sake of pouring into the flesh and blood of young people, ends in finishing them as lethal weapons that dream.

That which is capable of confronting today's condition, which envelops the distortions of a solidarity severed into pieces, is nothing other than the establishment of a new individual human image and the acquisition of that solidarity. I place that solidarity within the scope of my work. I attempt to press the limits of myself and of my material. From the nature of my work, living beings are my material. They are young living beings who hold their tongues. Jean Genet wrote: "Talent is courtesy with respect to matter; it consists of giving song to what was dumb. My talent will be the love I feel for that which constitutes the world of prisons and penal colonies."[2] These words, completely and exactly, lead to my determination. "One must," in Nietzsche's words, "strip the costume of barren perception designed by contemporary civilization" from these young people who shut their mouths before and after any action. Nietzsche also said: "My work is to reanimate with vitality a skeleton pieced together from the consciousness of being a victim. I am a man of simple sensual passion. The sense of the tragic increases and declines with sensuousness." Because I am, as in these words of Nietzsche, a man of sensual passion, my work in all its aspects is as follows: That I must continue still to learn many more things from chopping heads with a hoe. That, with my own will, I must grasp a lethal weapon in my hands. I must first attempt to recover these hands. These new hands for the sake of operating a machine must be backed up by the hands that have held a hoe; they are not hands that grieve over a labor accident. I must sever these slender fingers that play with scraps. "Work is *a priori* power and provocation in struggle with nature; it is the overcoming of resistance," said [Herbert] Marcuse.[3] This "provocation" is, in my own words, "dance." But a tongue that licks the wounds of this runaway mechanical civilization already exceeds the scope of our provocation. Politics that conceal in their breast a function stripped of meaning are nothing but a station for incompetent humans who have started to have doubts about themselves at their source. We must continue to open up the current situation with hands that hold a chalk eraser which wipes out signs of an impotent future, of that culture of mournful cries which exist in the skeleton of victim consciousness. I am placing in the body of my work an altar similar to asceticism in front of a human body purged of impurities. My work is to remove toy weapons from the limbs of today's youth, who developed in barren circumstances, and to finish them as naked soldiers, as a naked culture.

Today I do not know anything, in terms of the formation of alienation and the continuity of harshness that work imposes on a body, which ranks with pulling weeds in poor farm

6,000 BCE were found in a cave in Thailand. So generally speaking, the gourd was a known vegetable as early as the Jōmon period, and predated the invention of earthenware as a tool.[2] Perhaps it does not stand out compared to such staple crops as wheat or rice, but as a vessel it was a necessity for life that accompanied mankind daily for at least ten thousand years.

There are many ways to grow and cultivate, to utilize and process gourds, making it a dominant plant compared to others. It all begins with its shape, and the top three ways of using gourds as containers can be categorized as follows.

The first method involves cutting the gourd from the vine for use directly as a container. Maybe because this is the most common method, the English term for the plant is "bottle gourd." Tying a gourd at the waist to make a water flask is a common practice around the world. For instance, people in Santiago de Compostela, a city made famous by the Crusades, carried walking sticks with this sort of gourd on them. Two types of gourds commonly known as "bottle gourds" normally refer to a barbell-shaped gourd narrow in the middle with larger, bulbous ends.

The second variety is sliced horizontally into two halves for use as a bowl. A knife makes an incision on the tapered area at the center to form different shapes. If the cut is made closer to the bottom it becomes a plate, or a bowl when cut at its widest section. Sliced yet higher up the gourd, it can be used as a bottle.

The third type consists of a vertical division, where the two sides are finished as soupspoons or ladles. In this case, the larger bottom section is used to scoop up liquid, and the narrower upper section as a handle. North American gourds are only bulbous in one area, and ones with an especially long narrow portion are known as "dipper gourds"; they are also known by a similar name in Japan. Cut open along their length, they are used as rice scoops as well as soup ladles. Interestingly, when used for such purposes they are known as "round ladles," or *otamajakushi*—a homonym for "tadpoles," which are shaped somewhat like catfish.

5. The various treatments and uses for gourds described above can be found wherever gourds are grown across Africa, Asia, North and South America, Europe, and the Pacific Rim, thus giving rise to related mythology and folk beliefs around the world. For instance, in Africa the gourd is often seen as a feminine symbol, as it represents the mother's body. This is certainly related to the shape of the fruit, but others note that gourds produce countless seeds and are thus a symbol of fertility. Moreover, using gourds

land in summer. In the crude energy combined with autonomous rhythm supporting that labor, there is something that almost makes you cover your eyes. Young farmers lose their years inside that energy. Babies delivered there grow up playing even now with shit. The current situation is that a whole family finds recovery in an anal disease suffered by a six-year-old in a one-crop area of poor soil. The hands of parents are connected to hands that tease the gods. This phenomenon makes a design from a laughably black humor and that seems to me to be a mysterious dance.

Around the thirteenth year of the Showa period [1938], the one-crop areas of Tohoku were stricken with anal blockages. Those tearful voices must be recorded anew in the culture of preservation. Although they are today becoming an important accompaniment to my dance, they were such "primitive cries" that only now, twelve years since I started to live in Tokyo, have I been able to handle them cleverly. I am chewing on cries and the profundity of esoteric gestures by gazing closely and unceasingly at the mundane. I am inventing a walk molded of the present from atop the dark earth where dancing and jumping could not be united. In boyhood the dark earth of Japan was my teacher in various ways of fainting. I must bring to the theatre that sense of treading. I am a naked volunteer soldier who forces this treading to confront the handling of legs that have been domesticated by floors.

I use an initiation ceremony for youth as the altar of my work. It is perhaps akin to asceticism and can be called a coming-of-age ceremony. I would like to create such a dance made flesh and blood, which I would undertake with my own body, not by mutual understanding but by suffering the fear of believing and the act of continuing to experience. Believing people is today solitary work. Believing and continuing to live are myths of acts impossible to name. To risk. With hands that have gauged the weight of testicles, I substantiate a blind countenance.

I am dumbfounded by the bodies of young creatures who, bereft of any ethical echo, overrun the streets. I am making the subject of my work the warm sands, rapid vehicles, dramatic chases, and naked conversations that have removed the punishment of society from their shared reality of behaving like unlovable youth. I believe—through incessant conversation with young creatures who stand at the minimum distance from the primal experience and through work that plays with their bodies—that they can be perfected as my naked soldiers. Human remodeling will be accomplished only by getting involved with a dreaming lethal weapon that has long ignored the poverty of politics.

Originally published as "Keimusho e" in *Mita Bungaku*. Translated from the Japanese by Nanako Kurihara for *The Drama Review* 44, 1 (T165), Spring 2000, guest-edited by Nanako Kurihara.

1 Georges Bataille, *Erotism: Death and Sensuality*, trans. Mary Dalwood (San Francisco: City Lights Books, 1986), 17–18. Throughout, sources will be noted where available.

2 Jean Genet, *The Thief's Journal*, trans. Bernard Frechtman (New York: Grove Press, 1967), 110–11.

3 Herbert Marcuse, *Eros and Civilization: A Philosophical Inquiry into Freud* (Boston, MA: Beacon Press, 1974), 110–11.

as utensils and vessels for food is traditionally a woman's job. But surely this feminine association does not imply that humanity originates from the gourd.

Winding a cord around an immature gourd can form it into almost any shape. In China, techniques involving placing gourds into a mold and carving the surface are well developed. In addition, gourds can be utilized not just as water-resistant containers, but, as their surfaces are easily treated in many regions, they are decorated with drawings and patterns. Most of these designs are related to various local tales or customs, one such type being *Ōtsue*. Thus the gourd has been invaluable to humanity as a "body" for transmitting oral traditions

6. The gourd is also one of nature's musical instruments. When a dried gourd blows in the wind, the seeds inside rattle softly. In fact, the earliest use of the gourd as a musical instrument was probably as such a "shaker," which can be found in civilizations and cultures around the world. Sometimes they are fashioned specifically for ceremonial use as maracas. Thus gourds are vital plants not just as containers, but also as musical instruments.

Gourds are used around the world for percussion instruments as large as African drums or as small as maracas. In Hawaii they are essential as accompaniment to hula dancing, and in Latin American music they are rubbed on their curved surfaces to make a unique percussive sound. In Africa they are widely used not only as drums but to make such harmonic instruments as the *balafon* and *sanza* (thumb piano). Probably the most widely known stringed instrument using a gourd is the Indian sitar. In medieval Europe, the gourd was used as the body for string instruments as well. From Africa to Asia, the most prevalent shape for string instruments derives from the gourd. Gourds are also used as woodwind instruments throughout South and Southeast Asia, from India to Vietnam, but small gourds are also used as harmonic flutes in southern France and Corsica.

It is impossible to ascertain exactly when gourds were first used as musical instruments; however, this function definitely goes back at least as far as their use as a container. The gourd is doubtless the first plant used as a harmonic instrument. From tropical to temperate regions, it is still used as a musical instrument nearly everywhere across the globe, the music produced having a unique character not easily duplicated by other instruments. Without the gourd, music might not be what we know today.

THE TURNER DIARIES
by Andrew Macdonald

Epilog

Thus end Earl Turner's diaries, as unpretentiously as they began.

His final mission was successful, of course, as we all are reminded each year on November 9-our traditional Day of the Martyrs.

With the System's principal military nerve center destroyed, the System's forces poised outside the Organization's California enclave continued to wait for orders which never came. Declining morale, soaring desertions, growing Black indiscipline, and finally, the inability of the System to maintain the integrity of its supply line to its California troops resulted in the gradual erosion of the threat of invasion. Eventually the System began regrouping its forces elsewhere, to meet new challenges in other parts of the country.

And then, just as the Jews had feared, the flow of Organization activists turned exactly 180 degrees from what it had been in the weeks and months immediately prior to July 4, 1993. From scores of training camps in the liberated zone, first hundreds, then thousands of highly motivated guerrilla fighters began slipping through the System's diminishing ring of troops and moving eastward. With these guerrilla forces the Organization followed the example of its Baltimore members and rapidly established dozens of new enclaves, primarily in the nuclear-devastated areas, where System authority was weakest.

The Detroit enclave was initially the most important of these. Bloody anarchy had reigned among the survivors in the Detroit area for several weeks after the nuclear blasts of September 8. Eventually, a semblance of order had been restored, with System troops loosely sharing power with the leaders of a number of Black gangs in the area. Although there were a few isolated White strongholds which kept the roving mobs of Black plundvers and rapists at bay, most of the disorganized and demoralized White survivors in and around Detroit offered no effective resistance to the Blacks, and, just as in other heavily Black areas of the country, they suffered terribly.

Then, in mid-December, the Organization seized the initiative. A number of synchronized lightning raids on the System's military strongpoints in the Detroit area resulted in an easy victory

The Organization then established certain patterns in Detroit g which were soon followed elsewhere. All captured White troops, as soon as they had laid down their weapons, were offered a chance to fight with the Organization against the System. Those who immediately volunteered were taken aside for preliminary screening and then sent to camps for indoctrination and special training. The others were machine-gunned on the spot, without further ado.

The same degree of ruthlessness was used in dealing with the White civilian population. When the Organization's cadres moved into the White strongholds in the Detroit suburbs, the first thing they found it necessary to do was to liquidate most of the local White leaders, in order to establish the unquestioned authority of the Organization. There was no time or patience for frying to reason with shortsighted Whites who insisted that they weren't "racists" or "revolutionaries" and didn't need the help of any "outside agitators" in dealing with their problems, or who had some other conservative or parochial fixation.

The Whites of Detroit and the other new enclaves were organized more along the lines described by Earl Turner for Baltimore than for California, but even more rapidly and roughly. In most areas of the country there was no opportunity for an orderly, large-scale separation of non-Whites, as in California, and consequently a bloody race war raged for months, taking a terrible toll of those Whites who were not in one of the Organization's tightly controlled, all-White enclaves.

Food became critically scarce everywhere during the winter of 1993-1994. The Blacks lapsed into cannibalism, just as they had in California, while hundreds of thousands of starving Whites, who earlier had ignored the Organization's call for a rising against the System, began appearing at the borders of the various liberated zones begging for food. The Organization was only able to feed the White populations already under its control by imposing the severest rationing, and it was necessary to turn many of the latecomers away.

Those who were admitted-and that meant only children, women of childbearing age, and able-bodied men willing to fight in the Organization's ranks-were subjected to much more severe racial screening than had been used to separate Whites from non-Whites in California. It was no longer sufficient to be merely White; in order to eat one had to be judged the bearer of especially valuable genes.

7. The gourd was also used in ancient techniques for controlling the flow of water and air. If it hadn't been used to store and transport river water, humans would likely never have been able to migrate over long distances. In fact, such ancient methods were instrumental in humanity's spread around the globe. Capturing beasts was also an ancient technique for humanity, making the gourd a magical device for peoples around the world up to the present day. In Chinese celestial thought the gourd is a type of time machine, in which the flow is different on the inside and outside. If one accepts this observation, then there should be a Gourd Age in addition to the Stone Age. The Stone Age began when humans started fashioning implements out of stone, and ended when they ceased doing so, whilst the Gourd Age has no beginning and no end—because the gourd created mankind.

In *From Honey to Ashes*, the second volume of his four-part work of cultural anthropology entitled *Mythologiques*, Claude Lévi-Strauss attempted to understand the meaning of the gourd as a mechanism for controlling the flow of air and water. He recognized its utility as a container for holding water and as a musical instrument, also observing its third type of use: gourds filled with air can be used as floats or buoys in water. Gourds make different sounds when filled with water or air, and looking closely into the sounds made by gourds by the riverside in South African mythology, Lévi-Strauss noted that these myths corresponded with humanity's various mechanisms for coping with nature.

People living along rivers use ladles or oars to scoop water, propelling their boats forward and, as they row, making audible sounds for certain life-forms inhabiting the water. If one makes an audible sound, against the counsel of myths, one could very well be dragged into the water by a devil or monster and drowned. Snakes with gourd decorations inhabiting the Amazon River entice people near the water, and people making forbidden noises could end up falling in. In this way, if mythology ponders the human condition, so does the gourd.

Over three-quarters of Japanese catfish are this type of beast. One must presume that the motif of the gourd and the catfish existed prior to being incorporated in a fourteenth-century Japanese Zen painting. Catfish normally nest in the muck underwater, and are considered portents of earthquakes because it has been widely held since antiquity that, whenever catfish come to the surface, earthquakes follow. In contrast, dried gourds won't sink even if they fall into the river. The catfish and gourd have an opposite relationship—one that seemingly employs expressions of emotion and reason (or rational effort taken to the extreme). Attempting to capture

In Detroit the practice was first established (and it was later adopted elsewhere) of providing any able-bodied White male who sought admittance to the Organization's enclave with or hot meal and a bayonet or other edged weapon. His forehead was then marked with an indelible dye, and he was turned out and could be readmitted permanently only by bringing back the head of a freshly killed Black or other non-White. This practice assured that precious food would not be wasted on those who would not or could not add to the Organization's fighting strength, but it took a terrible toll of the weaker and more decadent White elements.

Tens of millions perished during the first half of 1994, and the total White population of the country reached a low point of approximately 50 million by August of that year. By then, however, nearly half the remaining Whites were in Organization enclaves, and food production and distribution in the enclaves had grown until it was barely sufficient to prevent further losses from starvation.

Although a central government of sorts still existed, the System's military and police forces were, for all practical purposes, reduced to a number of essentially autonomous local commands, whose principal activity became looting for food, liquor, gasoline, and women. Both the Organization and the System avoided large-scale encounters with each other, the Organization confining itself to short, intense raids on System troop concentrations and other facilities, and the System's forces confining themselves to guarding their sources of supply and, in some areas, to attempting to limit the further expansion of the Organization's enclaves.

But the Organization's enclaves continued to expand, nevertheless, both in size and number, all through the five Dark Years preceding the New Era. At one time there were nearly 2,000 separate Organization enclaves in North America. Outside these zones of order and security, the anarchy and savagery grew steadily worse, with the only real authority wielded by marauding bands which preyed on each other and on the unorganized and defenseless masses.

Many of these bands were composed of Blacks, Puerto Ricans, Chicanos, and half-White mongrels. In growing numbers, however, Whites also formed bands along racial lines, even without Organization guidance. As the war of extermination wore on, millions of soft, city-bred, brainwashed Whites gradually began regaining their manhood. The rest died.

The Organization's growing success was not without its setbacks, of course. One of the most notable of these was the terrible Pittsburgh Massacre, of June 1994. The Organization had established an enclave there in May of that year, forcing the retreat of local System forces, but it did not act swiftly enough in identifying and liquidating the local Jewish element.

A number of Jews, in collaboration with White conservatives and liberals, had time to work out a plan of subversion. The consequence was that System troops, aided by their fifth column inside the enclave, recaptured Pittsburgh. The Jews and Blacks then went on a wild rampage of mass murder, reminiscent of the worst excesses of the Jew-instigated Bolshevik Revolution in Russia, 75 years earlier. By the time the blood-orgy ended, virtually every White in the area had either been butchered or forced to flee. The surviving staff members of the Organization's Pittsburgh Field Command, whose hesitation in dealing with the Jews had brought on the catastrophe, were rounded up and shot by a special disciplinary squad acting on orders from Revolutionary Command.

The only time, after November 9, 1993, the Organization was forced to detonate a nuclear weapon on the North American continent was a year later, in Toronto. Hundreds of thousands of Jews had fled the United States to that Canadian city during 1993 and 1994, making almost a second New York of it and using it as their command center for the war raging to the south. So far as both the Jews and the Organization were concerned, the U.S.-Canadian border had no real significance during the later stages of the Great Revolution, and by mid-1994 conditions were only slightly less chaotic north of the border than south of it.

Throughout the Dark Years neither the Organization nor the System could hope for a completely decisive advantage over the other, so long as they both retained the capability for nuclear warfare. During the first part of this period, when the System's conventional military strength greatly exceeded the Organization's, only the Organization's threat of retaliation with its more than 100 nuclear warheads hidden inside the major population centers still under System control kept the System, in most cases, from moving against the Organization's liberated zones.

Later, when Organizational gains, together with growing attrition of the System's forces through desertions, tilted the balance of conventional strength toward the Organization, the System retained control over a number of military units armed with nuclear weapons and, by threatening to use these, forced the Organization to leave certain System strongholds inviolate.

Even the System's elite, pampered nuclear troops were not immune to the processes of attrition which sapped the System's conventional strength, however, and they could postpone the inevitable only temporarily. On January 30, 1999, in the momentous Truce of Omaha, the last group of System generals surrendered their commands to the Organization, in return for a pledge that they and their immediate families would be allowed to live out the remainders of their lives unmolested. The Organization kept its pledge, and a special reservation on an island off the California coast was set aside for the generals.

Then, of course, came the mopping-up period, when the last of the non-White bands were hunted down and exterminated, followed by the final purge of undesirable racial elements among the remaining White population.

From the liberation of North America until the beginning of the New Era for our whole planet, there elapsed the remarkably short time of just under 11 months. Professor Anderson has recorded and analyzed the events of this climactic period in detail in his History of the Great Revolution. Here it is sufficient to note that, with the principal centers of world Jewish power annihilated and the nuclear threat of the Soviet Union neutralized, the most important obstacles to the Organization's worldwide victory were out of the way.

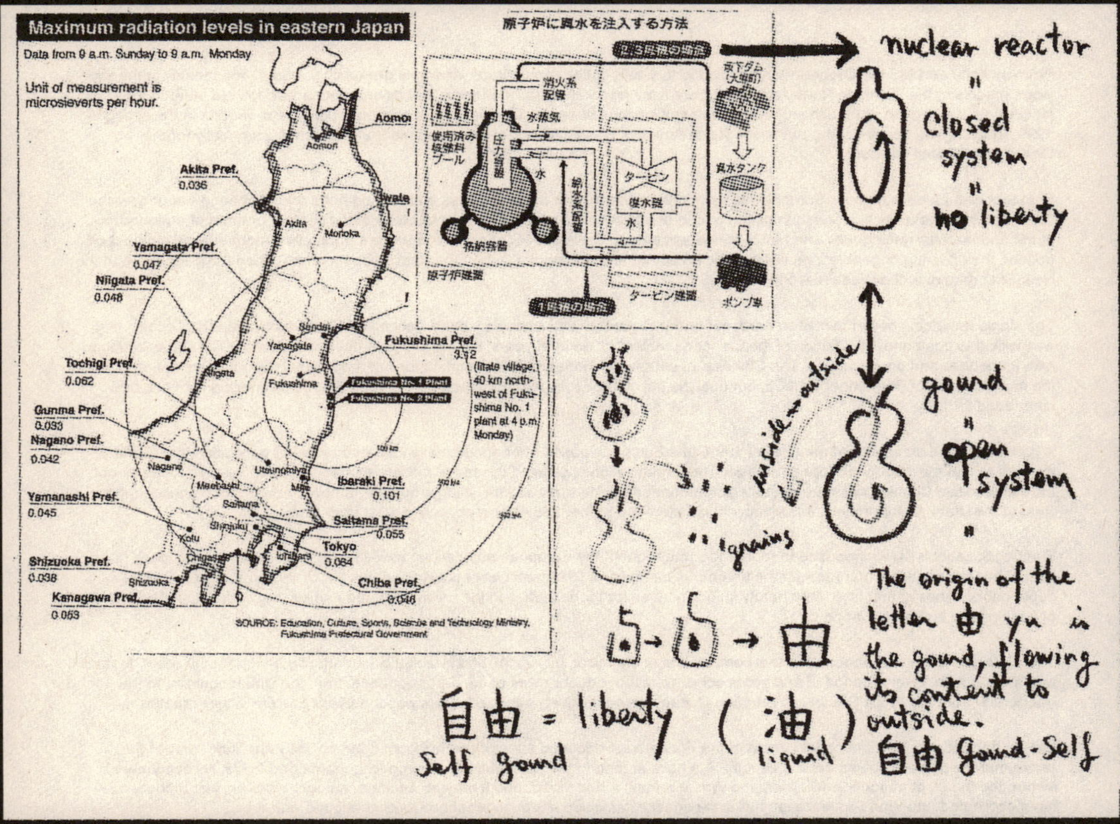

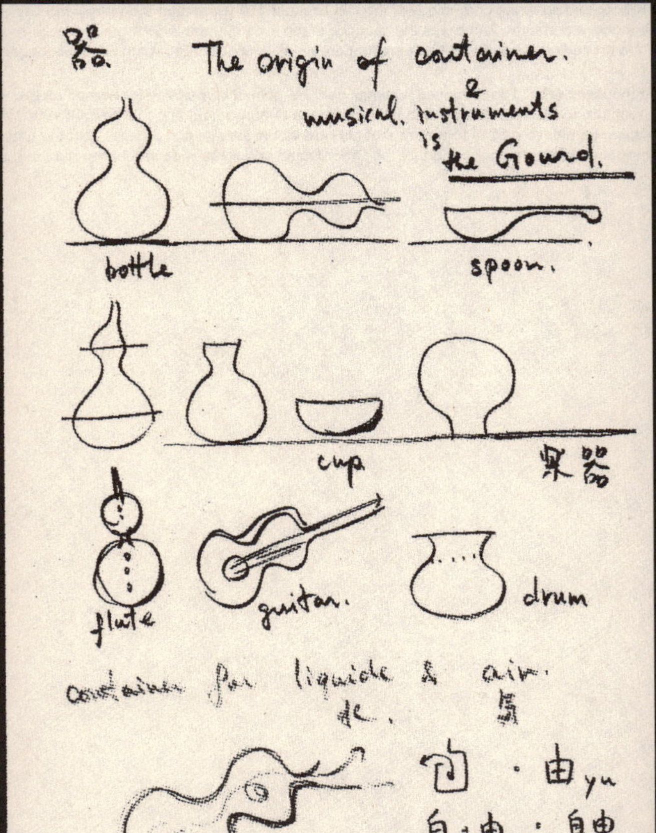

Chihiro Minato, gourd drawings

From as early as 1993 the Organization had had active cells in Western Europe, and they grew with extraordinary rapidity in the six years preceding the victory in North America. Liberalism had taken its toll in Europe, just as in America, and the old order in most places was a rotted-out shell with only a surface semblance of strength. The disastrous economic collapse in Europe in the spring of 1999, following the demise of the System in North America, greatly helped in preparing the European masses morally for the Organization's final takeover.

That takeover came in a great, Europe-wide rush in the summer and fall of 1999, as a cleansing hurricane of change swept over the continent, clearing away in a few months the refuse of a millennium or more of alien ideology and a century or more of profound moral and material decadence. The blood flowed ankle-deep in the streets of many of Europe's great cities momentarily, as the race traitors, the offspring of generations of dysgenic breeding, and hordes of Gastarbeiter met a common fate. Then the great dawn of the New Era broke over the Western world.

The single remaining power center on earth not under Organizational control by early December 1999 was China. The Organization was willing to postpone the solution of the Chinese problem for several years, but the Chinese themselves forced the Organization to take immediate and drastic action. The Chinese, of course, had invaded the Asiatic regions of the Soviet Union are. immediately after the nuclear strike of September 8, 1993, but until the fall of 1999 they had remained east of the Urals, consolidating the vast, new, conquered territory.

When, during the summer and early fall of 1999, one European nation after another was liberated by the Organization, the Chinese decided to make a grab for European Russia. The Organization countered this move massively, using nuclear missiles to knock out the still-primitive Chinese missile and strategic-bomber capabilities, as well as hitting a number of new Chinese troop concentrations west of the Urals. Unfortunately, this action did not stem the Yellow tide flowing north and west from China.

The Organization still required time to reorganize and reorient the European populations newly under its control before it could hope to deal in a conventional manner with the enormous numbers of Chinese infantry pouring across the Urals into Europe; all its dependable troops at that time were hardly sufficient even for garrison duty in the newly liberated and still not entirely pacified areas of eastern and southern Europe.

Therefore, the Organization resorted to a combination of chemical, biological, and radiological means, on an enormous scale, to deal with the problem. Over a period of four years some 16 million square miles of the earth's surface, from the Ural Mountains to the Pacific and from the Arctic Ocean to the Indian Ocean, were effectively sterilized. Thus was the Great Eastern Waste created.

Only in the last decade have certain areas of the Waste been declared safe for colonization. Even so, they are "safe" only in the sense that the poisons sowed there a century ago have abated to the point that they are no longer a hazard to life. As everyone is aware, the bands of mutants which roam the Waste remain a real threat, and it may be another century before the last of them has been eliminated and White colonization has once again established a human presence throughout this vast area.

But it was in the year 1999, according to the chronology of the Old Era-just 110 years after the birth of the Great One- that the dream of a White world finally became a certainty. And it was the sacrifice of the lives of uncounted thousands of brave men and women of the Organization during the preceding years which had kept that dream alive until its realization could no longer be denied .

Among those uncounted thousands Earl Turner played no small part. He gained immortality for himself on that dark November day 106 years ago when he faithfully fulfilled his obligation to his race, to the Organization, and to the holy Order which had accepted him into its ranks. And in so doing he helped greatly to assure that his race would survive and prosper, that the Organization would achieve its worldwide political and military goals, and that the Order would spread its wise and benevolent rule over the earth for all time to come.

The End

THE TURNER DIARIES
by Andrew Macdonald

Back Home

something as unpredictable as an earthquake is like trying to catch a catfish with a gourd, thus the logic of mythology and Zen koans meet through agnosticism.

8. Perhaps an accidental philosophy can be found within the humorous shape of the gourd. Speaking of which, let us return to the "Japanese Nuclear Power Comes with Catfish" illustration. At first blush, the image with the catfish on the top of a nuclear power facility appears to be precisely the opposite of the *Namazu-e* painting, because the catfish is subdued by a rock in the latter, whilst here the catfish presses down on the nuclear power plant; however, from an agnostic standpoint, both are saying the same thing. With the earthquake and tsunami now more than a year in the past, we still do not know what happened inside that reactor core.

People that build nuclear power plants on the shores of earthquake-prone countries are no different from those who walked with gourds by the water in the fourteenth century. Both are guilty of doing something that is forbidden in close proximity to water—probably because they made containers that violated the laws of nature. Sealed nuclear fuel containment compartments in nuclear reactors can never be opened up. The nuclear power plant with a catfish on the roof is a container in which nuclear fission takes place repeatedly in a sealed space. In and of itself, this is incompatible with natural containers premised on flow, so that when an accident happens and the inside is exposed, we once again awaken to the fact that it can only end in tragedy.

Can humanity endure peacefully through the Atomic Age? Will a man walking by the water trying to catch a beast with a gourd end up falling in? People born in the Gourd Age must once again look inside the gourd, for the seeds of hope might lay inside that little plant.

Curated by Chihiro Minato. Participating artists: Chen Szuting, Ting-Ya Chang, Daizaburo Harada, Kung Yi-Fang, Hsu Ming-Sheng, Shiro Takahashi.

1 The European and American sailing ships that knocked on Japan's door at the beginning of the modern era, especially those in Commodore Matthew Perry's armada that arrived at Kanagawa Ken in 1853 and forced the opening of the harbor, shaking the nation from top to bottom.

2 The Jōmon Period spanned from approximately 12,000 BCE to 300 BCE.

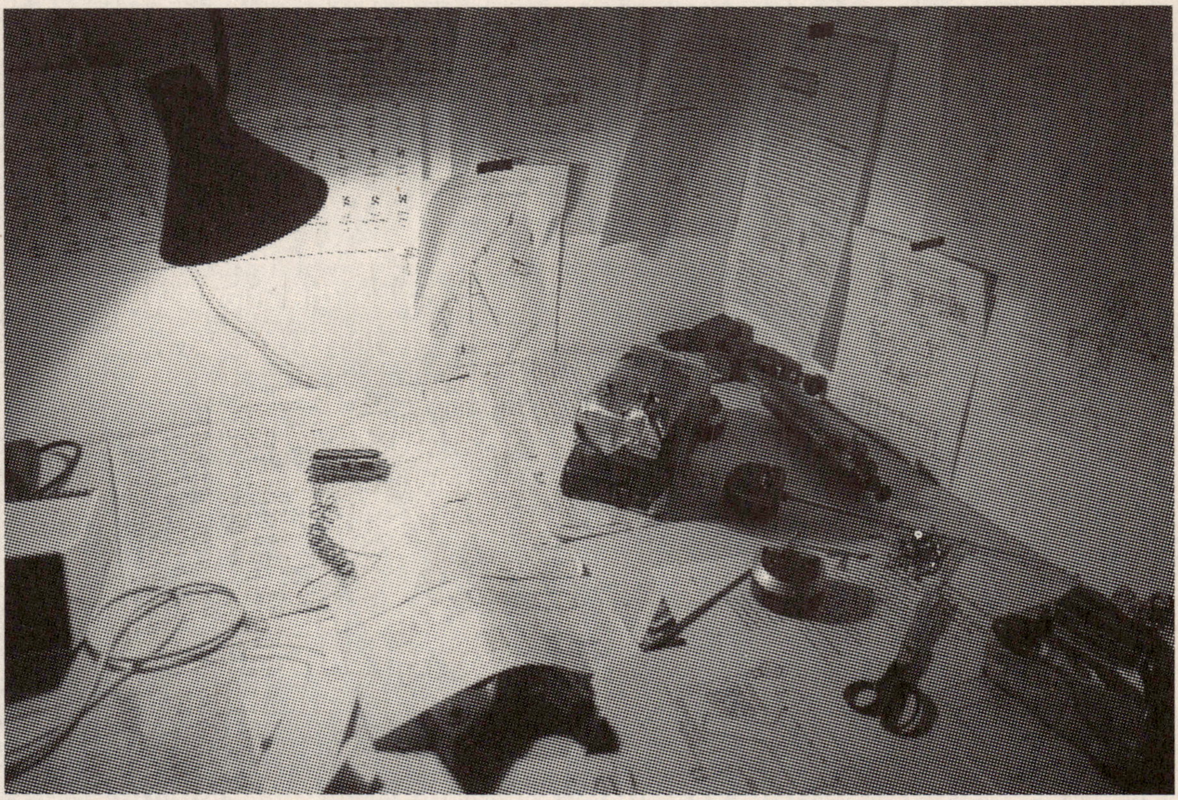

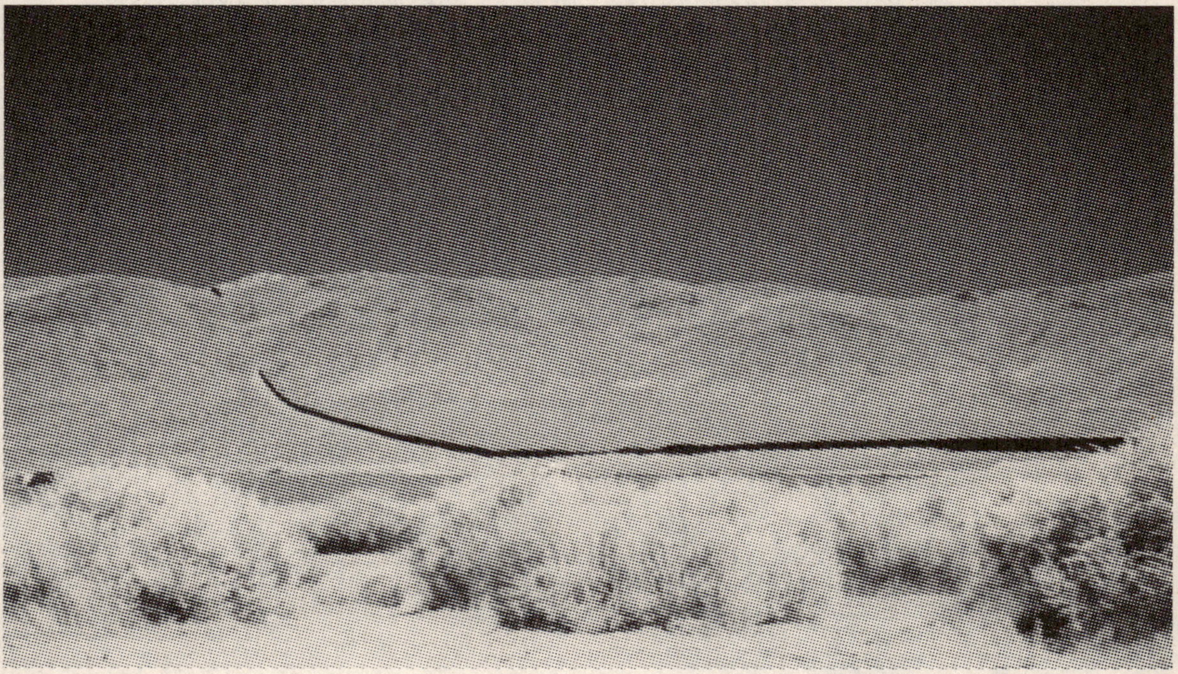

Yin-Ju Chen and James T. Hong, *The Turner Archives*, 2011, multimedia installation.

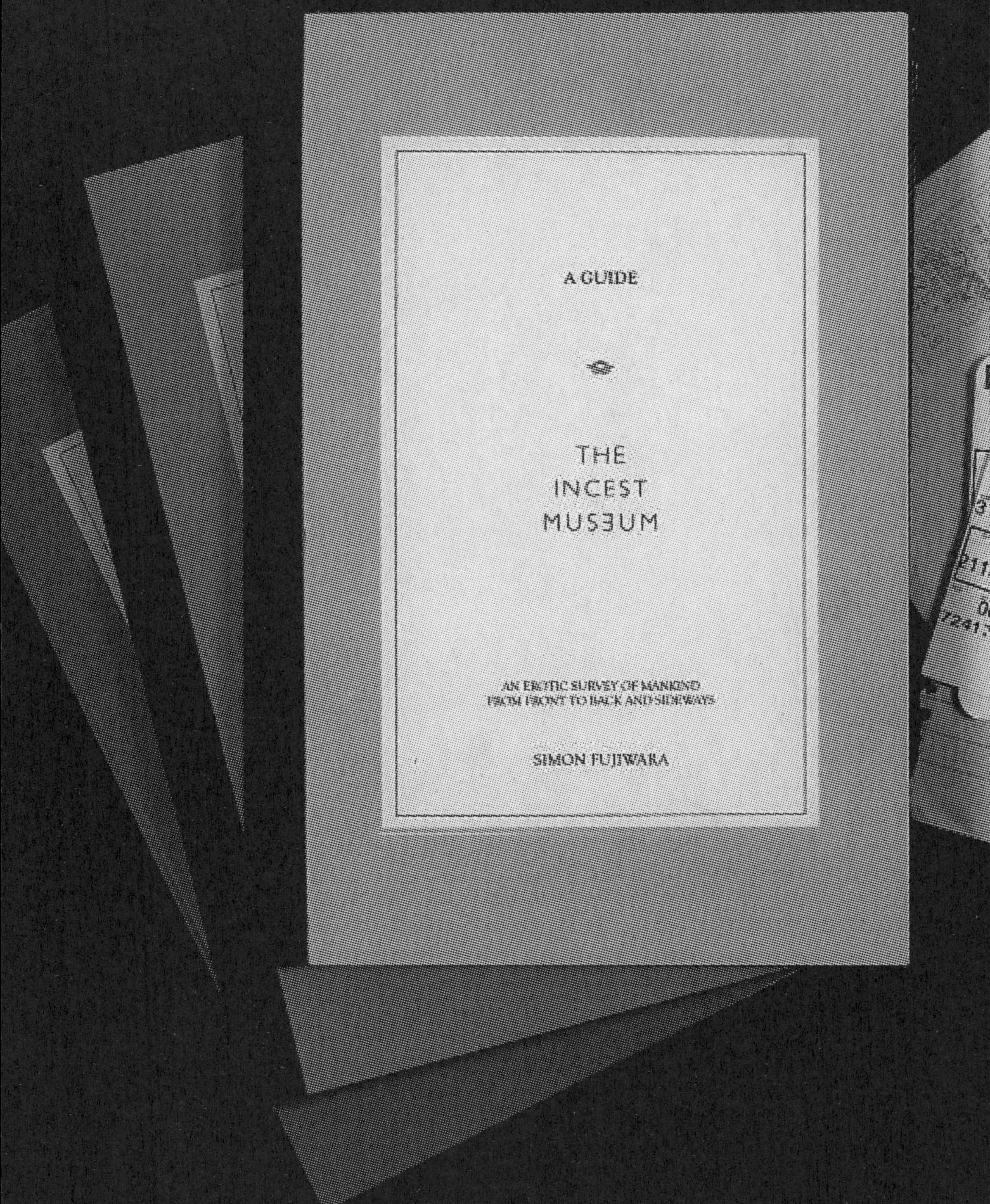
A GUIDE
THE
INCEST
MUSEUM
AN EROTIC SURVEY OF MANKIND
FROM FRONT TO BACK AND SIDEWAYS
SIMON FUJIWARA

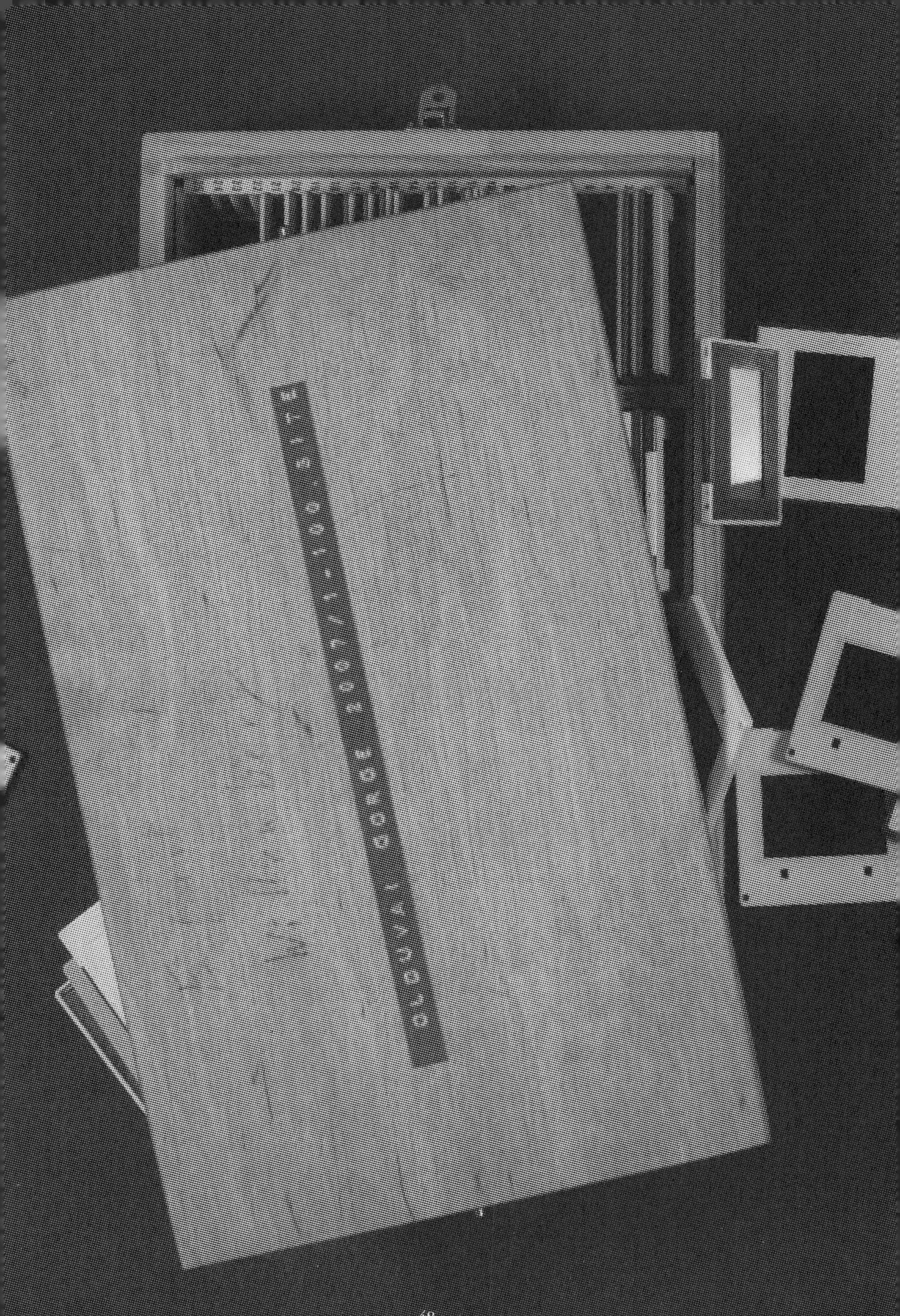

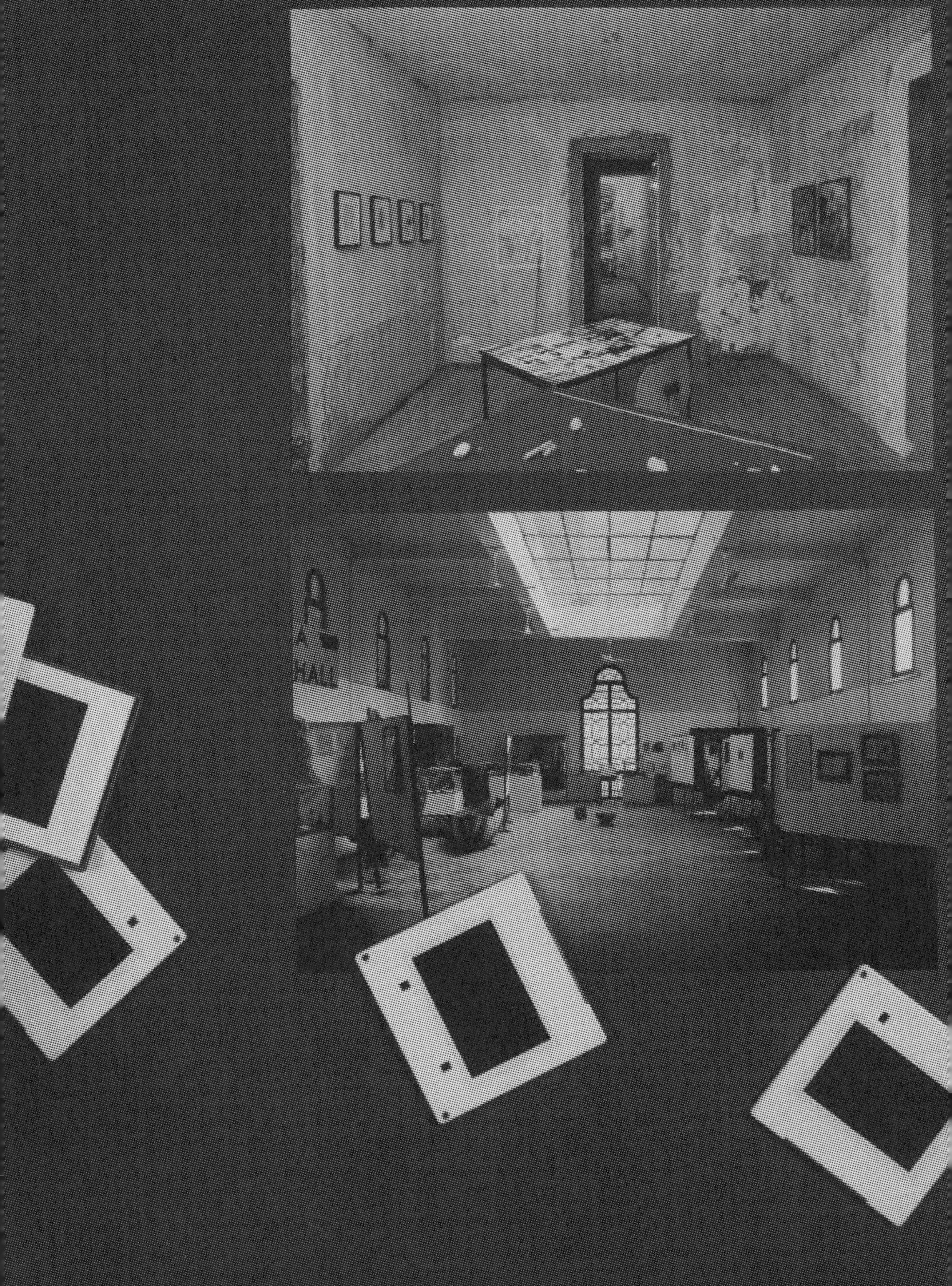

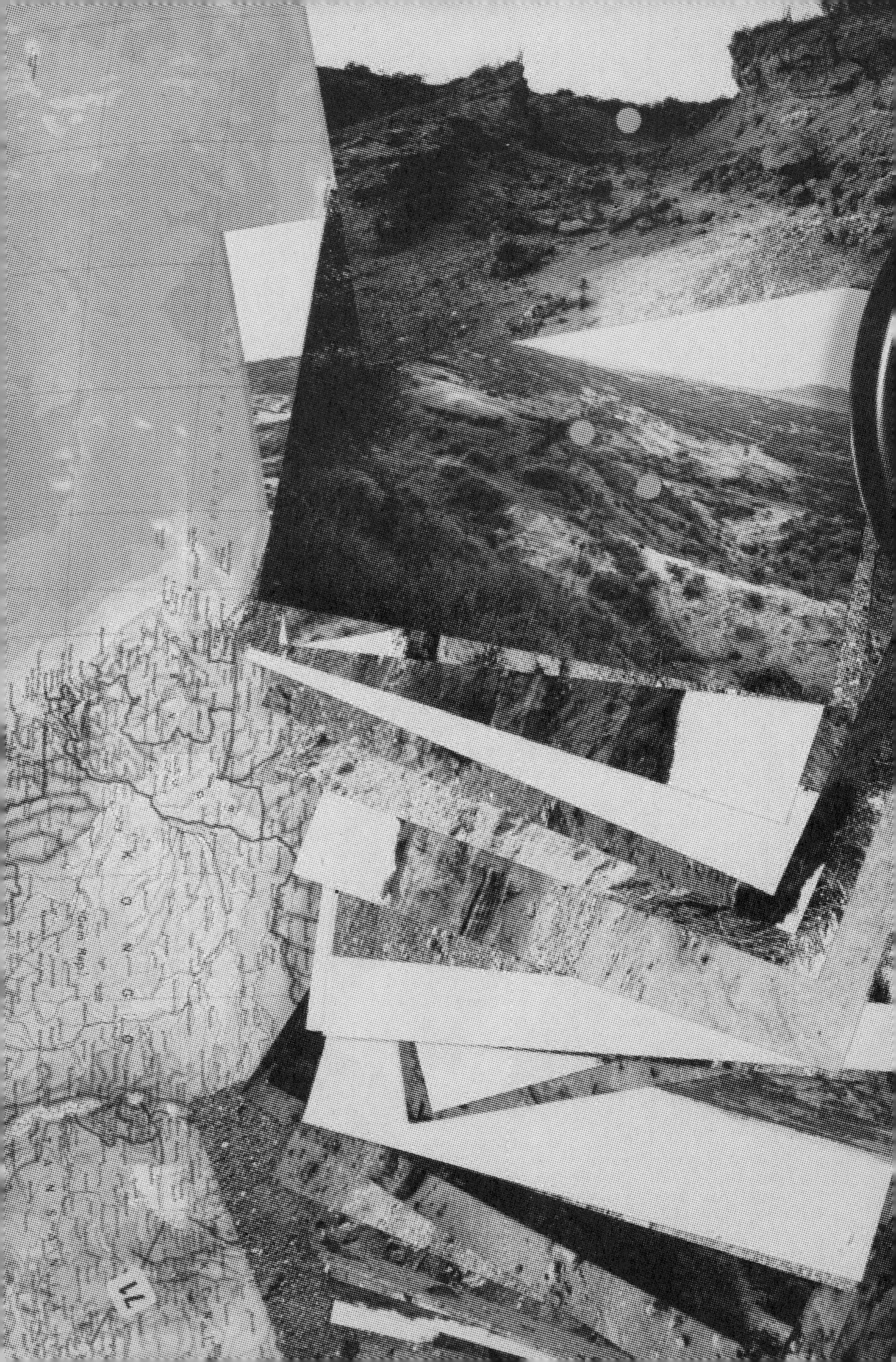

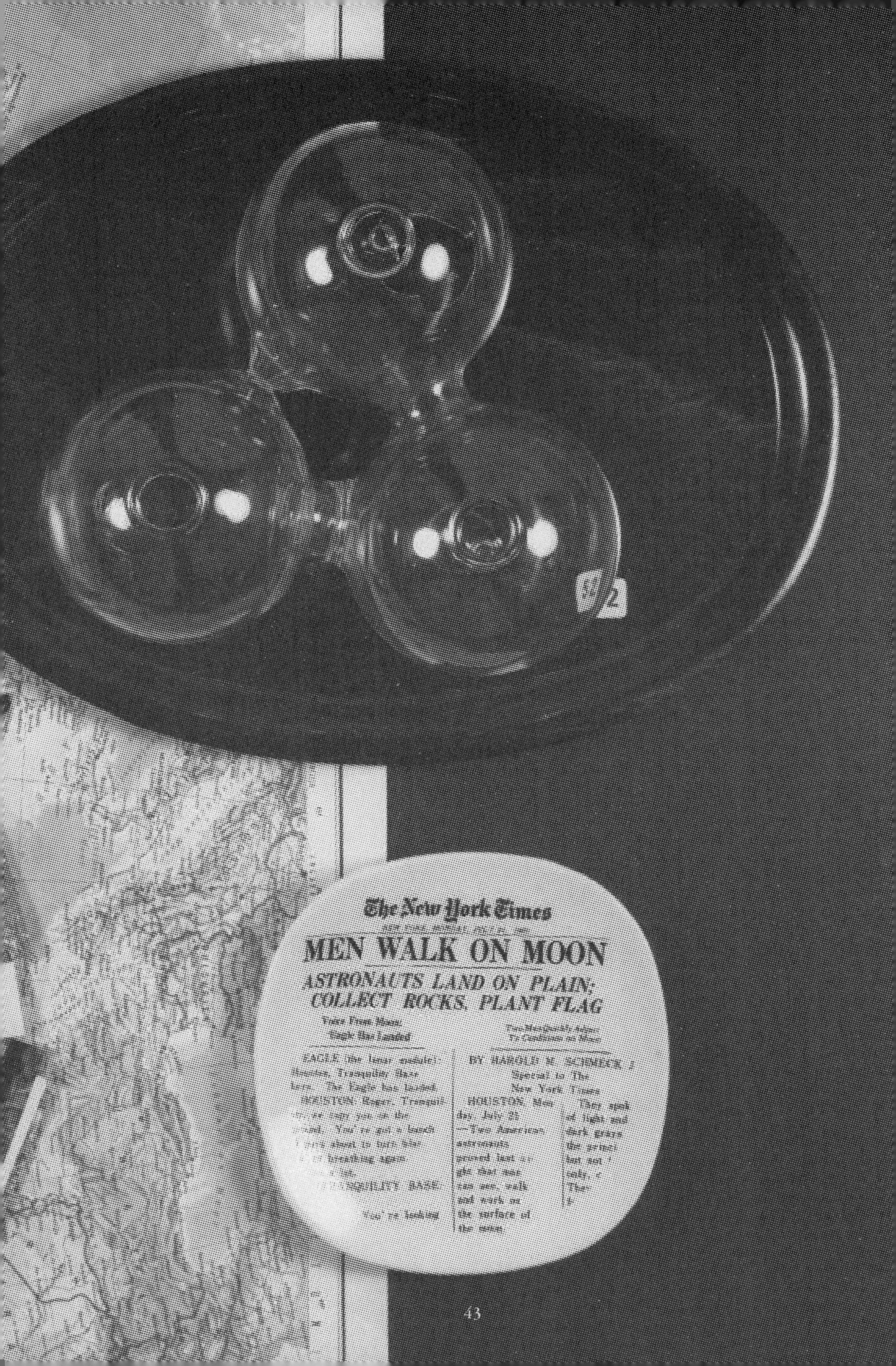
The New York Times
MEN WALK ON MOON
ASTRONAUTS LAND ON PLAIN;
COLLECT ROCKS, PLANT FLAG

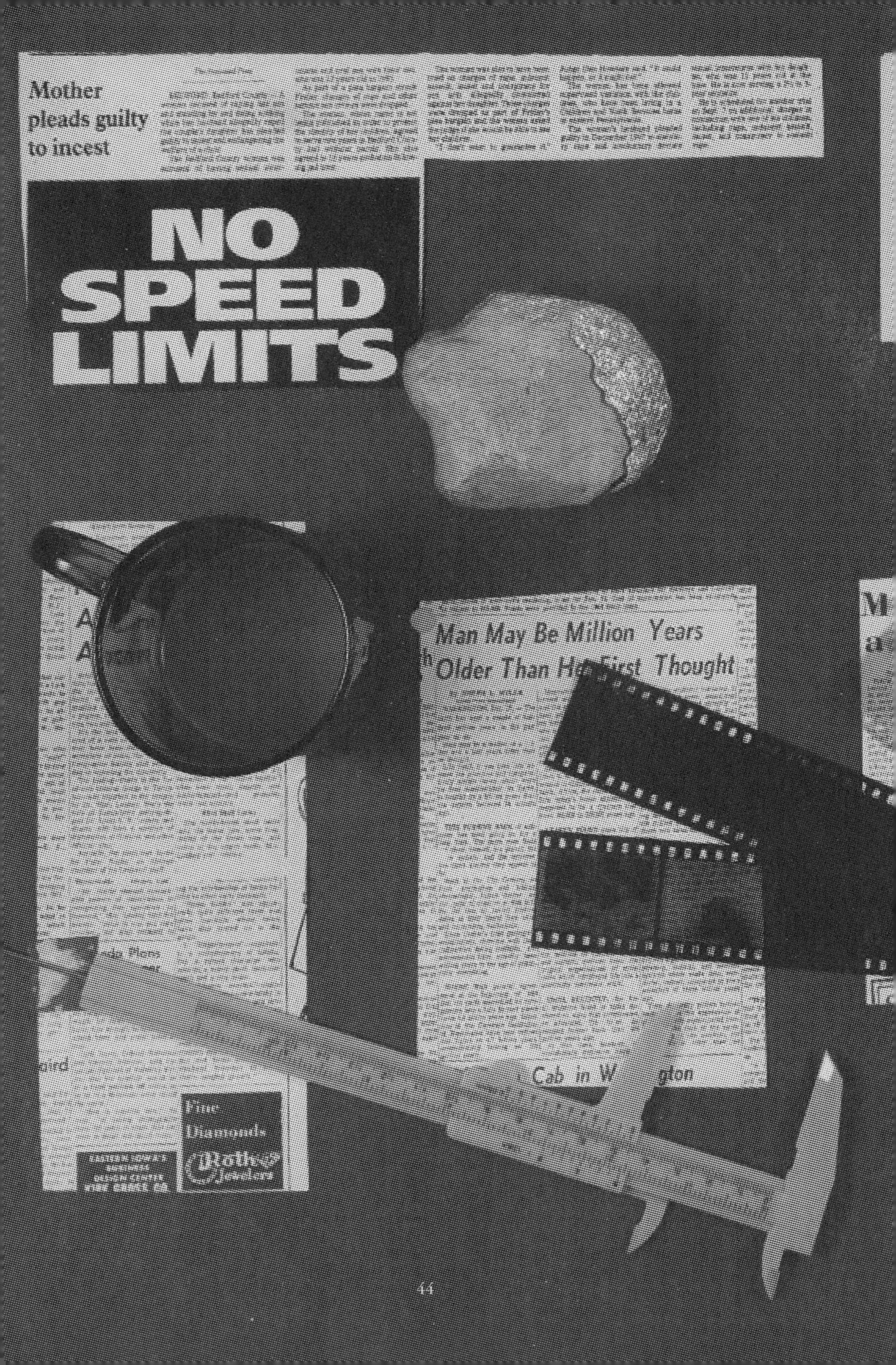
Mother pleads guilty to incest
NO SPEED LIMITS
Man May Be Million Years
Older Than H First Thought
Cab in W gton
Fine Diamonds
Roth Jewelers

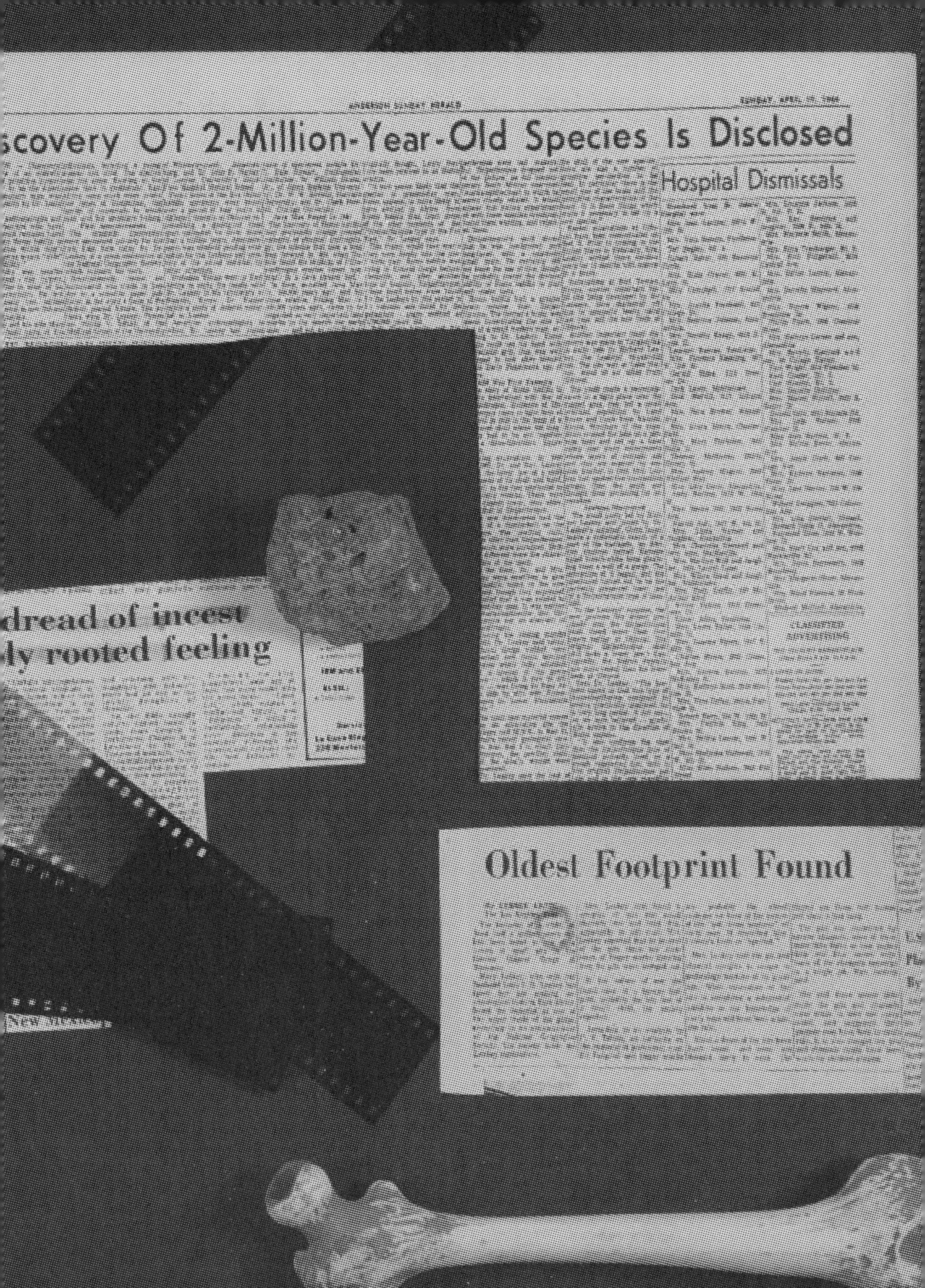

The Museum of Incest, Guide, revised October 2008.
This publication has been produced on the occasion of the exhibition *Simon Fujiwara: Since 1982* at Tate St Ive.

THE LIFE OF PARTICLES
A VISUAL RESEARCH PROJECT

Angela Melitopoulos and Maurizio Lazzarato

In contrast to Occidental music, Japanese music does not possess a harmonic system, the music does not blend sounds.

It compensates for this by modulating pure sounds.

The varied musical shifts affect frequency, tempo, timbre.

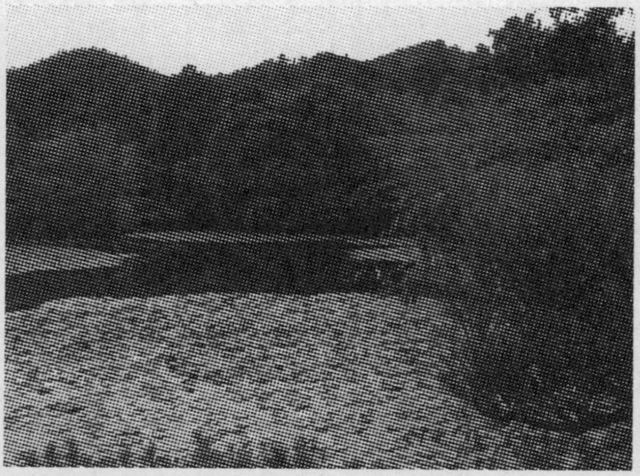

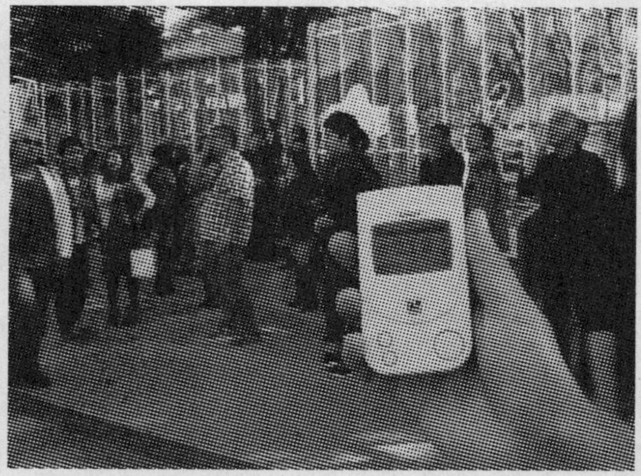

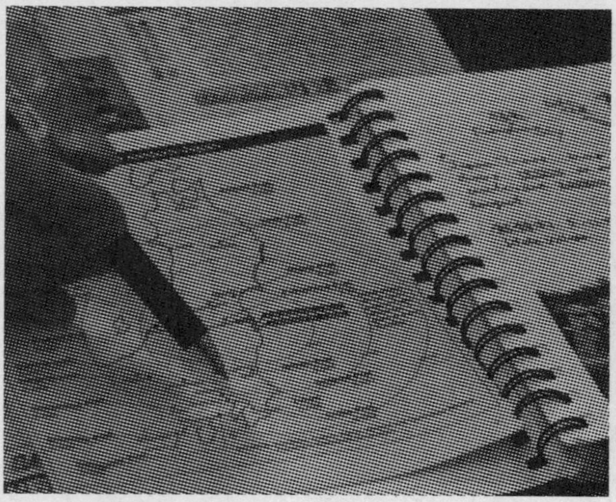

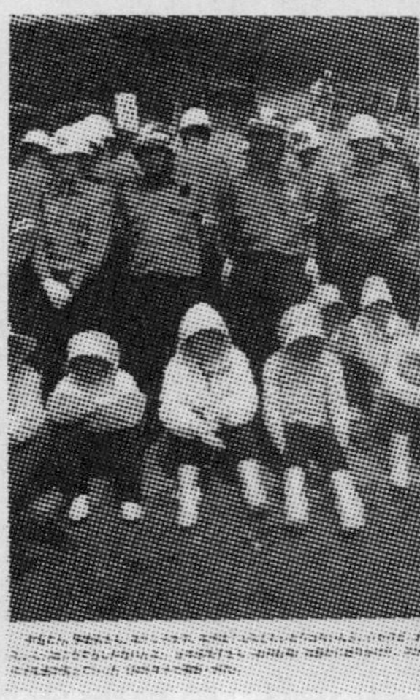

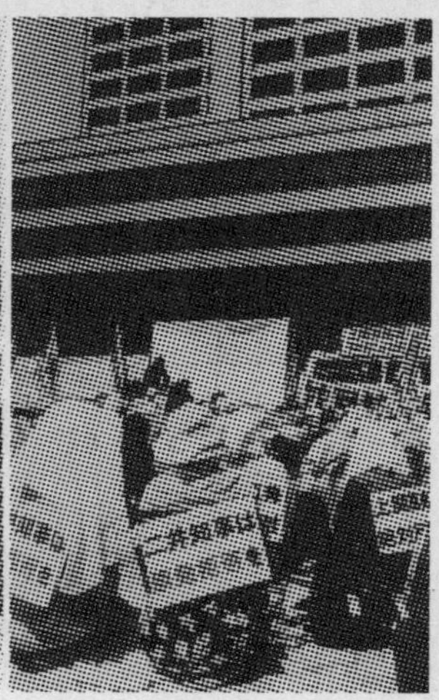

THE MUSEUM OF CROSS INGS

This method subtly integrates sounds and noise; the cries of insects that the Occident considers to be noise belong to this musical system.

The equivalent of a harmonic system is realized here, through the duration and quality of sounds that emanate quickly one after the other, so that they are perceived as a whole.

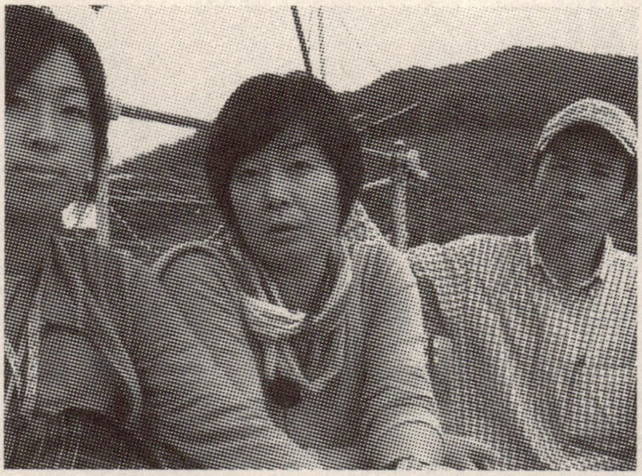

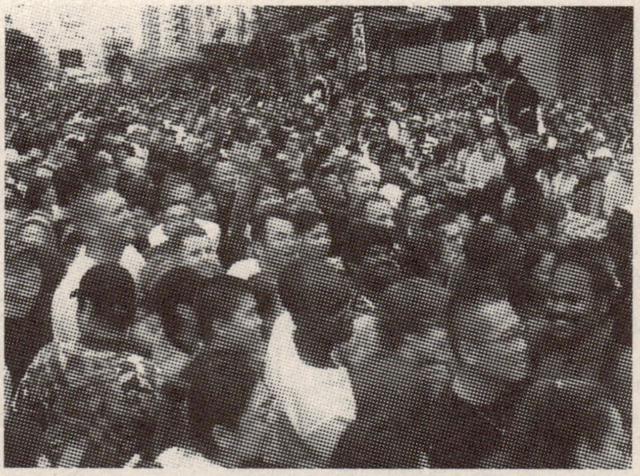

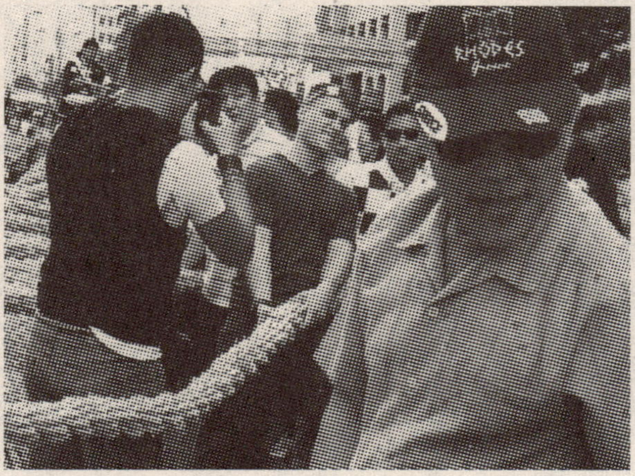

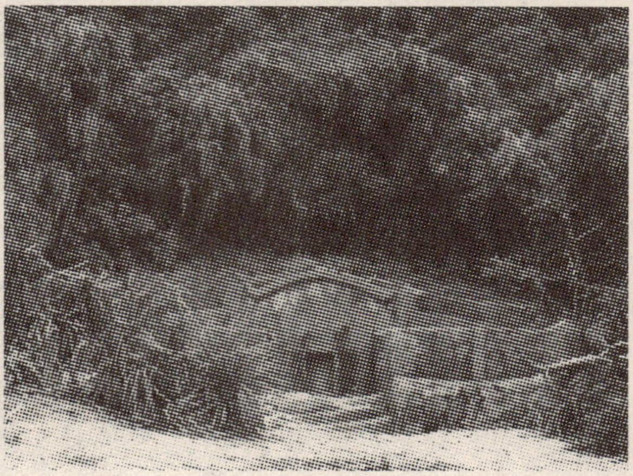

THE MUSEUM OF CROSSINGS

Anselm Franke and Hongjohn Lin

The Museum of Crossings is devoted to the crossing of borders. The first association refers to the physical crossing of boundaries, such as the borders of nation-states, which are crossed by tourists, entrepreneurs (and their money and goods), migrants and smugglers, and agents and spies. The spy perhaps best exemplifies what this museum is about: namely, that "borders" are zones of projections and mirror-effects, guarded by (often stereotypical) images and frames, which can be "passed" if one falls into a particular scheme, assumes a good camouflage, or acts like a legitimate "type." This is true not only of territorial borders, but of all borders of identity: borders are "mimetic zones" in which identity and deviation, similarity and difference, are guarded and negotiated. Above all, they are zones of contagion, of irreversible contact with alterity near and far, real or imagined, fictional or actual—and it is only because of this that they have become zones of control, of hygiene and paranoia, the site of racism, xenophobia, and the projective export and imputation of collective fears. *The Museum of Crossings* is devoted to different "morphologies" of crossing boundaries. It looks at borders as mimetic zones in which identity and alterity are in permanent exchange, and in which the imaginary and the fictional assume a powerful role. The monster in this context is a figure of mimetic and morphological powers who awaits those attempting to transgress normative or cosmological boundaries.

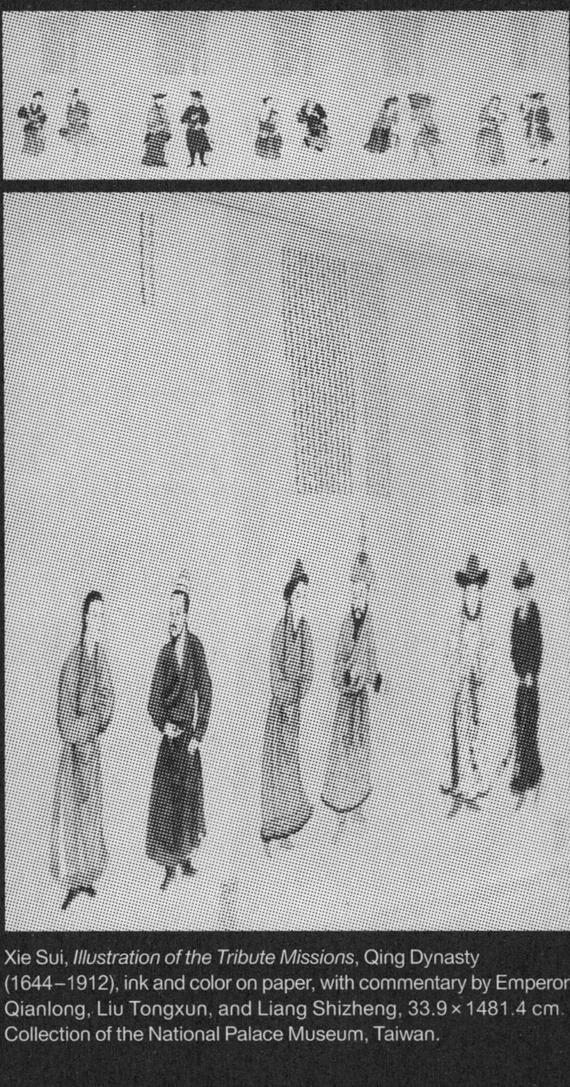

Xie Sui, *Illustration of the Tribute Missions*, Qing Dynasty (1644–1912), ink and color on paper, with commentary by Emperor Qianlong, Liu Tongxun, and Liang Shizheng, 33.9 × 1481.4 cm. Collection of the National Palace Museum, Taiwan.

Spirits are everywhere, in the grass, in stones, in the earth; and they protect man.

Some are particularly sensitive to these spirits, these people are called the "Saadaka."

The Saadaka who go mad are called "Kamidawari."

They are possessed by spirits, and in Europe, they would be classified as mentally ill.

In Okinawa we know that not all the Kamidawari are mentally ill.

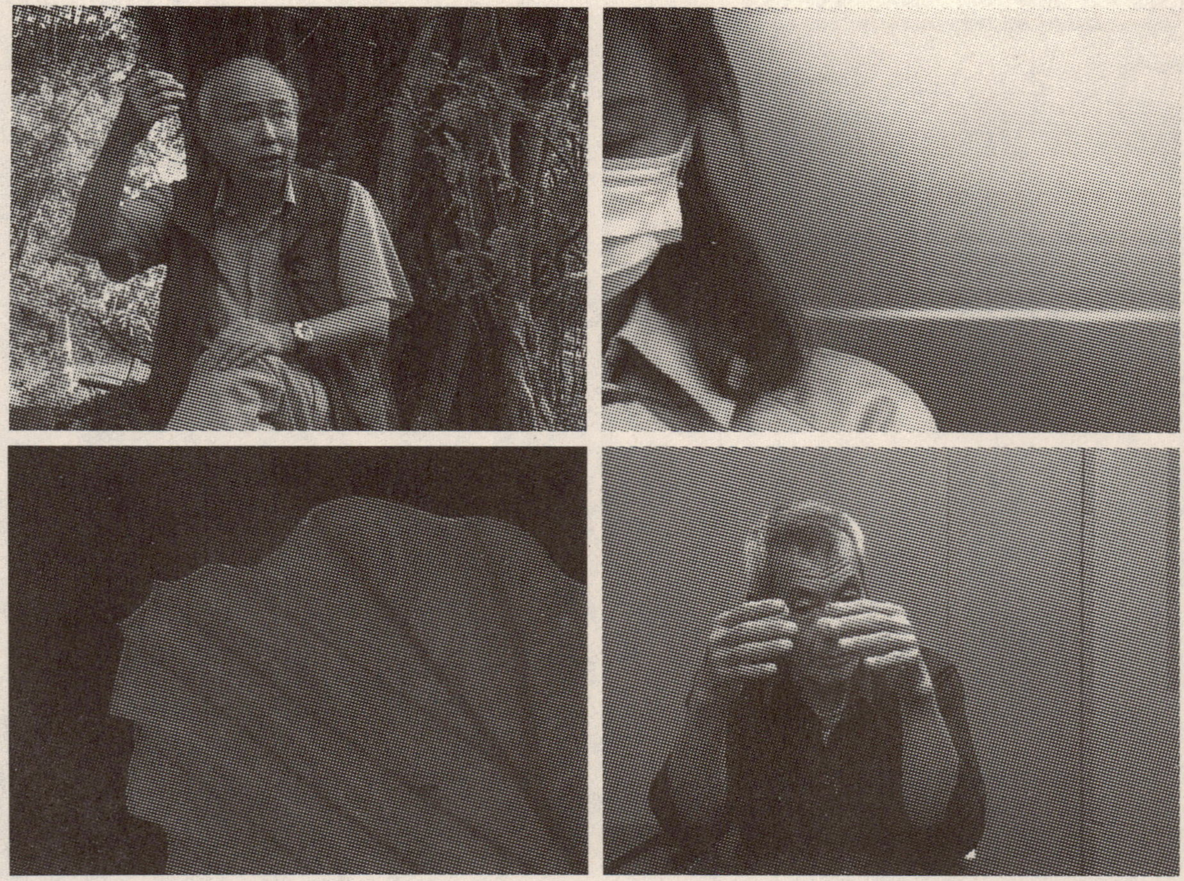

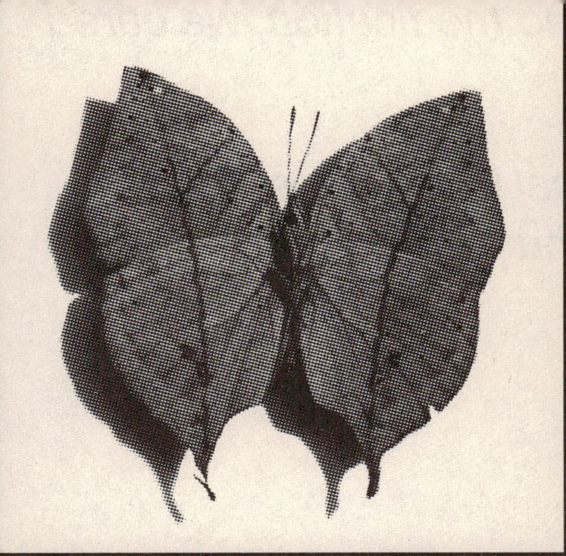

Dead Leaf Butterfly from Taiwan (*Kallima inachus formosanus Fruhstorfer*)

How is the border between the human and nonhuman guarded and upheld? Why is it that monsters are frequently hybrids, border-figures between human and animal, or between humans and machines? How can we image the passage, the process of crossing, between animal and human, between machine and man? In a different register: How does the symbolic order and cosmological representation change after acts of destruction and violence? And again: How are we to imagine the mimetic relation of any living organism to its environment, its “milieu”?

The Museum of Crossings is divided into two parts. The first part presents a series of “relational diagrams,” or “border mappings.” These are miniature stories and cartographies, organized along various lines of division in order to expose their very principles of construction. From the impact of the Bikini Atoll nuclear tests on cosmology, to the phenomena of mimicry in insects that visually “adapt” themselves to their environment, to the policing of the line between the normal and the pathological in psychiatry, to the “codes” of sexual politics, to so-called colonial mimicry and the apparently universal schemes of racism, a seemingly “natural” line of division in all cases is replaced with the always unstable and shifting distinction between “passive” and “active” agents, between a “figure” (active) and a “background” (passive), and their particular codependency.

The second part of the *Museum* attends to the specific case of George Psalmanazar, the bogus Taiwanese man who gained a reputation in learned social circles in early eighteenth-century London. His book *An Historical and Geographical Description of Formosa* (1704), portraying a bizarre wonderland of naked savages, floating villages, Satanism, cannibalism, and human sacrifice, never failed to satiate the curious desire for projecting the alterity of the other. Psalmanazar, despite having white skin and blond hair, could get by as Formosan, partly because of his hyper-exotic performance of eating raw meat and sleeping with his eyes open, and partly because of the lack of proper knowledge about Taiwan in particular and ethnicity in general. *The Museum of Psalmanazar* is intended to realize his fantastical Formosa, invoking the crossing of his spirit from early

In the past, when there was no medication, we cared for the Kami with prayer.

And now that we have medical techniques, we treat them by psychiatric means, but also with prayer.

Yoshihide Takaesu, MD
Director of a psychiatric hospital in Izumi, Okinawa

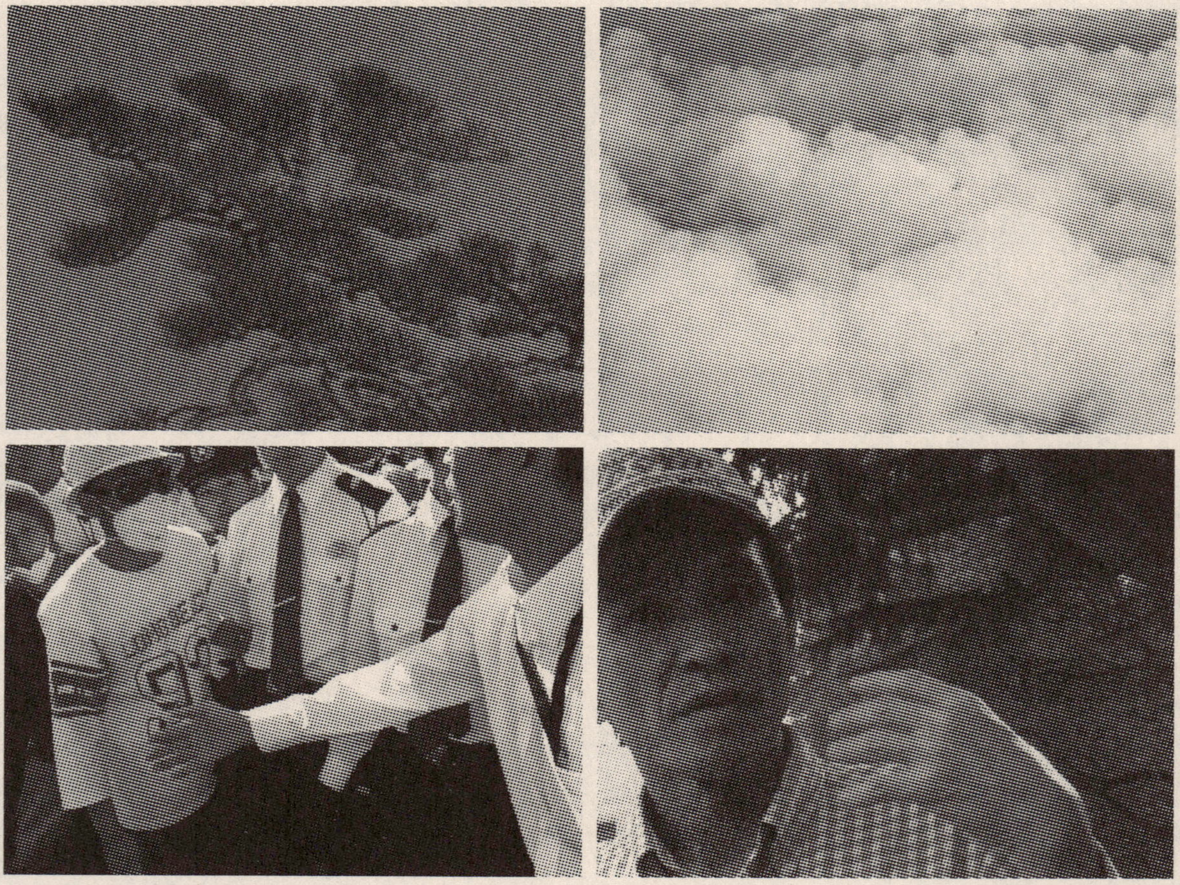

Angela Melitopoulos and Maurizio Lazzarato, *The Life of Particles,* 2011–2012, three-channel HD video installation, color, sound, 90 min.

Enlightenment London to the Taiwan of the present. Different display techniques, especially the shifting of foreground and background, are employed to recompose a skewed picture. The effect is to arrest the fleeting phantasmagorical images that have always divided the normal and the perverse, the primitive and the modern, the powerful and the empowered, and the one and the other in rendering cognitive relations at the crossroads of the fantastical and the real Taiwan.

Curated by Anselm Franke and Hongjohn Lin. Participating artists: Virlani Hallberg, Lin Swallow Y, Hongjohn Lin, Tsai Chih-Hsien.

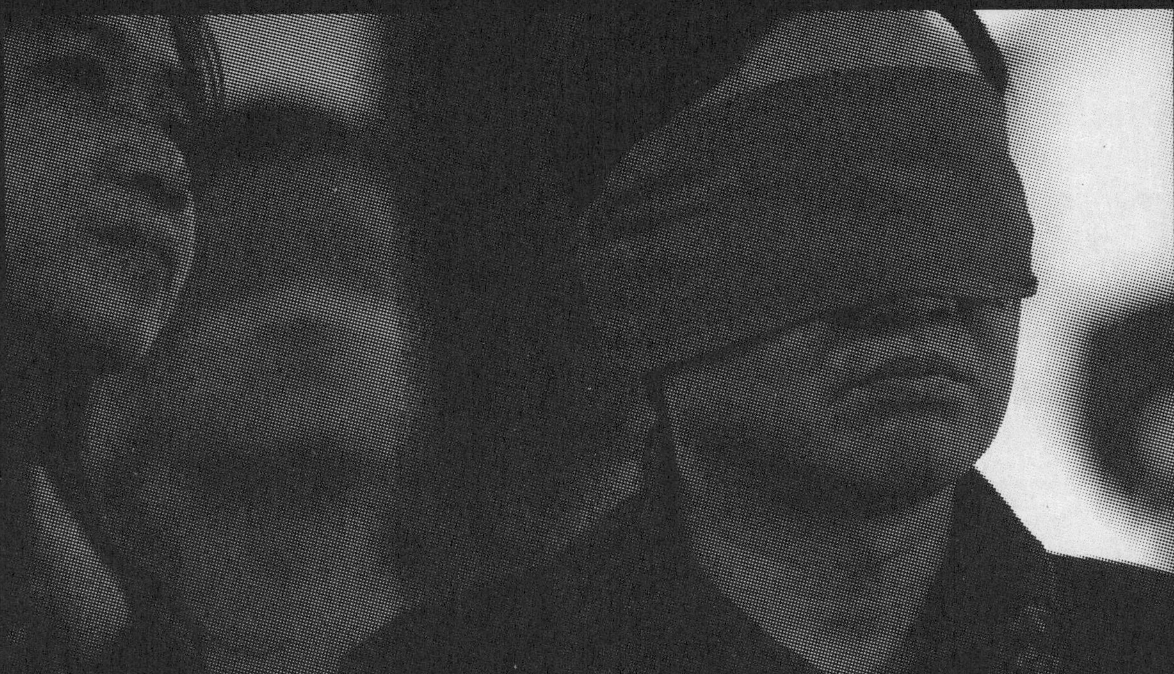

Virlani Hallberg, *Receding Triangular Square*, 2012, HD video, color, sound. *RTS* juxtaposes Daoist rituals and traditional healing methods from Taiwan's aboriginal cultures with Western-style psychiatry. The film investigates different ways of crossing boundaries to the "other side"—the side of ancestors and spirits, of the psyche, of unspeakable experiences. The connection to the "other side" can no longer be taken for granted. It has to be questioned, made, and remade.

THE LAST WILL AND TESTAMENT OF ME, A POOR, SINFUL, AND WORTHLESS CREATURE COMMONLY KNOWN BY THE ASSUMED NAME OF GEORGE PSALMANAZAR

George Psalmanazar

George Psalmanazar was a bogus Taiwanese man who gained a reputation in learned social circles in early eighteenth-century London. His book *An Historical and Geographical Description of Formosa* (1704), portraying a bizarre wonderland of naked savages, floating villages, Satanism, cannibalism, and human sacrifice, never failed to satiate the curious desire for projecting the alterity of the other. Despite having white skin and blond hair, Psalmanazar managed to get by as Formosan, partly because of his hyper-exotic performance of eating raw meat and sleeping with his eyes open, and partly because of the lack of proper knowledge about Taiwan in particular and ethnicity in general. As part of the Taipei Biennial 2012, *The Museum of Psalmanazar* is intended to realize his fantastical Formosa, invoking the crossing of his spirit from early Enlightenment London to the Taiwan of the present. To this day the real identity of Psalmanazar remains unknown, though his accent caused some to believe he was French. Ultimately, he was a man who identified more with the fictitious than with the original and the real. The following excerpt from his book *Memoirs of* **** (1765)—which was to be published posthumously, though it was still signed with his alias—is his last will and testament, in which he confesses to having been a fraud.
—Hongjohn Lin

Thy ever blessed and unerring Will, Oh most gracious, though offended God! be done by me and all the world, whether for life or death.

Into thy all-merciful hands I commit my soul, as unto a most gracious Father, who, though justly provoked by my past vain and wicked life, but more especially so during the youthful sallies of a rash and unthinking part of it, has yet been graciously pleased, by thy undeserved grace and mercy, to preserve me from the reigning errors and heresies, and the more deplorable apostasy and infidelity of the present age, and enabled me to take a constant and steadfast hold on the only author of our salvation, thy ever adorable and divine Son Jesus Christ, our powerful and meritorious Redeemer, from whose alone, and all-powerful intercession and merits […]

I desire that my body may be kept so long above ground as decency or conveniency will permit, and afterwards conveyed to the common burying-ground, and there interred in some obscure corner of it, without any further ceremony or formality than is used to the bodies of the deceased pensioners where I happen to die, and about the same time of the day, and that the whole may be performed in the lowest and cheapest manner. And it is my earnest request that my body be not enclosed in any kind of coffin, but only decently laid in what is called a shell of the lowest value, and without lid or other covering which may hinder the natural earth from covering it all around.

[…]

But the principal manuscript I thought myself in duty bound to leave behind, is a faithful narrative of my education, and the sallies of my wretched youthful years, and the various ways by which I was in some measure unavoidably led into the base and shameful imposture of passing upon the world for a native of Formosa, and a convert to Christianity, and backing it with a fictitious account of that island, and of my own travels, conversion, and etc. All or most of it hatched in my own brain, without regard to truth and honesty. It is true, I have long since disclaimed even publicly all but the shame and guilt of that vile imposition, yet as long as I knew there were still two editions of that scandalous romance remaining in England, besides the several versions it had abroad. I thought it incumbent upon me to undeceive the world, by unravelling that whole mystery of iniquity in a posthumous work, which would be less liable to suspicion, as the author would be far out of the influence of any sinister motives that might induce him to deviate from the truth. All that I shall add concerning it is that it was began about twenty-five years ago with that view, and no other, during a long recess in the country, accompanied with a threatening disease, and since then continued in my most serious hours, as any thing new presented itself; so that it hath little else to recommend itself but its plainness and sincerity, except here and there some useful observations and innuendoes on those branches of learning in which I had been concerned, […] in the producing a more perfect body of Universal History, and more answerable to its title than that which hath already passed a second edition. And these, I thought, might be more deserving a place in that narrative, as the usefulness of them would in a great measure make amends for the small charge of the whole. If it therefore shall be judged worth printing, I desire it may be sold to the highest bidder, in order to pay my arrears for my lodgings, and to defray my funeral; and I further request that it be printed in the plain and undisguised manner in which I have written it, and without alteration or embellishment. I hope the whole is written in the true, sincere spirit of a person awakened by a miracle of mercy, unto

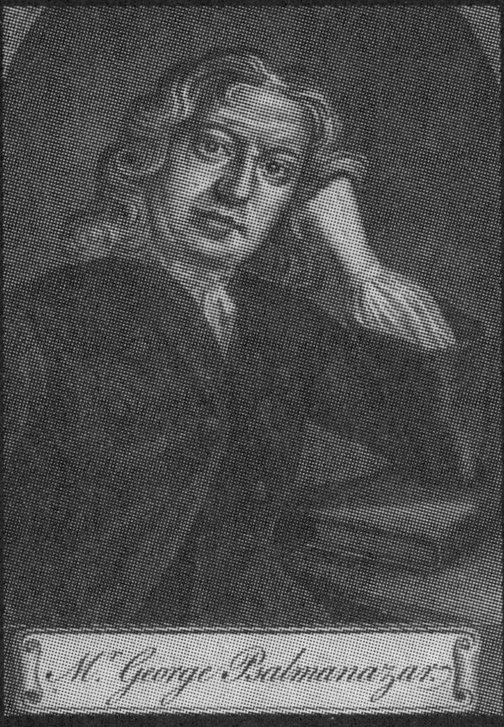

a deep sense of his folly, guilt, and danger, and is desirous, above all things, to give God the whole glory of so gracious a change, and to show the various steps by which his Divine Providence brought it about.

The whole of the account contains fourteen pages of Preface, and about ninety-three more of the said relation, written in my own hand with a proper title, and will be found in the deep drawer on the right hand of my white cabinet. However, if the obscurity I have lived in, during such a series of years, should make it needless to revive a thing in all likelihood so long since forgot, I cannot but wish that so much of it was published in some weekly paper as might inform the world, especially those who have still by them the above-mentioned fabulous account of the Island of Formosa, which I have long since owned both in conversation and in print that it was no other than a mere forgery of my own devising, a scandalous imposition on the public, and such, as I think myself bound to beg God and the world pardon for writing, and have been long since, as I am to this day, and shall be as long as I live, heartily sorry for, and ashamed of.

These I do hereby solemnly declare and testify to be my last Will and Testament; and in witness thereof have thereto set my name, on the 23rd day of April, in the year of our Lord 1752, O. S. and in the 73rd year of my age.

TIME OF NO SHADOWS (1959–2004)

Chang Chao-Tang

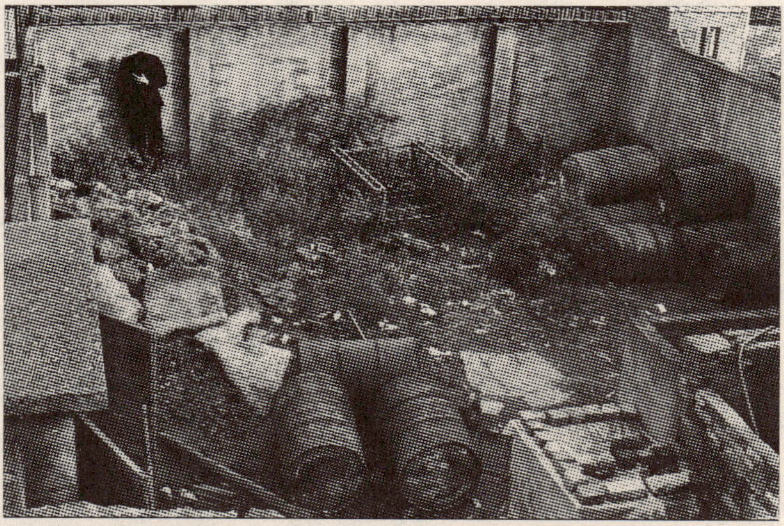

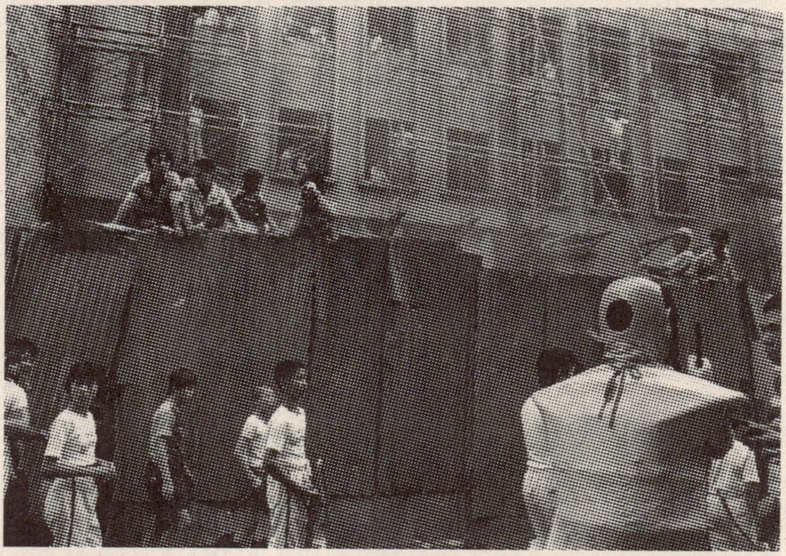

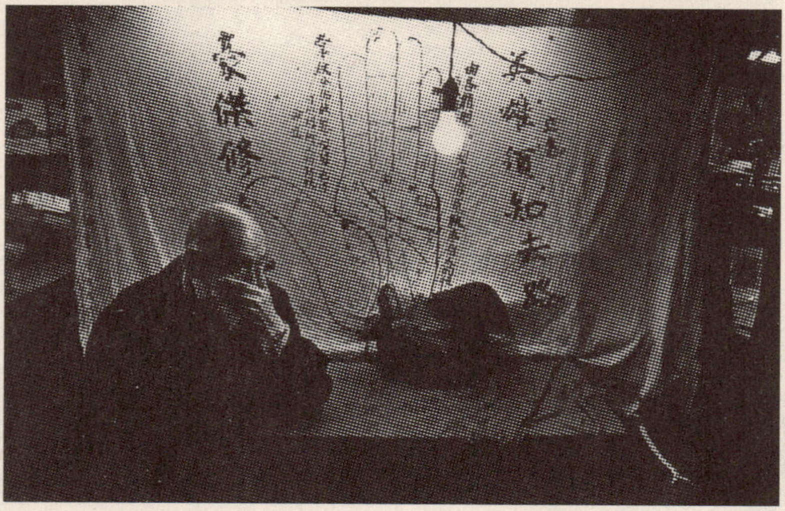

Fig. 1 *Panchiao, Taiwan 1964.*
Fig. 2 *Taipei, Taiwan 2000.*
Fig. 3 *Wanhua, Taiwan 1983.*

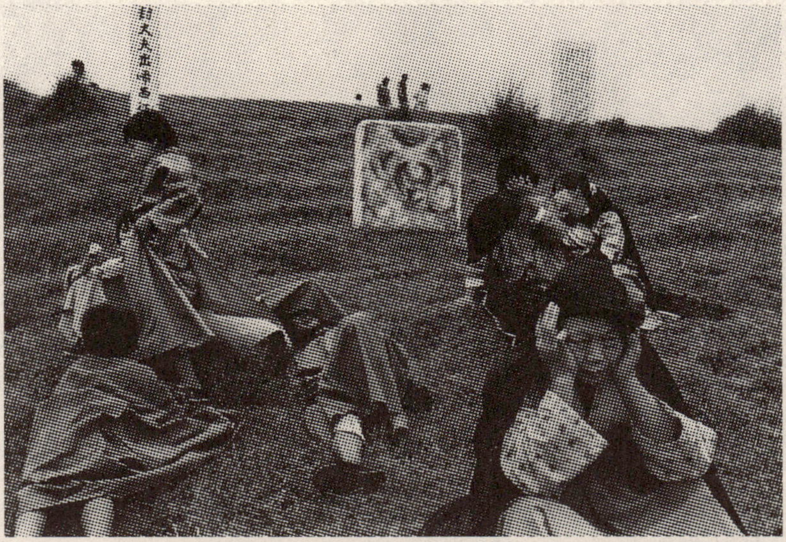

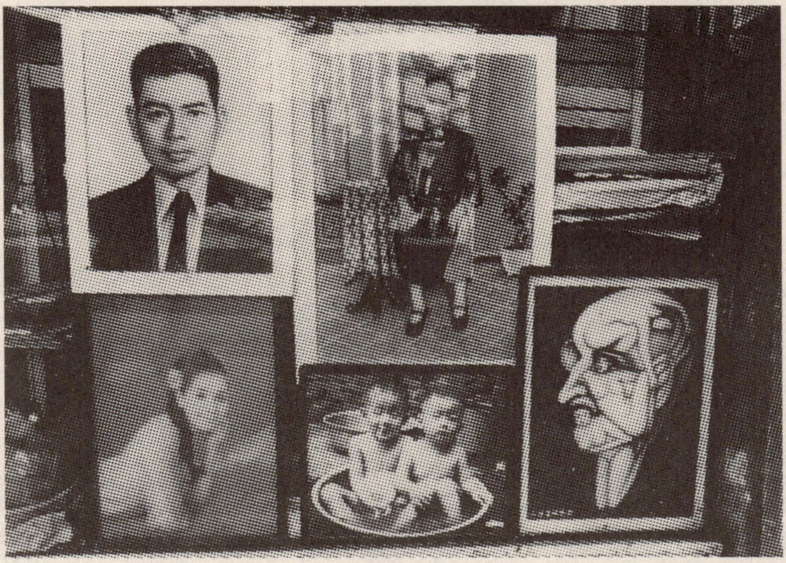

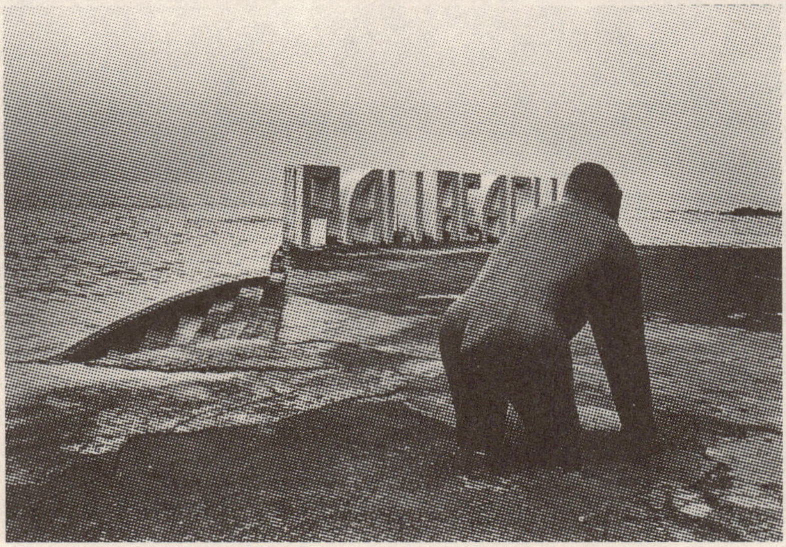

Fig. 4 *Chingtienkang, Taiwan 1985.*
Fig. 5 *Sansia, Taiwan 1980.*
Fig. 6 *Wanli, Keelung, Taiwan 1996.*

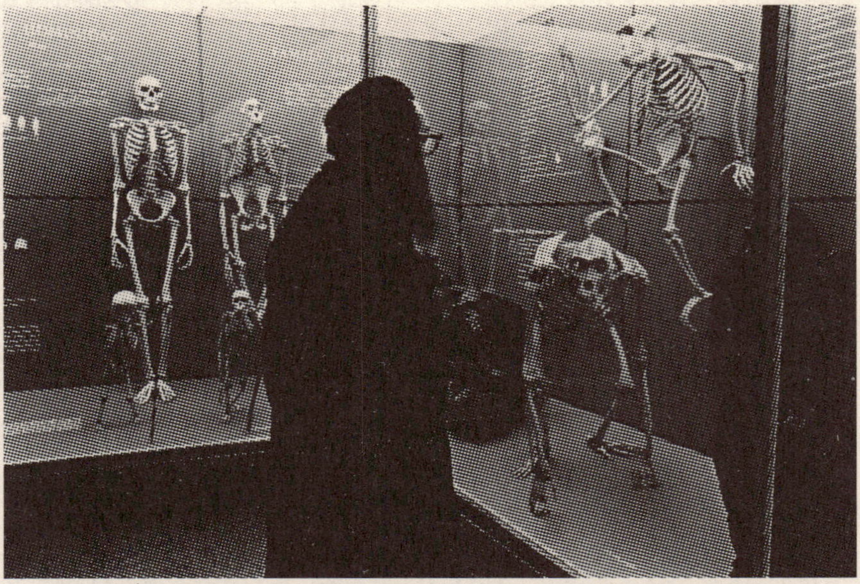

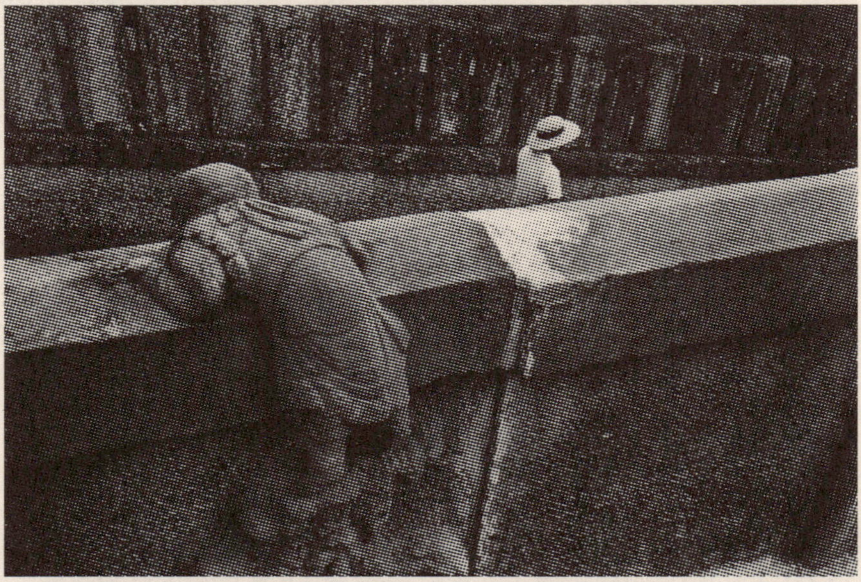

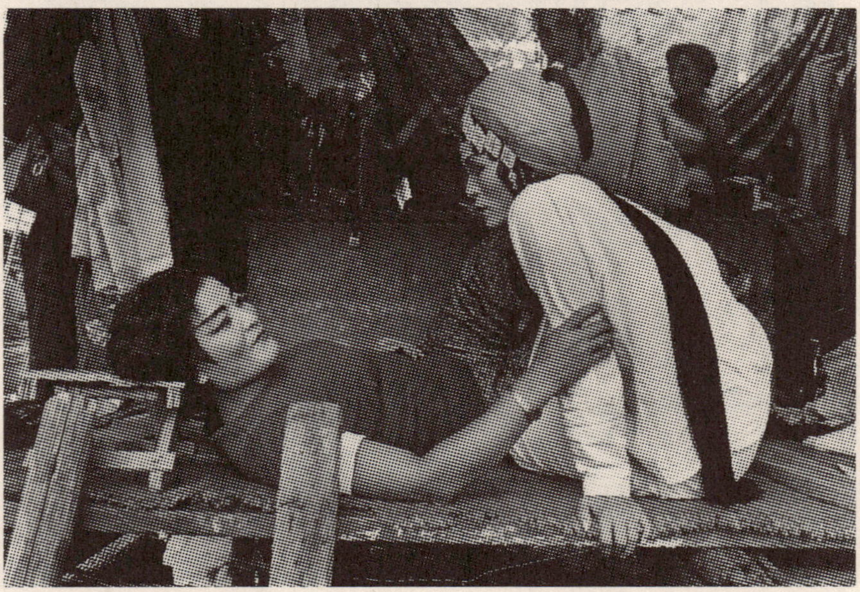

Fig. 7 *New York, USA 1998.*
Fig. 8 *Kyoto, Japan 2004.*
Fig. 9 *Keelung, Taiwan 1974.*

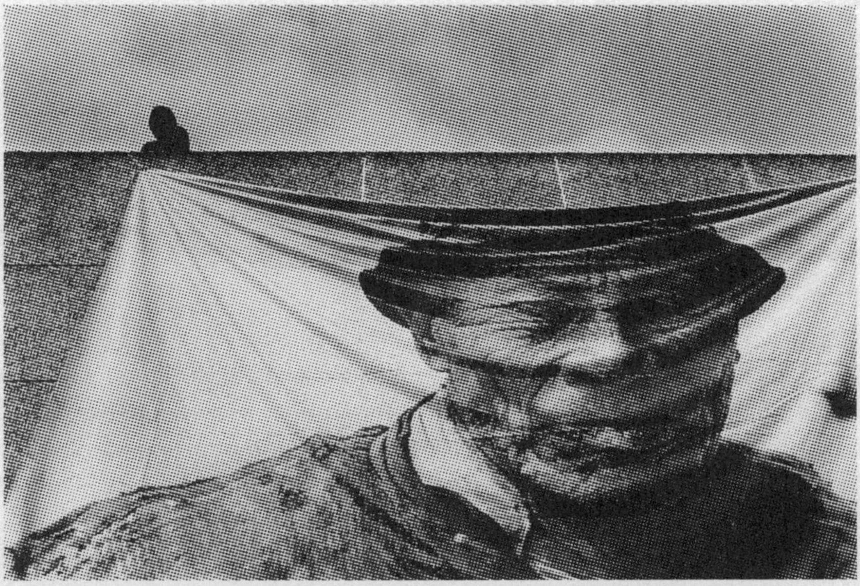

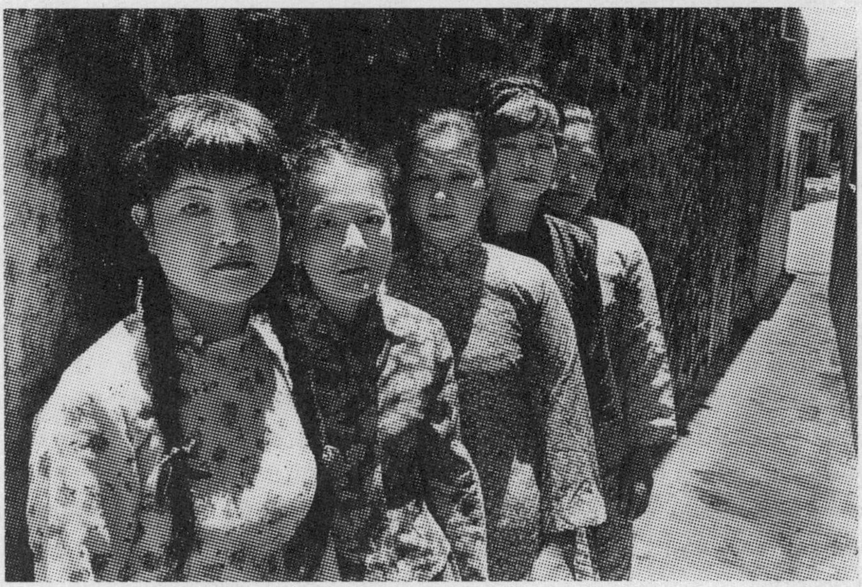

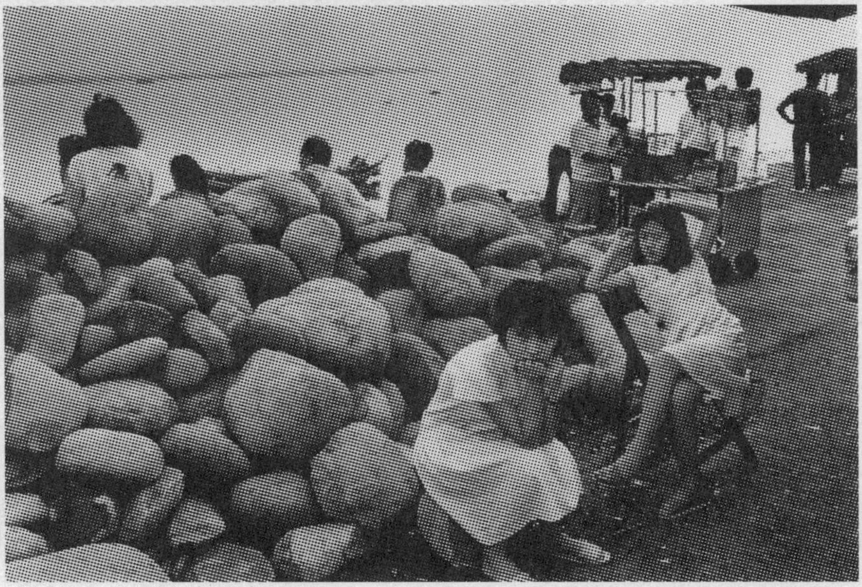

Fig. 10 *Tainan, Taiwan 2004.*
Fig. 11 *Penhu Island, Taiwan 1983.*
Fig. 12 *Tanshuei, Taiwan 1987.*

THE MANIPULATIONS OF TIME

Henri Lefebvre

What has not been written on time and space, generally defined as given, distinct, separate essences (or substances)? Up until the modern era, space was generously attributed to the human race, and time to the Lord.

This separation is in the process of being filled in, though more than one lacuna remains. The history of time and the time of history hold another mystery. The genesis of social time remains obscure. The history of time and the time of history should include a history of rhythms, which is missing. There are certain benefits, however. Time is at once fleeting, ungraspable (even for the self of psychology), and grasped, timed, timed *chronometrically*. A philosophical paradox, but one that goes further than philosophy: time, number, and drama concern life. In historical time, what is the role of history in the forms of memory, recollections, narratives? Are there not alternatives to memory and forgetting: periods where the past returns—and periods where the past effaces itself? Perhaps such an alternative would be the rhythm of history …

CAPITAL AND LIFE (THE LIVING)

It has often been said: "Capitalism makes masters and slaves, the rich and the poor, the propertied and the proletariat …" This is not wrong, but it does not suffice for measuring the evil power of *capital*. It constructs and erects itself on a contempt for life and from this foundation: the body, the time of living. Which does not cease to amaze: that a society, a *civilization*, a culture is able to construct itself from such disdain. This leads us to remark:

1

that the disdain conceals itself beneath an ethic (in the moral sense);

2

that it makes up for itself with ornaments: refinements in hygiene, the proliferation of sports and sporting ideology;

3

that if this contempt has played a big role in history, in the foundation of this society (in the nineteenth century, still the so-called Victorian period), and if some of it remains, it is fading, exhausting itself. It has transformed itself in a way that is subversive and even *revolutionary* in advancing into the unknown: the exaltation of *life*.

The domination-exploitation of human beings begins with animals, wild beasts and cattle; the humans associated with these creatures inaugurated an experience that would turn back against them: killings, stockbreeding, slaughters, sacrifices, and (in order better to submit) castration. All these practices were put to the test and succeeded. The castration of beasts, what power! And what a symbol of anti-nature! *Nature* gave way to representations, to myths and fables. The earth? Those who cultivated it loved it; they treated it as a generous divinity. The living (except those who accepted domestication, such as cats and dogs) provided raw material, a *primary substance* [matière prémière] that each society treated in its own way.

After which *human beings* separated themselves from each other: on the one hand the masters, men worthy of this name; and on the other, the subhumans, treated like animals, and with the same methods: dominated, exploited, humiliated. Whose fault is this? A bad question. Not that of the animals or their assimilated equivalents. Especially given the progress, the advances that this situation achieved: in knowledge, technology, world exploration, and

THE MUSEUM OF RHYTHM

the mastery of the natural. Man made himself *master* and *possessor of nature*, of the sensible, of substance. It was through this that he divided himself against himself, in realizing himself. Thus did capitalism!

One could, to supplement the concepts with images, depict capital: a chain of bacteria that grabs passing matter, that feeds itself by dividing itself, that multiplies by dividing itself. A false image: bacteria produces the living by absorbing the inert. Meanwhile, capital grows to make the void: it kills things around it on a planetary scale. Both in general and in detail. Capital does not construct. It produces. It does not edify; it reproduces itself. It simulates life. Production and reproduction tend to coincide in the uniform! Traditionally, we take it out on the *rich*, on the *bourgeois*. Thus the object of action is displaced. We forget that the guilty party is not even *money*, it is the functioning of capital! Which sublimates concepts. Images do not supplant concepts; however, in saying *true* or *real*, concepts simplify reality in their own way. Never has a handful of *property owners* dominated the world. There are always associates; they always have numerous auxiliaries with them. Today it is the technocracy, the *specialists* for whom communication relays speech and renders dialogue useless. Plus all those who occupy themselves with *cultural* production, who occupy themselves with things and suchlike. Just as the aristocracy had hordes of vassals, of valets and subjected peasants around it. Without which neither it, nor its reign, nor its society (which otherwise had grandeur, charms, and splendor) could have lasted.

Capital has something more than maliciousness, malignance, and malevolence about it. The wills, the wishes of the property owners are not there for nothing: they execute. Through them, the death-dealing character of capital is accomplished, without there being either full consciousness or a clear intuition of it. It kills nature. It kills the town, turning itself back against its own foundation. It kills artistic creation, creative capacity. It goes as far as threatening the last resource: nature, the fatherland, roots. It delocalizes humans. We adopt technology at the slightest suggestion. Yet technologies do not emerge from the living. Communication? It remains formal, we have seen; content? neglected, lost, wasted away. Technologies kill immediacy (unless the speed of cars, planes, or automatic cameras pass for a return to the immediate; but that isn't saying much). The impact of technological conquests does not make the everyday any more *alive*; it nourishes ideology.

Yet another paradox, which is to say an affirmation that is at once truthful and unexpected. Capital kills social richness. It produces *private* riches, just as it pushes the *private* individual to the fore, despite it being a public monster. It increases political struggle to the extent that states and state-apparatuses bow down to it. Social richness, however, dates from an earlier time: gardens and (public) parks, squares and avenues, open monumentality, and so forth. Investment in this domain, which is sometimes reliant on democratic pressure, grows rarer. What sets itself up is the empty cage, which can receive any commodity whatsoever, a place of transit, of passage, where the crowds contemplate themselves (example: the Beaubourg Centre, the Forum in Paris, the Trade Centre in New York). Architecture and the architect, threatened with disappearance, capitulate before the *property developer*, who spends the money.

Like creative pre-capitalist architecture, so-called *tribal*, which is to say communal, forms of social life have been ruined on a world scale. Without replacement, except by a gestating *socialism*. Capital! The majority of readers of Marx have read this as "The Capitalists," while the concept designates an entity, a weird being which has a terrible, monstrous existence, both very concrete and very abstract, very efficient and very effective—but which exists through the heads and hands that incarnate it. One could well say: "It's not their fault … it's fate! Necessity, in short, the ineluctable!" But this necessity has a name. It is the *real*, the entity that functions and creates through actors and social and moral relations. The *personalization* of capital, a theoretical error, can lead to practical (political) errors. It would suffice to change the *established* people for society to change. We risk passing over the essential and leaving

MUSEUM OF RHYTHM: A CONSTELLATION OF ANOMALY

Natasha Ginwala

The Greek term for a water clock, *clepsydra*, literally means "to steal water" or "water thief." As the earliest time-keeping devices, water clocks assumed contrasting forms in different parts of the world, yet all measured time-flow with a perpetually leaking vessel. Be it an earthen bowl or the complicatedly geared elephant clock from al-Jazari's twelfth-century manuscript, the rhythmic intermittence of time was gauged as a sequence of programmatic departures and replenishments—a liquid time that must be released in order to exist cyclically.[1] Are those fugitive rivers of time the pages of history or its unchronicled interstices?

The defining authority and control of space has generally been attributed to humanity. Time, however, was thought to belong to the realm of divinity—until it was captured by a universally applicable measure of clocks.[2] The time of history and the history of time remain deeply entangled. Official accounts, which we accept as situated pasts, have been composed at a certain pitch, tempo, and frequency. When arranged as a linear progression, history is heard as a brutal drone. Just as the striking of a tuning fork releases a swarm of collisions that are received as a steady hum by the human ear, the construction of modernity has involved a systemic muting of imprints that run alongside proclaimed universals. Even the vector of modern monstrosity has been made impenetrable—a medley of masks that can no longer reveal a face. The effects of this positivist temporality resonate as a false note unto which we are made shadow dancers.

Surrounded by political, cultural, and civilizational collapses on a global scale, we are now faced with the sheer facticity that there is no stable ground upon which history can be sited. Only a lingering identification with its memorized tempo endures. Within a seismic contemporaneity, the imaginative potential of telling time may no longer lie in minor dissections of petrified chronicles, but rather in reconsidering the entirety of history's sensual complex—the rhythm of history.

The fundamental incompatibility of a surfaceless history and its parallel staging of false universals have led to an unrelenting estrangement between self and world(s). This cannot play out as a dialectical conflict, but only as a the functioning of the *thing* to persist. The thing, which is to say the entity that reifies … Not the object in its usual, empirical and philosophical sense, but the "Thing" …

"You are exaggerating! You are allowing yourself to be carried away by your metaphors! Who would you have believe that people, the brave people, you and I, move alongside this legendary monster, this dreadful entity that you describe? No, capital does not sow death! It produces, it stimulates invention … "

Dear speaker, advocate of capital, it is not directly a question of the people. It is not their fault because there is no fault, there is *something* that functions implacably and produces its effects. The brave people, as you said, not only move alongside the monster but are inside it; they live off it. So they do not know how it works. The informational reveals only tiny details and results. Would one of your cells, if it put itself to it, understand your body? These people who moreover move everyday alongside infamous events, great abuses and horrors, find themselves neither horrified nor infuriated by them. They are facts. They were taught that these are simple facts among many others and so it's fine … The people of our country let themselves play, through their representatives, a role on the world stage that it is better to abstain from qualifying: they let thousands of other brave and simple people of the Third World die of hunger, while here abundance reigns! But do you finally see what the monstrous efficiency of the monster reveals: the situation of the human race, threatened with disappearance, to a large extent unconscious and marching lightheartedly, in quick time to military music along the road of death?

The rhythm that is proper to capital is the rhythm of producing (everything: things, men, people, and so forth) and destroying (through wars, through *progress*, through inventions and brutal interventions, through speculation, and so forth). It is often said: "Yes, it was like this or that in the old days; then the world changed …" This isn't wrong, but it does not go beneath the surface; in fact there were, as we have seen, great rhythms of historical time: apology for the body and following that negation of the body; exaltation of love and pleasure then depreciation and apology for frivolity; taste for and then refusal of violence; and so forth. Capital replaced these alternatives with the conflicting dualities of production and destruction, with increasing priority for the destructive capacity that comes at its peak and is raised to a world scale. Which, on the negative side, therefore plays the determining role in the conception of the world and the worldly.

All this is nothing new; it has been said and re-said. Why repeat it? Because these *truths* or these *ideas* have penetrated badly into consciousness—which consciousness? *Social*? Philosophical? Political? Let us say immediately, in order to bring the discussion to a close: political. In a way that was unforeseen, over the course of centuries, political consciousness has suffered a decline, though not without leaving its marks. The social? *Socialism*? The *socialisms* have not yet gained in prestige or in clarity. Perhaps ancient truths will come to pass through a language other than that of the modern, and the position in favor of the *social*.

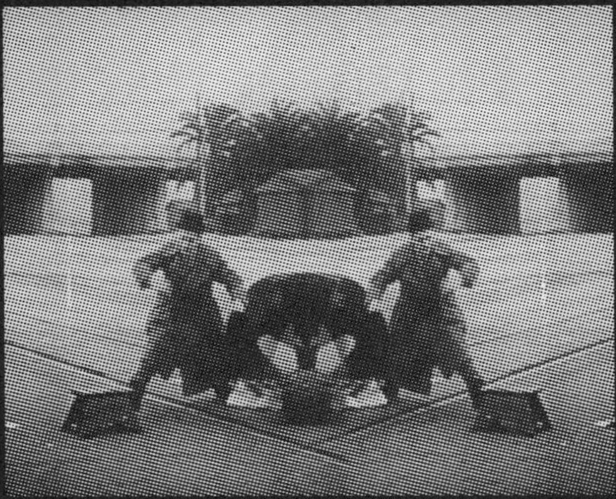

Ken Jacobs, *Ontic Antics Starring Laurel and Hardy: Bye, Molly*, 2005, video still, black and white, color, sound, 90 min.

state of phantasmagoria—in which people and things occupy a place in time, which is incommensurable with the one they have in space(s) of a world.[3] As Proust has noted, these are the things that exist viscerally in our midst but whose time is the multitudinous past or future. And, perhaps even more precarious are thing-scenarios that resound in our present as *timeness* but remain incapable of delivering a graspable form.

In a decorporeal time, the sighting of rhythm forms lends flesh to temporality. For the figurative demands of rhythm urge us to inhabit history rather than simply becoming transcribed subjects of it. A Bakhtinian swallowing of "the world" in order to compel histories to speak from the gut—as an uncanny polyphony of *self-worlds*.[4] It is from such a conflated morphology that nonlinear futures may come to be read.

And They Keep Missing the Train

In *Ontic Antics Starring Laurel and Hardy: Bye, Molly,* we encounter the classic double act: Laurel and Hardy, conducting routines of loopy clumsiness in their are failed attempts to reach Pottsville. Troubling and troubled bodies, they ironically represent the collapses of industrial capital preceding an era of economic stagnation. The space of celluloid is thus resonant with the waves of a socioeconomic temporality.

Ken Jacobs splinters the original comedy, *Berth Marks* (1929), such that slapstick turns into an account of immanent impossibility and trapped hysteria. Montaging the wheels of a steam locomotive, Laurel is poised to step onto the train (but almost never managing to do so), and Hardy is crashing everywhere. They lose themselves, almost cause a riot, and cannot remain intact. As these beautiful losers are frozen in folly, the universe around them continues to shudder as though on the brink of depression.[5]

Ken Jacobs's films compose worlds of polyrhythmic seeing—anomalies of movement set in conscious displacements of time. Challenging the precision of vision as well as the architecture of cinematic apparatus, Jacobs deploys projection to recompose the material syntax of filmic time.

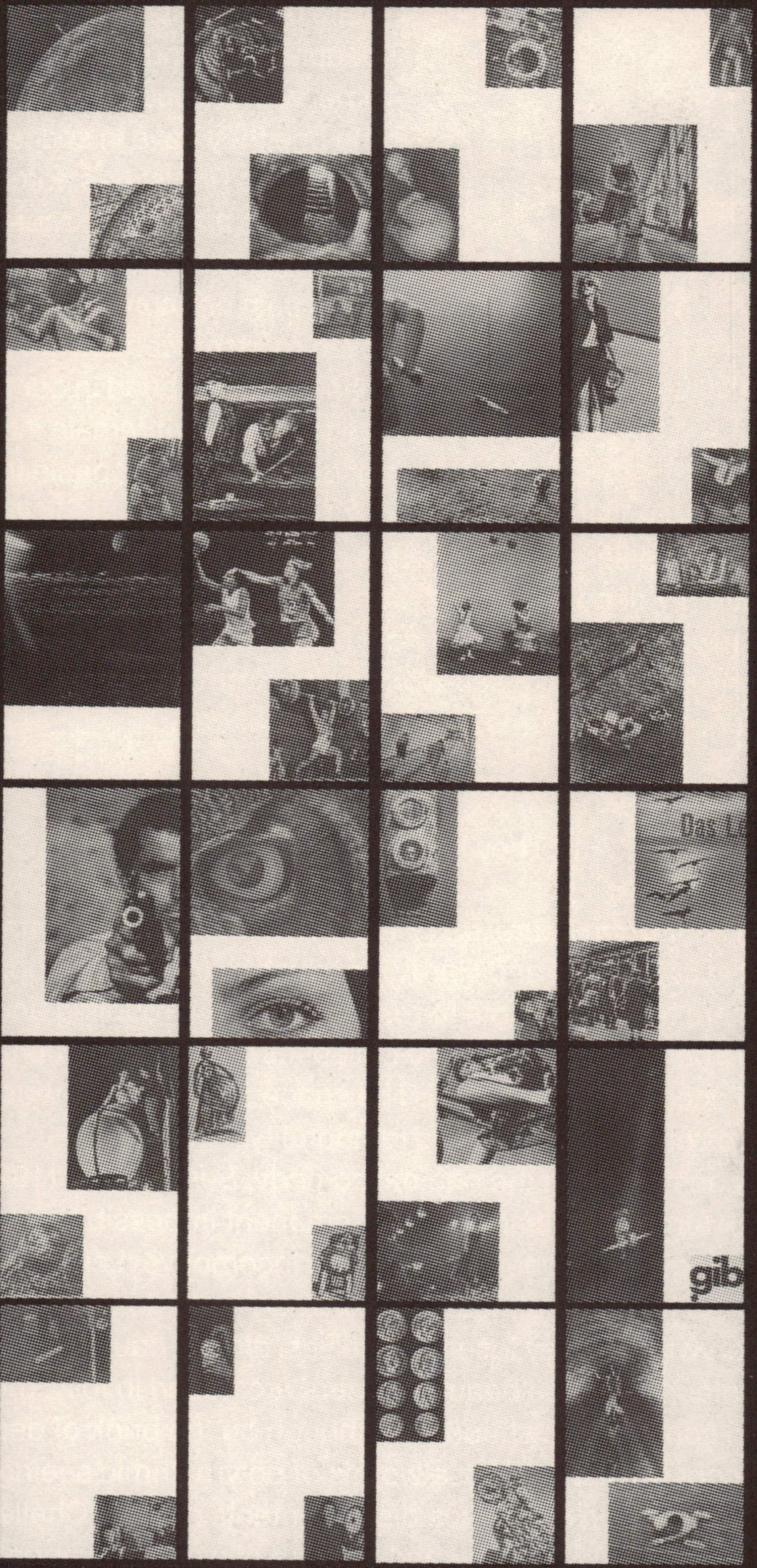

Gerhard Rühm, *RUND*, 1950–1998, fotomontage, collage on thin cardboard, series of twenty-four works, each 29.7 × 21 cm. Courtesy: Christine König Galerie, Vienna.

He thereby conceives registrations of missing images caught in fissures of a master narrative. Dislodged from a visual thread, the frame is meticulously inverted, flipped on its side, compressed / de-compressed, and further, treated to *explosions* such that it must be consumed as an array of abstract throbs that endure and test endurance.[6] In Jacobs's films, there is no ultimate image to be found, only a *body-in-pieces*. The image appears as a phantasmal fragment that reveals Modernity's violent assertions, and the past appears as an incessant pile of wreckage.[7]

Aura, Blind Spot, and Inapproachability

In Walter Benjamin's reading of the aura as an "apparition of a distance, however close it may be," the aura is constituted as an always-open phenomenon, which is a notation of inapproachability.[8] As a strange weave of space and time, the aura is an ambiguous surrounding that appears and disappears. In "The Work of Art in the Age of Mechanical Reproduction," Benjamin indicated *the decline of the aura*, and yet this decline may be read as a pattern of deviations, inclinations, and semblances by which the auratic continues to inflect the present in new ways.

The scotoma, constituted as blind spot, is never an absence. It is a catchment area inscribed by subterranean shocks of involuntary memory.[9] Hence, it is not a simple lack of sight, but an assembly of projection forms that are counterpoints to an external reality. This sounding together of autonomous voices upon a contrapuntal plane is what exceeds optical consciousness. The blind spot as source-space carries out a destruction of origins by alternating relations with *Now-time* and construction sites of *the Then*. Read as a Benjaminian form, it is "a whirlpool in the river of becoming [that] pulls the emerging matter into its own rhythm."[10] And like the aura, it is "that of which our eyes will never have their fill."

Tomo Savić-Gecan's practice performs this kind of "excess zone." The artist stitches a parallelity that defies agreed upon codifications of a singular body-space, to structure bodies-between-spaces-and-times. In the spirit of conjoined star systems that maintain a synchronized life despite being light-years apart, the artwork renders deliberate attunements between social horizons separated by time and place. Bringing about a mutant association between Biennial visitors, a specific frequency in air traffic, and the water mass of air, Savić-Gecan ultimately lends the quality of porosity to *The Museum of Rhythm*, drawing it into a membrane-form, continually affected by an elsewhere.

One may never be sure when the artwork works, since it is a silently breathing effection. One engages with the weight and texture of value, non-image, aesthetic exposure, and, finally, also nothingness as phenomenal presence. When conceiving of history-telling as a sedimentary site rather than a narrative arc, the artist's role in the construction of an imagined place ruptures the self-enclosed skin of time, allowing for epistemic disobediences to address that which is a remainder—the realm of inconceivability.

Of Equal Temperament and Law of Contagion

In the sixteenth century, two prominent figures—musicologist and mathematician Prince Zhu Zaiyu of the Ming dynasty in China, and Vincenzo Galilei, an Italian lutenist and music theorist—both established the system of twelve-tone equal temperament.[11] Zhu Zaiyu drew from the acoustic calculations of early pitch pipes and calendric recordings found in *Yuelü*, the ancient ritual tone system, finally inventing the formulation with an eighty-one-bit abacus.[12] In the late Renaissance, Galilei studied string tension and proposed a system of equal intervals for tuning the lute. With this equal-tempered scale, he challenged still-dominant Pythagorean traditions in music theory.

While both figures—almost contemporaneously—altered tuning history, it is unlikely that the two knew of one another. It would seem that as two strings vibrate at an equal harmonic ratio, the temperaments of thought-matter and events of history also arrive at intersections of sympathetic time. It is at such a juncture that modern rationality collapses, to be taken over by the very gestures of nonconformity it has stifled.

A music score by Taiwanese composer Su-ti Chen titled *Breezes Through The Banana Leaves* is exhibited alongside geographer Herman Moll's *A New Map of The Whole World With Trade Winds* (1736), as an emplacement outlining a "third" fictional cartography. The first is a sonic act that maps the surrender of banana leaves to the irrational call of the wind, depicted as a string of music notes leaping across the page. The second is a re-charting of the world through the observational plotting of variable seasonal winds and a shower of arrows outlining their shifting pattern. This map was realized by the same figure who earlier plotted fanciful cartographies for Daniel Defoe's *Robinson Crusoe* and Jonathan Swift's *Gulliver's Travels*.

While Su-ti Chen provides a topographical sketch of the banana field as a breeze-induced score, Moll's map is also a score for empires colonizing territorial pockets, composed in the pitch of wind pressure arrows piercing the belly of his world atlas. If we go by the Law of Contagion as it relates to magical thinking, once these materials become co-actors within a shared biosphere, they continue to affect one another's given temperament even after physical contact has been severed.[13] The act of placing beside is seen here as an interruption rather than an expression of direct association. It argues for a transgressive geography between time, place, and things of incommensurate worlds.[14]

With each airplane from Los Angeles that lands in Taiwan's Taoyuan International Airport, the level of humidity in the exhibition gallery will change slightly.

Tomo Savić-Gecan, *Untitled*, 2012.

Tuning Bodies in the World / The World as Tuned Body

Around the time of the horse-drawn wagon, Frank B. Gilbreth and Lillian M. Gilbreth began elaborate experiments in time-motion by turning the laboring body into a measurable entity. Their aim was to find "the one best way" to work.[15] For the National Conference of the Western Efficiency Society in 1917, they authored a pamphlet titled *Measurement of the Human Factor in Industry*. It proclaimed, "Measurement on machines that are obsolete is of little value. Measurement of human beings is valuable forever."[16] Half a century earlier the Victorian polymath Francis Galton made a similar claim to popularize anthropometry.

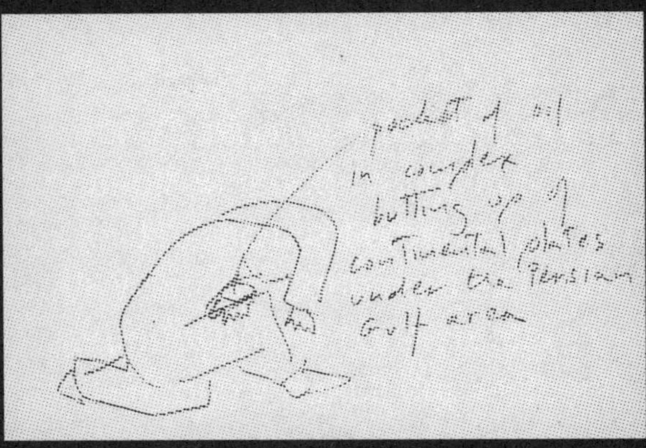

Simone Forti, from Guest Editorial, *Contact Quarterly*, Winter Issue, 1990. Courtesy of the artist.

Between 1910 and 1924, the Gilbreths operated as a consulting firm. They studied the relationship between effort and fatigue and instituted the most efficient work motions for a range of professions, from bricklaying to typing, fencing, and surgery.[17] A selection of Gilbreth chronocyclographs presented in *The Museum of Rhythm* expose snapshots of motion paths formed by small electric lamps usually fastened to workers' hands or fingers. Long exposures to a chain of light circuits turn bodies into incandescent streaks or a frenzy of scratches on a plate of darkness. The luminosity of a golfer's swing and a hand-drill operator thus come to resemble a neighboring display of theosophical body-aura diagrams. Though these materials are fundamentally incompatible, both study corporeal potential as a flow of vibrations to be disciplined into *higher forms*—be it through the problematic principles of clairvoyance or the scrupulous ordering of work-motions for female typists. The latter involves a total mechanization of the body to operate as a tool of highest efficiency, while the former treats the body-flesh as an inferior "receiver" for an idealized astral body.

Clashes between inherent and acquired bodily rhythms are a fundament of socializing the self. A hierarchy of gesture and mimetic tendencies frame a dominant mode of being-in-a-world. It is through an economy of bodies brought into a prescribed rhythm that the time regimes of encultura-tion processes and civilizational enterprise proliferate. Henri Lefebvre points out in his writings on rhythmanalysis that "humans break themselves in *[se dressant]* like animals."[18] Through a set of consecrated rites of presenting ourselves and presenting others to the world, *dressage* reduces unforeseen behavior to thrust us into deterministically rhythmized beings. Our bodies, like those of animals, are found to have a use-value only once they are broken in or trained to operate efficiently in society.[19] In contrast, the untrained body, or the trained yet defiant body, is cast as dysfunctional—forced into modernity's scenes of "aberration."

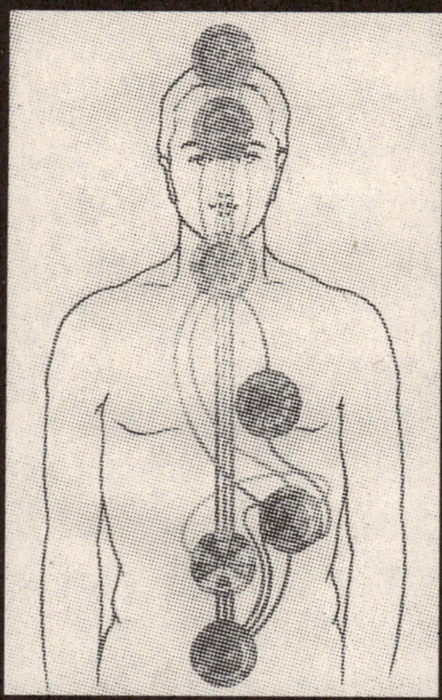

C. W. Leadbeater, *The Chakras*, 1927, The Theosophical Publishing House. Image: from Chakras, Human Aura as per e-journal essay.

Dancing Discontinuously

In Jean Painlevé's *Acera or the Witches Dance*, acera (a type of mollusk) first appear as floating balls and then slowly emerge from protective shells into amoeba-like ambiguous forms. With open circulatory systems and rasping tongues that combine digestive and sensory capabilities, in a conventional sense these creatures could well be considered phenomenal aberrations.

As this surrealist science documentary journeys through mollusk life history, we see these invertebrates open diaphanous flaps to perform an ecstatic ballet that is also a complex mating ritual. They copulate in a chain pattern; first there are three, then five, playing hermaphroditic double roles. Moving between states of continuity and discontinuity, it is a choreography that blurs life, death, and unison. It brings to mind Bataille's configuration of death and the erotic: "We are discontinuous beings, individuals who perish in isolation in the midst of an incomprehensible adventure, but we yearn for our lost continuity."[20]

To maintain an asymmetrical relationship with one's world by performing as a nonconforming body is also a refusal to succumb to a milieu of biosocial rhythms. While prescribed states of *normalcy* continue to govern as the violent skin of modernity, gestural defiance and inner mutations interrupt this encrusted skin. Such departures are easily categorized as transgressions of a primitive subjectivity that is fundamentally opposite to Modernism. But this is a limited reading, since transgression is what profoundly discredits a way of life reduced to servile forms. For in its abject and revolting avatars there is a radical de-linking from predictable patterns of sociality, and a posture of dissidence. Within the arena of historicization, transgressive acts sound parallel collisions as an articulation of "possible worlds." Their shattering effect, rupturing the ceiling of false rationalisms, is akin to breaking the surface of water with a vibrating tuning fork.

To Cast into States

For *The Museum of Rhythm*, Francisco Camacho has conceived a new form of swimming. *The 360° Stroke* is a hybrid swimming stroke that involves a rotation of the body in a style similar to water combat moves deployed in training the US Marine Corps. As the linear figuration of a swimmer's body is turned into a cyclical form, the bodily experience in water invites a seeing-thinking "in the round." The result is a strange condition of watching the world and, in turn, being watched by it through associative spinning. This looping through water in the manner of a helix and primeval nature clocks sets forth a novel attitude towards our very physicality as well as its horizon of aqueous sociality.

The human body is not designed to be in water, yet our civilizational connections with aquatic resources have historically demanded a culture of swimming. As a prehistoric phenomenon, some of the earliest avatars of

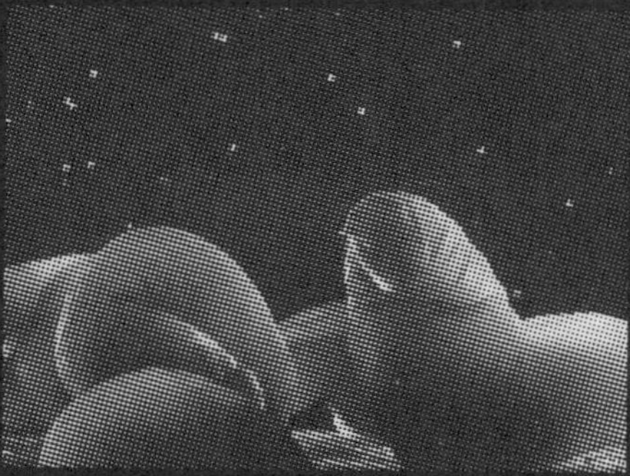

Jean Painlevé, *Acéra or the Witches Dance*, 1972, film still. © les documents cinématographiques, Paris.

swimming pools can be seen at sites of the Indus Valley Civilization (such as Mohenjo-Daro) and the widely scattered Roman baths. Camacho inscribes the given rhythmic scheme of swimming history with another logic, one that provides a visceral exercise in unlearning what has been made a common standard.

By proposing this swimming stroke along with a manifesto describing swimming as an artistic practice, the artist offers a new social imaginary and an arrival at bodily commonality from a place of deep-seated turning. It may also be thought of as an act of syncopation—a new accent or attitude that "disturbs" regular pacing and generic movement flows. The body thus becomes an *offbeat* presence and a counter-surface.

In his influential treatise "Techniques of the Body," sociologist Marcel Mauss dealt with the way societies teach men to use their bodies.[21] In his lectures on *descriptive ethnology* at the Institut d'Ethnologie of the University of Paris, he persuaded ethnographers to move from concrete to abstract considerations when exploring technical facts of cultural behavior. When studying the activity of swimming as a historical and ethnographic question, he observes: "In my day swimmers thought of themselves as a steamboat. It was stupid, but in fact I still do this: I cannot get rid of my technique."

What are museums meant to teach? Conceived as early sites of civilizing rituals and coinciding with the historic invention and application of the guillotine, the museum has a consuming relationality with the behavioral codes of modernity, morality, and enlightenment ideals. As a speculative

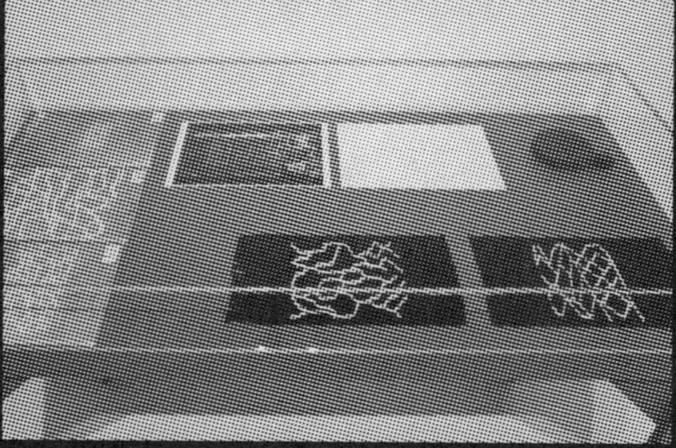

In November 2011, the Google satellite located "White Lines" in the Gobi Desert. News reporters, scientists, military strategists, UFO enthusiasts, etc., made several attempts to understand the true nature of this abstract pattern in desert sands. However, it continues to confound us. The geographic coordinates deliver a digital view but there is no material experience for this absurd geography—as a whole. For *The Museum of Rhythm*, Justice Abusa, a textile artist in Accra (Ghana) was commissioned to create a Kente textile inspired by these Google satellite images. This process of material transfer may be considered an exercise in *rhythmanalysis*—converting a gathering of pixels into fabric, through a traditional weaving technique.

Further, a wood block sourced in the winter of 2007 while researching hand-printed textiles in Gujarat (India) bears an uncanny resemblance to these "White Lines." The motif-surface is solid yet it manages to capture that fluid arrangement on arid ground. A tool to render design impressions on cloth—this wood block comes to stand as a "positive" object for disappeared negatives. These artefacts along with image documents (a hysterical CNN weather reporter and satellite views) are gathered as semi-fictional evidence as well as witness figures within a vitrine display in *The Museum of Rhythm*.

museum, any pedagogic function in this case involves subversion rather than a confirmation of museal history. Through the training in *The 360° Stroke, The Museum of Rhythm* brings about a physical non-synchronicity by re-crafting an essential life skill: swimming.

On Sequentiality: From the Head of a Frog into the Idealized Head of Apollo

J. C. Lavater's *Essays on Physiognomy* (1789–1798) surveys morphological transfer: from states of animality toward the formation of so-called ideal human types. The basis for his study was that a greater knowledge of mankind would emerge from the thesis that God created Man in his own image. Lavater hence attempted to capture human portraits as an amalgamation of the moral, the intellectual, and the animal. A fine balance of virtue and vice would therefore be recognized as markings upon the corporeal exterior of humanity—foreheads, noses, chins, and eyes becoming coded scripts of "natural inclinations." In one depiction, a raven's beak fuses with a male profile in a physiognomical reading of his character and inner spirit. This sort of proto-animation is also seen in a twenty-four–stage transformation from the head of a frog to the idealized head of Apollo.

The Museum of Rhythm brings together a colored drawing of Lavater's Frog-to-Apollo head (1797) with Eadweard Muybridge's motion studies of *Boys Playing Leapfrog*—part of his pivotal Animal Locomotion series (1872–1885). As this renowned electro-photographic investigation meets another predecessor of human-animal behavioral sequencing, one is reminded of the complex theatrics that accompanied the construction of these modern scientific documents. Experienced here as a qualitative "leaping" from one state of being into a rationalized other.

From there on, the production of a sequence around the frog leitmotif becomes obsessive—perhaps dissonant even. A wooden frog-shaped *guiro* (a popular souvenir and percussion instrument largely exported from Southeast Asia) is exhibited beside a copy of George Orwell's *Some Thoughts on the Common Toad* as well as the endangered Taipei Grass Frog's call. As Orwell presents a lucid account of the habitat and movements of the common toad, the resonant body of the Frog Guiro calls to be "croaked." Meanwhile, we never see that rare Taipei Grass Frog but only hear a recording made by local amphibian experts. An accompanying factsheet claims it was popularly known as "Thunder God Frog."

Circulations of the Circular

Some of the oldest uses of the word "rhythm" indicate a pause or a steady limitation of movement.[22] In the seventh century BC the Greek poet Archilochos was determined to "understand the rhythm that holds mankind in its bonds." While the master of ancient tragedy, Aeschylus (525–456 BC), lamented in his *Prometheus Bound*, "I am bound here in this rhythm."[23] Hence, rhythm is understood not as a condition of stillness per say, but as a social architecture of recurring time. As temporal phases that subject human as well as nonhuman bodies to factors of "eternal recurrence" they play out as a dramaturgy of cycles—alternating between confinement and renewal. And it is within cyclical dramaturgies as such that rhythm inscribes figure-ground relationship(s).

In *RUND* (1950–1998), we travel from the moon's surface into an escalator tunnel, James Bond's gun barrel, a hula-hoop, an enormous leaking stomach, a tennis court, and onward into what appears to be a mineshaft. Gerhard Rühm's photo collage series made across five decades bears the sensibility of a graphic score that mediates conditions of "roundness"—articulations of circuits, cycles, spheres—and eventually, the status of thinking/making as acts of spinning "around."

The circle comes to serve as an elemental habitat but also a passage. A reminder that the whole can no longer be portrayed as a large round whole.[24] Instead there is an observation of the thing via circumambulation—since the empty center can only be conceived through remnants that surround it. Rühm's dizzying arrangement generates a field of reciprocal belonging as surfaces pass through surfaces. As a founding member of the *Wiener Gruppe* he fundamentally addresses the erotics of language, here as a relation between tensions.

Roland Barthes has stressed that when writing is animated by truth, at a certain moment—be it as the deepest crises (or epiphany)—our relation with that instant is brought about by a change in the language of rhythm.[25] Rhythmic tendencies de-center image-body relations in order to reproduce them as "new events."[26] As a constituting principle, rhythm maintains history as *living form*. Rather than a predominant pulse, its truth is a shifting unity composed of something radically other. And this may be understood as the contiguity of fiction. Ultimately, rhythm is also an accretion—a phenomenon of endurance and, arguably, endurance itself.

Curated by Natasha Ginwala. Participating artists: Erick Beltrán, Francisco Camacho, Hanne Darboven, Juan Downey, Simone Forti, Frank B. Gilbreth, Lawrence Abu Hamdan, Channa Horwitz, Ken Jacobs, Katarzyna Kobro, Labour Exchange Band, Richard Lin, Jean Painlevé, Gerhard Rühm, Tomo Savić-Gecan, Yashas Shetty, among others.

1 al-Jazari, *The Book of Knowledge of Ingenious Mechanical Devices*, 1206, interpreted in the following article: *The Machines of Al-Jazari and Taqi Al-Din*, Prof. Salim T. S. Al-Hassani, http://www.muslimheritage.com/topics/default.cfm?ArticleID=466.

2 Henri Lefebvre, *Rhythmanalysis: Space, Time and Everyday Life* (New York: Continuum, 2004), 51.

3 See Gilles Deleuze, *Cinema II: The Time-Image* (New York: The Athlone Press, 1989; reprinted 2000), 39.

4 See Mikhail Bakhtin, *Rabelais and His World* (Bloomington, IN: Indiana University Press, 2009).

5 This is noted from the artists' statement on the film, Electronic Arts Intermix (EAI).

6 Referring to Ken Jacobs's development and performance of pyrotechnic effects as filmic experience.

7 See Linda Nochlin, *The Body in Pieces: The Fragment as A Metaphor of Modernity* (New York: Thames & Hudson, 1994), 7.

8 Walter Benjamin, "Little History of Photography," trans. Edmund Jephcott and Kingsley Shorter, in Benjamin, *Selected Writings, Vol. 2* (Cambridge, MA: Harvard University Press, 2005), 518. Translation modified.

9 Walter Benjamin, "On Some Motifs in Baudelaire" (1939), in *Illuminations: Essays and Reflections*, ed. Hannah Arendt (New York: Houghton Mifflin Harcourt, 1968), 157–59.

10 Georges Didi-Huberman, "The Supposition of The Aura: The Now, The Then, And Modernity," trans. J. M. Todd, in *Walter Benjamin and History*, ed. Andrew Benjamin (New York: Continuum, 2005), 4.

11 Vincenzo Galilei was the father of the eminent astronomer, mathematician, physicist, and philosopher Galileo Galilei.

12 See Gene J. Cho, *The Discovery of Musical Equal Temperament in China and Europe in the Sixteenth Century* (Lewiston, NY: E. Mellen Press, 2003).

13 See James George Frazer, *The Golden Bough: A Study in Magic and Religion* (Cambridge: Cambridge University Press, 2012). First published in 1890.

14 See Elizabeth A. Povinelli, "Radical Worlds: The Anthropology of Incommensurability and Inconceivability," *Annual Review of Anthropology* Vol. 30 (October 2001): 319–334.

15 *Original Films of Frank B. Gilbreth* (Part 1), 1910–1924, presented by James S. Perkins in collaboration with Dr. Lillian M. Gilbreth & Dr. Ralph M. Barnes, Chicago Chapter of the Society for the Advancement of Management, Perlinger Archives. See http://archive.org/details/OriginalFilm.

16 Frank B. Gilbreth & Lilian M. Gilbreth, *Measurement of the Human Factor in Industry* (The Library of Congress, 1917). See http://archive.org/details/measurementofhum00gilb.

17 Ibid.

18 Henri Lefebvre, *Rhythmanalysis: Space, Time and Everyday Life*, 39.

19 Ibid, 40.

20 Georges Bataille, *Death and Sensuality: A Study of Eroticism and the Taboo* (New York: Walker and Company, 1962), 15.

21 Marcel Mauss, "Techniques of the Body," *Economy and Society* 2:1 (1973): 70–88.

22 Curt Sachs, *Rhythm and Tempo: A Study in Music History* (New York: Norton, 1953).

23 Some scholars have raised questions around the authorship of this work. For the purposes of this essay we shall side with the argumentation of Aeschylus as author.

24 Peter Sloterdijk, *Spheres Theory: Talking to Myself About The Poetics of Space*, see http://beyondentropy.aaschool.ac.uk/?p=689

25 Roland Barthes, *Critical Essays* (Evanston, IL: Northwestern University Press, 1972).

26 Susanne K. Langer, *Feeling and Form: A Theory of Art, Developed from Philosophy in a New Key* (New York: Scribner, 1953), 126. http://yondentropy.aaschool.ac.uk/?p=689

NOTES FROM THE AURAL CONTRACT AUDIO ARCHIVE: A CONTEMPORARY CHRONOLOGY OF FORENSIC LISTENING

Lawrence Abu Hamdan

1984

A radical form of listening took shape in Britain in 1984. This sonic avant-garde was not attached to any nameable cultural shift or trend, but in fact owed its origin to the passing of the Police and Criminal Evidence Act (PACE). The legislation marked a crucial shift in the conventions of testimony and what the law recognized as "truth," stretching the juridical ear beyond speech acts into speech itself—not simply hearing words spoken aloud, but actively listening to the process of speaking itself.

Code E of PACE required police interview rooms to be equipped with audio recording machines, so that all interrogations could be recorded. This legislation was seen as a solution to claims that the police were falsifying confessions and altering statements made during interviews, as prior to this point all statements were simply written down "verbatim" by the police officers and then signed off on by the suspect.

Were it not for a handful of linguists practicing a rare strand of forensic phonetic analysis, PACE would have remained a simple and transparent article of legal reform. Instead, the act exponentially increased the use of speaker profiling, voice identification, and voice prints, in order to, among other things, determine regional and ethnic identity as well as to facilitate so-called voice lineups. Emerging out of this legislation, this scientific field marked the voice as a new medium through which to conduct legal investigations.

Prior to PACE, if it was suspected that someone's voice was on an incriminating recording—for example, a bugged telephone conversation in which there was discussion of an illicit act, or a CCTV surveillance tape of a masked bank robber shouting "hand over the money"—that person was asked to come to the police station and give a voluntary voice sample. After PACE, doing so was no longer voluntary, and all such recordings were added to a growing sonic archive that was permanently accessible to forensic phoneticians and audiologists.

By rapidly increasing the application of forensic listening in legal investigations, PACE widened the attention of the law to include not only the voice but also many of the other sounds that constitute our sonic environment. Soon, the forensic listener was required not only to identify the voice on a recording but also the sounds in the background, so as to ascertain where, by what brand of machine, and at what time of day a recording was made. PACE was the catalyst that enabled a complete spectrum of sonic frequencies to take the witness stand and testify.

JP French Associates, the UK's most prominent independent forensic audio laboratory, has worked on over five thousand cases since 1984. Its founder, Peter French, told me in reference to PACE that "whereas up to that point … I had a trickle of work coming in, all of a sudden it was as though there had been a thunderstorm and it started raining cassette tapes."

1990

While Dr. French was wading through his flood of cassettes in the wake of the PACE storm, a team of forensic listeners in Nevada was busy selling out the profession. The 1990 trial of the heavy metal band Judas Priest was to be forensic audiology's fifteen minutes of fame and the beginning of its unshakable reputation as a pseudoscience. The civil trial examined whether the band was responsible for an incident in 1985 in which twenty-year-old James Vance and eighteen-year-old Raymond Belknap shot themselves in Sparks, Nevada with a gun that belonged to Vance's stepfather. In their suit, the families of the two young men alleged that subliminal messages hidden throughout the band's 1978 *Stained Class* album contributed to the suicide of Belknap and the severe injuries sustained by Vance, who died before the trial commenced.

Prior to his death, Vance had convened with lawyers, singing for them parts of his favorite Judas Priest songs. This led to the song "Better By You, Better Than Me" becoming the focus of analysis for the court's designated forensic listening expert, William Nickloff, a self-help tape producer who used the most up-to-date digital sonic waveform analysis technology to wow the judge with a performance of microscopically precise sonic attention. Nickloff's testimony resulted in Judas Priest's lead singer Rob Halford taking to the dock to give an a cappella rendition of the song in its entirety. Afterwards, Halford faced a grueling cross-examination in which he was asked a series of questions about when, where, and why he chose to inhale and exhale during his singing. The court also devoted particular attention to Halford's "meeeee'ya," his way of singing "me." In response to the intense scrutiny of his vocal chords and enunciative patterns, Halford simply said, "It's just the way I've always sung it really."

Never before was Halford's singing process subjected to such specialist attention. However, the outcome of all Nickloff's "high-tech" listening was the rather ambiguous identification of seven instances when the album played backwards yielded the subliminal message: "Do it!" "Do what?" we may ask. The case was thrown out of court when Halford decided that forensic audiology was not altogether that difficult, and after a quick listen to his album backwards, he took it upon himself to present the more meaningful fragments he had found to the court with a boom box pointed directly at the judge. When the band's song "Exciter," for example, was played backwards, the lyrics "Stand by for Exciter / Salvation is his task" could be heard as "I asked for a peppermint / I asked for her to get one."

The most important thing about this trial for me is that it became a trial in the first place—that such a claim was taken so seriously as to be entertained by a judge representing the American legal system. Perhaps the law here entertained the idea of Judas Priest as subliminal culprits because of a certain quality in the way it interpellates its own subjects by soliciting their obedience and subjugation. The law believes that if it can operate subliminally, so too can other sonic practitioners, such as heavy metal bands and self-help tape producers.

1998

American forensic audiologists were still blushing with embarrassment over the subliminal listening craze of the early 1990s (which also witnessed the trials, for example, of the band AC/DC and the Mountain Valley Television Corporation) when a Romanian practitioner, Catalin Grigoras, began to reinstitute the radicality of his field, proving once again that "noise speaks" by relentlessly listening to the hum of Romania's national electrical grid.

Grigoras theorized that the humming of electrical mains could be used as evidence to authenticate recordings—that is, to determine their time and date and whether they had been edited or otherwise altered. Based on Grigoras's results, forensic audio labs across the world realized that the hum of the mains operates like sonar, as a sonic mapping device. The sound source emitted by the state (through the national grid) can be retrieved via a recording and analyzed to provide information and evidence on unlawful activity. Peter French describes the current juridical application of Grigoras's experiments:

> If you give us a digital recording made anywhere in an urban environment in the UK, we can in principle tell you exactly when it was

> made. The way we do that is by recording mains electricity hum 24/7. In this country we have an alternating mains current and ours alternates at a nominal value of 50Hz per second. However, that's only a nominal value; in fact, at any moment in time it might be 49.6, or it might be 50.3. So there are micro-fluctuations in the rate of alternation that alter unpredictably minute by minute. So by recording the mains hum all around the clock all through the year, if someone gives us a digital recording—which always invariably has mains hum on it, either because the device was plugged in or because it inducts it off nearby cables or the lights in a room—we look at the fingerprint of the mains hum and correlate that with the database of our recordings, match the fingerprint, and tell you exactly when the recorded event occurred.

The legal application of Grigoras's experiment shows us that mains electricity no longer simply hums. It now testifies. Forensic listening now has the power to discern which of the vast and heterogeneous frequencies of the sonic world can be legally meaningful. As forensic listening advances, we will see even more radical practices of listening emerge, each one working to amplify more and more of our sonic environment into the range of legal audibility and legal affectivity.

2003

By 2003, the US and the UK were entrenched on two fronts in the War on Terror. These wars forced mass migrations that became the catalyst for immigration authorities around the world to turn to forensic speech analysis to determine which individuals had been displaced as a result of the catastrophic invasions and which were simply migrants posing as refugees. On a scale similar to the 1984 PACE act, this produced a huge proliferation of forensic listening, this time employed to help determine the validity of asylum claims made by thousands of people without identity documents, particularly in Australia, Belgium, Germany, the Netherlands, New Zealand, Sweden, Switzerland, and the United Kingdom.

In these circumstances, the interview process between the immigration authorities and the asylum seeker is recorded, and the claimant's voice is then analyzed by phoneticians, often in independent laboratories in Sweden; these, in turn, contract regional phoneticians to assess whether the voice and accent correlate with the claim of national origin. The confidence in, and the rapidly increasing predominance of, this kind of investigation within immigration law is troubling, given that its accuracy has been called into question by many forensic linguists, phoneticians, and other practitioners around the world. These skeptics are demanding substantial reforms to the techniques employed; a group of them even wrote a set of "Guidelines for the Use of Language Analysis in Relation to Questions of National Origin in Refugee Cases." One of the main concerns of this group of linguists is to advocate for the idea that citizenship is a bureaucratic distinction that cannot be registered in the voice of a citizen.

In extensively researching this politically potent form of listening, I heard many accounts of instances of vocal discrimination that were shocking—none more so than in the case of Mohammad, a Palestinian asylum seeker who, after immigration authorities lost his Palestinian identity card, was forced to undergo an accent test to prove his origins. Subsequently, he was told that he was lying about his origins because of the way he pronounced the word "tomato." Instead of "*bandora*," he said "*banadora*." This tiny "a" syllable is the sound that provides the UK border agency with the apparent certainty of Mohammed's Syrian origin. The border agency designates this syllable as that of a Syrian national, implying that this vowel in the word "tomato" is coterminous with Syria's borders.

But locating this Syrian vowel in the speech of a Palestinian surely proves nothing more than the displacement of the Palestinians themselves. In other words, the instability of an accent, its borrowed and hybridized phonetic form, is testament not to someone's origins but to the unstable and migratory living patterns common to those fleeing from conflict and seeking asylum, often spending years getting to this country living in diversely populated camps along the way.

Is it not more likely then that a genuine asylum seeker's accent would be an irregular and itinerant concoction of voices, a biography of a journey, rather than an immediately distinguishable sound, a pure voice that avows its unshakable roots in a single place?

The fact that this syllable designates citizenship—more so than an identity card that contradicts it—forces us to rethink how borders are being made perceptible and how configurations of vowels and consonants are made legally accountable.

AFTERWORD: TAIPEI BIENNIAL

Fang-Wei Chang

The Taipei Biennial of 2012 was an encapsulation of the successive stages through which it had previously evolved from 1996 to 2012, and the beginning of a new transition. Organized by the Taipei Fine Arts Museum (TFAM), the Taipei Biennial has been running for over a decade. Compared to other biennials established around the 1990s, when the popularity of biennials began to surge worldwide, its total budget is not at all high, averaging NT$37 million (about €750,000).[1] The limited budget has kept the Taipei Biennial at a medium scale, with a compact structure and a precise focus. For Taiwan, the Taipei Biennial serves as a channel for accessing and understanding the newest trends in global art, and its organizational process has become a platform for cultivating art administrators and professionals.

At the Taipei Biennial international seminar in 2000, Peter Doroshenko voiced a question that is of concern to many in the field: "Is the biennial dead? If not, in what form should it appear?"[2] In *A Brief History of Curating*, Daniel Birnbaum also noted: "The successful museum has become a corporation, the biennale is in crisis."[3] Even though many people remain skeptical of biennials, they continue to thrive, like a cat with nine lives, as more second-tier cities eagerly jump on the bandwagon. Biennials still capture the imagination of many municipal decision-makers, who see them as an important means for increasing the prestige of their cities.[4] Precisely what impact is the global biennial boom having on international contemporary art and culture? What else can a biennial bring us? The last few editions of the Taipei Biennial have attempted to respond to these key issues.

Let us look back on the history of the Taipei Biennial. For the inaugural event in 1996, six Taiwanese curators and scholars developed the biennial along the theme of "The Quest for Identity." If any common thread unified the next eight biennials, it was that each one took Taiwan as its point of departure for exploring the realities of globalized (capitalist) political and economic survival in the current age. Each biennial has also engaged in a subtle dialogue with the one that preceded it, forming an interpenetrating thread both interesting and deeply meaningful. This is perhaps the special quality most readily observable from a preliminary examination along a linear timeline.[5] Of course, as an exhibition mechanism, this quality is not immune from deliberate manipulation, but it is worthy of further consideration and self-reflection.

The Taipei Biennial can perhaps be roughly divided into two periods: 1998 to 2006, and 2008 to 2012. The curatorial structure began with a single-curator model in 1998, then adopted a co-curator model for the next six biennials, before returning to the structure of one curator in 2012. As for the exhibition venue, from 1998 to 2006, it was confined to the museum itself. This fact had little connection to any conceptual perspective, but had to do with limitations in personnel, exhibition infrastructure, and budget. That is to say, keeping the biennial inside the museum building was one of the strategies for keeping costs down. Yet many still hoped and imagined that the biennial would leave the conventional "white box" of the museum and spread out into the city, and in 2008 the Taipei Biennial genuinely fulfilled these expectations, an achievement previously unattainable due to timing and geographical and social conditions. The 2008 edition was co-curated by Vasif Kortun, who had previously curated two Istanbul Biennials—amassing considerable experience in expanding exhibition sites beyond the doors of a museum—and Manray Hsu, who had previously co-curated the 2000 Taipei Biennial. Furthermore, the Taipei Flora Expo (located in the area surrounding TFAM) was in its preparatory phase at the time, providing a relatively ample supply of both human and material resources. Thus, the 2008 biennial can be seen as a watershed in terms of both resources and curatorial strategy.

As for the content of previous Taipei Biennials, TFAM director Chang Chen-Yu defined the theme of the first biennial in 1996 as "The Quest for Identity," outlining an effort to articulate the contemporary art situation in Taiwan. The theme of the 1998 biennial, "Site of Desire," expanded the scope of the biennial to encompass northeast Asia, examining the pursuit of material desire in the context of industrialization and national development. The 2000 biennial, with the theme "The Sky is the Limit," erased geographical boundaries and content restrictions, transforming a dance with the monster of runaway globalization into a graceful waltz of freedom—addressing the subject of globalization from an optimistic, positive stance. The 2002 biennial followed its clamorous predecessor with an exhibition strategy that appeared on the surface to harken back to classicism, but in fact—by exploring the theme of the "Great Theatre of the World" in both discourses and actual presentation—it envisaged the "audience" becoming the protagonist of the contemporary art exhibition, as interactive, participatory art increasingly became the trend of the future. The theme of the 2002 biennial foreshadowed the distinctive theatricality that would take shape in the Taipei Biennial over the ensuing decade, reaching its apex in 2008 and 2010. The 2004 Taipei Biennial, with the theme "Do You Believe in Reality?," zoomed in on everyday realities, stressing the insertion of art into civic consciousness and social participation. The 2006 biennial, with the theme "Dirty Yoga," considered the increasing worldwide popularity of yoga as a metaphor for desire and the pursuit of universality. To a certain degree, this musing upon "hybrid culture"—initiating an extreme clash of values that resulted in a wealth of possibilities—echoed the previous biennials, with their implicit explorations of sensual passion. In the 2008 biennial, a considerable quantity of archived interviews and site-specific video art incorporated non-artists into the artistic process, and documented their inclusion. This edition of the biennial examined the artistic nature of politics—reflecting, criticizing, and underscoring new issues arising from free-market capitalism and globalization.[6] The works in the 2010 biennial went further, incorporating the public in the creative process through numerous participatory events, and transforming a series of lectures into a gray zone of theatrical performances, incidents, and artworks.

Certain aspects of the three Taipei Biennials since 2008 can also be seen as examples of self-reflection on the event itself. That is, these exhibitions experimented with and reflected on the very form and nature of biennials. In particular, Taipei Biennial 2010 presented a powerful challenge to the exhibition mechanisms and logic of beholding that characterize the modern era, attempting to reply to the "political art" of 2008 with "politics in art." Both of these orientations referenced how art is produced and manufactured. As if summing up the biennials of previous years, 2012's theme "Death and Life of Fiction" served as a broad platform for depicting modern history and for contemplating humanity's multifaceted pursuit of knowledge and perception, encompassing anthropology, theosophy, science, art, politics, and economics. Viewed overall, this process of development may not have been intentional, yet it was certainly not entirely coincidental either. As a microcosm of the evolving global biennial phenomenon, the Taipei Biennial has concretely reflected nearly twenty years of contemporary art development and local social realities, and has been at the forefront in exploring local issues and forms of artistic expression.

After this evolution, what can the Taipei Biennial do next? This is the question arising from the Taipei Biennial and from biennials in general. Although every biennial is different, the focal point of biennials around the world has begun to shift. In recent years, biennials have gradually become major venues for dialogue, debate, and reflection on contemporary art. Some have become vehicles for rumination on the current state of biennials themselves. What is most often observed is that biennials are becoming platforms where artists attempt to grapple with current socioeconomic conditions from both a global and local perspective. Some biennial curators are even engaging in intensive spatiotemporal examinations of their host institutions.[7]

The previous Taipei Biennials consistently maintained an intimate dialogue between changing political, economic, and social developments within the context of globalization and the evolving state of contemporary art. The 2000 Taipei Biennial addressed the issue of globalization with a relatively optimistic, positive stance, but the 2008 Taipei Biennial engaged in stringent criticism of neoliberalism. These two very different postures were connected to the realities of politics, economics, and society at the time the biennials took place. Taipei Biennials of the past have been able to engage in such dialogues independently and openly. In 2008, for example, some of the artworks broached political issues that were sensitive for the local community (such as a site-specific installation by Burak Delier in the indigenous community of Xizhou along the banks of the Xindian River), but from preparatory phase to final presentation, neither the museum nor the government interfered with these projects. In a two-week period in September 2008, seven biennials opened in Asia. The Taipei Biennial stood out among this crowd because many projects (especially the site-specific installations) could only be exhibited in Taipei, while the other biennial sites in Asia rejected works that addressed sensitive political issues or works deemed inappropriately provincial in orientation. This concretely demonstrated the Taipei Biennial's distinctive timeliness and local relevance. The 2010 and 2012 Taipei Biennials were also unique among Asian biennials in that the former explored "the politics of art" based on "institutional critique" as a supporting framework, while the latter critiqued modern society and history, examining modernity through the metaphor of monsters. This was a substantive reflection of the increasing maturity of Taiwanese democracy.

1 In 1998 the Taipei Biennial cost approximately NT$22 million, and in 2000 it exceeded NT$23 million. By 2012, the biennial, spanning three above-ground museum floors plus space at the Shilin Paper Mill, cost over NT$40 million. This cost estimate is the "core budget," exclusive of electricity fees and museum staff salaries (but inclusive of fees for personnel hired specially for the biennial).

2 The 2000 Taipei Biennial seminar was held at TFAM on September 10, 2000.

3 Daniel Birnbaum, "The Archeology of Things to Come," in *A Brief History of Curating*, ed. Hans Ulrich Obirst (Zurich: JPR, 2009), 238–9.

4 During the early period of the global groundswell of interest in biennials in the 1990s, the initial idea was to mount festival-style biennials to help promote tourism in the host cities, so these cities would gain a higher visibility and local artists would receive greater exposure. But interestingly, statistics indicate that at biennials all over the world, the majority of visitors come from the local population. (See Sabine B. Vogel, *Biennials—Art on a Global Scale* [Wien: Springer-Verlag, 2010], 93.) The Taipei Biennial has never been a festival-style art fair, nor has its impact been sufficient to serve as a significant part of the city's marketing strategy.

5 A conversation between 2006 Taipei Biennial co-curator Jun-Jieh Wang and Manray Hsu also reveals clear connections between the 2006 and 2004 biennials. See *Pots Weekly*, issue 437.

6 In the 2008 exhibition guide, the curators stated: "The 2008 Biennial deals with a constellation of related issues arising from neo-liberal capitalist globalization as seen in Taipei and internationally, such as urban transformation, the dire circumstances of foreign labour forces, divided nations and micro-nations, permanent conditions or war, ecological collapse, global unrest, as well as opportunities for change." *2008 Taipei Biennial Exhibition Guide.*

7 Generally speaking, from the various Asian biennials of 2010 one can broadly discern new elements and potential future directions for the global biennial movement. In an interview, one of the curators of the 2010 Shanghai Biennale, Gao Shiming, declared his intention to "engage in reflection on the biennial system." Meanwhile, at the Taipei Biennial 2010, co-curators Hongjohn Lin and Tirdad Zolghadr made a clear break with the past, exploring ways to transcend conventional biennial operations from the inside out, be it the selection of artists and works, organizational methods, themes, events, or preparatory processes.

MODERN MONSTERS /
DEATH AND LIFE OF FICTION
TAIPEI BIENNIAL 2012

CURATOR OF TB12
Anselm Franke, curator and art critic, born 1978 in Germany, lives and works in Berlin.

CHIEF EDITOR
Brian Kuan Wood, writer and editor, born 1978 in USA, lives and works in New York.

AUTHORS
Nabil Ahmed, artist, curator and writer, born 1977 in Bangladesh, lives and works in London.

David Barton, art critic and scholar of comparative literature, born in Canada, lives and works in Jhongli.

Bavand Behpoor, art theorist, artist, and critic, born in Iran, lives and works in Tehran and Munich.

Fang-Wei Chang [張芳薇], curator, born in Taiwan, lives and works in Taipei.

Mark Fisher, writer and editor, born 1968, lives and works in Suffolk and London.

Jow-Jiun Gong [龔卓軍], art critic and theorist, born 1966 in Taiwan, lives and works in Tainan.

Jiang Gui [姜貴], writer, born 1908 in China, died 1980 in Taiwan.

Lawrence Abu Hamdan, artist and writer, born 1983 in Jordan, lives and works in London.

Henri Lefebvre, French Marxist philosopher and sociologist, born 1901, died 1991 in France.

Daisy Li [李蝶衣], graduate student in art history, born 1986 in Taipei, lives and works in Taipei.

Andrew Macdonald (a pen name for William Luther Pierce), physicist and writer, born 1933, died 2002 in USA.

Masao Matsuda [松田政男], political activist and film critic born 1933 in Taiwan, lives and works in Tokyo.

Reza Negarestani, philosopher and writer, born in Iran, lives and works in Seremban.

George Psalmanazar, writer, born 1679[?] in France, died 1763 in UK.

Ian Svenonius, musician and writer, born 1968 in USA, lives and works in Washington, DC.

Hijikata Tatsumi [土方巽] (a pen name for Hijikata Tatsumi [米山九日生]), choreographer and the founder of Butoh, born 1928 in Japan, died 1986 in Tokyo.

Michael T. Taussig, anthropologist, born 1940 in Australia, lives and works in New York.

Sophie Wahnich, historian, lives and works in Paris.

Alberto Toscano, sociologist, cultural critic, philosopher, lives and works in London.

David Der-Wei Wang [王德威], scholar of comparative literature and literary criticism, born 1954 in Taiwan, lives and works in Cambridge, MA and Taipei.

ARTIST PARTICIPANTS
John Akomfrah, born 1957 in Ghana, lives and works in London.

Maria Thereza Alves, born 1961 in Brazil, lives and works in Berlin.

Adam Avikainen, born 1978 in USA, lives and works in Minnesota.

Ashish Avikunthak, born 1972 in India, lives and works in Calcutta.

Eric Baudelaire, born 1973 in USA, lives and works in Paris.

Fernando Bryce, born 1965 in Peru, lives and works in berlin.

Chang Chao-Tang [張照堂], born 1943 in Taiwan, lives and works in Taipei.

Chen Chieh-Jen [陳界仁], born 1960 in Taiwan, lives and works in Taipei.

Yin-Ju Chen [陳瀅如], born 1977 in Taiwan, lives and works in Taipei.

Yu-Cheng Chou [周育正], born 1976 in Taiwan, lives and works in Taipei.

Jason Dodge, born 1969 in USA, lives and works in Berlin.

Jimmie Durham, born 1940 in USA, lives and works in Berlin and Rome.

Harun Farocki, born 1944 in German-annexed Czechoslovakia, died 2014 in Germany.

Omer Fast, born 1972 in Israel, lives and works in Berlin.

Peter Friedl, born 1960 in Austria, lives and works in Berlin.

Simon Fujiwara, born 1982 in UK, lives and works in Berlin.

Andrea Geyer, born 1971 in Germany, lives and works in New York.

Yervant Gianikian, born 1942 in Italy, lives and works in Milan.

Angela Ricci Lucchi, born 1942 in Italy, lives and works in Milan.

Virlani Hallberg, born 1981 in Indonesia, lives and works in Berlin and Stockholm.

Hsu Chia-Wei [許家維], born 1983 in Taiwan, lives and works in Taipei.

Hannah Hurtzig, born in GDR, lives and works in Berlin.

Luis Jacob, born 1971 in Peru, lives and works in Toronto.

Maryam Jafri, born 1972 in Pakistan, lives and works in New York and Copenhagen.

Chia-En Jao [饒加恩], born 1976 in Taiwan, lives and works in Taipei.

Rajkamal Kahlon, born 1974 in USA, lives and works in Berlin.

Kao Chung-Li [高重黎], born 1958 in Taiwan, lives and works in Taipei.

Joachim Koester, born 1962 in Denmark, lives and works in Copenhagen.

Jompet Kuswidananto, born 1976 in Indonesia, lives and works in Jakarta.

Marysia Lewandowska, born 1955 in Poland, lives and works in London; Neil Cummings, born 1947 in UK, lives and works in London.

Liu Ding [劉鼎], born 1976 in China, lives and works in Beijing.

Joven Mansit, born 1984 in Philippines, lives and works in Manila.

Angela Melitopoulos, born 1961 in Germany, lives and works in Berlin.

Maurizio Lazzarato, born 1955 in Italy, lives and works in Paris.

Jakrawal Nilthamrong, born 1977 in Thailand, lives and works in Bangkok.

Boris Ondreička, born 1969 in Slovakia, lives and works in Bratislava.

Willem Oorebeek, born 1953 in Holland, lives and works in Brussels.

The Otolith Group, founded in London in 2002.

Pak Sheung-Chuen [白雙全], born 1977 in China, lives and works in Hong Kong.

Pratchaya Phinthong, born 1974 in Thailand, lives and works in Bangkok.

Roee Rosen, born 1963 in Israel, lives and works in Tel Aviv-Yafo.

Andreas Siekmann, born 1961 in Germany, lives and works in Berlin.

Elisa Strinna, born 1982 in Italy, lives and works in Venice.

Sun Xun [孫遜], born 1980 in China, lives and works in Beijing.

Teng Chao-Ming [鄧兆旻], born 1977 in Taiwan, lives and works in New York and Taipei.

Rosemarie Trockel, born 1952 in Germany, lives and works in Cologne.

Anton Vidokle, born 1965 in Russia, lives and works in New York; Hu Fang [胡昉], born 1970 in China, lives and works in Guangzhou.

Danh Vo, born 1975 in Vietnam, lives and works in Berlin.

Wei-Li Yeh [葉偉立], born 1971 in Taiwan, lives and works in Taipei.

CURATORS OF MINI-MUSEUMS

THE MUSEUM OF RHYTHM
Natasha Ginwala, curator and researcher, born 1985 in India, lives and works in Berlin.

THE MUSEUM OF ANTE-MEMORIALS
Eric Baudelaire (see Artist Participants).

THE MUSEUM OF THE MONSTER THAT IS HISTORY
James T. Hong, filmmaker and artist, born 1970 in USA, lives and works in Taipei.
Anselm Franke (see Curator of TB12).

THE MUSEUM OF GOURD
Chihiro Minato [港千尋], photographer, writer, critic, and curator, born 1960 in Japan, lives and works in Tokyo.

THE MUSEUM OF THE INFRASTRUCTURAL UNCONSCIOUS
Territorial Agency, independent organization, founded by architects and urbanists *John Palmesino and Ann-Sofi Rönnskog* in 2007.
Anselm Franke (see Curator of TB12).

THE MUSEUM OF CROSSINGS
Anselm Franke (see Curator of TB12).
Hongjohn Lin [林宏璋], artist, curator, and art critic, born 1964 in Taiwan, lives and works in Taipei.

MODERN MONSTERS /
DEATH AND LIFE OF FICTION
Taipei Biennial 2012
09.29.2012–01.13.2013

Director of Taipei Fine Arts Museum
Hai-Ming Huang

Museum Development Board
Ming-Hsing Liu, Tsun-Lin Liao, Chien-Kuo Liu, Lily Chang, Fang-Wei Chang, Yu-Ming Lin, Ping-Chung Yu, Jen-Kui Chen, Yu-Chen Pai

EXHIBITION TEAM
Curator
Anselm Franke

Assistant Curator
Heidi Ballet

Curatorial Assistant
Chun-Chi Wang

Director of Taipei Biennial and International Projects Office
Fang-Wei Chang

Exhibition Assistant
Kat Siao

Exhibition Officers
Yi-Ting Lei, Mei-Ching Fang, Shu-Ting You, I-Ying Chiang, Tzu-Hsiu Su

Exhibition Coordinators
Jade Wang, Singer Hsu, Sabrina Yen

Project Assistants
Eve June Liu, Hui-Ting Huang, Wei-Ching Chuan, Chia-Ling Lee, Chih-Ying Lee, Wan-Yi Chang, Pei-Shin Hung, Kai Nien, I-Huei Lin, York Chu, Fei-Hao Chen, Selene Hung

Exhibition Display Officers
Chien-Hau Feng, Han-Yu Chih

Exhibition Design
Anselm Franke and Zak Group in collaboration with CoDKT

Public Relations
Li-Wei Lu, Shun-Wen Yang, Chia-Ching Chang

Technical Coordinators
Hong-Tu Chen, Herman Wang, Mason Tseng, Yi-Chen Lin

Electricity and Lighting Technicians
Chang-Wei Tseng, Feng-Huang Tsai, Chong-De Liu, Yu-Cheng Chang

General Affair Officers
Yu-Ming Lin, Yun-Nuo Liao, De-Shuin Jao, Ming-Yu Chang

Accountants
Ping-Chung Yu, Zoe Li

Government Ethics Officer
Yu-Chen Pai

Information Technology
Yen Lin, Chien-Nan Liao

Photographers
Chih-Ho Chen, Yung-Jen Chen

Documentary Video
Life Scenery Films Ltd.

EDUCATIONAL PROGRAM
Educational Program Supervisor
Chien-Kuo Liu

Lectures and Seminar Executive
Su-Fong Wang

Guided Tour Coordinators
Judy Hsiao, Luso, Li-Ya Chuang, Swee Shi, Hsuan-Chun Lin

Special Project
Chiung-Yu Chen, Hsuan-Chun Lin, Janet Chia-Hui Lin

PUBLICATIONS
Journal Publishers
Hai-Ming Huang, Taipei Fine Arts Museum
Markus Dreßen, Anne König, Jan Wenzel, Spector Books

Chief Editors
Anselm Franke, Brian Kuan Wood

Executive Editor
Yen-Ing Chen

Design and Art Direction
Zak Group assisted by Rohan Hu

Design Executive
Rohan Hu (Chinese)

English Copyeditor
Michael Andrews

Chinese Copyeditors
Yi-Ning Shen, Fang-Wei Chang

English to Chinese Translators
Sylvie Lin, Yi-Ning Shen, Eric Chang, Wanling Chen, Wei Yu, Jessie Kuo, Stacey Ma, Ya-Wen Chen

Chinese to English Translators
Brent Heinrich, Julie P. White, Eric Chang

Japanese to Chinese Translator
Tze-Chien Liu

Japanese to English Translator
Yuki Nakayama

Printer
Chia Shin Printing CO., LTD., Taipei, Taiwan

Published by
Taipei Fine Arts Museum
181, Zhong Shan N. Road, Sec. 3, Taipei 10461, Taiwan, R.O.C.
T: 886-2-2595-7656, F: 886-2-2594-4104
www.tfam.museum

Spector Books
Harkortstraße 10, 04107 Leipzig, Germany
T: 49-341-2645-1012, F: 49-341-2122-411
www.spectorbooks.com

Distribution
USA, Canada: RAM Publications+ Distribution Inc., www.rampub.com
UK, Japan: Anagram Books Ltd, www.anagrambooks.com
Australia, New Zealand: Perimeter Distribution, perimeterdistribution.com
Germany, Austria, France: GVA, Gemeinsame Verlagsauslieferung Göttingen GmbH&Co. KG, www.gva-verlage.de
Switzerland: AVA Verlagsauslieferung AG, www.ava.ch
Other Countries: Motto Distribution, www.mottodistribution.com

Published on the occasion of the Taipei Biennial 2012.

ISBN 978-3-944669-56-4

p. 29
Preface to Whirlwind (Originally titled *A Tale of Modern Monsters*, in a collector's edition by Spring Rain Pavilion)–Jiang Gui
Originally published in 1959 (written 1952), edition by Spring Rain Pavilion. Translated from the Chinese by Brent Heinrich for *Whirlwind* (enlarged edition, Taipei: Chiu Ko Publishing, 2009), 7–10.

p. 33
Headless Landscapes–Jow-Jiun Gong
Translated by Heinrich Brent

p. 80
In Defense of the Terror: An Intolerable Revolution–Sophie Wahnich
First published by Verso Books © 2012

p. 88
The Bloody Latte: Vampirism as a Mass Movement–Ian Svenonius
From Ian Svenonius, *The Psychic Soviet* (Chicago: Drag City Press, 2006).

p. 114
Yaoyan Films and Strategies–
Chen Chieh-Jen. This text supplements the conversation regarding *yaoyan* films included in Hannah Hurtzig's installation work *The Waiting Hall: Scenes of Modernity*. Most of Chen Chieh-Jen's writings in this text are from his lecture entitled "Jiang Wei-Shui's Public Funeral: A Documentary —Discussing Image and Sound as an Action to Subvert and Make Qualitative Change," delivered at the China Academy of Art on June 6, 2011. Translated by Eric Chang.

p. 122
Talking Rubbish: Wei-Li Yeh and Others–Daisy Li. *Talking Rubbish* is a peer-reviewed academic journal specializing in antiquity-like rubbish, criticism, theory and creative writing, published by the Antiquity-Like Rubbish Research & Development Syndicate Press. These excerpts were taken from *Talking Rubbish, vol. 3*, published for the Taipei Biennial 2012.

p. 135
Powers of The False (Notes from a Journal)–Eric Baudelaire
Translated from the French by Matthew Cunningham

p. 152
Taipei Notes: 2011.11.19–2011.11.28–
Pak Sheung Chuen
Translated by Julie P. White

p. 157
Secret Room—Landscape—Power: Wakamatsu Films and Liberation of Sex–Masao Matsuda. Translated by Yuki Nakayama

p. 192
Sixteen Professions–Hu Fang
Translated by Melissa Lim, except No. 8, 9, and 16 translated by RB Baron.

p. 221
How to Catch a Beast: A Brief History–
Chihiro Minato
Translated from the Chinese by David J. Toman

p. 222
To Prison–Hijikata Tatsumi
Originally published as "Keimusho e" in *Mita Bungaku*. Translated from the Japanese by Nanako Kurihara for *The Drama Review* 44, 1 (T165), Spring 2000, guest-edited by Nanako Kurihara.

p. 260
The Manipulations of Time–
Henri Lefebvre. Translated by Stuart Elden and Gerald Moore. "The Manipulations of Time" is the sixth chapter in Henri Lefebvre's *Elements of Rhythmanalysis: An Introduction to the Understanding of Rhythms* (London: Continuum, 2004), originally published as *Éléments de rythmanalyse: Introduction à la connaissance des rythmes* (Paris: Éditions Syllepse, 1992).

Organized by

臺北市立美術館
TAIPEI FINE ARTS MUSEUM

Official Support

文化部
MINISTRY OF CULTURE

台北市文化局
Department of Cultural Affairs
Taipei City Government

TAIPEI

International Support

ifa Institut für Auslands-
beziehungen e. V.

Mondriaan Stichting
(Mondriaan Foundation)

BRITISH
COUNCIL
英國文化協會

GOETHE
INSTITUT

Special Projects Sponsor

iaspis

震旦 AURORA

Assisted by

當代藝術基金會
Contemporary Art Foundation

竹圍工作室

ACKNOWLEDGEMENTS

We would like to sincerely thank the following individuals and organizations, whose generous help has made this exhibition and publications possible.

INSTITUTION / ORGANISATION
Aanant & Zoo; Art Book Cologne; Art Resource, NY; Atomic Engergy Council; Aurora Group; Bamboo Curtain Studio; Beitou Museum; Bentley Park Suites; Boston Public Library; Central Weather Bureau of Taiwan; Chinese Taipei Film Archive; Chiu Ko Publishing; Christine König Galerie, Vienna; CNAP (centre national des arts plastiques); Cornell University; David M. Rubenstein Rare Book & Manuscript Library; David Rumsey Map Collection; Department of Botany Taiwan Forestry Research Institute; Drag City Press; Duke University; Earthly Clinic; Estate of Hanne Darboven; European Space Agency (ESA); Faculty of Mass Communication and Journalism, Thammasat University; Formosa Filmedia Co.; Fraenkel Gallery; Galerie Urs Meile; gb agency, Paris; GMVZ; Goethe-Institute Taipei; Gourd Art Museum; Guan Lo Yin; HCT LOGISTICS CO., LTD.; Hiroshima Peace Memorial Museum; Institute of History and Philology; Jan Mot, Brussels; Jiu Xiang Ju Books; Kavalan Tribe; Kheel Center, The University of Florida; Konrad Fischer Galerie; La Synagogue de Delme; Les Documents Cinématographiques, Paris; Library of Congress, USA; Long Fa Tang; Madukismo Sugarcane Factory (Yogyakarta); Ministry of Foreign Affairs, Republic of China (Taiwan); Mondriaan Foundation; Monitor Gallery; Museum Associates / LACMA; Museum of Bamboo Art, Nantou; Museum of Modern Art (MoMA), New York; Muzeum Sztuki (Łódź); National Aeronautics and Space Administration (NASA); National Archives USA; National Archives and Records Administration, Washington DC; National Palace Museum; National Taiwan University, Department of Psychology; Nederlands Instituut voor Beeld en Geluid; Nederlands Instituut voor Mediakunst; Numthong Gallery; Paul Sacher Foundation, Basel; Peng Ming Min Foundation; Peters Edition Limited, London; Quality Information Publishers; Rijksakademie van beeldende kunsten; Scala, Florence; Schott Music, Mainz; Science & Society Picture Library; Shangh ART Gallery; Tainan Veterans Home; Taipei Artists Village; Taipei City Archives; Teater Garasi (Yogyakarta); The BOX Gallery; The British Library; The Freesound Project; The Getty Research Institut; The Juan Downey Estate; The Press of the Nova Scotia College of Art and Design; The Seismological Center; The Theosophical Society; The University of Chicago Library; Trees Music & Art; Trouble Magazine; Verso Books; Wellcome Library; π Animation Studio

AND
Justice Abusa; Robert Adams; Putri Adju (Ark Gallery, Jakarta); Lee Ambrozy; Dorothy Amenuke; Angela Anderson; Michael Andrews; Kaim Ang; Thomas Argiro; Lewis Baltz; Wolfgang Becker; Markus Bernhard (Goethe-Institut Taipei); Nathalie Boutin; Frauke Breede (Galerie Thomas Zander, Cologne); Stefan Britton; Annett Busch; Joel Ruiz Butuyan; Cai Zhen-Yu; Christian Casse; Francois Casse; Chang Cheng-Jen; Chang En-Maan; Chao Hsia-Hsien; Lee Chatametikool; Mortimer Chatterjee (Chatterjee and Lal, Mumbai); Dan Chen; Rita Chen; Chen Qibang; Chen Fang-Ming; Zian Chen; Chen Szu-Ting; Chen Xindong (Chen Xindong Gallery, Beijing); Amy Cheng; Chien Fan Chen (Department of Botany Taiwan Forestry Research Institute); Katy Shiu-Chih Chien; Ben Chou; Chu Po-Ying; Yung-Feng Chung (Labour Exchange Band); Jean-Marie Courant; Matthew Cunningham; Deng Da-Xin; Guillaume Désanges (Trouble); Marck Dickenson (Neue Alte Brücke, Berlin); Pauline Doutreluingne; Marilys B. Downey; Bassam El Baroni; Fan Xiao-Lan; Feng Zhi-Ming; Chiara Figone (Archive Books, Berlin); Gridthiya Gaweewong; Ginger Glacier's eggs; Lina Gopaul; Jow-Jiun Gong; Solène Guillier; Guo Jau-Lan; Alexander Hahn (Aanant & Zoo, Berlin); Heide Häusler (Sprüth Magers, Cologne); Nanna Heidenreich; Lorenz Helbling (ShanghART Gallery, Shanghai); Margareta Helleberg (Moderna Museet, Stockholm); Eva Häfler (Christine König Galerie, Vienna); Manray Hsu; Merak Huang; Kwang-Kuo Huang; Huang Yan-Yan; Hung Kan (curator for Gourd art museum); Nabu Husungan Istanda; Lori G. Juvida; Max Kahlen; Kammarheit; Michael Keevak; Irfan Khatri; Christine König (Christine König Galerie, Vienna); Nanako Kurihara; Kung Yi-Fang; Panai Kusui; Tara Lal (Chatterjee and Lal, Mumbai); Jamaludin Latief; David Lawson; Miriam Lazoff; Lee Penghsiang; Ding-Li Lee; Li Jie-Hua; Li Ran; Maggie Liao; Filiep and Mimi Libeert; Patrizia Libralato (Birch Libralato, Toronto); Lin Hsiao-Wei (The Seismological Center, Central Weather Bureau of Taiwan); Millie Tien-Hui Lin; Lin Zhen-Yun; Lin Guang-Ron; Aimèe Lin; Pei-Yu Lin; Andrea Lissoni; Lisa Luo (British Council, Taipei); Esther Lu; Carol Yinghua Lu; Evonne Mackenzie (British Council, London); Giovanni Majer; Inge Maruyama (Stiftung Museum Kunstpalast, Düsseldorf); Charles Mazé; Mister Michael; Mister NY; Jan Mot; Marc Mozga; Chris Mullen (Wellcome Library, London); Ng Yan Yan; Sonja Oehler; Reiko Ogura; Louie Ojeda; A-Yu Pan; Qing-Shui Pan; Wu-Ji Pan; Hila Peleg; Capucine Perrot; Radim Peško; Raquel Pinto; Yu-Xun Peng; Ella Raidel; Jan Ralske; Ching-Yueh Roan; Laurie Robins; Jeffrey Rosen (Misako & Rosen Gallery, Tokyo); Arin Rungjang; Murayama Sachiko; Gerald Salgado; Ewa Sapka-Pawliczak; Rizky Sasono; Erika Satoh; Radovan Scasascia; Kai-Fong Shi; Benedicte Sehested; Shi Pei-Jun; Margaret Shiu; Ana Sokoloff; Stefanie Schulte Strathaus; Dr. Su Sheng-Chieh; Kuen-Lung Su; Monika Szewczyk; Nina Tabassomi; Yudi Ahmad Tajudin; Alexander D. Tan; Suehli Tan; Marshal Tie Jia (Temple of the Empress of Heaven (Mazu), Beigan Township Chinbi Village); Barbara Thumm (Galerie Barbara Thumm); Miguel Tomacruz; Tsai Chuen-Horng; Arthur Tsay; Bahrul Ulum; Julie Ulvestad; Rene Vienet; Heidi Voet; Kai Vollmer; Chia Chi Jason Wang; David Der-Wei Wang; Wang Jiang-Xiong; Wang Shao-Gang; Hui-Min Wei; Wei Yan-Nian; Wei Sung (Goethe-Institut Taipei); Camille Weiner; Malwina Woest (Eidotech); Nicole Wolf; Wang Wei-Lian; Wu Shu-Lun; Wu Hsuan-Hsuan; Xiao Ling; Yuan-you Xuan; Kai Yen; Yang Yi-Ju; Yang Du; Pauline Yao; Yu Shan-Lu; Zheng Mei-Ling; Zheng Yong-Chang; Zhou Rui-Fa; Jim Zhu; Arnas Ziedavicius; Tirdad Zolghadr; Theus Zwakhals (Netherlands Media Arts Institute)

NX